**Jean-Louis Gardies
Rational Grammar**

Analytica

Investigations
in Logic, Ontology and the Philosophy of Language

Editors:
Ignacio Angelelli · Austin (Texas/USA)
Joseph M. Bocheński · Fribourg (CH)
Christian Thiel · Erlangen

Editor-in-chief:
Hans Burkhardt · Erlangen

Philosophia Verlag München Wien

Jean-Louis Gardies

Rational Grammar

Translation by Kevin Mulligan

The Catholic University of America Press
Washington, D.C.

Philosophia Verlag München Wien

CIP-Kurztitelaufnahme der Deutschen Bibliothek:

Gardies, Jean-Louis:
Rational grammar / Jean-Louis Gardies. Transl. by Kevin
Mulligan. – München · Wien : Philosophia Verlag, 1985.
– Washington, D.C.: Cath. University of America Press.
  (Analytica)
  Einheitssacht.: Esquisse d'une grammaire pure <engl.>
  ISBN 3-88405-013-3 (Philosophia Verlag)
  ISBN 0-8132-0611-1 (Catholic University of America Press)

Library of Congress Cataloging in Publication Data

Gardies, Jean-Louis.
  Rational grammar.
  Translation of: Esquisse d'une grammaire pure.
  Bibliography: p.
  1. Grammar, Comparative and general.   I. Title.
P151.G3613   1985   415   84-23002
ISBN 0-8132-0611-1

Available in North and South America from
The Catholic University of America Press, Washington, D.C.

Translated from the French by Kevin Mulligan
Originally published under the title
Esquisse d'une Grammaire Pure
Librairie Philosophique J. Vrin, Paris, 1975

ISBN 0-8132-0611-1
ISBN 3-88405-013-3

Typesetting: FotoSatz Pfeifer, Germering
Manufactured by H. Mühlberger, Augsburg
Printed in Germany 1985

Table of Contents

Preface to the English Translation   9

Introduction   11
The Different Senses of the Term 'Language':
Language and Grammar   11

Chapter One. The Level of Grammar   16
Recognition of the Pre-Logical Level of Grammar   16
Logic and the Definition of 'Meaningful Expression'   20
Grammar and the Notion of Grammaticality   25
The Boundary Between the Grammatical and the Logical   33

**Chapter Two. Meaning Categories and Degrees
of Grammaticality**   39
The Husserlian Notion of 'Semantic Category'   39
The Antinomies and the Grammatical Requirements to which
they Give Rise   43
The Conflict of Grammatical Requirements   46
Languages and their Goals   49
Conclusions of the First Two Chapters   59

Chapter Three. Name, Proposition, Functor   63
On the Distinction Between the Three Categories   63
The Methods of Verifying Syntactic Connection According to
Ajdukiewicz and Bar-Hillel   69
Criticisms of these Methods   75

Chapter Four. The Verb   86
Verb and Function   86
The Case of Impersonal Verbs   89
The Different Senses of the Verb 'to be'   95
The Reduction of the Verb to the Copula-Predicate Form   101
Traditional Definitions of the Nature of the Verb   106
Number and Position of the Arguments   111

Chapter Five. Person, Tense, Number   126
Impersonal and Tenseless Propositions   126
Person   127
Tense   135
Gender and Number   146
Categories Between Number and Gender Foreign to
Indo-European Languages   149

Chapter Six. The Moods   155
The Fundamental Status of the Non-Indicative Moods:
Optative, Imperative, and Related Moods   155
The Special Case of the Interrogative   165
The Distinction Between Moods and Modalities   172

Chapter Seven. The Name   176
What we Shall Understand by 'Name'   176
Names of Individuals (1): Proper Names   178
Names of Individuals (2): Definite Common Names   182
Names of Individuals (3): Indefinite Names   184
Participle, Adjective and Relative Clause   185
Names of Properties or Relations – Names of Classes   190
Names of States of Affairs   193
The Subjunctive as the Nominalisation of a State of Affairs   197
Quotation Marks   201
The Confusion Between a Proposition, its Name, the State
of Affairs it Asserts, and the Name of this State of Affairs   205

Chapter Eight. Negation and Conjunction   213
Coordination and Subordination   213
Negation and the Conjunctions Applied to States of Affairs
and Propositions   220
Extensionally Defined Conjunctions and Strict Conjunctions   232
Remarks and Warnings   238

Chapter Nine. Adverbs and That-Clauses   248
The Two Possible Expressions of Modality   248
Definition of the Adverb   255
The Specific Nature of the Completive Construction   257
The Case where the Distinction Between the Two Expressions
of Modality is no Longer Possible   259

Chapter Ten. Aspects of Aspect   263
Aspectualizers and Grammar   263
Aspectualizers and the Semantics of Modal Propositions   273

Chapter Eleven. Conclusion   284
The Technical Schema of Communication   284
The Linguistic *A Priori*   293
The Structure of Discourse and the Structure of Thought   300
Logic and its Mathematical Heritage   303
The Structure of Discourse and the Structure of its Object   305
The Arbitrariness of the Linguistic Sign   311

Bibliography   319

Index   329

Preface to the English Translation

This book appeared originally in French in 1975. The text has been modified in some respect for this English translation, although the original intentions remain the same. The most important changes – the transformation of Chapter Three and the addition of two new chapters dealing with the adverb and the completive proposition (Chapter Nine) and with aspect (Chapter Ten) – have been introduced solely in order that the whole remains as faithful as possible to the original project.

It will perhaps – indeed certainly – be felt to be a matter for regret that we have not defined or further specified the exact status of the *a priori* structures so frequently mentioned in the text. We accept this criticism without hesitation, for our aim here has been to *describe* or, more simply still, to point out something that in the course of our analyses we have frequently encountered. It has seemed much too early to make any sort of claim about the status of such structures if we are to avoid falling almost immediately into the trap of making claims that are without any philosophical foundation. We do not pretend to know any more about the *a priori* of grammar than about the *a priori* of law that was the subject-matter of an earlier book (*Essai sur les fondements a priori de la rationalité morale et juridique*, 1972). It is only by pushing ahead cautiously and slowly with the precise analysis of individual points that one can hope, not to answer the question as to the nature of *a priori* structures, but at least to throw light, step by step, on the right way to approach this question, something we have tried to do, albeit very apprehensively, in subsequent investigations.

I am grateful to Kevin Mulligan for his careful translation and for his suggestion that this book be translated into English.

Jean-Louis Gardies

Introduction

The Different Senses of the Term 'Language': Language and Grammar

The notion of grammar refers us immediately to that of language, a term which, depending on whether it is employed by logicians, linguists or philosophers, can be taken in many different ways. It therefore seems necessary, before embarking on the investigation announced in our title, to give a provisional definition of what the word 'language' will be taken to mean here – provisional because it is not impossible that the course of our analyses will provide some reasons for calling into doubt a hitherto accepted terminology. The most narrow definition of the term *language* restricts its application to those languages which are sometimes called *natural* and which André Martinet has shown to be characterized by a *double articulation,* in a classic analysis which we shall here simply summarise.[1] This double articulation allows a natural language to express an infinite number of messages by means of a number of signs that is not merely finite but in fact very limited.

The *first* articulation is the segmentation of the message to be expressed into units of sense, called *morphemes* by some linguists and *monemes* by others. French, for example, does not possess a single sign for the expression of 'le soleil brille', another for the expression of 'j'ai faim', a third for the expression of 'la marquise sortit à cinq heures'. In other words French does not possess an infinite number of signs corresponding biunivocally to the infinite number of possible messages. Instead it provides us with the means of articulating each of our messages by arranging in sequence a selection of some of the thousands of morphemes it puts at our disposal. Thus in order to say 'le soleil brille' we decompose the semantic unity of the proposition into at least four morphemes which, beneath their phonic expression, are already equipped with a certain sort of sense – the definite article 'le', the noun 'soleil', the stem of the verb 'briller' and the form of the latter when conjugated in the present. Each of these four morphemes is already equipped with a certain sense and it is the articulation of these four

11

meaningful elements (an articulation which is of course quite different from any simple addition, heap or sum), which enables us to fit together the global meaning of the whole proposition.

The *first* level of articulation makes it possible to form an infinite number of messages from a basic number of meaningful elements – a number not small, but at least finite. The *second* level of articulation is based on the segmentation of each of these morphemes or monemes into *phonemes*. French does not have as many basic sounds as there are morphemes to be expressed; rather, natural languages effect the expression of the different morphemes with two or three dozen differently articulated phonemes, without there being in general any meaning-relation between each constituent phoneme and the meaning expressed by the morpheme thereby constituted (onomatopoeia is an exception). We find the sound 'l', which occurs at the beginning of the definite article 'le', in the middle of the word 'soleil', but this does not establish any sort of semantic connection between these two words. In many languages the combinatorial possibilities of some thirty phonemes suffice to express thousands of morphemes which in their turn combine to form the infinite variety of possible messages.[2]

The now standard terms 'first articulation' and 'second articulation' should not suggest that there is any analogy between the two levels, nor should they mask the radically different nature of each. For while the first level of articulation constitutes a whole meaning by combining elements that are themselves already meaningful, the second associates each of these meaningful elements with a combination of material elements that have no meaning in a relation that is to some extent unmotivated.

We have summarised André Martinet's analysis in order to emphasize that, although some authors are agreed in reserving the term 'language' for the designation of systems of signs that are doubly articulated, others go further and designate in this way systems employing less than two levels of articulation. Such systems can of course be divided into three groups:

(1) *Systems of signs that are not articulated at all.* The system of signs peculiar to traffic-lights can be considered as a language in which there correspond to the three propositions:

- you may proceed
- you may only proceed if you are already in gear
- you may not proceed

the three signs *green, amber, red,* without any articulation. An analogous, though slightly richer system would be the set of optical systems recognized in the Highway Code. Such a language can of course only express a finite number of messages.

(2) *Systems of signs that employ only the first level of articulation.* A good example is provided by any logico-mathematical ideogram. Thus the language of arithmetic and algebra is articulated in the sense that the mathematician does not have one sign in order to express '5 is greater than 3', another for '3 is greater than 2', and a third for '2 is equal to 1 plus 1'. In his 'language' (which differs from a natural language also in the superficial respect that it is first and foremost a set of *written* signs) the mathematician will, for example, write $5 > 3$, an expression which can be broken down into at least four morphemes constituting a whole proposition: the ideogram '5', the ideogram '>', the ideogram '3', and finally that morpheme which is the *position* of each of the three signs relative to one another (which alone enables me to say that that number which is greater than the other is 5 and not 3). Now each of these four morphemes is such that it cannot be segmented a second time.[3] Only by resorting to artifice can the sign '5' or the sign '>' be decomposed into elements that could be found in the make-up of other arithmetical ideograms. This absence of any second level of articulation is responsible for the fact that, although the system of arithmetical/algebraic ideograms is quite capable of expressing an infinity of propositions, the propositions it can express must be selected from a very restricted range, unless one is prepared to entertain the construction of an ideogram-system that is clumsy in the extreme, a system containing thousands of ideograms, corresponding to the thousands of morphemes that natural languages are capable of expressing through the articulation of some thirty of phonemes.

(3) *Systems of signs that employ only the second level of articulation.* Examples can be found amongst the systems of optical signals in use in the different navies before the development of radio communication. Many of these systems, it is true, were based on a simple alphabetic transcription of a written message; some of them, on the other hand, had their own completely *sui generis* mode of functioning, – for example semaphore, which succeeded in expressing a certain number of propositions about the force and direction of the wind simply by combining three elementary signals – a cylinder, a cone with its tip turned towards the sky, a cone with its tip turned down – distributed along a

vertical line. Here the elements of the second level of articulation, although optical and not phonetic, are nevertheless semantically just as arbitrary as is the combination of phonemes into morphemes in a natural language.

Now the account of grammar to be given in what follows leads us to refuse to reserve the term 'language' for the designation of systems with double articulation and to extend it to cover *at least* all those systems, singly or doubly articulated, which employ the first level of articulation. If it is true that, in the ordinary use of the words, 'grammar' implies a reference to a 'language', then we do not see any need to call unarticulated systems 'languages' (though we do not see any objection to doing so either) – and for the simple reason that these have no grammar, since they are, precisely, without articulation. Grammar, perhaps not always in the current sense of the word but at least in the only sense in which we can speak of *pure* or *rational grammar* is essentially a set of rules governing what, following Martinet, we have called the first level of articulation, that is, the segmentation of a message into the primary elements of meaning. Thus we can admit that systems of signs that enjoy only an articulation of the second sort have hardly any more of a grammar than systems that are entirely without articulation and we have therefore no interest here in claiming for such systems the name 'language', even if we have no definite reason for refusing them this name.

With this summary definition of what we shall call *language* it remains only to point out that the first two chapters of this book constitute a sort of introduction, both historical and theoretical, to the problems raised by the notion of grammaticality and to the history, in particular the recent history, of the forms these problems have taken and of the different attempted solutions. The elucidation of these questions is a preliminary stage in our inquiries. Without it we could not start that account of a pure, rational grammar promised in the title and which the remaining chapters of the book attempt to set forth.

Notes

1 A. Martinet, "La double articulation linguistique" (see bibliography, p. 324).
2 It would be wrong to regard double articulation as a privilege restricted to natural languages. A singly articulated artificial system such as that of the ideograms of arithmetic and algebra which we shall deal with soon can, if one wishes, be provided with a second, for example oral,

articulation. This is what happens when we read the proposition '5 > 3' as *five is greater than three*. For here, in contrast to the case where writing is a transposition of oral expressions from a natural language, it is the oral expression which is the transposition of a written expression whose self-sufficiency is such that it is not read in the same way by a Frenchman, an Englishman, a German, etc., even though it always *can* be read by any of these.

[3] The decimal notation makes it possible to form all numbers from the symbols for zero and for the first nine whole numbers, but this cannot possibly be considered as the sign of a second level of articulation. The way a number such as 235 is written has nothing to do with what is here called the second level of articulation, as is shown particularly by the fact that the three numerals 2, 3 and 5 are by no means without meaning. The way '235' is written pertains entirely to the first level of articulation and an expression such as 235 > 207 must be analysed as a singly articulated combination of the different morphemes 2, 3, 5, 7 etc.

Chapter One
The Level of Grammar

"What a funny watch!", she remarked. "It tells the day of the month, and doesn't tell what o'clock it is!"

"Why should it?" muttered the Hatter. "Does *your* watch tell you what year it is?"

"Of course not", Alice replied very readily, "but that's because it stays the same year for such a long time together."

"Which is just the case with *mine*", said the Hatter.

Alice felt dreadfully puzzled. The Hatter's remark seemed to her to have no sort of meaning in it, and yet it was certainly English.

Lewis Carroll, *Alice in Wonderland*, ch. 7.

Recognition of the Pre-Logical Level of Grammar

The project of establishing a pure, rational grammar has much in common with the hope of establishing a natural law. These ambitious dreams crop up again and again in the history of philosophy; the most recent outburst of interest in rational grammar occurred during the first quarter of the twentieth century. The problem of grammar presented itself in a quite novel way as a result of the development of logic itself: the characteristic tendency of the axiomatic method to make all the presuppositions of a given language explicit and to take nothing for granted necessarily led to a rediscovery of the fact that the distinction between truth and falsity only makes sense within certain limits, limits which might be called *syntactic* or *grammatical*.

The outlines of the problem are the same for both natural language and the simplest sorts of formalized languages. A tautology such as

$$Cpp[1]$$

can manifest two quite different contrasts. It contrasts with a propositional form such as

$$Cpq$$

16

which, if certain suitable substitutions are carried out, *may* lead to contradictions. Secondly, C*pp* contrasts with a propositional form such as

K*p*N*p*.

which, whatever substitutions we make, will always yield a false proposition. That this double contrast or opposition only makes sense because of certain syntactic rules means that it is possible to group together

C*pp*
C*pq*
K*p*N*p*, etc.,

and to distinguish these from series of symbols such as

*p*KN
*p*C*q*
*q*CC, etc.

These latter expressions do not deserve to be called either *true* or *false*. They are beyond truth and falsity because they lack the syntactic minimum which makes this distinction possible.

In *The Sophist*[2] Plato noted that an analogous situation arises in everyday language. In Theaetetus' dialogue with the stranger the latter points out to Theaetetus, who is seated, that the obviously true proposition

Theaetetus sits

and the obviously false proposition

Theaetetus (whom I am talking to at this moment) flies

have in common 'a certain character', namely of being true or false, a character that authorises us to group them together in the class of words 'which, when spoken in succession, signify something, fit together' and so to oppose them to those 'which mean nothing when they are strung together', which, the stranger says, 'you may utter ... all one after another, but that does not make a statement'. Aristotle, in *De Interpretatione*,[3] was even to give an example of such a string of words which, since they fail to satisfy the minimal conditions for syntactic coherence, escape the true-false alternative: '*of Philo is* or *of Philo is not* do not form either a true or a false proposition'.

This awareness of the necessity of a grammar of meanings as a preliminary to logic proper is, then, by no means new in the history of philosophy. Thus it is all the more remarkable that neither during the period in which Plato and Aristotle wrote nor later did anyone succeed in, or even dream of outlining, for a given language, the laws of this συμπλον, and this is in spite of the fact that Plato, probably in the wake of many others, had underlined the indispensable character of this weaving together of significant terms. If the reply to Plato's challenge is to be found anywhere, it is in the work of the Stoics who, long before the Romans, created what is commonly known as *grammar*. Strangely enough, syntactic considerations are nearly completely absent from the work of Euclid. All his axiomatic constructions implicitly presuppose grammatical conditions which he never attempts to identify.

But it would be wrong to criticize Euclid. The greatest logicians of the nineteenth century were to overlook the level of grammar and the nature of its justification, indispensable though this seems today. Frege himself, for all his scrupulousness and the radical nature of his reflections on logic, failed to get to the heart of the matter. It seems that logicians were woken from their grammatical slumbers by two more or less independent events: by the discovery of the antinomies within their systems and by the warning addressed to them by Husserl in his *Logische Untersuchungen (Logical Investigations)*.

Husserl there develops his famous distinction between *Unsinn* and *Widersinn;* the logical opposition between sense *(Sinn)* and absurdity *(Widersinn)* presupposes the distinction between *Sinn* and *Widersinn* on the one hand, and the properly syntactic notion of nonsense or senselessness *(Unsinn)* on the other hand. The function of grammar is to define those laws in virtue of which an expression avoids this basic sort of nonsense, whereas the function of logic is to define those laws in virtue of which expressions which, for syntactic reasons, are already free of nonsense also avoid absurdity. The former, Husserl writes, are laws

which govern the sphere of complex meanings, and whose role it is to divide sense from nonsense, are not yet the so-called laws of logic in the pregnant sense of this term; they provide pure logic with the *possible meaning-forms,* i.e. the *a priori* forms of complex meanings which are significant and unified, whose '*formal' truth* or *objectivity* the 'logical laws' in the pregnant sense of the term they govern. The

18

former laws guard against nonsense *(Unsinn)*, the latter against formal or analytic absurdity or countersense *(Widersinn)*. If the laws of pure logic establish *what an object's possible unity requires in virtue of its pure form*, the laws of complex meanings set forth the requirement of merely *significant unity*, i.e. the *a priori* patterns in which meanings belonging to different semantic categories can be united to form one meaning, instead of producing chaotic nonsense.[4]

The distinction between the true and the false, or in particular between the apodictic and the non-apodictic can only be made if there are 'possible meaning-forms' and these can belong only to an *a priori* grammar; logic as the 'pure theory of validity' presupposes a 'pure morphology of meanings'.[5] Faced with examples such as *a round or, a man and is, king but or like and,* "it is apodictically clear that no such meaning can exist, that significant parts of these sorts, thus combined, are incompatible with one another in a unified meaning", writes Husserl. But expressions such as *a round square, wooden iron, all squares have five angles,* even if one tends to describe them as senseless or nonsensical, nevertheless belong to "a sub-domain of the significant"; indeed they are "names or sentences as genuine as any". The indisputable absurdity of such expressions involves of course, as in the previous case, a certain form of incompatibility. But, Husserl makes clear, "the judgement of incompatibility is here concerned, with objects, in the previous case with ideas".[6]

The weakness of logico-mathematical systems was for a long time the fact, that, in their efforts rigorously to delimit the sphere of logical operations and procedures, logicians covertly assumed that the formulation of syntax would take care of itself; and syntax was abandoned to this intuition, an intuition which was then deliberately deprived of any guiding role. It is for this reason, Husserl tells us, that such basic syntactic rules are the last things one will think of when one speaks of logical laws; "one will think exclusively of the quite different laws, infinitely more interesting in our cognitive practice, that are concerned only with significant meanings and with their *objective possibility and truth*".[7]

Husserl returns to this theme in *Formal and Transcendental Logic:* our logico-mathematical systems take great care to reject expressions such as *no square has four angles, all A's are B and some are not B,* propositions for which the question of grammatical correctness does not arise. Because of this such systems are guided, says Husserl, less by "grammar (a word which brings *de facto* historical languages and their grammatical description to mind)" than "by the grammatical itself".[8]

19

Thus, in the name of requirements internal to logico-mathematical systems themselves, Husserl is led to rehabilitate the idea of a *grammaire générale et raisonnée* which was so dear to the rationalism of the seventeenth and eighteenth centuries. For, he writes, "the older grammarians instinctively concentrated their attention on the sphere of laws we have described, even if they were unable to bring it to full conceptual clarity". The distinction between *a priori* and empirical elements applies not only to the domain of logic, i.e. the domain of expressions which are already grammatically well-formed, but also to that of the merely grammatical. This or that grammatical detail, to be found in a given language, may equally well belong either to "chance peculiarities ... of nationality and national history, of the individual and his life-experience" or to "universal ... traits of human nature". But it may also belong to that *a priori* without which the distinction between the true and the false would lack all sense. The difficulty here, as Husserl notes, is due to the paradoxical fact that this *a priori* domain is so fundamental that its trivial yet ubiquitous presence has often escaped the attention of even the most rigorous axiomatisers. "Nevertheless its systematic demonstration, theoretical pursuit and phenomenological clarification remains of supreme scientific and philosophical interest, and is by no means easy".[9]

The task of this pure logical grammar will be to "lay bare an ideal framework which each actual language will fill up and clothe differently, in deference either to common human motives or to empirical motives that vary at random". Indeed, Husserl goes on, to the extent that

each language is bound to this ideal framework, theoretical research into the framework must accordingly be one of the foundations of the scientific clarification of all language as such.[10]

Logic and the Definition of 'Meaningful Expression'

At first glance it does not seem as though Husserl has had any success in encouraging linguists to work out a rational grammar; but it would be wrong to conclude that his suggestions have served only to feed further the speculations of philosophers. In one definite respect Husserl has had a definite influence not only on the course of philosophy but also on science itself. Logicians did not remain deaf to Husserl's reproaches:

It is not at all remarkable that, till this day, no logicians, not even Bolzano, have succeeded in ... forming the idea of a purely logical theory of forms. Logic accordingly lacks its prime foundation; it lacks a scientifically strict, phenomeno-logically clarified distinction between primitive meaning-elements and meaning-structures, as well as a knowledge of the relevant laws of essence.[11]

But Husserl provided more than a denunciation of the deficiencies of the logic of his time and general indications as to how to go about reducing all "the structure of the essential laws of meanings" to "a minimum number of independent elementary laws"[12]; he provided instructions as to how this reduction could be carried out, even specifying its two phases:

(1) First, one would have to fix "*the primitive forms of independent meanings, of complete propositions with their internal articulations and the structures contained in such articulations*".

(2) Then one would have to fix "*the primitive forms of compounding and modification* permitted by the essence of the different categories of possible members;" for, as he points out, "complete propositions may also become members of other propositions".

In this way Husserl defines the recursive method which, on the basis of a finite number of rules, is capable of yielding in a law-governed manner the infinite number of grammatically possible propositions. Indeed by using the method he indicates one could obtain "a systematic survey of the boundless multitude of further forms which are *derivable by way of repeated compounding or modification*".[13]

Not only did Husserl define the method, he also succeeded in furnishing an outline of how to put the method into practice in a text which we shall reproduce in full before commenting on it:

For example, to each of two nominal meanings M and N there belongs the primitive form of connexion M *and* N together with the law that the result of a connection is in its turn a meaning of the same category. The same law obtains if, instead of nominal meanings, we take those of other categories, for example, propositional or adjectival meanings. Any two propositions connected in the form M *and* N yield a new proposition; any two adjectives a new adjective ... Again, to any two propositions M, N there correspond the primitive forms of connection *if* M *then* N, M *or* N such that the result is itself a proposition. To any nominal meaning S and to any adjectival meaning p there belongs the primitive form Sp (for example, *red house*), the result being a new meaning fixed by law in the category of nominal meaning. We could in this manner give many other examples of primitive forms of connection.[14]

The entire text amounts to an enumeration of rules which today would be set out, somewhat more drily, as follows:

(1) If *'M'* is a name and if *'N'* is a name, *'M and N'* is a name.
(2) If *'M'* is a proposition and if *'N'* is a proposition, then *'M and N'* is a proposition.
(3) If *'M'* is an adjective and if *'N'* is an adjective, then *'M and N'* is an adjective.
(4) If *'M'* is a proposition and if *'N'* is a proposition, then *'if M then N'* is a proposition.
(5) If *'M'* is a proposition and if *'N'* is a proposition, then *'M or N'* is a proposition.
(6) If *'S'* is a name and if *'p'* is an adjective, then *'Sp'* is a name.[15]

Husserl points out in the next paragraph that once the primitive forms have been defined it is always possible to 'progressively substitute for a simple term a combination exemplifying just these forms' and so to establish an unlimited number of new forms by means of a 'conjunctive combination.' He gives the following examples:

(M and *N)* and *P*
(M and *N)* and *(P* and *Q)*
{*(M* and *N)* and *P*} and *Q*,

which he applies explicitly to propositions but which, in line with his intentions, might equally well have been applied to names and adjectives. Besides conjunctive combination he also mentions the possibilities of combinations which are opened up by 'disjunctive and hypothetical combinations of propositions'. He underlines the fact that such compoundings may be repeated indefinitely and so make it possible to obtain "insight into *the a priori constitution of the domain of meanings in respect of all those forms which have their a priori origin in its basic forms*".[16]

It has seemed important to analyse in some detail what Husserl said in order to be able to emphasise the historical point that his appeals were actually understood and his suggestions followed. An effort was made to fill the breach in the edifice of logic which had been noted by Husserl in the critique he had directed at logic, first of all, it seems, by the Warsaw School. Indeed it seems to have been acquainted with the *Logical Investigations* which led Leśniewski to his conception of what he called *meaningful expression*[17] and to his awareness of the necessity of a definition of this type of expression as the basis of all logical construction. Łukasiewicz, who accords the honour of inventing the term *meaningful expression* to Leśniewski, does not himself make any special mention of what this expression owes to Husserl's distinction between *Sinn, Unsinn* and *Widersinn*. But Leśniewski recognized his debt and explicitly refers in his *Grundzüge eines neuen Systems der Grundlagen der Mathematik*[18] to the 1913 edition of the *Logical Investigations;* Tarski, as assistant and so close a collaborator of Leśniewski, has confirmed that this influence is a matter of historical fact.[19]

From this point on the creators of logico-mathematical systems were to endeavour to define the conditions under which it can be established without any reference to intuition whether an expression is or is not meaningful before tackling the construction of the logical system itself. We need only compare the text quoted above in which Husserl sketched out some rules intended to establish the syntactic correctness of a language with the recursive definitions on which an author like Łukasiewicz bases a simple system such as his *propositional calculus*. It would be difficult to deny the direct line which goes from Husserl to Łukasiewicz by way of the recognized intermediary, Leśniewski:

"The expression x is a meaningful expression", writes Łukasiewicz, *"if and only if one of the following conditions are satisfied:*
(1) x is a lower-case letter;
(2) x is the negation of a meaningful expression;
(3) x is an implication with arguments which are meaningful expressions;
(4) x is an alternation with arguments which are meaningful expressions;
(5) x is a conjunction with arguments which are meaningful espressions;
(6) x is an non-conjunction (exclusion) with arguments which are meaningful expressions;
(7) x is an equivalence with arguments which are meaningful expressions."[20]

There are of course certain differences between the texts of Husserl and Łukasiewicz:
(1) The syntactic rules outlined by Husserl concern, it seems, ordinary language, whereas the rules proposed by Łukasiewicz deal with the much poorer language of the calculus of propositions.

(2) Hence the rules proposed by Łukasiewicz suffice to account for the syntactic correctness of *every* meaningful expression of the language to which they apply. This was not Husserl's intention.

(3) Not only are the rules proposed by Łukasiewicz complete with respect to their object but they are very much more rigorously defined, an advance in rigour due as much to an improvement in methods and analyses as to the greater simplicity of the language chosen.

In spite of these differences the procedure remains fundamentally the same. Łukasiewicz takes over Husserl's idea that it is not necessary to give explicit definitions of meaningful expressions, it is enough to give recursive definitions. Thus each of the seven rules set forth by Łukasiewicz – except for the first, which clearly only applies to an elementary, unanalysed propositional form – not only makes it possible to obtain complex propositional forms from simple propositional forms but also highly complex forms from complex forms. These seven rules suffice to check the syntactic correctness of any of the infinitely many propositional forms which go to make up the calculus of propositions. Thus the expression

NEKC*pq*A*qr*D*pr*

is *meaningful,* in accordance with the second case provided for by Łukasiewicz if and only if the form

EKC*pq*A*qr*D*pr*

is a *meaningful expression.* This latter expression is *meaningful* if and only if, in accordance with the seventh case provided for by Łukasiewicz,

KC*pq*A*qr*

on the one hand, and

D*pr*

on the other hand are *meaningful expressions.*

Now D*pr* is a *meaningful expression,* in accordance with the sixth case, if and only if both *p* and *r* are *meaningful expressions p* and *r* are lower-case letters and so conform to the first case provided for by Łukasiewicz.

KC*pq*A*qr* is a *meaningful expression,* in accordance with the fifth case, if and only if

C*pq*

on the one hand, and

Aqr

on the other hand are *meaningful*. C*pq* is seen to be a *meaningful expression* by consulting first the third and then the first case, A*qr* by consulting first the fourth and then the first case.

Grammar and the Notion of Grammaticality

This way of building up well-formed expressions fully meets the expectations a linguist rightfully has of a grammar. "An acceptable grammar" writes Noam Chomsky "must give a precise specification of the (in general, infinite) list of sentences (strings of symbols) that are sentences of this language."[21] The fact that this list is *in general* infinite means that, although it is not impossible to imagine languages containing only a finite number of sentences, this is certainly not the case with natural languages, nor even with the majority of known, formalized languages. Now "one requirement that a grammar must certainly meet is that it be finite. Hence the grammar cannot simply be a list of all morpheme (or word) sequences, since there are infinitely many of these."[22]

This is the very simple reason that prevents us from thinking of a grammar as a simple 'dictionary of sentences'. It is of course possible to construct artificially certain finite languages such as those imagined by Chomsky[23], which admit as expressions all and only those expressions containing at most three elements, which might be *a, b,* and their repetitions. The grammar would then be constituted by the simple list of the following fourteen combinations: *a, b, aa, bb, ab, ba, aaa, aab, aba, baa, abb, bab, bba, bbb.* In natural languages, on the other hand, we are always able to form entirely new sentences, whatever the previously established list of sentences might be. That this is the case is due in particular to the fact that "it is impossible to fix an upper limit to the length of sentences. Given a grammatical sentence of any length, it is always possible to construct another, equally grammatical, by inserting in it at appropriate points an adjective, a subordinate clause etc".[24]

This feature of grammar has been recognized ever since the historical

25

origins of the development of grammars. Thus in the Sanskrit tradition around two centuries before Christ, a commentator on Panini, Patañjali, explicitly underlined the remarkable fact that one can only account for the infinite variety of expressions by specifying a finite number of rules. Evoking the legend of the deity who had not succeeded, in over a thousand years, in teaching all the grammatical expressions by means of enumeration, he concludes: "But how, then, are grammatical expressions acquired? Some work containing general rules and exceptions has to be composed." Many centuries later, while the Indians were inventing the positional notation of number, another Indian, the grammarian Bhartrhari was establishing a parallel between this possibility of accounting for an infinite number of sentences on the basis of a few rules and the use of position to construct the infinite series of the whole numbers on the basis of a few numbers.[25]

These characteristics are all to be found in a logical system such as the calculus of propositions, in which normally a *substitution rule* is allowed, a type of insertion analogous to that found in ordinary language and which, when repeated indefinitely, makes it possible to construct a proposition that is as long as one wants. For, as its name indicates, this rule permits us to substitute for any elementary variable in a theorem an arbitrary well-formed expression without altering the truth-value or, *a fortiori,* the purely syntactic correctness of the entire proposition.

Thus as soon as one refuses to restrict one's attention to languages containing a finite number of expressions one must think of a grammar, whether of natural or formalized languages, as "a finite mechanism capable of generating an infinite set of sentences", a form of words which, as Chomsky uses them, is a deliberate return to Wilhelm von Humboldt's way of characterizing what is essential to every language, "the infinite use of finite means".[26]

Chomsky gives some artificial and hence ideally simple examples of such a use, such as the following four languages which we shall list in order of complexity.

(1) First, what is probably the simplest conceivable sort of such languages with an infinite number of expressions. It contains all and only the strings containing an arbitrary number of occurrences of the same sign, for example the letter *a: a, aa, aaa, aaaa,* etc.[27]

(2) The language Chomsky sometimes calls L1, containing the set of strings of *n* occurrences of *a* followed by *n* occurrences of *b: ab, aabb, aaabbb,* etc.

(3) The language Chomsky sometimes calls L2, containing the set of expressions made up of a string of an arbitrary number of the signs *a* and *b* in any order followed by the same string in reverse: *aa, bb, abba, baab, aabbaa*, etc.

(4) The language Chomsky sometimes calls L3 formed by the set of expressions containing a string of an arbitrary number of the signs *a* and *b* in any order and the repetition of the same string: *aa, bb, abab, baba, aabaab*, etc.

Nothing could be simpler than setting up the recursive grammar of each of these four languages:

(1) Two rules suffice here:

a is a well-formed expression;
if *x* is a well-formed expression, *ax* is a well-formed expression.

(2) Here also two rules suffice:

ab is a well-formed expression;
if *x* is a well-formed expression, *axb* is a well-formed expression.

(3) The grammar of L2 may be described with the help of four rules:

aa is a well-formed expression;
bb is a well-formed expression;
if *x* is a well-formed expression, *axa* is a well-formed expression;
if *x* is a well-formed expression, *bxb* is a well-formed expression.

(4) The grammar of L3 can be represented in one rule:

if *x* is a sequence of the signs *a* and *b*, the number and order of which are arbitrary, *xx* is a well-formed expression.[28]

We can see that, for three of these four grammars, those containing two or four rules, the first or the first two rules give the explicit definition of the elementary case (s) on the basis of which the second or the last two rules make it possible to construct all the other expressions by repeated application.

These recursive rules vary of course from language to language. Even while we were emphasizing the analogy between the calculus of propositions and natural languages we could not hide the differences. Within Indo-European languages the most obvious recursive elements are, for example:

the use of the relative pronoun, *the woman who was playing with the child that was carrying a sweater that had a colour that* ..., etc.;

the use of noun complementation (the logical rigour of which can vary), *the brother of the father of the cousin of the grandmother of* ...;

the use of the conjunctions *and* and *or* to connect adjectives;

the use of the *same* conjunctions to connect propositions, a feature of both natural languages and of the calculus of propositions.

It is thus quite normal for the grammarian to be of the opinion that "one of the main tasks of syntax will be to determine what elements are recursive in different languages and to specify the exact form of the rules which introduce them".[29]

This does not mean that the exploitation of recursivity in natural languages has no limit. The examples of *who* and *of* above show that if the recursivity of these forms is abused then one arrives very quickly at expressions that cannot keep our attention. Expressions such as *the brother of the father of the cousin of the grandmother* ... are usually only employed in order to produce a comic effect. But this comic effect is based on the contrast between the possibility of extending the recursive procedure indefinitely and our limited ability to maintain an intuitive grasp of such extensions. The recursive character of the grammar of historical languages explains why there is in these languages "an infinite sub-set of grammatical sentences, obtained by the application of the familiar rules of grammar and which nevertheless are, because of their great complexity, unpronounceable or incomprehensible, even if they have a perfectly clear sense".[30] Thus ordinary language is in practice led to limit the use it makes of the recursivity of its rules, to an extent that is difficult to specify because it depends so much on circumstance. In written language, since the reader who has lost the thread of an argument can always turn back a page, there is of course much less need to limit the repeated exploitation of recursive rules, whereas spoken language rarely makes use of the same elements more than two or three times in a row.

The grammarian is indeed obliged to take account of the gap between what Chomsky calls the *competence* that provides a speaker with his possession of these recursive rules, and *performance,* a gap beyond which he cannot pass. The point is not that creativity is bound up with the speaker's ability to deviate from the rules, *creativity* is rather, to use

Chomsky's expression, *rule-governed*. Competence, as this is established by the combinatorial interplay of grammatical rules, opens up possibilities which are indeed infinite. But these pure possibilities rapidly find themselves blocked by the empirical fact which is the instrumental imperfection of the speaker, listener or reader. These are limitations which the grammarian has no right to ignore, but he can explain them only by turning to psychology, physiology or sociology. Formalized languages, however, know nothing of these limitations for it is formalization that allows the logician or mathematician to analyse any finite expression, whatever its length, and to apply one and the same recursive rule an arbitrary number of times without there being any need for any intuition or grasp of meaning to accompany these operations.

It is this recursivity of grammatical rules that the expression *generative grammar* rightly seeks to emphasize, an expression Chomsky provides with the following commentary which leaves no doubt about his meaning. "In general, a set of rules that recursively define an infinite set of objects may be said to *generate* this set."[31] Chomsky, then, like Husserl, is right to trace his ideas back to the grammatical rationalism expounded from the seventeenth to, at least, the nineteenth century, from *The Port-Royal Grammar* to Wilhelm von Humboldt's essay *Über die Verschiedenheit des menschlichen Sprachbaues,* before linguists deliberately took the step of devoting themselves almost exclusively to reconstituting the historical evolution of languages and to the observation of their geographical variations. Husserl, it should be remembered, had congratulated himself long before Chomsky on the similarity between his ideas about grammar and those of Humboldt.[32]

The notion of well-formed expression in the vocabulary of contemporary logic corresponds almost exactly to what Chomsky today calls grammaticality. Indeed, so close is the correspondence that some commentators on Chomsky's work can assume a near-equivalence between the two terms in his thought. "A sentence is called grammatical in a given language", writes Nicolas Ruwet[33], "if it is well-formed; it is called ungrammatical or non-grammatical if it deviates in some way or other from the principles defining grammaticality in the language".

It will be pointed out that Chomsky himself has emphasized the danger of confusing *grammaticality* and *interpretability* or *meaningfulness*.[34] Although the two English phrases:

colourless green ideas sleep furiously

and

furiously sleep ideas green colourless,

are, if they are taken literally, equally nonsensical, one can admit the grammatical correctness of the first, where the second must be recognized to be fundamentally incorrect.[35] Hence the *grammatical* and the *meaningful* must be distinct. Another demonstration of the non-coincidence of the two terms is also given by Chomsky: the existence of expressions which, although indisputably ill-formed, are meaningful and, what is more, completely free of any ambiguity, such as:

Read you a book on modern music

or

The child seems sleeping.

But within logic this distinction between grammaticality and interpretability, or meaningfulness was effected a long time ago. It was the recognition of this distinction which seems to have pushed logicians in the direction of abandoning the locution 'meaningful expression', suggested by Leśniewski, with all its Husserlian overtones, in favour of the much simpler *'well-formed formula'*, which has the clear advantage of expelling all properly semantic considerations. As well as the examples just quoted, there is the even more radical example of Carnap's, suggested thirty years earlier:[36]

Piroten karulieren elatisch

Although none of these three words is to be found in a dictionary, it is possible to establish that the expression is German, if, Carnap explains, one knows that "'Piroten' is a plural noun, 'karulieren' a verb (third person, plural, indicative) and 'elatisch' an adverb", all of which is already displayed by the very forms of the words in a language like German. Since our Indo-European languages admit as sentences expressions consisting of a name followed by a verb which agrees with the name in person and number, and which is itself followed by an adverb, we are justified in calling the above expression *well-formed* whereas the term *meaningful expression* would be clearly inappropriate (since, as we see, the meanings of the individual words and hence the meaning of the whole sentence do not exist). Thus in order to understand that one is dealing with a sentence it is not only not necessary to understand the sentence, it is not even necessary to be acquainted with the meaning of any of its constituent terms.

It is much easier for the logician than for the grammarian to furnish examples of sentences which are not interpretable but are nevertheless grammatical: to the extent that it remains *formal,* logic comprises *only* expressions of this type. On the other hand the logician would find it more difficult than the grammarian to come up with examples of sentences which are a-grammatical yet interpretable. There are two main reasons for the difference between the logician and the grammarian as far as this last point is concerned:

(1) On the one hand, the formalized languages studied by the logician were constructed with the maximum degree of rigour and economy; all redundancy is strictly avoided; hence it is difficult to correct the suppression or displacement of a sign by appeal to context. If an expression is not well-formed the most a logician can do is to indicate the minimum number of modifications necessary to 'restore' syntactic correctness.

(2) On the other hand we are normally acquainted with formalized languages, as has just been pointed out, independently of any acquaintance with what they do or can signify. This has two consequences in the present connection:

(1) where the logician has not eliminated or bound his variables he will certainly be at a loss if he has to come up with an expression which is simply meaningful, whether or not it is also supposed to be grammatical;

(2) if the notion of interpretability is widened so as to allow, for example, that an expression like

Cpp

has a sense then, in most cases, the reader of the logical formula will not have at his disposal a network of meanings dense enough to enable him to locate this sense, to see through and correct its defective expression. Someone who hears or reads an a-grammatical sentence in a natural language, on the other hand, is guided in his corrections by the small number of possible senses suggested by the intrinsically well-formed elements of which the total expression is composed.

But these differences between the positions of the linguist and the logician are of little consequence in the present context. Every logician will agree with Chomsky that it is harmful to confuse 'intuition about linguistic form', which is indispensable to whoever wants to set out a grammatical system with recursive rules, with 'intuition about meaning'. Faced with a sentence like that from Carnap, what would we do without the first, but also what would we do with the second? It is possible to be interested in a logical system without taking the trouble to define the rules of well-formedness for expressions in this system and this involves deciding to trust one's intuitive and spontaneous grasp, not of meaning, which often does not exist at all, but of linguistic form. "The major goal of linguistic theory", Chomsky very rightly points out, "is to replace this obscure reliance on intuition by some rigorous and objective approach".[37]

But do the claim that "the notion of grammaticalness cannot be identified with that of meaningfulness"[38] and the refusal to admit that "grammatical sentences are those that have semantic significance"[39] permit one to conclude roundly that "grammar is autonomous and independent of meaning"?[40] The fact that it is possible to develop syntaxes without any corresponding semantics (as in the four languages thought up by Chomsky which we mentioned above) does not authorize any assimilation of languages which signify in a natural or an artificial way to this particular case. That grammar should endeavour to be independent of meaning shows that its aim is, as it must be if it is to deserve any autonomous existence, to acquire the status of syntax. This ambition is essential to grammar: if grammar could not successfully be *formulated* without any reference to meaning,[41] it would not exist and the present work would be without a subject-matter. On this point Chomsky can declare, without any fear of contradiction, "I am not acquainted with any detailed attempt to develop the theory of grammatical structure in partially semantic terms".[42]

But except for the unusual case of sign-systems defined without any concern for considerations of meaning, it is well known that the primary concern of those involved in constructing the syntaxes of natural languages and, indeed, of most artificial languages was to take into account semantic considerations – a concern that went hand in hand with the scrupulous elimination of just these considerations from their basic syntactic vocabularies. For syntax is syntax only to the extent that it is expressed in terms that abstract from and leave aside, all semantic considerations. The ambiguity here is due to the fact that it is precisely the task of grammar to define, independently of meaning, the basic conditions of the possibility of meaning. It would be rash and naïve to conclude from this that grammar scorns meaning. On the contrary, the

32

task of the grammar of a language that serves communication or calculation is to identify in an explicit fashion those prior – and hence necessary but not sufficient – conditions of the meaningfulness of expressions that go under the name of *rules of well-formedness.*

The Boundary Between the Grammatical and the Logical

If, however, we are to be able to consider syntactic correctness as the first level of intelligibility, it seems we must be able to identify a clear boundary between this level and the next level up. But where do the grammatical conditions on intelligibility stop and those which, in formalized and natural languages, are a matter of logic or simply of common sense begin? Are the degrees of intelligibility necessarily so numerous that it becomes difficult to isolate the point at which one goes beyond syntax? Is it, for example, possible to distinguish rigorously between the features of the grammatical *form* of expressions and the features of the logical laws of their *transformations,* to use a distinction set out in several different places by Carnap?

The answer to the question depends on the sort of language under consideration. In the case of a formalized language, axiomatic rigour is nowadays such that the syntax and the logic of a system are strictly separated. The rigour of the distinction is not merely a result of the methods used nowadays; it is the result of the nature of the object involved.

Let us look again at an example which is ideal because of its very simplicity, the calculus of propositions. Axiomatic presentations of this calculus normally begin with a recursive definition of *well-formed formula.* Definitions of terms obtained from the primitive non-defined terms normally come after and occasionally immediately before the definition of well-formed formula. These definitions have no creative role of their own within the calculus of propositions, do not contribute to the system's completeness; their principal merit is that they transform certain expressions into other expressions which are intuitively more accessible. It seems, then, that they may belong indifferently either to syntax or to logic. Rules of inference or axioms, on the other hand, always follow after the recursive definition of well-formedness has been given.

It is therefore tempting to assume that it is the presence of axioms that marks the difference between logic and syntax. For, as we have seen, syntax provides rules whereas logic, though it adds new rules, the rules of inference, does so in such a way that the new rules can only be used once the axioms are given. But to make the presence of axioms the key characteristic of logic is to confuse what is essential to logic with its axiomatic presentation. Yet it has been known since the work of Gentzen[43] that this is not the only possible presentation of logic and that the logic of propositions can be based on a simple set of rules without the help of a single axiom. In the method of *natural deduction* there are no more axioms at the level of logic than there are at the level of grammar. Should one conclude that the method of natural deduction abolishes the distinction between syntax and logic, a distinction which is, in any case, fragile, since it is bound up with a mode of presentation which is easily dispensed with?

In fact, for the calculus of propositions, the distinction between syntactically correct expressions, that is to say, expressions formed with the help of completely grammatical rules, and tautological expressions (which in an axiomatic presentation are obtained from axioms by using rules of inference distinct from the axioms themselves) can be made quite rigorously, independently of the method of presentation employed: logically valid expressions, here tautologies, form a sub-set of the set of well-formed expressions so that with the help of a recursive definition of well-formed expressions and a *truth-table* it is possible to allot any expression to one of the following three categories to the exclusion of the other two categories:

(1) The set of expressions which are not well-formed expressions (formulae) of the calculus of propositions.

(2) The set of well-formed expressions of the calculus of propositions which are not theorems of the calculus.

(3) The set of theorems of the calculus of propositions.

The last two sets together constitute the set of well-formed expressions of the calculus of propositions.

Thus within an elementary system such as the calculus of propositions the boundary between the requirements of logic and the requirements of grammar is clearly marked, so clearly marked that it is possible to graft different logics onto one and the same grammar. In order to illustrate this suggestion we might think it is enough simply to mention again the example of the recursive definition of meaningful expression cited above, that is to say, the grammar Łukasiewicz introduces as the basis of his two-valued logic. For Łukasiewicz bases not merely one but at least two logics on this grammar: a two-valued logic isomorphic with the classical systems of Frege and Russell, and a three-valued logic which differs from the latter not only in that certain theorems of the first logic do not appear in the second but also in the fact that two theorems, one belonging to the two-valued logic and the other to the three-valued logic are morphologically identical yet nevertheless admit very different interpretations.

No doubt those who want to regard definitions of terms as a matter of grammar can argue at this point that, in Łukasiewicz's systems, it is not merely the number of axioms that changes as we pass from two-valued to three-valued logic; rather, they might point out, Łukasiewicz is led to transform certain definitions, those of disjunction, conjunction und equivalence.[44] It might also be pointed out that, to the extent that two-valued logic simply adds an axiom to those of three-valued logic and so contains all the theorems of the latter in addition to its own, one cannot really speak here of two rigourously distinct systems founded on one and the same grammar.

Analogous difficulties arise if one considers the hierarchy of logics weaker than classical two-valued logic, for example what are normally called *absolute logic, minimal logic,* and *intuitionist logic.*

For when one passes from one of these systems to the next one and from the last to classical logic what one finds is, on the one hand, the same theorems as before together with the new theorems belonging to each new system, and on the other hand, at least in a number of cases, modifications of the definition of a well-formed expression. These examples, then, provide only a very imperfect illustration of the possibility of establishing a rigorous boundary between what characterizes grammar and what characterizes logic.

However, in order to establish the *possibility* of completely isolating the conditions of meaningfulness that constitute the level of grammar from additional conditions (i.e. in the present case, from logical conditions), it would be enough to construct a system satisfying the following double condition:

(1) That the specification of a well-formed expression and the definitions of the derived terms are strictly identical to those of the classical calculus of propositions;

(2) That the set of theorems of this system lies entirely outside the set of theorems of this calculus. Thus by comparing this system and the classical system of the calculus of propositions we would find that we have

two systems that are entirely distinct from one another even though they share the same grammar.

It is easy to construct such a system. We could, for example, raise to the level of a system the set of antilogistic propositional forms, that is to say propositional forms whose truth-tables show falsehood on every line in accordance with the classical matrices of the calculus of propositions. Such a system can be set up either by using rules and axioms or, if one prefers, by using the method of natural deduction. The demonstration of consistency and completeness is then so easy that we can spare going into the details.

The possibility of constructing such a system shows that the justification for our talk of a *level of grammar* has its basis in our ability, at least in certain privileged cases, to isolate this level from other levels of meaningfulness. This does not of course mean that we can conclude that the level of grammar can always be easily distinguished, whatever the language, from the levels of logic or common sense. The possibility we have noted of constructing systems exhibiting a sharp, unique boundary between logic and what is purely grammatical will not prevent us – as we shall see later – from concluding that, in the case of natural languages, it is impossible to establish a rigorous dividing line which would tell us where grammar ends and where the next fundamental structures of rationality begin.

Notes

1 We shall use here the symbolism developed by Łukasiewicz. It should be borne in mind that (1) the symbol for the connective does not occur between but before the two variables whose connection it expresses; (2) N is the symbol of negation, C of implication, K of conjunction, A of disjunction (non-exclusive disjunction, alternation), D of incompatibility (non-conjunction), E of equivalence.

2 Plato, *The Sophist,* 261e–263b, pp.304–10.

3 Aristotle, *De interpretatione,* 2, p.16a.

4 Husserl, *Logical Investigations,* IV, Introduction, Eng. trans. p.493 [Findlay's translations have been modified where necessary. – Tr.] We shall refer to the text of the second edition of Husserl's *Logical Investigations* (1913/21) and pass over the historical question about the extent to which the remarks of Husserl in which we are here interested are already to be found in the first edition (1900/01) or only in the second. On this question the reader is referred to S.-Y. Kuroda, "Edmund Husserl, *Grammaire générale et raisonnée* and Anton Marty" 1973, pp.169–75.

5 Ibid., p.493.

6 Ibid., IV, §12, Eng. trans. p.517 and §14, Eng. trans. p.521.

7 Ibid., IV, §14, Eng. trans. p.522.

8 Husserl, *Formal and Transcendental Logic*, Part I, a, ch.1, §22.

9 Husserl, *Logical Investigations*, IV, §14, Eng. trans. p.524.

10 Ibid., IV, §14, Eng. trans. p.526. For Husserl the 'ideal framework' mentioned in the text is not to be identified purely and simply with what is universal and common to different grammars. On the contrary, he regards this framework as forming only a part of universal grammar. For when each grammar fills up the ideal framework with different empirical materials it does this partly as a reflection of randomly variable motives but partly also as a reflection of universal human motives. Thus for Husserl the domain of pure grammar is included in that of universal grammar but the latter is not included in the former.

11 Ibid., IV, n 3, Eng. trans. p.528.

12 Ibid., IV, § 13, Eng. trans. p.518.

13 Ibid., IV, §13, Eng. trans. p.519.

14 Ibid., IV, §13, Eng. trans. pp.519–21. [For the first occurrence of 'nominal meanings' in this quotation Findlay has 'propositions'. – Tr.]

15 There is certainly much that remains to be settled as far as most of these rules are concerned:

(a) Husserl does not explain what he takes to be the status of adjectives.

(b) He makes no distinction between the different sorts of conjunction; he follows ordinary language in remaining undisturbed by the different roles of 'and' in connecting propositions, names and adjectives.

(c) The sixth rule, as formulated by Husserl ('to any nominal meaning S, and any adjectival meaning p...'), is a challenge to the theory of types.

But even if one were to admit that Husserl were wrong on each of these points (a conclusion we would not want to draw in a hurry) it should not be forgotten that he is here giving only a sketch which, as such, has the merit of paving the way for more rigorous formulations.

16 Ibid., IV, §13, Eng. trans. p.521.

17 Cf., for example, Łukasiewicz, *Elements of Mathematical Logic*, Author's Preface to the first edition, p.XI.

18 In: *Fundamenta Mathematica*, 14, 1929, p.14.

19 Cf. "The Concept of Truth in Formalized Languages", in: *Logic, Semantics, Metamathematics*, p.215.

20 Łukasiewicz, *Elements of Mathematical Logic*, ch. 2, p.37.

21 Chomsky and Miller, I,3 pp.284f.

22 Chomsky, *Syntactic Structures*, 3.1, p.18.

23 Nicolas Ruwet, *Introduction to Generative Grammar*, 1973, ch.1, 4.1, p.25.

24 Ibid., p.24.

25 Cf., J.F. Staal, *Word Order in Sanskrit and Universal Grammar*, Foundations of Language Supplementary Series, vol. 5, Dordrecht: Reidel, 1967, p.5. The parallel mentioned here is probably much more than a comparison; should not the very invention of counting, one might ask, be considered quite simply as the invention of a grammatical instrument? This would presuppose that its inventors were aware of the grammatical necessity of accounting for a system of infinitely many objects by means of the combination of a finite number of rules. Thus the invention of counting in the Indian tradition might be a by-product of the prior discovery of the essential recursivity of grammar.

26 Cf., for example, Chomsky, "The Formal Nature of Language", in: Lenneberg, ed., p.408.

27 Cf., Chomsky and Miller, I,3. Language L1, L2 and L3 are mentioned on p.285 of this work and in Chomsky, *Syntactic Structures*, 3.2, p.21.

28 For the grammars of the first three languages we follow Chomsky in Chomsky and Miller, pp.285f and in *Syntactic Structures*, p.34. We have simply modified the presentation of the rules in order to bring out the similarity with logical systems.

29 N. Ruwet, *Introduction*, ch.1, 4.1, p.27.

[30] Ibid., ch.1, 4.2, p.27.

[31] Chomsky, "The Formal Nature of Language", p.439, note 12.

[32] Cf., for example, Chomsky, *Cartesian Linguistics*, pp.19–27 and Husserl, *Logical Investigations*, IV, note 4, Eng. trans. p.529.

[33] N. Ruwet, *Introduction*, ch.1, 3.1, p.15.

[34] Chomsky, *Syntactic Structures*, 2.3, p.15.

[35] We do not agree with Roman Jakobson when he criticizes this passage from Chomsky (see his "Boas' View of Grammatical Meaning" (1959). Jakobson's aim is to show that the sentence

Colourless green ideas sleep furiously

is indeed perfectly meaningful provided one refuses to 'censure pedantically every metaphorical expression'. Because of its polemical form, Jakobson's requirement runs the risk of masking the difference between literal and metaphorical expression. No *censure* is involved in observing that metaphorical speech consists largely in allowing the speaker to cease to observe what logicians call type distinctions, which in literal speech are normally binding. Thus Chomsky's example has no literal meaning (this is Chomsky's point) even if one or more metaphorical meanings can be found for it. The example in fact brings us up against the problem of degrees of grammaticality to be dealt with in the next chapter.

[36] Carnap, *Logical Syntax*, Introduction, p.2.

[37] Chomsky, *Syntax Structures*, 9.2.1, p.94.

[38] Ibid., 10, p.106.

[39] Ibid., 9, p.94.

[40] Ibid., 2, p.17.

[41] The extent to which a syntax can emancipate itself from all reference to meaning will already be apparent from Łukasiewicz's recursive definition of a meaningful expression in the calculus of propositions (cf. above p. 23). It is even more apparent in the definition of the same expression given by Stanislaw Jaśkowski:

An expression is meaningful if and only if the following four conditions are satisfied:
1. It contains no other symbols than the capital letters N, C, A, K, D, E and the lower-case letters.
2. The capital letter N does not occupy the final position.
3. The number of capital letters other than N is one less than the number of lower-case letters.
4. In every segment of the expression that begins at an arbitrary point and continues to the end of the expression the number of capital letters other than N is less than the number of lower-case letters (quoted by J. Łukasiewicz in "Ein Vollständigkeitsbeweis des zweiwertigen Aussagenkalküls", in *Comptes rendus des Séances de la Societé des Sciences et des Lettres de Varsovie*, XXIV, 1931, Cl. III).

This ostentatious rejection of all reference to meaning nevertheless expresses precisely the *conditions of* meaning.

Let us note in passing that one peculiarity of Jaśkowski's definition is that it is not strictly speaking *recursive;* it proceeds by simply giving a structural description. This shows that at least in certain circumstances it is possible to imagine a grammar that does not proceed recursively but which nevertheless makes possible the construction of an infinite number of sentences. The link between a procedure's recursivity and its generation of an infinite number of sentences is less rigorous than Chomsky sometimes makes it out to be.

[42] Chomsky, *Syntactic Structures*, 9.2.1, p.93.

[43] M.E. Szabo, ed., *The Collected Papers of Gerhard Gentzen*, 1969.

[44] Cf. Łukasiewicz, *Elements of Mathematical Logic*, ch. 2, p.36 and ch.3, p.80.

Chapter Two
Meaning Categories and Degrees of Grammaticality

London is the capital of Paris, and Paris is the capital of Rome.

Lewis Carroll, *Alice in Wonderland*, ch.2

The Husserlian Notion of 'Semantic Category'

According to Leśniewski, his conception of *semantic categories* (*semantische Kategorien*), sketched out in 1922, goes back to the tradition of Aristotelian categories as well as to that of the 'parts of speech' of traditional grammar and to the work on 'meaning categories' (*Bedeutungskategorien*) of Edmund Husserl, who wanted to make these the foundation of his pure logical grammar.[1]

Husserl's own starting point was a distinction, which has been traditional since the Greeks, between *categorematic* and *syncategorematic* expressions.[2] For not every grammatical symbol can be said to have an independent meaning: hence all those signs will be called syncategorematic "which only have complete significance together with other parts of speech, whether they help to arouse concepts as mere parts of a name, or contribute to the expression of a judgement (i.e. of a statement) or to the intimation (*Kundgebung*) of an emotion or of an act of will (i.e. to a formula for a request or for a command)."[3] Quite distinct from syncategorematic signs or expressions are those which already have an autonomous sense, for example 'categorematic expressions of presentations or names' or 'categorematic expressions of judgments or propositions'.[4]

To what extent did Husserl follow the traditional distinction, and how far did he thereby modify it?

(1) For him, as for the ancient grammarians, what characterizes categorematic terms is that their meaning is an integral whole; as Priscian put it 'hae solae ... plenam faciunt orationem'.[5] Syncategorematic terms, on the other hand, owe their name ('consignificantia', in Priscian's

translation), to the fact that they only acquire a sense when combined with other terms.

(2) It is surprising that, in view of their adherence to this criterion, the ancient grammarians often held that names and verbs were the only two sorts of genuine categorematic expressions in language. "Names and verbs", says Avicenna, "both have a perfect sense".[6] In view of such failures to apply the distinction properly it is not difficult to understand why it has been violently criticised:[7] by itself the verb has a complete meaning only when it constitutes a proposition by itself, and this, as we shall see, is uncommon. Husserl, therefore, allows as categorematic terms not names and verbs but names and propositions, for only these are in accordance with the logic of the completeness criterion.

Although Husserl mentions the view that syncategorematic terms are 'quite meaningless' since only the whole expression 'really has a meaning',[8] he goes on to qualify this view almost immediately:[9] it would be an exaggeration to say that a syncategorematic term, like a grammatical conjunction, is entirely meaningless when considered by itself. To be more exact, what one should say is that it cannot have an independent meaning, that is to say: "cannot constitute the *full, entire meaning* of a concrete act of meaning". The dependent or incomplete meaning which characterizes syncategorematic expressions "can only be realized in a non-independent part-act in a concrete act of meaning", and hence "can only achieve concreteness in relation to certain other complementary meanings, can only 'exist' in a meaningful whole".

But to admit the existence of dependent meanings is, at the same time, to refuse to see language and discourse as any sort of simple combination of elements, it is to admit that "to each case of dependent meaning ... a law of essence applies, a law regulating the meaning's need of completion by further meanings, and so pointing to the forms and kinds of context or connection (*Zusammenhang*) into which it must be fitted".[10] The way in which the joint contributions of the different elements can combine to form a unified meaning is the very opposite of the mode of connection characeristic of an arbitrary mixture, sum or heap. Certain combinations are excluded as impossible and their impossibility is not based simply on the concrete sense of the sentence. It is not logical coherence that is important here but the coherence dictated by the grammatical meaning categories; the impossibility does not attach to what is singular in the meanings to be combined but to "the essential *kinds,* the semantic categories, that they fall under".[11]

Thus the impossibility of certain grammatical combinations cannot by any means be based on the mere incompatibility of the concrete terms occurring in the sentence. The proposition

This giant is small

owes its logical absurdity to the combination of two incompatible terms but, for all that, remains grammatically correct. The grammatical absurdity of a proposition is established only when every substitution for terms belonging to one semantic category of another term belonging to the same semantic category leaves the proposition's absurdity unaffected. If we replace *giant* in our example by *doctor, armchair* or *dog,* or if we replace the adjective *little* by other adjectives such as *brown, intelligent* or *sexagenarian,* the sentence *may* be meaningful. It is therefore grammatically correct and so its grammaticality is a matter only of the semantic category of its terms.

If we consider, with Husserl, a propositional form such as *this S is p,* we see that "we cannot substitute any meaning we like for the variables 'S' and 'p'". If we choose for 'p' the adjective *green,* then we can choose for 'S', Husserl continues, the words *trees, gold, algebraic number n* or *blue raven.* Ill-fitting although *green* and some of these nominal expressions are, to the extent that they are nominal expressions a certain unity of sense, what we shall call, 'grammatical combination', is nevertheless preserved.

Where nominal material stands, any nominal material can stand, but not adjectival, nor relational, nor whole propositional material. But where we have materials from one of these categories, it can always be replaced by other material of the same kind, i.e. always from the same category and not from another. This holds of all meanings whatsoever, whatever the complexity of their form.[12]

If, on the other hand, one takes an expression such as:

if the or is green
A tree is and[13]

then no matter what substitutions are attempted – for example the substitution for *is green* of any other combination of copula and adjective, or for *tree* of any common noun, for *and* of any conjunction – it remains impossible to provide these expressions with a meaning. This demonstrates that the observation of the *a priori* laws concerning the semantic categories of the expressions of a language is a necessary condition of its intelligibility. Husserl concludes

Hence arises the great task equally fundamental for logic and for grammar, of setting forth the a priori constitution of the realm of meanings, of investigating the a priori system of formal structures which leave open all material specificity of meaning in a theory of the forms of meaning.[14]

This task, which is a central feature of pure or rational grammar, will consist first of all in dividing all the expressions of a language into classes such that:

(1) Two expressions belonging to the same class can always be substituted for one another without the context becoming an incoherent heap of expressions.

(2) Two expressions belonging to two different classes never allow this possibility.

In addition to carrying through this division, pure or rational grammar must specify the properties of each of these classes, that is to say the *a priori* laws governing the combinations of any expression in each of these classes with any expression of some other determinate class.

After Husserl this notion of *semantic category* was redefined in what is without doubt the most rigorous and faithful fashion by Ajdukiewicz as follows:[15]

The word or expression A, taken in sense x, and the word or expression B, taken in sense y, belong to the same semantic category if and only if there is a sentence (or sentential function) S_A in which A occurs with meaning x, and which has the property that if S_A is transformed into S_B by replacing A by B (with meaning y) then S_B is also a sentence (or sentential function). (It is understood that in this process the other words and the structure of S_A remain the same.)

This definition takes as its starting point and clarifies the definition which Tarski had given and described as being only approximate:[16]

Two expressions *belong to the same semantical category* if (1) there is a sentential function which contains one of these expressions, and if (2) no sentential function which contains one of these expressions ceases to be a sentential function if this expression is replaced in it by the other.

Tarski also points out that the relation of belonging to a common semantic category is reflexive, symmetrical and transitive. It is therefore an equivalence relation, partitioning expressions into mutually exclusive classes, a point already implicitly contained in Husserl's analyses.

The Antinomies and the Grammatical Requirements
to which they Give Rise

The agreement between what Husserl and Leśniewski say about semantic categories goes no further. Leśniewski did not simply adopt Husserl's concept. Leśniewski's aim was to solve a problem posed within logic by Russell at the beginning of the century, a problem which was far from being at the centre of Husserl's preoccupations. Leśniewski's originality was to make use of a concept which Husserl had elaborated at a simple level of intuitive rationality, in order to resolve the problem of the antinomies raised by Russell. Russell had drawn Frege's attention to the antinomy of *the class of classes which are not members of themselves* shortly before the publication of the second volume of the *Grundgesetze der Arithmetik*. Not only Frege's own view of classes but also Cantor's notion of a set were victims of this antinomy. Shortly afterwards the problems multiplied when Russell showed that the level of predicates was subject to antinomies (the antinomy of the predicate *impredicable*). Russell's well-known response to these problems was the *theory of types*. And because this theory is put forward as a set of grammatical rules, Russell, as well as Husserl, must be accorded the merit of having put grammar back at the centre of modern logic. When applied to the concept of class the theory of types allows only individuals as members of classes of the first level, then only classes of the first level as members of classes on the second level and, in general, only classes of level n-1 as members of classes on level n. Similarly the argument of a first-order predicate can only be an individual; the argument of a second-order predicate can only be a first-order predicate; or in general terms, the argument of a predicate of order n can only be a predicate of order n-1.

The immediate advantage of the theory of types was, as Carnap notes,[17] to correct Frege's mistaken admission that all expressions are necessarily true or false, an admission forcing him to call any expression false containing a predicate combined with an argument from the wrong level or type. The introduction of rules such as those suggested by Russell opened up a domain for logic where the law of the excluded middle could henceforth hold without any exceptions: the true-false alternative holds only for syntactically well-formed expressions; apart from these we need only remember that there are expressions which lack sense and which Frege was obliged to count as belonging to the class of false propositions.

Leśniewski's objection to the notion of type as it is to be found in

Principia Mathematica is that, to paraphrase a formulation of Tarski's, it is a simple prophylactic measure against possible antinomies within the deductive sciences, whereas

the theory of semantical categories penetrates so deeply into our fundamental intuitions regarding the meaningfulness of expressions that it is scarcely possible to imagine a scientific language in which the sentences have a clear intuitive meaning but the structure of which cannot be brought into harmony with the above theory.[18]

Fiercely 'intuitionist' as he claimed himself to be, Leśniewski was not satisfied with the relatively pragmatic presentation of Russell's theory.[19] In this respect he was much happier with the Husserlian notion of semantic category. But Husserl's presentation of the notion does not show how the antinomies were to be avoided. This is achieved by Leśniewski's transformation and clarification of the notion which does without what Russell – with an eye to the impression his first formulation of the theory of types might make – called 'a simple *ad hoc* hypothesis intended to avoid contradictions'.

Russell was later to come round to the point of view of Leśniewski when he emphasized the need for a philosophical grammar, although there seems to be no question of any influence. But Russell's examples clearly illustrate the differences between the understanding of grammaticality of the logician who has come up against the antinomies and Husserl's view of the matter. Russell and Husserl agree that although "'Brutus killed Caesar' is significant, ... 'Killed killed Caesar' is nonsense, so that we cannot replace 'Brutus' by 'killed', although both words have meaning".[20] But other expressions Russell mentions, such as

virtue is triangular[21]

quadruplicity drinks procrastination[22]

are not in his eyes completely grammatical whereas, as we have seen, the analogous expression

the algebraic number *n* is green

served Husserl as an example of a syntactically correct expression.

The well-formedness of *virtue is triangular* is, for Husserl, due to the fact that *virtue* is a noun and *triangular* an adjective and that the syntactic form of the expression 'A is b', in which A is a noun and b an adjective, is grammatically correct. Similarly in *quadruplicity drinks procrastination* the verb *drink* calls for a subject and an object which must both be nouns, and this is indeed the case in this example. If we wanted to begin to put this in logical terms we might say that what we have here is a functor with two nominal arguments, and since we do indeed have two nominal terms to fill the argument places we must admit that the expression is well-formed. 'Killed killed Caesar', however, will clearly not be well-formed, because 'Killed' is not a nominal term.

But the simple distinction between names, verbs, adjectives, etc., that Husserl takes over from ordinary language seems totally inadequate if one's aim is to avoid the risk of encountering contradictions. The semantic categories of Indo-European languages turn out to be insufficiently precise to serve as means of calculation, as the Greeks realized. It is not enough to say that *virtue* is a noun and *triangular* an adjective; it is necessary to go a step further and point out that *is triangular* is a first-order predicate, that is to say, a predicate requiring an individual as its argument (*such and such an object is triangular*); however, *is a virtue* is a second-order predicate, as in *To be courageous is a virtue*; in this example *To be courageous* is a first-order predicate. A first-order predicate cannot take a predicate of any order as its argument. It is not enough to distinguish names from adjectives; it is necessary to distinguish within the class of names between names of individuals, class-names, names of classes of classes, etc., names of relations between individuals, names of relations between relations, etc.

In short, Husserl's understanding of grammaticality in the *Logische Untersuchungen* is such that, like Bolzano earlier, he would not have recognized the precise difference of kind that we would have to allow for today, after Russell, between the two expressions *round square* and *green virtue*.[23] Today we see that the first expression merely offends against geometry, where the second infringes type distinctions. It is false that a square is round, whereas the question about the truth or falsity of the claim that virtue is green cannot even be posed. Similarly, on Husserl's view, in the example from Carnap

Piroten karulieren elatisch (Pirotes karulize elatically)

the grammatical well-formedness of the expression is guaranteed simply by the fact that the form of the words used clearly indicates their verbal, adverbial or nominal nature. If, on the other hand, we take into account type distinctions, we will be obliged to note that, although, 'Piroten' does indeed appear to be a name, we have no means of knowing whether it is the name of an individual; and also that we have no means of specifying the nature of the predicate formed by the verb 'karulieren'. The fact that the sense of the words is not apparent is not, by itself, the main problem. But although the disappearance of sense in our example is without any effect on the indication that an expression belongs to this or that large semantic category (name, verb, adverb), it does, unfortunately, mean that the indispensable indication of the type or level involved disappears.

The Conflict of Grammatical Requirements

At this stage in our investigations we may, it seems, safely conclude that, after Husserl had simply sketched out the main features of grammaticality, authors such as Leśniewski were led to clarify and develop the nature of grammaticality, as a reflection of purely logical requirements. But before concluding that the inquiry begun in the *Logische Untersuchungen* is merely incomplete, it would be wise to turn to the linguists to see whether they are prepared to accept the developments of the notion of *semantic category* which we find in Leśniewski and his disciples. We shall see that there is on this point not so much a theoretical disagreement with the logicians as a divergence of interests.

There is, to begin with, a large area of agreement between logicians and at least some linguists. When Chomsky wants to show that the grammaticality of an expression cannot be based on a criterion of statistical frequency he gives an example to which neither Husserl nor any other logician could find anything to add:[24] in the context 'I saw a fragile –' the words *whale* and *of* may have equal (i.e. zero) frequency in the past linguistic experience of a speaker who will yet 'immediately recognize that one of these substitutions but not the other gives a grammatical sentence'. This shows that, as far as semantic categories are concerned, possibility and a certain degree of probability must be strictly distinguished. Chomsky is here in agreement with Husserl that empirical observation is totally unable to determine the characteristic combinations of categories so radically different from one another as name and proposition. So complete is the agreement on certain points that one finds Chomsky using examples which are nearly identical with those of Husserl, just as Husserl himself employed examples to be found in Bolzano.[25]

On the other hand, as far as certain other points are concerned, linguists would find Hussel's distinctions too simple and those of the logicians too fine. Thus, within the school of generative grammar, Ruwet[26] emphasizes that "it is important to sub-categorize the verbs ... by means of rules that refer to the context" in order to "be able to exclude from the grammar sentences like 'the order admires the boy', 'the boy frightens the cake'." In Husserl's eyes, however, such sentences would have been perfectly grammatical.

Type distinctions would rule out the first example since the verb *admire* requires as its first argument (or subject) an individual, which an order cannot be; but they do not allow us to describe the second example as ungrammatical: the verb *frightens* takes as its second argument (or object) an individual, and this is a role the term *the cake* can easily play.

Thus insofar as Indo-European languages frequently violate type distinctions, such distinctions are of no interest to grammarians, whose concern is not to refine a logical tool but to account for the structures of languages as they are. And the distinction employed by some grammarians between the categories of animate and inanimate beings, fundamental though it may appear to be to the grammarian, is of hardly any interest at all as far as most logicians are concerned and is, in their eyes, as little justified. The theory of types was invented in order to avoid the antinomies, that is to say, in order to exclude the possibility of proving in certain cases that a proposition is both true and false at the same time. And as long as the terms in propositions are of the appropriate types, there is no reason to think that sentences such as *the boy frightens the cake* will ever lead to antinomies. The simplest strategy then, is to regard this proposition as (1) a syntactically well-formed proposition which (2) happens to be false.

Thus we find ourselves faced with various accounts, not of grammaticality itself, but of the criteria of grammaticality. Husserl's account is easily distinguished from the others by virtue of the fact that it is less demanding than the other two; it appeals to a smaller number of rules; it is a slighter grammar. On the other hand, nearly all the requirements of a Husserlian grammar have found a place both in the tradition of generative grammar and in the foundations of contemporary logic. But in their definitions of their additional requirements logicians and linguists do not seem to be able to agree, and we shall try to show that it is essential that they cannot agree.

The amelioration of the instrument or tool of grammar which is the aim of logicians' investigations really involves a transformation of the very concept of language. As Tarski has stressed, universality is one of the essential features of colloquial language, for which there is nothing that cannot be said. What this means is that "it would not be in harmony with the spirit of this language if in some other language a word occurred which could not be translated into it". "It could be claimed", he continues, "that, if we can speak meaningfully about anything at all, we can also speak about it in colloquial language".[27]

But this privilege of colloquial language, its universality, is a mixed blessing. One of its effects is that in ordinary language one finds not only propositions or, more generally, expressions, but the names of these propositions or expressions, propositions containing these names and, again, the names of these propositions. And it is presumably "just this universality of everyday language which is the primary source of all semantical antinomies".[28]

The antinomy of the liar in its simplest form, as given by Tarski,[29] who was himself following Łukasiewicz, may be described as follows. Consider the sentence

C is not a true sentence

in which the symbol C designates precisely this sentence; we can establish by inspection that

(1) 'C is not a true sentence' is identical with C.

But the general definition of a true sentence

x is a true sentence if and only if p

in which 'x' is the name of the sentence 'p', allows us to write

(2) 'C is not a true sentence' is a true sentence if and only if C is not a true sentence.

Since (1) allows us to replace "'C is not a true sentence'" in (2) by 'C' we finally have

C is a true sentence if and only if C is not a true sentence.

and this is clearly contradictory.

The contradiction is equally clearly due to the universality of colloquial language, which allows a speaker to speak *about* the very language *in* which he is speaking. But does this not tend to show that "every language which is universal in the above sense and for which the normal laws of logic hold must be inconsistent"?[30] It is certainly possible to introduce into the grammar of a language rules which would eliminate the risk of any such contradictions. But to do this would be to form a hierarchical language, that is to say, a language lacking the universality of a natural language. The student of a formalized language must rigorously distinguish between the formalized language about which he speaks and the language in which he speaks, whether this is another formalized language or a natural language. The names of the expressions of the language he is studying do not belong to this language, any more than do descriptions or names of the structural connections between these expressions; these names belong to the metalanguage and it is only by observing this hierarchy of distinctions that the possibility of contradictions is excluded.[31]

The attempt to combine in one language the advantages of universality with those of non-contradiction seems, therefore, to be necessarily condemned to failure. Just such a project seems to have been Leśniewski's initial goal and was to give rise to his later disillusioned remarks on the pernicious influence of one-sided preoccupations with philosophical grammar;[32] it was to lead him to severe judgments about his first "stubborn effort logically to subjugate colloquial language and bend it to theoretical ends for which it was never created".[33] A language rich enough to incorporate its own semantics is condemned to contradiction. As soon as one renounces the infinite task of resolving colloquial languages into a hierarchy of levels each of which would provide the metalanguage for the next lower level, all hopes for the sort of radical rationalisation involved in providing a language with its own semantics must be given up. It is utopian to want to subjugate colloquial languages and formalized languages to each other's purposes. The choice that has to be made is between a language which is universal and inconsistent and a language which pays for its consistency by not being universal.

Languages and their Goals

We are led, then, to the consideration of the goal or goals of language. Language is first and foremost, it seems, a means; it is, we might say, almost a technique – provided we add that it belongs to that group of techniques whose acquisition, in the most typical cases, does not come about through artificial acts of invention or teaching. As a technique, it must be considered not exclusively but principally as the employment of certain means in order to achieve a certain end. But if the requirements of natural languages and those of formalized languages clash, then we have a conflict and hence a divergence of goals. "A language", writes Carnap, "... is a system of sounds, or rather of the habits of producing them by the speaking organs, for the purpose of communicating with other persons, i.e. of influencing their actions, decisions, thoughts etc. Instead of speech sounds other movements or things are sometimes produced for the same purpose".[34] The *basic* goal of language in all known civilisations – whether it is functioning to address another person, in an order, a prayer, in advice, or in the giving of instructions – seems to be that of communication. Does this mean that communication is the only goal of every conceivable language?

The fact that we are here ignoring other functions of language does not mean we fail to recognize their existence. There is no doubt that, at least in most cases, it would be very difficult to interpret a cry of pain simply as an appeal to another person for help, as a way of alerting someone else to one's own distress. It may well be a pure expression of pain, an expression that one cannot exactly imagine describing as disinterested but whose goal belongs more to the sphere of magical behaviour. Yet although the cry of pain provides relief, it is not a technique for providing relief. Let us recognize once and for all that the use of language is sometimes simply a response to a pure need for expression. This is indeed the first justification for certain grammatical moods such as exclamations or wishes, which do not even have to be addressed to anyone. Even within the range of the indicative mood, most societies are familiar, in one form or another, with types of expression that are nearly completely separated from any message whatsoever: certain forms of poetry or, at a less exalted level, chatter. Yet it will be recognized that if language differs from mere cries this is because satisfaction of the need for expression represents in language a sort of secondary employment of what is primarily a means of communication; language here turns aside from its normal goals.

But over and beyond communication language is capable of responding to new goals when, instead of using as a means of expression a temporal succession of symbols, words, gestures or those 'signals by drums, flags, trumpets, rockets' mentioned by Carnap,[35] it employs symbols which constitute meaning not by succeeding one another in time but by their spatial arrangement, as is the case with writing. With the transition from time to space two new possibilities for language are opened up; the awareness of these two possibilities will provide written language with two new goals, the second grafted onto the first.

The first of these two goals goes back to the very invention of writing: it is very probably the reason why writing was invented. The spatial arrangement of symbols has the advantage over their strictly temporal deployment that it provides the expressed symbol with a certain stability. The written symbol is always there, even when I have forgotten all about it, for the very simple reason that, since the action of writing is itself, like all my actions, temporally located, I can only write in space as a result of the accumulation of the effects of successive actions. And this of course presupposes that these effects are not themselves simply arranged in a temporal order of succession. Sounds do not allow themselves to be accumulated any more than the signs one might want to make on the surface of calm water. It is for this reason that symbolization in space proceeds from the medium of sand to that of, say bronze: a minimum of resistance by some material is the condition of all spatial expression.

But what here appears to us to be the condition of spatial expressibility must historically rather have been the purpose for which spatial expression was invented. If stability is the *sine qua non* of the spatiality of expression, the civilisations which have acquired writing probably only made use of the spatial form of expression initially because of the gain in stability. The power that writing has to retain a message and to preserve it against all sorts of deformation is what alone made possible those bureaucracies which, in their turn, were necessary for the establishment of the great empires at the dawn of history. That the disposition of symbols in space was initially envisaged only because of the stability with which this endowed them shows itself in the fact that the writing-systems of all known civilisations, rather than emancipating themselves from this linearity to which symbols are necessarily restricted by temporal expression, have only succeeded in reinventing a spatial equivalent of the one-dimensionality of time. Whether it proceeds from left to right as in the West, from right to left as in Semitic languages, from top to bottom as in Chinese, or from bottom to top as in some pre-Columbian writing systems, the line appears to be a more or less universal historical institution. Liberated in principle from the constraint of the impossibility of pronouncing two elements at once, an impossibility which made it necessary to order the elements 'one after the other along the chain of the spoken word [*parole*]',[36] writing has, paradoxically, pushed to one side the advantages of spatiality – evidence that the original aim was to attain stability and that spatial expression was the means to this end, rather than the other way round.[37]

Onto this function of fixing messages which is peculiar to written languages, another function has increasingly come to graft itself – a function which was almost totally unknown to Greek civilisation, which has its beginning during the first thousand years A.D. in the Indian and Arab civilisations and which has become increasingly widespread in the West ever since the Middle Ages. Written language serves not only to communicate, but also as a means of calculation.

Our everyday reasoning, as this is to be met with in ordinary language, is always reasoning about something, it has an object, whether or not this reasoning finds expression in signs. Hence if I want to communicate to another person the progress of my reasoning, I can do so only by urging him to go through the steps of the argument himself. Ordinary language does not make available any means of compelling the mind of another person to follow directly the course of my own reasoning. If the other person does not succeed in grasping intuitively whatever it is that is the object of my process of reasoning, if he cannot reinvent my reasoning on his own account, he will not understand. For the language in which I express my arguments is not identical with the process of reasoning itself. It is for this reason that, in such ordinary languages as those of arithmetic or Euclidean geometry, all teaching is maieutic; the object meant transcends the signifier used; there is a gap between sign and thing that reduces the pedagogue to the approach Frege described as follows: "there is nothing for it but to lead the reader or hearer, by means of hints, to understand the words as is intended".[38] Thus if I reason as follows:

Men are numerous
The Andorrans are men
Therefore the Andorrans are numerous

no-one will be able to follow me directly in my conclusions, for there is no meaningful process of reasoning which corresponds to these sentences and which can be intuitively grasped simply by following the indications provided by them. Indeed my listener or reader may even accuse me of *verbalism*, i.e. make the classical objection that I am operating on words rather than reasoning about things. Thus everyday reasoning is distinguished by the fact that it concerns an object which is the object of the speaker's thoughts or words but is not otherwise indicated.

The characteristic feature of a calculus, on the other hand, is precisely that it substitutes operations on signs for reasonings about what the speaker has in mind: it is the 'reduction of the theory of things to the theory of signs' by means of symbols 'so selected and perfected that the theory, combination, transformation, etc. of signs can serve to do what would otherwise have to be done by conceptual operations'.[39] The *operation* that replaces reasoning in this way is a tranformation of the different material signs – whether these be the pebble which gave its name to the calculus, the elements of the abacus which replace the fingers of the child or of the oriental book-keeper, or the ideograms manipulated in writing.

The discovery of the possibilities of developing languages whose essential function is to make possible not communication but calculation, i.e. whose signs were defined sufficiently rigorously for it to be possible to substitute simple rules governing their transformation for the reasonings that ordinary language had hitherto sought to designate has been belated, timid and gradual. Although this discovery is still going on it seems to have begun, as far as the West is concerned, with arithmetical operations: the exploitation of numeration of position by the principle of carrying over from the thirteenth century onwards; progress in establishing the most convenient direction for arithmetical operations (from right to left or from left to right?); the invention of the basic notations and ideograms of classical algebra $(+, -, =, \sqrt{}, \text{etc.})$ from the end of the fifteenth century; the process of perfecting the algorithms discovered by the Arabs and the Indians; the employment of the law of distributivity of multiplication relative to addition, etc.

Classical algebra, especially after Descartes and Viète, is a language which has ceased to be a means of communication in order to become a means of invention. An algebraic operation, a calculation, may very easily be the work of a single person who has no intention of allowing anyone to follow in his footsteps. It is of course true that formalized languages are very suitable instruments as fas as that particular sort of communication we call persuasion is concerned. A formalized proof or demonstration even possesses an efficaciousness not displayed by ordinary demonstrations. But demonstration in its most general sense, unlike communication, does not essentially presuppose two knowing subjects.

The fact that a formalized demonstration can nevertheless be exceptionally persuasive is due to the fact that, based as it is on material operations which belong to the order of what is empirically observable, it no longer requires that perpetual recourse to the object signified or meant without which the process of ordinary demonstration does not make sense. The superiority of formalized demonstration, which is responsible for the belief among some of its adepts that it is the only legitimate form of demonstration, is due to the fact that it is the only form of demonstration that is not maieutic. It does not involve inviting the interlocutor to attempt to reconstruct for himself a process of reasoning whose main steps can only be pointed out to him indirectly. Rather, it carries out under his very eyes *real* transformations which make possible the transition from one term to another. It is paradoxical that formalized languages, which are not initially set up for communicative purposes, should subsequently turn out to be the only definitive instruments of persuasion, precisely because their primary function was not that of communicating something to someone. In formalized languages the sign has won its autonomy; the operations on signs have a definitive, probative force which they alone possess.

Thus it is necessary to distinguish rigorously between two possible functions of language: the function of communication, which may well be regarded as the historically basic function of non-artificial languages, and the historically more recent function of calculation characteristic of the artificial languages which, since the Middle Ages, have based themselves on a revival of those ideograms that were held to have disappeared once and for all in favour of a uniformly phonetic type of writing.

It is doubtful whether one and the same instrument can carry out these two functions; the perfection of an instrument of communication is measured by the universality of its capacity for expression; the perfection of an instrument of calculation, on the other hand, can only be recognized when it has first been established beyond all doubt "under what conditions the transformation of one or more expressions into another or others may be allowed"[40] in such a way that, given such and such a proposition composed of such and such a group of signs arranged in such and such a way we may infer such and such another proposition composed of such and such another group of signs arranged in such and such another way. Historically, then, we have two functions – universality and operational reliability – which, as we saw above, cannot be combined.

Does this distinction between the two functions not imply that *language* means two very different things which it would be dangerous to confuse?

(1) A language is a system of signs adapted for communication; the essential feature of signs is to signify something other than themselves and language is just such a system of signs.

(2) A language is also a system of signs which lend themselves to certain transformations carried out according to rules; but the signs of this language, unlike those of the first, are not called signs because they signify something else. They may, of course, designate an object in certain cases; but in other cases they may well signify nothing at all. In this sense, as Carnap puts it,[41]

the system of rules of chess is also a calculus. The chessmen are the symbols (as opposed to those of the word-languages, they have no meaning).

The word 'symbol' means that what is so qualified is a *something* which has no other reality than that of being a possible object of a certain number of substitutions, of replacements or displacements, fixed at the beginning by the rules of the system or game.

But whether the role of signs is to signify something to another person or whether they are fashioned in such a way that they make it possible to arrive by means of operations and transformations at ideas which would otherwise have been accessible only via long and difficult trains of argument and processes of reasoning – each of the two cases together with the goal that corresponds to it is such that it must *follow certain rules*. The fact that some rules are *in part* common to these two types of language is doubtless due to the fact that both are products of the same sort of intuitive rationality. And it is also due to the historical fact that language as a system of calculation was developed on the basis of language as a system of communication. English logicians, for example, discovered in the middle of the nineteenth century that the same law of distributivity of multiplication over addition which had been discovered by the Italian algebraists at the end of the fifteenth century is also exhibited by the relations holding between the connective *or* and the connective *and* in ordinary languages (at least in certain senses).

But the fact that these rules were partially common has sometimes been responsible for the illusion that they could become wholly or completely shared and that a sort of universal calculus or *mathesis universalis* might equally well serve as a mode of universal communication. For a long time it was thought that the only difference between formalized and colloquial languages was the greater precision of the former. A system whose purpose is communication could only profit by eliminating the ambiguities that the clumsy adjustments of history have not been able to rid it of; ambiguity is as harmful for communication as it is for calculation. And natural languages could only profit from the discoveries that resulted from the developments of formalized languages. But it is very unlikely that natural languages could have any interest in adopting distinctions which in formalized languages serve to make these languages operational, in view of the fact that, in order to become operational in this way, natural languages would have to renounce their flexibility and that universality which remains the essential property of a good system of communication.

Thus the grammar of language as a system of communication cannot pretend to be capable of being organized as an algorithmic system such that every grammatical expression falls under the principle of the excluded middle, even though this requirement seems to be the fundamental justification for the underlying presence of syntactic structure in formalized systems. But if the criterion of the grammaticality of a sentence is no longer the fact that this sentence is necessarily true or false,[42] to what new criterion shall we appeal in order to satisfy the requirements of grammar? If we can no longer define all the formal conditions that a sentence must satisfy in order to be capable of interpretation, but only some of these, if we can no longer determine the complete list of necessary and sufficient conditions for a sentence to be interpretable without affecting the universality of language, where must we draw the line around that list of merely necessary conditions that we call *grammar?*

This poses the problem, familiar to grammarians, of degrees of grammaticality. For either grammaticality can be defined by the possibility of applying the principle of the excluded middle as is the case with the specification of well-formedness in the calculus of propositions – and then there is a clear, unique boundary between the grammatical and the non-grammatical; or one can only speak of degrees of grammaticality between which we must choose.

We shall illustrate this idea by reference to the four sentences:

(1) Peter prefers this apple to that one.
(2) This pear prefers this apple to that one.
(3) The flavour prefers this apple to that one.
(4) Peter prefers to this apple.

It is obvious that, of all these four sentences, only the first really makes sense, because it alone satisfies the following three conditions:

(a) The verb *prefer* must have a subject and two objects: *x prefers y to z*. Logically speaking *prefer* is a predicate that takes three arguments.

(b) The arguments of the predicate *prefer* may always be names of individuals; although the first argument can only be the name of an individual, the last two arguments, which grammarians usually call *complements,* may easily be names of predicates[43] (the object of my preference need not be an individual; it may be a quality).

(c) If the sentence containing *prefer* is to have a sense, this name of an individual may only designate an individual endowed with that minimum of personality that enables him to act on his preferences, in short, an *animate being.*

None of our four sentences except the first satisfies all three conditions; the second sentence does not meet condition (c); the third does not meet either (b) or (c); the fourth does not meet (a). Shall we then say that only the first of our four sentences is grammatical? Husserl would have considered the first three sentences as completely grammatical, although two of them hardly make any sense at all. As to the logician, he might be tempted to introduce considerations of types that would lead him to make a distinction which, in the eyes of the grammarian, will certainly seem quite arbitrary; he will be led to deny the grammaticality of the third sentence while at the same time admitting that of the second sentence. Thus Husserl would, it seems, have made do with rule (a), the logicians with (a) and (b), certain grammarians with (a) and (c);[44] some writers, finally, would require that all three conditions be satisfied.

There is therefore some arbitrariness involved in the plurality of levels between which we must choose. Should one leave to grammar or to good sense the task of determining that the subject of verbs such as *love, prefer, admire, want, fear,* and the direct objects of verbs as *convince, astonish, delight, seduce,* must be individuals belonging to the category of animate beings and of excluding as ungrammatical

This picture loves Peter,

or

Peter seduces this picture?

Such specifications can of course be incorporated into an account of what is grammatical. Indeed there is nothing to prevent us from going further; we can so structure our grammar that sentences such as the following which, in one way or another, are contradictory, turn out to be non-grammatical:

> It rains every time it does not rain.
> The sum of the angles of a triangle is equal to three right angles.
> The father of Peter is at the same time his son.

Nothing prevents us going even further and bringing within the domain of grammaticality everything that pertains to common sense except for considerations such as that just mentioned of the inevitable renunciation of universality.

In practice the grammarian – whose task is by and large that of accounting for systems with which we are familiar – will be obliged to specify in certain cases the semantic category of those names that are allowed to play this or that grammatical role if the syntax he is studying is itself not indifferent to such distinctions. Thus French distinguishes in certain circumstances between the case where the complement does and does not designate an animate being:

animate	*non-animate*
je suis content de lui	j'en suis content
(I am happy about him)	(I am happy about that (e.g. about that fact))
je pense à lui	j'y pense
(I am thinking about him)	(I am thinking about it (this job))
qui vois-tu	que vois–tu?[45]
(who do you see?)	(what do you see?)

It is therefore not surprising that grammarians have been led to recognize that the description of natural languages 'requires that we generalize the grammatical-ungrammatical dichotomy, developing the notion of degree of grammaticalness';[46] that they do not hesitate to speak of semi-grammatical sentences.[47] or sentences that are *more* or *less grammatical* than others. Thus in the study of natural languages they substitute for the ideal of a unique grammar the representation of a hierarchy of grammars, distinguishing for example as does Chomsky, between 'context-dependent grammars' and 'context-free grammars'[48] depending on their intrinsic strength.

The difficulty of drawing a single boundary between what is and what is not grammatical within a natural language is increased by the fact that this boundary itself shifts as the language is used in different ways. Scientific uses of French or English are governed much more strictly than their poetic uses. To admit type distinctions, for example, would mean ruling out most metaphors, all those that go beyond comparing individual objects with individual objects or, more generally, go beyond comparisons of terms of the same type. Thus we could no longer say

Jealousy is cruel as the grave

Generosity triumphs.

It is difficult to see what a poetry would look like that conformed to type distinctions; it would certainly cease to be an 'art of suggestion'.

Conclusions of the First Two Chapters

Let us now sum up some of the conclusions we seem to have been led to by the analyses of these first two chapters.

(1) We have seen that it was possible to imagine linguistic systems in which the grammatical level can be rigorously isolated from higher levels of intelligibility.

(2) On the other hand, in the majority of known linguistic systems, in particular those of natural languages, the transition from what is simply grammatical to less elementary forms of rationality is a gradual one, and it is not possible to determine a unique boundary.

(3) In addition, although it is certainly impossible to define a common body of grammatical structure with which both logicians and linguists could make do, the very requirements with which the two groups are concerned may then lead them to go beyond this common basis and develop descriptions of various additional degrees of grammaticality that lead to their paths diverging.

In view of these conclusions the object of the following chapters will be to try throw some light on this common body of grammatical structure even if, once we reach certain cross-roads, we attempt to make some incursions into domains where the paths of logic and grammar diverge or, more simply still, into domains where, even if the paths have not diverged historically, the possibility of such a divergence is nevertheless inscribed in the order of things.

Notes

1. "Grundzüge eines neuen Systems der Grundlagen der Mathematik", *Fundamenta Mathematica* 14, 1929, p.14.
2. Husserl, *Logical Investigations,* IV, §4 Eng. trans. Vol. II, p.499f.
3. A. Marty, quoted by Husserl, ibid., Eng. trans. p.499.
4. Husserl, ibid., Eng. trans. p.500.
5. Quoted by Roland Donzé, *La grammaire générale et raisonnée de Port-Royal,* 1967, note 36, p.198.
6. Ibid.
7. In fact, in order to remain consistent, the ancient grammarians were often obliged to add that name and verb were categorematic in that they succeeded in forming a complete meaning when combined together to make a proposition. But does this not deprive the term 'categorematic' of all sense? Would it not have been more satisfactory in these circumstances to accord the status of categorematic expression only to propositions?
8. Husserl, *Logical Investigations,* IV, §4, Eng. trans. p.500.
9. Ibid., IV, §7, Eng. trans. p.506.
10. Ibid., IV, §10, Eng. trans. p.510.
11. Ibid., IV, §10, Eng. trans. p.511.
12. Ibid., Eng. trans. pp.511f.
13. Ibid., Eng. trans. p.512.
14. Ibid., Eng. trans. p.513.
15. "Syntactic Connexion" in: S. McCall. ed., *Polish Logic 1920–1939,* Oxford: Clarendon Press, 1967, p.208.
16. "The Concept of Truth in Formalized Languages", in: *Logic, Semantics, Metamathematics,* p.216. Ajdukiewicz's article appeared in 1935; the original Polish edition of Tarski's article appeared in 1933.
17. Carnap, *The Logical Syntax of Language,* ch.3, p.137. We here follow Carnap's interpretation. Just how true it is that Frege made the mistake Carnap accuses him of is a historical question we cannot go into here. It should be noted, however, that in "Begriff und Gegenstand" of 1892 (in Geach and Black, ed.) Frege gives examples of propositions that are neither true nor false but meaningless ('weder wahr, noch falsch, sondern sinnlos'). It is therefore somewhat misleading to say, as does Carnap, that

> Russell was the first to make the threefold distinction that has become so important for the further development of logic and its application to empirical science and philosophy, between true, false and meaningless expressions.

18. Tarski, "The Concept of Truth in Formalized Languages", p.215. Although Tarski was later to abandon this view (cf. ibid., Postscript, p.268), this formulation seems to capture Łukasiewicz's thoughts on the matter.
19. Leśniewski, "Grundzüge eines neuen Systems der Grundlagen der Mathematik", p.78. The final passage of this work is worth quoting in full:

> I would see no contradiction in wanting to assert that whilst constructing my system I go in for a fairly radical 'formalism' precisely because I am a stubborn 'intuitionist'. By setting out various deductive theories, I attempt to give expression in a series of propositions to a series of thoughts I have about this or that topic, and to derive some propositions from others in such a way that they harmonize with the modes of inference *(Schlußweisen)* which I intuitively regard as binding for me. I know of no more effective method of making the reader acquainted with my 'logical intuitions' than the method of 'formalisation' of the deductive theories that are to be set out and which, however, by no means cease to consist of genuine meaningful propositions under the influence of such a 'formalisation'.

[20] Russell, "Logical Atomism" as repr. in: D. Pears, ed., *Russell's Logical Atomism*, London: Fontana, 1972, p.155; and in *Logic and Knowledge*, p. 206.

[21] Russell, *The Principles of Mathematics*, 2nd ed., Introduction, 1937, p.xiv.

[22] Russell, *An Inquiry into Meaning and Truth*, 1940.

[23] Cf. Bolzano, §67, pp.88f. These examples of Bolzano's coincide almost exactly with those given by Husserl – whether due to recollection or coincidence we do not know – but without mention of Bolzano.

[24] Chomsky, *Syntactic Structures*, p.16.

[25] 'The blue crow is green' served Husserl, as we have seen, as an example of a well-formed expression. 'The black crows are white' is put to the same use by Chomsky (cf. Chomsky and Miller, I,3). It will be noticed that Chomsky's is the better example of the two. Husserl's sentence has the disadvantage that it combines two quite different sorts of 'absurdity':

(1) the logical absurdity of saying that a crow that is not green is green

(2) the empirical absurdity (if this is the correct expression) whose basis is the recognition that there are no such things as blue crows.

[26] *Introduction to Generative Grammar*, ch. 3, p.93.

[27] Tarski, "The Concept of Truth in Formalized Languages" p.164. This privilege of universality enjoyed by natural languages was also recognized by Louis Hjelmslev whose research in linguistics led him independently – and simultaneously – to the same conclusions as Tarski. "By everyday language", Hjemslev writes, "one understands *a language into which all other languages can be translated* ... in everyday language one can formulate anything at all, if necessary in a very roundabout way and at the price of paying very close attention". (Hjelmslev, *Le Langage*, Minuit, 1966, p.139.) We have preferred to refer to Tarski because he seems to have pursued further than Hjelmslev the analysis of all the implications of this universality.

[28] Ibid.

[29] Ibid., p.158.

[30] Ibid., pp.164f.

[31] Ibid., p.167. The point developed by Tarski here was first made by Leśniewski. It is clear that the universality of language is bound up not with just any logical antinomy but precisely with those that Carnap, following Peano and Ramsey, called 'syntactic antinomies' and for which Tarski, following Leśniewski, used the more suitable term 'semantic antinomies'. In order to obtain a semantic antinomy it is necessary to speak about the expressions of a language, to designate these, and so to move to the metalanguage, whilst the logical antinomies in the narrow sense such as that of the class of non-self-membered classes may be obtained without making the transition to the metalinguistic level. A grammar of the sort in which the logician may be interested must clearly be constructed so as to avoid both sorts of antinomy.

[32] Cf. E.D. Luschei, *The Logical Systems of Leśniewski*, Amsterdam: North-Holland, 1962, ch.2, pp.23ff.

[33] Ibid., p.20.

[34] *Introduction to Semantics*, p.3.

[35] Ibid.

[36] F. de Saussure, *Cours de Linguistique Générale*, 1966, ch.5, p.170.

[37] The institution of the written line is, apparently, historically prior to the process in which written language came gradually closer to oral language, as ideograms – the hieroglyphs of Egypt, and the Chinese and cuneiform writing systems – progressively changed into phonetic writing systems. Of course once one has phonetic writing it is not surprising that the writings form should be linear, for it is bound to the one-dimensionality of phonic material.

[38] "Begriff und Gegenstand", in: Geach and Black, eds., p.43.

[39] Lambert, *Neues Organon*, vol.2, 1764, §§23f, p.16. Quoted by Husserl, *Logical Investigations*, I, §20, Eng. trans. p.305.

[40] Carnap, *Logical Syntax*, §2, p.4.

[41] Ibid., p.5.

[42] This is true whether or not the verification of a sentence occurs within the system or by reference to experience.

[43] We postpone for discussion at a later stage the question whether the verb *prefer* contains the same functor when its complements are names of individuals as it does when they are names of predicates.

[44] We prefer our example here to the very similar example given by Chomsky in *Syntactic Structures* (5, note 7, pp.42f; 7, pp.78f). The sentence 'John admires sincerity' is, Chomsky tells us, more grammatical than 'sincerity admires John' which is more grammatical in its turn than 'sincerity admires eat' or 'of admires John'. The difference between Chomsky's example and our own is that the latter brings out a divergence between the logician and the grammarian concerning degrees of grammaticality. In this sense the term 'degree' is not the ideal metaphor for what we want to say here, as it risks suggesting the idea of a linear progression and masks the existence of bifurcations.

[45] Cf. Ruwet, *Introduction to Generative Grammar*, ch.1, p.36 from whom we borrow the last two examples.

[46] Chomsky, *Syntactic Structures*, 5, p.36, note 2.

[47] Ibid.

[48] Cf. especially Chomsky and Miller, II,3 and II,4.

Chapter Three
Name, Proposition, Functor

On the Distinction Between the Three Categories

Our investigation will be restricted, to begin with, to the grammar of the indicative mood. Not because the indicative is the only mood which is of interest; our spontaneous use of language shows that this is not the case; it is as natural to give someone an order or to make a request as it is to convey an indication of something to him. But between orders and requests on the one hand, and indication on the other, there is a fundamental difference, clearly perceived by the Greeks. As Aristotle put it, it is only in *declarative* or apophantic discourse "that there resides truth and falsity. Thus a prayer is a sentence, but is neither true nor false".[1]

The main reason for beginning with the indicative is a practical one: at least in most Indo-European languages, the indicative enjoys a privileged position; its grammar is better developed than that of other moods; and what is known of the evolution of language seems to indicate that the use of the indicative is becoming more extensive and that there is, if not a decline, at the very least a contraction in the use of the other moods. And, of course, the indicative is the mood *par excellence* of the theoretical attitude which is required by science. On this point Aristotle's exhortation –

Let us therefore dismiss all other types of sentence but the proposition, for this last concerns our present inquiry, whereas the investigation of the others belongs rather to the study of rhetoric or of poetry,[2]

– has been taken only too seriously. To the extent that its ambitions have been extensional, modern logic has exploited the privilege accorded by Aristotle to the indicative and confirmed its primacy over other moods. Only during the last thirty years have logicians begun to take an interest in the other moods.

There seem to be two ways of *indicating* something to another person. I can first of all point out some object to him: without saying a word I can

63

merely point with my finger towards some object; in other cases, in order to reduce the ambiguity which arises from the fact that a series of different objects lie in the direction indicated by my finger, I may accompany my gesture with verbal indications about the object designated. Thus I will say not 'this', but 'this tree'. In other cases I may abstain from both gestures and demonstratives and yet designate by means of an indication or series of indications ('the tree of such and such a species, of such and such a height, which is to be found at such and such a spot', etc.) which I judge to be sufficient to eliminate doubt or error as to the identity of the object I have in mind.

The second way of bringing something to the attention of another person is to state a proposition. Now as Husserl points out,[3] "in the judgment a state of affairs [*Sachverhalt*] ... becomes intentionally objective to us"; it is therefore not an object that could be sensibly perceived and which we could therefore point to with a finger. If it rains outside I may of course point my finger to the sky I see from my window and refer by saying 'the rain'. But if, on looking at the sky, I state 'it is raining' I no longer refer to or designate something, rather, I express a proposition, which will continue to be true or false and which claims to make known the fact that it is raining. Of course, as is apparent from our example, the state of affairs and what was designated are not without some connection. But what distinguishes assertion and statement from designation is that "what 'appears' before us, or becomes intentionally objective to us, is not the existent sensible object but the fact that *this is*".[4] Further on, Husserl writes:

Just as it is not the same, in terms of intentional essence, whether one perceives an existent or judges that it exists, so it is not the same if one names an existent as existent, or says or predicates of it that it exists.[5]

After Bolzano, Husserl and Leśniewski, then, it must be admitted that

nominal acts and complete judgments never can have the same intentional essence, and hence that every transformation or modification of one into the other, though preserving a common core, necessarily works changes in this essence.[6]

Apart from the function of designation carried out in language by names and the function of asserting or stating which is the job of propositions, there are hardly any other acts the contents of which are wholly and properly indicative, so that it is legitimate to conclude that with these two sorts of linguistic items we have the only two known types of categorematic expression. Thus not only is the distinction between name and proposition by no means arbitrary, but the designations and assertions expressed by these two types appear to be the only real structures of indication (in the full and proper sense of the word) that we could ever encounter.

The only point which, in our opinion, is open to discussion, is whether it is not necessary to be even more restrictive in the use of the term 'categorematic'. Without actually using the term, Plato, in *The Sophist*,[7] seems to be in favour of some such restriction: if it is characteristic of indicative discourse that it is either true or false, we seem to be compelled to recognize that 'a statement never consists solely of names' –

And again, if you say 'lion stag horse' and any other names given to things that perform actions, such a string never makes up a statement.

This refusal to see in names anything more than syncategorematic expressions is also to be met with in *The Port-Royal Grammar*:[8]

there is never a nominative which lacks a relationship to some verb either expressed or understood, because the purpose of speech is not only to indicate conception, but also to express what is thought about what is conceived, and this latter purpose is what is marked by the verb.

More recently, a similar view has been put forward in the *Tractatus Logico-Philosophicus*[9] of Ludwig Wittgenstein: names are there regarded as simple signs designating objects which are elements of a situation; but just as an object cannot be conceived of independently of the state of affairs within which it combines with other objects, so too it is only within the body of the proposition that the name has a sense; more exactly, a name corresponds to a particular object only if it is itself part of a proposition.

When considered independently of their role in propositions it does seem that names and the designation accomplished with their aid belong to very elementary situations such as that of a child who, on seeing the moon or a bird, says simply: 'the moon' or 'the bird'. But expressions of this sort may well be exclamations rather than indications effected by referring expressions. Adults, who are accustomed in the majority of cases to more practical behaviour, are less likely to see the point of such pure designation and reserve the use of names for the designation of objects whose names form part of their statements.

In any case, there is no great distance between those who, like Plato or Arnauld, consider names to be syncategorematic and only propositions to be categorematic, and those who, like Husserl or even Peirce,[10] consider both to be categorematic, although the disagreement is by no means devoid of interest. For the completeness of the meaning of an expression is something which admits of degrees.

It would be over-simple to adopt a strict dichotomy between what does and what does not have a complete meaning. A name such as 'the father of this child' clearly has a meaning which is more complete than is the case with the syncategoremes (or, as linguists say, morphemes or monemes) such as 'the', 'father', 'of', of which it is composed. Yet each of these morphemes is, as we have seen, far from being devoid of all meaning. The degree zero of meaning is met with only at the level of *phonemes,* which make up the expression of morphemes.[11] Between the phoneme, which is deprived of any meaning, and the proposition, which has a complete meaning, we must situate the morpheme and the name as occupying intermediate positions: a name has the advantage over a morpheme that it suffices to designate its object; but unlike a proposition, it cannot teach us anything, since by itself it conveys neither message nor information. In view of this it seems that it is a matter of convention whether the boundary between what is *syncategorematic* and what is *categorematic* coincides with that between name and proposition, or with that between morpheme and name.

We shall adhere to Husserl's terminology, since this, more than that of Port-Royal, influenced the Warsaw School. But this should not blind us to the justification of Aristotle's remark:[12]

Nouns and verbs, provided nothing is added, are like thoughts without combination or separation; 'man' and 'white', as isolated terms, are not yet either true or false. In proof of this, consider the word 'goat-stag'. It has significance, but there is not truth or falsity about it, unless 'is' or 'is not' is added, either in the present or in some other tense.

Our decision to classify *name* and *proposition* together as categorematic expressions does not signify that, in another sense, names do not deserve to be classified as *syncategoremes* as much as *verbs* and opposed, in the way Aristotle suggests, to *propositions*.

We will say, then, that apart from names and propositions there are only syncategoremes, that is, terms which lack an independent meaning. As Husserl notes:[13]

Isolated syncategorematica such as *equals, together with, and, or* can achieve no fulfilment of meaning, no intuitive understanding, except in the context of a wider meaning-whole.

If these syncategorematic terms are not, for all that, deprived of meaning, then this is because we know that they are capable of completion. A conjunction such as *and,* standing by itself, only appears to us to have sense because we are able, for example, to sketch or anticipate in some other way the schema of two propositions that it might conjoin. This possibility of anticipation apart,

no syncategorematic meaning, no act of dependent meaning-intention, can function in knowledge outside of the context of a categorematic meaning.[14]

One might be tempted to compare Husserl's ideas with the famous formulation from *The Port-Royal Grammar*: 'The only rule is to consider what is said and that of which it is said. The first is always the attribute and the second the subject.' In the light of what has been said so far this requires some comments:

1. What is said is not the attribute but the proposition as a whole; in the proposition *Peter is tall* what I say of Peter is not *tall,* nor even *is tall,* but rather *Peter is tall.*

2. That of which something is said is not only the subject, or, rather, it is only the subject in propositions which cannot have an object. If I say that *Peter prefers Jack to Paul* I say this both of Peter, who does the preferring, and of Jack, who is preferred, as well as of Paul, with respect to whom Peter's preference for Jack is exercised.

The Port-Royal formulation has, then, to be modified so that it is the proposition as a whole which is *what is said,* and every name in the proposition with the role of an argument *what it is said of.*

Apart from these two fundamental categories of name and proposition, a third category may be admitted, the category of what the

Warsaw School called *functors*. This consists of certain syncategorematic terms or combinations of such terms. The classification developed by the Polish School, from Leśniewski to Ajdukiewicz, distinguishes three classes of functors:[15]

(1) *Nominal functors,* that is to say, functors which together with their arguments form names. This category can be subdivided according to the number and semantic category of the arguments. Thus the expression 'the fact that' will be said to be a nominal functor with a single propositional argument, since it forms from a clause a term which functions as a name. Logicians today tend to call nominal functors, whose arguments are also nominal, *operators*.[16]

(2) *Propositional functors,* that is to say, functors which, together with their arguments, form propositions. This category, like the first, can be sub-divided according to the number and semantic category of the arguments of each functor. Thus the most common sort of negation can, be considered as a propositional functor with only one propositional argument, since it takes an affirmative proposition as its argument, and makes from this a new (negative) proposition.[17] Most conjunctions on the other hand, in so far as they form compound propositions from two elementary propositions, are what today are generally called *connectives,* that is to say, propositional functors with two propositional arguments. Those terms which are grammatically classified as *verbs* are for the most part propositional functors with nominal arguments, and are sometimes called *predicators:* the verb *walk* is a propositional functor with one nominal argument; the verb *love* has two nominal arguments; the verb *prefer,* three, etc. Some verbs are propositional functors with both nominal and propositional arguments, as in the sentence.

Peter promises Paul that he will visit him tomorrow,

where the verb *promise* may be regarded as a propositional functor with three arguments, the first two of which are clearly nominal (*Peter, Paul*) and the third propositional (*that Peter will visit Paul tomorrow*).[18]

(3) But there are other functors which result neither in a proposition nor in a name and so fall into neither of the two categories just mentioned. This is the case with all those functors which, taken together with their arguments, form expressions which are still syncategorematic, are, in other words, still functors. A large number of what grammarians call

adverbs fall squarely into this category. Thus an adverb such as *passionately* is a functor which takes another functor (for example, *love*) as its argument, in order to make a new functor *(love passionately)*. In this example the functor arrived at by completing the first functor is propositional, having two nominal arguments, whereas the first functor is functorial, having only one argument which is itself a functor. (We shall, in general, talk of 'functorial functors' rather than 'functor-forming functors', of 'propositional functors' rather than 'proposition-forming functors', etc.)

The Methods of Verifying Syntactic Connection According to Ajdukiewicz and Bar-Hillel

This classification, sketched by Leśniewski, allowed Ajdukiewicz[19] in 1935 to perfect a formalized system for ascertaining or verifying the syntactic connections between expressions. Although the system was further developed after 1953 by Bar-Hillel[20] in such a way as to increase its flexibility and so bring it closer to natural languages, we shall here first outline Ajdukiewicz's method before taking into account these developments and introducing some criticisms and suggestions of our own.

In the system of syntactic verification developed by Ajdukiewicz the two basic categories, corresponding to Husserl's categorematic meaning-categories, are name and proposition or sentence. The names, and the propositions, are represented by the letters n *(name)* and s *(sentence)* respectively; the functors are represented by fractions: as the numerator of these fractions there stands a letter (n or s) or a new fraction, designating the semantic category (name, proposition, or functor) of the term which results when the functor is supplied with its arguments; the symbols for the denominator indicate the nature (nominal, propositional, functorial) of the arguments of the functor.

Thus to a propositional functor with one propositional argument such as negation, there corresponds the symbol $\frac{s}{s}$; to a propositional functor with only one nominal argument – as, for example, in the case of some intransitive verbs – the symbol $\frac{s}{n}$. As for the adverb *passionately* in the expression *love passionately*, since it yields a propositional functor with two nominal arguments, the numerator of the fraction which represents it can be written $\frac{s}{nn}$, and since its only argument is itself a propositional functor with two nominal arguments, the denominator will have the same form. Hence this adverb may be symbolized as:

$$\frac{\dfrac{s}{nn}}{\dfrac{s}{nn}}$$

If every categorematic expression may be divided into two parts, functor and argument or arguments, Ajdukiewicz's method would require that for every analysable categoreme the arguments are always written immediately after the functor. This is just as in the notation devised by Łukasiewicz for the propositional calculus where, for an expression such as

$$(p \vee q) \supset p,$$

one writes first the symbol for implication, then the antecedent of this implication, which, since it is itself a meaningful expression, begins with the symbol for disjunction, as in:

$$CApqp.$$

Under each of the symbols ordered in this way the corresponding notation for syntactic verification must be indicated. The constant C is a propositional functor with two arguments; the same is true of the constant A; the variables p and q designate elementary propositions; we can therefore write:

$$
\begin{array}{cccccc}
C & A & p & q & p \\
\dfrac{s}{ss} & \dfrac{s}{ss} & s & s & s
\end{array}
$$

The rule for verifying the syntactic connection of such an expression is to examine the sequence of symbols from left to right, stopping when a fraction is found which is immediately followed by the same symbols as those which occur in its denominator; this is the case, in our example, for the sequence of expressions

$$\frac{s}{ss} \; ss$$

The string picked out in this way is then replaced by the numerator of the fraction with which it begins. In our example, after replacing this string by s there remains:

$$\frac{s}{ss} \; s\,s$$

which, by applying the same rule again, can be replaced in its turn by s.

Any expression whatsoever will be called *syntactically connected* or *normal* if it can be reduced by a finite number of operations to a single letter, either s or $n,$ so indicating whether it is propositionally or nominally categorematic.

This method is applicable both to the expressions of a formalized language, as in the example just looked at, and to the expressions of ordinary languages. Thus if we consider:

The lilac smells very strongly and the rose blooms,

this may be represented as follows:

The lilac smells very strongly and the rose blooms.

$$\frac{n}{n} \quad n \quad \frac{s}{n} \quad \frac{s}{\frac{s}{\frac{s}{n}}} \quad \frac{s}{\frac{s}{n}} \quad \frac{s}{ss} \quad \frac{n}{n} \quad n \quad \frac{s}{n}$$

The principal functor is the conjunction *and,* a propositional functor with two propositional arguments; we shall therefore, in our representation of the process of verification, write it first. The word *very* is a functorial functor with the functor *strongly* as argument. The new functor, *very strongly,* formed with the help of the functor *very,* is also a functorial functor with the functor *smells* as argument. The functor obtained from these *smells very strongly* is itself a functor, but a propositional functor with one nominal argument. This explains both the notation we have employed, following Ajdukiewicz, for each of the terms, and the order in which they are set out, each functor being immediately followed by its argument(s):

$$\frac{s}{ss} \quad \frac{\dfrac{\dfrac{s}{n}}{\dfrac{s}{n}}}{\dfrac{s}{n}} \quad \frac{\dfrac{s}{n}}{\dfrac{s}{n}} \quad \frac{s}{n} \quad \frac{n}{n} \quad n \quad \frac{s}{n} \quad \frac{n}{n} \quad n$$

Which can be simplified step by step in the following manner:

$$\frac{s}{ss} \quad \frac{\dfrac{s}{n}}{\dfrac{s}{n}} \quad \frac{s}{n} \quad \frac{n}{n} \quad n \quad \frac{s}{n} \quad \frac{n}{n} \quad n$$

$$\frac{s}{ss} \quad \frac{s}{n} \quad \frac{n}{n} \quad n \quad \frac{s}{n} \quad \frac{n}{n} \quad n$$

$$\frac{s}{ss} \quad \frac{s}{n} \quad n \quad \frac{s}{n} \quad \frac{n}{n} \quad n$$

$$\frac{s}{ss} \quad s \quad \frac{s}{n} \quad \frac{n}{n} \quad n$$

$$\frac{s}{ss} \quad s \quad \frac{s}{n} \quad n$$

$$\frac{s}{ss} \quad s \quad s$$

$$s$$

The result shows both that the expression is well-formed, and that it constitutes a proposition.

As we have seen, Ajdukiewicz's method involves a transformation of the natural order within sentences, in that every functor must come immediately before its arguments. This transformation does not, of course, occur in those formalized languages which follow the Polish tradition inaugurated by Łukasiewicz, where functors always immediately precede their arguments. Languages constructed on the model of many vernacular languages, in which there is a classical distinction between the positions of the arguments before and after a functor do, however, allow such a transformation. Bar-Hillel avoids the need to admit any transformation by suggesting that the argument represented by the denominator of the fraction standing for the functor be put between parentheses where the argument precedes the functor and between square brackets where it follows the functor.

Thus the example borrowed from Ajdukiewicz will be represented henceforth as follows:

$$\text{The}\quad\text{lilac}\quad\text{smells}\quad\text{very}\quad\text{strongly}\quad\text{and}\quad\text{the}\quad\text{rose}\quad\text{blooms}$$

$$\frac{n}{[n]}\qquad n\qquad \frac{s}{(n)}\qquad \frac{\dfrac{s}{(n)}}{\left(\dfrac{s}{(n)}\right)}\;\Bigg/\;\left[\dfrac{\dfrac{s}{(n)}}{\left(\dfrac{s}{(n)}\right)}\right]\qquad \frac{\dfrac{s}{(n)}}{\left(\dfrac{s}{(n)}\right)}\qquad \frac{s}{(s)\,[s]}\qquad \frac{n}{[n]}\qquad n\qquad \frac{s}{(n)}$$

But this modification of the notation brings with it another modification. For, as we have seen, as long as the order suggested by Ajdukiewicz was adhered to, it was necessary only to run through the sequence of signs from left to right and stop at the first fraction which was followed immediately by the same symbols as those occurring in its denominator. In this way an automatic procedure was available whereby either confirmation of the expression's syntactic connection was arrived at by a single route, or this connection was ruled out by the impossibility of arriving at a single letter. But if we apply this uniform procedure from left to right to our example, bearing in mind that certain arguments now occur to the left of the functor on which they depend, then, as is easily seen, a small number of operations quickly brings us to the following sequence:

$$s\;\frac{\dfrac{s}{(n)}}{\left(\dfrac{s}{(n)}\right)}\;\frac{s}{(s)\,[s]}\;s$$

which makes it impossible to proceed any further and risks making the expression appear non-grammatical.

Thus Bar-Hillel's suggested modification destroys the automatic nature of the procedure. Henceforth, in order to justify the grammaticality of our example a choice between different alternatives will be available provided certain others are ruled out. It is of little importance which of the two expressions *the lilac* or *the rose* is established first as a nominal expression and which second, and the same is true of the propositions conjoined by *and*. What is important is that our procedure should not lead us to admit as intermediate expressions sequences of signs such as *lilac smells, rose blooms* or *the lilac smells*. Although these might well be well-formed outside the present context, they are not well-formed here, since the expression *very strongly* applies not to the proposition *the lilac smells* but to the condition marked by the verb *smell*.

One of the advantages of the modification suggested by Bar-Hillel is that, besides the gain in economy, it restores to grammar a certain ambiguity of which it had been stripped by Ajdukiewicz. For the automatic nature of the procedure he established is of course foreign to the grammars of vernacular languages. The latter operate in a far more hesitant fashion. The reader or speaker establishes the way a sentence is structured first and foremost by reference to the syntactic context, that is to say, by an exploration of the possible combinations to which the sentence as a whole lends itself. Only formalized languages in general avoid the necessity of such a trial and error approach. This is due both to the simplicity of their vocabularies and to the degree of rigour their authors intended such instruments of calculation to possess. To put this sort of automatic procedure, which is peculiar to formal languages, at the heart of natural languages – and this is the upshot of Ajdukiewicz's method – would be to betray their real grammar. Bar-Hillel's revisions, by restoring to language one of its main sources of ambiguity, bring us much closer to this real grammar.

But Bar-Hillel's reform goes further than we have suggested. It is not only by an exploration of the *syntactic* context, as in our first example, that the grammaticality of a sentence is verified. Such verification also involves the *semantic* and even the *pragmatic* dimensions of discourse; not least because what may give pause to a reader or listener, even before the question of different possible combinations of arguments and functors arises, is the nature of the functors themselves. Thus to use Bar-Hillel's example, in the expression:

Paul thinks that John sleeps

the word *thinks*, when taken out of context, may be understood sometimes as an intransitive verb ("I think, therefore I am"), to be written $\frac{s}{(n)}$, and sometimes as a transitive verb depending not only on the subject but also on the object of thought: $\frac{s}{(n)\,[n]}$. The word *that* can be interpreted either as a conjunction introducing a clause, or as a demonstrative: *that John over there, the one I am pointing to*. Now an exploration of the syntactic combinations is enough to eliminate the possibility of an intransitive use of the verb *thinks* in the present context. But the choice between

Paul thinks that John sleeps

and

Paul thinks (that) that John over there sleeps

will almost certainly be made on the basis of semantic or pragmatic considerations deriving from the general context, from the way the speaker has pronounced the given sentence, or even from the gesture with which he may have accompanied it.

Criticisms of these Methods

The method summarized briefly here is open to two criticisms. The one to be dealt with first concerns the adaptions suggested by Bar-Hillel; the second concerns a feature already to be found in Ajdukiewicz.

Bar-Hillel himself notes that everyday languages do not make do merely with being able to position arguments to the immediate left and right of functors – the only possibility allowed for by this method. In his example:

Paul strangely enough refused to talk,

the argument of the functor *strangely enough* is the proposition *Paul refused to talk* which rather than being unequivocally to the left or to the right of the functor falls both partly to the left and partly to the right. In certain cases it is not the argument but the functor which is thus 'divided', for example in propositional negation in French, where the verb which is the main functor of the proposition is flanked by the two words *ne* and *pas*. It may even happen that a functor is not marked by any sign (how then, we might wonder, is it noticed?), as is the case with the conjunction *that* (which is without any doubt a nominal functor with a propositional argument) in

Paul thinks John is sleeping.[21]

Some formalized languages, for example algebraic notation, where the multiplication sign is traditionally omitted, provide another example.

Thus the advantage promised by Bar-Hillel's modification, although it takes us close to an exact description of everyday language, is largely illusory, since such an approximation cannot be completed. Indeed the effort to achieve descriptive exactness risks drawing attention away from one of the most important features of Ajdukiewicz's notion, which is to underline the functional nature of the majority of linguistic expressions. What is important is not that the arguments or complements of a verb lie to its left or right, but that the proposition constituted around a verb be seen as a function assigning to such arguments taken in its domain (in this case the subject and complements of the verb) one of the two values (true or false) of its range. It is this functional aspect which Ajdukiewicz's notation underlines by having the denominator designate the domain or domains and the numerator the range. But it is a weakness of this notation that the only way of expressing the functional nature of the proposition is by placing the argument to the right of the functor; the flexibility suggested by Bar-Hillel is merely an expedient which, as we have seen, cannot deal with all the constructions in which the function can occur.

In fact the whole merit of Ajdukiewicz's notation lies in its expression of three things; and the whole weakness of this notation – a weakness only attenuated by Bar-Hillel – lies in its inability to express the third of these sufficiently clearly. The two features which the method does successfully indicate, are the domain and range of the function; but the third element which remains to be provided is the arrangement of the signs corresponding to the function, something which, as we have seen, cannot be reduced to the two possibilities: left or right of the functor. It is therefore important to remove the constraints imposed by the notation of Ajdukiewicz and Bar-Hillel and to replace the way they express the three sorts of information which must be provided by a simple ordered triple[22] indicating:

(1) the (ordered) set of domains;
(2) the range;
(3) the rule governing the distribution of the signs.

It is then possible to express the functional nature of, for example, propositional negation in French by indicating, (1) that its argument is a proposition, (2) that once furnished with its argument this functor itself forms a proposition, and finally (3) by specifying the different ways in which the arrangement of functor and argument can occur, ways which differ according to the different features of the propositions which serve as arguments.[23] In this way the advantages of the original method are retained, yet one has available the much more developed methods for the expression of rules that are, as the example of negation clearly shows, indispensable to an analysis of everyday language.

Such a modification of the method also enables us to deal with a case which is easily imaginable and which we shall soon meet, where two functors with the same number and type of arguments and which form the same type of expression nevertheless differ fundamentally in the rule governing the distribution of signs. In such a case the two functors must be considered as belonging to two distinct families, although this would have been disguised by the notation of Ajdukiewicz. For the latter's method provides only one rule (and Bar-Hillel's suggestions allow only a slight increase in flexibility) for every class of functors characterized by the same initial domain and range, while a *function* is characterized by more than these alone.

We have gone into this first question in some detail, even though it is less fundamental than a second question – to be raised now – because the answer to the latter presupposes a grasp of the first. A major criticism which can be made of Ajdukiewicz, as well as Bar-Hillel, who follows him completely on this point, is that he does nothing to remove the ambiguity which attaches to the use of the term *name*. There are at least two things the term might be taken to mean, which logical and philosophical reflection should always keep separate:

(1) The term may, first of all, – and here we are following the Husserlian tradition – be reserved for categorematic expressions which suffice to designate a single object; in this sense 'Paul', 'that man there', 'the fact that it is raining', are *names*. But the word 'homme' (man) by itself is not a name, insofar as its syncategorematic nature prevents it from designating any single object whatsoever.

(2) The grammar of Indo-European languages nevertheless describes as names *(nom, Name),* or more exactly as common nouns, *(nom commun, Gemeinname)* words such as 'man' which designate not individuals but at best classes, and which make up designations which have always been called names when combined with articles (in French) and perhaps with other particles or without the article (in English).

That Ajdukiewicz does not distinguish between the two is evident from the example we have borrowed to illustrate his method. For we have seen how he used the same letter – *n* – both for common nouns such as 'lilac' and 'rose' and for the genuine categorematic nominal expressions, 'the lilac' and 'the rose'. This ambiguity does not present any difficulties in most formalized languages for the simple reason that these normally have nothing which functions as a common noun. But difficulties do begin when natural languages are being analysed, for there common nouns do indeed have an important role.

Where *name* and *common noun* are not distinguished the sequences of words.

lilas sent
man loves woman
poor a man[24]

must be considered to be as grammatical as

the lilac smells
this man loves this woman
a poor man,

since (keeping to Bar-Hillel's notation)[25] the first three sequences will have the following representations:

$$n \frac{s}{(n)}$$

$$n \frac{s}{(n)[n]} n$$

$$\frac{n}{[n]} \frac{n}{[n]} n$$

which reduce easily to *s* in the first two cases and to *n* in the third case.

If, on the other hand, we introduce a distinct designation, and provisionally we shall employ the Greek letter v for what traditional grammar has called *common nouns,* and reserve the letter n for the categoreme *name,* then the *article* and *demonstrative* may be represented by $\frac{n}{[v]}$, i.e. when followed by a common noun they constitute a genuine *name.* Similarly the majority of *adjectives* may be represented as $\frac{v}{[v]}$ or $\frac{v}{(v)}$: when followed or (in French) preceded by a common noun *(poor man, homme pauvre)* they constitute a *common noun.* In this way the ill-formedness of the expressions above will show itself immediately in the notation, since none of them can be reduced to a *basic category:*

$$v \ \frac{s}{(n)}$$

$$v \ \frac{s}{(n)[n]} \ v$$

$$\frac{v}{[v]} \ \frac{n}{[v]} \ v$$

The introduction of distinct symbols for *name* and *common noun* allows us to consider the proposition 'of' (*de* in French) as a nominal functor with a common noun and a name as arguments. The expression

the husband of Joan

must then be represented, and simplified, as follows:

$$\frac{n}{[v]} \ v \ \frac{v}{(v)[n]} \ n$$

$$\frac{n}{[v]} \quad v$$

$$n,$$

and not as:

$$\frac{n}{[v]} \ v \ \frac{n}{(n)[n]} \ n$$

$$n \ \frac{n}{(n)[n]} \ n$$

$$n.$$

The alternative, which is to treat the preposition 'of' as a functor whose arguments are genuine *names,* would oblige us always to recognize as grammatical such sequences of words as

Peter of John.

Unless the difference between common noun and name is admitted, it also becomes impossible to give an account of the distinction between *restrictive* and *non-restrictive relative clauses*[26] which appears in certain languages (though marked in different ways: for example by the use of the subjunctive or the indicative mood, by the presence of absence of a comma before the relative pronoun). In the non-restrictive case, e.g.

This man, who is thirty-two years old,

the first argument or, as grammarians put it, the antecedent, of the relative is already a genuine name, which by itself designates this man – independently of any indication of his age. The relative pronoun here is then a nominal functor with two arguments the first of which is a name *(this man)* whereas the second may be considered a propositional functor with a nominal argument (*is thirty-two years old*):

$$\frac{n}{(n) \quad \left[\dfrac{s}{(n)}\right]}$$

In the case of the restrictive relative, on the other hand, as in the title of Victor Hugo's novel

The man who laughs,

the article together with the common noun 'man' does not yield a categorematic term which is capable of picking out anyone at all. To do this the article must combine with the common noun 'man who laughs'. The relative pronoun is then a functor which makes a simple common noun by taking a common noun *(man)* and a propositional functor with a nominal argument:

80

$$(v) \quad \overline{\left[\dfrac{s}{(n)}\right]}^{\nu}$$

In spite of the notation which we have been provisionally making use of here in order to bring out the role of common nouns, the need which we have emphasized of distinguishing the latter from genuine names by no means commits us to recognizing the common noun as a third basic category. There is certainly no difficulty in principle in introducing a third category, so that besides propositions (which, semantically, involve a truth value) and genuine names (which refer to things or objects), we would have common nouns (which, as already noted, would refer to classes).[27] But we can also treat the common noun not as a third basic category but as a simple functor which takes a name as an argument to make a proposition: thus the common noun *man* is that functor which, taking the noun *Peter* as its argument, forms the proposition *Peter is a man*.

This treatment of the common noun as a functor brings out concretely the necessity – which was the subject-matter of the first criticism we made above – of giving up the notation of Ajdukiewicz (and that of Bar-Hillel) which would only allow us to represent the functorial nature of the common noun as:

$$\frac{s}{n}$$

and so leaves us no way of distinguishing it from predicates with one nominal argument.[28] But this involves a considerable departure from our intuitions, which do not allow us to group together a common noun such as 'man' and a verb in the third person singular such as 'walks', even though both are capable of forming propositions with the help of some nominal argument: 'Peter is a man' and 'Peter walks'. For although domain and range are the same in each case, what varies is the rule which governs the formation of the expression. In the one case the argument is placed *before* the intransitive verb, in the other case the common noun requires the verb 'to be'. In general, the methods of Ajdukiewicz and Bar-Hillel do not suffice for the expression of this rule.

Nevertheless, in those many cases where the context excludes any possible confusion between two functors, which differ only in the rules governing the way they are formed, it will be convenient to use one of the two available methods for the sake of simplicity. And for our final point in this chapter we shall in fact use Bar-Hillel's method.

The notation of functors with several arguments poses a problem which is best illustrated by means of an example. A predicate such as 'loves' may be interpreted either as a *propositional* functor with two nominal arguments:

$$\frac{s}{(n)\,[n]}$$

or as a *functorial* functor with one nominal argument, in which latter case it may take one of two forms:

$$\frac{\frac{s}{(n)}}{[n]} \quad \text{or} \quad \frac{\frac{s}{[n]}}{(n)}$$

The distinction is by no means artificial, nor are the two forms interchangeable. For the analysis of the grammaticality of the expression

Jack, who loves Mary

requires us to adopt the first of the two forms for 'loves':

$$n \frac{n}{(n)\ \left[\dfrac{s}{(n)}\right]} \quad \frac{\frac{s}{(n)}}{[n]}\ n$$

simplifying to:

$$n \frac{n}{(n)\ \left[\dfrac{s}{(n)}\right]} \frac{s}{(n)}$$

and thus to

$$n$$

whereas in order to establish the grammaticality of the expression

Jack, whom Mary loves,

we are obliged to use the second form:

$$n \, \frac{n}{[n] \; \left[\dfrac{s}{[n]}\right]} \qquad n \; \frac{\dfrac{s}{[n]}}{[n]}$$

$$n \, \frac{n}{(n) \; \left[\dfrac{s}{[n]}\right]} \qquad \frac{s}{[n]}$$

n.

Transposition of the latter without making use of Bar-Hillel's notation presents so few difficulties as to justify our not setting out here what it would involve. It is enough to note that, depending on which of its two arguments it is supplied with first, the transitive verb 'loves' may be used to form either the intransitive verb 'Jack loves' – which will then lack an argument-complement – or the intransitive verb 'loves Mary' – which will lack an argument-subject.

Notes

[1] Aristotle, *De interpretatione*, 4, p.17a.
[2] Ibid., p.17a.
[3] Husserl, *Logical Investigations*, V §28, Eng. trans. Vol. II, p.611.
[4] Ibid.
[5] Ibid., §35, Eng. trans. p.630.
[6] Ibid., Eng. trans. p.628.
[7] Plato, *The Sophist*, 262a-c.
[8] Arnauld and Lancelot, *The Port-Royal Grammar*, 2nd part, ch. 24, p.171.
[9] English trans. by Pears and McGuinness, 1961; cf. in particular propositions 2.021, 3.202, 3.26, 3.3. This is not the place to challenge the philosophy which can be glimpsed behind Wittgenstein's refusal to accord an independent meaning to names. This is a theme we shall not deal with until our conclusion, ch.X, pp. 306–308, below.
[10] Peirce's position is made all the more difficult to interpret by the substantial evolution it underwent. In some of his writings the distinction we have here described as that between *names* and *propositions* is to be found described as the distinction between *Rheme* and *Dicent*. Later, around 1906, Peirce prefers the terms *Seme* and *Pheme*: 'By a *Seme* I mean

anything which serves for any purpose as a substitute for an object of which it is, in some sense, a representative or sign. The logical Term, which is a class name, is a Seme. Thus the term 'The Mortality of man' is a *Seme*. By a *Pheme* I mean a sign which is equivalent to a grammatical sentence...', quoted by Ogden and Richards, 1966, p.285. [By 1908 at the latest Husserl had given up the view that names are categorematic, according to the description of his views given by Erich Heinrich in a dissertation done under Husserl *Untersuchungen zur Lehre vom Begriff,* Göttingen, 1910, p.62/3. Heinrich's source is Husserl's logic lectures of 1907/8. The change in Husserl's views is set out also in the masterly first appendix to *Formal and Transcendental Logic* (English translation, 1969, Nijhoff, The Hague) entitled *Syntactic Forms and Syntactic Stuffs,* especially in §1. This appendix is based on logic lectures of 1910/11. – Tr.]

[11] Husserl was perfectly aware of the different ways in which an expression may be incomplete *(ergänzungsbedürftig)* insofar as it is meaningful. In the *Logical Investigations* he stresses, for example, the radical difference between incomplete yet meaningful forms such as 'aber' or 'des Vaters' and phonetic elements that are without any meaning at all such as 'bi' in 'billig' and 'bissig'. (Cf. S.-Y. Kuroda, "Edmund Husserl, *Grammaire générale et raisonnée,* and Anton Marty", 1973. pp.189f.)

[12] Aristotle, *De interpretatione,* 1. 16a.

[13] *Logical Investigations,* IV, §9(b), Eng. trans. p.508.

[14] Ibid.

[15] Although the term 'functor' was introduced by Kotarbiński, it seems that, as he himself points out, it was Leśniewski who is responsible for its fully generalized use. The birth of the notion of functor also poses a very delicate problem in the history of logic. Although priority of general use seems to be due to the Warsaw School, this is apparently due in part to the fact that, in the wake of Kazimierz Twardowski, the teacher at Lwow of Łukasiewicz and Leśniewski, this school had a place within the philosophical and logical tradition inaugurated by Bolzano's *Wissenschaftslehre.* For it seems that it is in this work that the first sketch of what was to become the notion of functor is to be found (cf. for example Bolzano §58).

[16] Cf. for example H.B. Curry and R. Feys, *Combinatory Logic,* 1968, p.24.

[17] What is said here about negation and the connectives is merely provisional. We shall have to come back to this issue. It may therefore be surprising that we seem to admit here what we shall later, at least in part, reject. The fact of the matter is that it is too early to introduce certain distinctions that will later come to appear indispensable.

[18] See note 17.

[19] "Syntactic Connection", in *Polish Logic,* 1967, 207–31.

[20] Cf. especially "A quasi-arithmetical notation for syntactic description", 1953.

[21] Ibid., pp.53f. where, however, Bar-Hillel proposes an analysis from which we diverge.

[22] This has been done, in particular, by Richard Montague, *Formal Philosophy,* 1974.

[23] There can be no question of going into any detail about such a rule. It may be enough to note that in French the main functor of the negated proposition can only be flanked by *ne...pas* if this main functor is a predicator (a *verb,* let us say). If the main functor is a connective (for example a *conjunction*) one may, for example, let the whole negated proposition be preceded by *it is not the case that.* But even for simple negation there are other cases that should be looked at.

[24] Bar-Hillel puts this objection to himself: "It is obvious that the categories dealt with so far are too gross to be applicable to ordinary languages; according to such an application *Man knew that John was a poor Paul* would also have to be considered a sentence, a thing which most people would hesitate to do" (Ibid., p.49).

[25] Surprising though this may seem, we have retained Bar-Hillel's notation here even after criticizing it. For in all those cases where the relation of the functor to its arguments is sufficiently well expressed by the mere position on the left or right hand side, Bar-Hillel's

notation has the pedagogical advantage that it is immediately comprehensible, in spite of its brevity. We shall therefore stick to this notation and to that of Ajdukiewicz, except where the weakness we have pointed out would conceal a confusion.

[26] The grammaticalization of this distinction in French has been studied by Jean-Claude Pariente who attributes it chiefly to Beauzée's *Grammaire générale* (1767). See Pariente, "Grammaire, logique et ponctuation", 1979.

[27] Ajdukiewicz himself admitted the possibility of admitting categories other than *name* and *proposition* as basic: "If the concept of syntactic connection were to be defined in strict generality, nothing could be decided about the number and kind of basic semantic and functor categories, since they may vary in different languages. For the sake of simplicity, however, we shall restrict ourselves (like Leśniewski) to languages having only two basic semantic categories, that of sentences and that of names." (*Polish Logic*, p.209f.) One can find for example in the work of David Lewis the adoption of the *common noun* as a basic category in addition to *proposition* and *name*. Cf. *Montague Grammar*, ed. B. Partee.

[28] In the present case, where we have encountered no more than two types of propositional functor with one nominal argument, we may (following Richard Montague) surmount the difficulty by separating numerator and denominator in one of the two cases by a double bar. But this would be evidently nothing more than an expedient, sufficing to distinguish but not to explicate the diversity of rules. Montague himself underlines the originality on this point of this method relative to that of Ajdukiewicz, and takes care to add: "The fact that we need only two copies is merely an accident of English or perhaps of our limited fragment; in connection with other languages it is quite conceivable that a larger number would be required." To which he adds in a note: "It was perhaps the failure to pursue the possibility of syntactically splitting categories originally conceived in semantic terms that accounts for the fact that Ajdukiewicz's proposals have not previously led to a successful syntax." (*Formal Philosophy*, p.249.)

Chapter Four
The Verb

We next went to the school of languages where three professors sat in consultation upon improving that of their own country. The first project was to shorten discourse ... by leaving out verbs and participles, because in reality all things imaginable are but nouns.

Jonathan Swift, *Gulliver's Travels,* Part III, ch.5.

Verb and Function

Following Frege, we can consider every proposition of a language as a function, provided this language (whether formalized or not) has some basis in intuition. If we bear this in mind, then it seems clear that, in the case of natural languages, what the Indo-European tradition among others calls *the verb* is what in most cases plays the role of the functor in this function.

Mathematical logic today has completely adopted the extension of the notion of function suggested by Frege. As it was understood within mathematics towards the end of the seventeenth century, the function in its classical form

$$y = f(x)$$
$$y = f(x, z)$$

already indicated that it was a relation. Such expressions signify that to every value of x, or to every pair of values of x and z, there corresponds a determinate value of y. Now this notion can be extended beyond the domain of numerical functions, that is of those functions whose arguments belong to the set of real numbers. In the case of the propositional function, for example, the subject and the complements of the verb will take the place of the independent variables and the dependent variable will have only one or the other of two values: *the true* or *the false.*

It will be useful to look at one of Frege's own examples.[1] The proposition

Cato killed Cato

may be interpreted in four different ways:

(1) The functor *killed* with two nominal arguments may be held to take as arguments *Cato* and *Cato,* just as in other contexts it might have taken *Cain* and *Abel* or *Brutus* and *Caesar, Ravaillac* and *Henry IV* or, quite generally, any pair made up of a murderer and his victim. One might then write

killed (Cato, Cato).

(2) The functor *killed himself* may be held to take as its only nominal argument *Cato,* just as elsewhere it might take *Cleopatra* or *Judas.* One might then write

killed himself (Cato).

(3) It is also possible, as Frege points out, to take *killed Cato* as a functor in its own right, with Cato as its only argument:

killed Cato (Cato).

(4) Or, conversely, *Cato killed* may be taken as the functor and *Cato* as its only argument:

Cato killed (Cato).

The last two interpretations may well appear somewhat artificial, although in principle, whatever the clear theoretical advantages of the first two, all four are legitimate. For the argument is that part of the function which is *taken to be replaceable,* and the functor that part which is *taken to be constant.* So that in any function, merely by considering as replaceable any symbol which had been taken to be irreplaceable, the original function may be transformed into a new function endowed with an additional argument.[2]

Thus every simple proposition in a natural language may be interpreted as a function with *n* arguments, where *n* stands for a natural number: the verb has the role of functor and the subject and complement that of arguments. The possibilities we have looked at of arbitrarily varying parts of a sentence in order to arrive at different interpretations, are based on the logical fact that any function with *n* arguments may be transformed into a functor with n-1, n-2, n-3, arguments, provided that n-1, etc., are not less than 0. This is doubtless the reason which makes *a priori* possible the tendency which verbs have of incorporating their complements, a tendency exhibited by some languages more than others, and often underlined by grammarians. But even if it is always possible to consider the proposition *Cato killed Cato* as a function with two arguments, it is difficult to see how it could be treated as a function with more than two arguments;[3] it is not possible to analyse any function with n arguments as a function with n+1 arguments. Let us, therefore, call the *maximum* number of arguments which can be made out in a proposition which is considered as a function, the *normal* number of its arguments.

In general, then:

(1) The verbs or verbal expressions, *run, be ill, blush, lie,* are functors with only one nominal argument.

(2) The verbs *love, wound, conquer, manufacture,* are functors with two nominal arguments, although there is always the possibility in ordinary language of treating them as functors with only one argument; one can say of someone: 'he loves'.

(3) The verbs *give, persuade, prefer, promise,* are functors with three arguments which in languages such as French or English are called subject, and direct and indirect object (complements).

(4) Grammatical forms with more than three arguments are rare and in general are obtained by composition: if I say *the points* A *and* B *are at the same distance from one another as* C *and* D then the italicized expression designates a functor with four arguments.

Thus if the verb is considered as the functor of a propositional function then there is a law, formulated by Tarski,[4] which holds of it:

the functors of two primitive sentential functions belong to the same category if and only if the number of arguments in the two functions is the same, and if any two arguments which occupy corresponding places in the two functions also belong to the same category.

This allows us to classify verbs using the method which, as we have seen, is valid for every possible functor, on the basis of the number of their arguments and of the semantic category to which these arguments belong.

When classifying verbs in this way it is important not to be misled by certain homonyms in everyday language. The semantic category of a term such as the verb *prefer*[5] is not to be determined by stating that it is a functor with three arguments. For the word covers at least two different functions:

(1) In the proposition *I prefer Paul to Philip* the verb *prefer* is a functor with three nominal arguments.

(2) But in the sentence *I prefer walking to working* the verb *prefer* is a functor with three arguments, only one of which is nominal, the two others being often considered propositional.[6] Rather than pursue this and other distinctions here it will be convenient to postpone going into the analysis of semantic categories until we have taken into account the principles of the *theory of types*. Until then we shall merely group a sentence such as *I prefer justice to charity* with sentences such as that in (1), even though neither *justice* nor *charity* are of the same type as *Paul* or *Philip*.

This view of the verb brings us back to an opposition traditional amongst grammarians between the verb and the name. The basis of the difference between verb and name is to be found in the fact that the latter has an independent meaning; it is categorematic, to use Husserl's term, or saturated *(gesättigt)* in the terminology of Frege. The verb by itself, on the other hand, because it is syncategorematic, is essentially unsaturated. Only when the verb is completed by its *complements* (in a wide sense of the term in which the subject is considered as the first of the complements of the verb) is there a genuine categorematic expression, the proposition. Hence although the verb is to be distinguished from the name, it must also be distinguished from the proposition of which it is a part, that is, the complete function of which it is a functor.

The Case of Impersonal Verbs

But is the verb taken on its own necessarily *ungesättigt?* Are there not verbs which at least in certain cases make do without any complements at all and which are therefore categorematic? The question amounts to asking whether we should follow the long tradition which denies the uniqueness and irreducibility of impersonal verbs. Plato[7] claimed that "a statement never consists solely of names ... nor yet of verbs apart from names". Every proposition, he said, must have a subject; the combination of a name and a verb, as in *the man learns,* forms "the most simple and the first of all imaginable sorts of discourse". For as The Stranger put it to Theaetetus: "Whenever there is a statement, it must be about something; it cannot be about nothing". And the statement *Theaetetus sits* is only a statement because it is about Theaetetus.

Aristotle was to follow Plato[8]: the verb "indicates in every case something which is affirmed of some other thing". "It is always a sign of something said about something else; i.e. of something either predicable of or present in some other thing". From Priscian to Scaliger and Sanctius, the "most able grammarians", as Lancelot put it in his *Nouvelle méthode pour apprendre facilement et en peu de temps la langue latine,* all share the point of view to be found in *The Port-Royal Grammar*[9]:

there is ... no verb which lacks its nominative, either expressed or understood, because the nature of the verb being affirmation or assertion, it is necessary that there be something of which one affirms, this being the subject or the nominative of the verb.

Thus Husserl, when he points out that "each expressed statement contains at least one name"[10], is no innovator. And the idea is to be found again in Sapir: "There must be something to talk about and something must be said about this subject of discourse."[11]

It should be noted first that the problem of impersonal sentences presents itself in very different terms to the contemporary logician. The ways in which post-Aristotelian logic tried to reduce every proposition to a combination of a subject and a predicate by means of the copula *est* are well-known. We shall come back to this topic when we look at the verb *to be,* and we shall see that there is no obstacle of a logical nature to treating any proposition whatsoever as a sequence consisting of subject, copula and predicate, provided the function in question has at least one argument. Where this is the case, then, as Aristotle mentions:[12] "there is no difference ... at all between saying *man walks* and *man is walking*"; or, to recall the excample of *The Port-Royal Logic*:[13] "to say *Peter lives* is the same as to say *Peter is living"* (Pierre est vivant). But in order to reduce every proposition to a predicative judgment in this way it is necessary, as has been pointed out ever since Plato, that the predicate can be affirmed or denied of a subject; there must, that is, be a subject, or – in other words – the verb considered as a function must have at least one argument.

The logicians' claim to be able to reduce every judgment to the subject-copula-predicate form is to be explained in part by their strong denials that such clearly impersonal expressions as *it is raining, it is snowing,* are basic and by their contrived efforts to reveal a hidden subject which, they claim, is implicitly presupposed:

il (it) takes the place of the nominative, i.e. *pluie* (rain), *neige* (snow), *grêle* (hail), etc. which are included with their substantive verb *est* (is) or *fait* (makes or does) as if one were to say *il pluie est* (literally: it rain is), *il neige se fait* (literally: it snow occurs).[14]

And even Bolzano[15], with his project of reducing every proposition to what he considered to be its normal form (*A has b*), puts forward the following analysis of the expression *it is snowing*:

The representation (*Vorstellung*) of a fall of snow has objectivity (*hat eine Gegenständlichkeit*).

The existence of such impersonal locutions was the main reason which effectively prevented the logical reduction of every proposition to the classical predicative form. This reduction did not require that the proposition contain objects, but it did presuppose the existence of at least one subject.[16] Hence the observation made by the less systematic and more honest writers

that there are indivisible judgments which have neither subject nor predicate and that these should be distinguished from judgments of predication where the assertion is analysed.[17]

If, following Frege, every proposition is analysed as a function with n arguments, a genuinely impersonal proposition is a function where $n = 0$; that is to say, a function which is composed of a functor only. Contemporary logic has no reason to reject such functions for they raise no difficulties whatsoever. Their only peculiarity is that, since they cannot be analysed into distinct functions and arguments, they do not belong to what is called the functional calculus or calculus of predicates. Moreover, since every function with one or more arguments can be considered as a function with a smaller number of arguments, every proposition may, if necessary, be treated as an impersonal proposition. But although the distinction between function and arguments is then not drawn, such a proposition does not thereby cease to be amenable to logical treatment; rather, it falls into the province of the calculus of propositions.[18]

In fact the existence of ultimately unanalysable impersonal propositions seems to correspond to one way in which the existential field of our knowledge is spontaneously structured. "The universe", as Russell and Whitehead point out,[19] "consists of objects having various qualities and standing in various relations". Can one go one step further and say that the universe consists *only* of objects having various qualities and standing in various relations? If this were the case, then everything in the universe could be expressed in terms of functions containing at least one argument. And this would amount to a denial of the intentional object of impersonal propositions.

When a subject has perceptual experience he certainly isolates objects in the flux of this experience, that is to say, he isolates those islands of resistance which enjoy a certain perceptual autonomy and maintain their unity through changes they themselves undergo and through the changes of the subject. The natural tendency of perception is to attribute qualities to these objects, to observe their interplay, and, above all, to establish the relations holding between them. On this point it seems that our perception does indeed structure itself in the way indicated by Russell and Whitehead: objects show themselves; we are able to designate them. But we designate them above all in order to describe them, not only with reference to what is peculiar to each object, but also with reference to the network of relations they enter into.

But our sense experience does not always succeed in structuring itself in this way. The perception of an object presupposes a certain intellectual grasp of what is given perceptually and this is not something which is always available. I perceive certain phenomena which no amount of attention permits me to isolate or pick out in a 'single ray' of consciousness; it is the objects that have the upper hand: I am merely amongst them, or simply in front of them. I am not in the presence of objects to which I can attribute certain properties or between which I can discern relations. This is the case wherever we are submerged in something: atmospheric phenomena such as wind, rain, cold, heat, or affective states which overcome a subject entirely, such as shame, remorse, pity. And indeed these constitute the domain of privileged examples of impersonal verbs. The object *par excellence* of the impersonal verb is everything which 'can be distinguished only with difficulty in the content of our consciousness',[20] that which we cannot dominate visually, which is such that we cannot single it out at a glance and in which we are submerged.

This had indeed been suspected by those authors who had searched most diligently for an implicit subject in impersonal propositions. Thus Ueberweg described the subject of impersonal propositions as 'the totality of being which surrounds us', and it was described by Lotze as the 'reality which contains everything', and by Prantl as the 'surrounding perceptual world'.[21] Although the victims of a prejudice which obliged them to search for a subject-predicate form, these writers nevertheless came very close to an exact analysis of what is the case.

In Husserl's immediate circle it was Alexander Pfänder who saw most clearly the real nature of impersonal propositions. Their uniqueness, he explains,[22] is due to the fact that

qualities and processes can be thought of in isolation, without being subordinated to any sort of object of which they would be the properties and activities.

The domain of impersonal verbs, Pfänder continues, is to be found wherever

such qualities and processes present themselves or seem to present themselves in our experience by themselves, without any things or objects to which they are attached.

This formulation requires only two qualifications:

(1) Pfänder's mode of expression lends itself to ambiguity; the fact that a quality or relation is thought of independently of any object is characteristic of a certain sort of *nominalisation,* to which we shall return when we deal with names. The expression used by Pfänder runs the risk of referring to the case where a predicate is nominalised, something which has little if anything to do with impersonal propositions.

(2) Besides the remarkable formulations we have quoted, Pfänder also employs in the same paragraph a number of other, rather disappointing formulations, and it is difficult to see how they might be reconciled with one another. Thus he writes that in *it is raining* the real subject of the verb is the name which designates "that position in the world around us which we have in mind".[23] It is difficult to see here why, in spite of what Pfänder says elsewhere in the same paragraph, an impersonal proposition should require a subject at all, or why circumstantial indications, however

necessary they are for many propositions which do have a subject, should be promoted to do the job of a subject only in the case of the so-called *impersonal* propositions.[24]

Certain writers have tended to mix up two very different questions under the heading of *the problem of the universality of the subject-predicate construction:*

(a) The question of the possibility of impersonal propositions; that is to say, the question whether the subject-predicate distinction is dispensable. To this we have given an affirmative answer.

(b) The question of the possibility of a language dispensing completely with the subject-predicate distinction, that is to say, of an *entirely* impersonal mode of expression. To this question, it seems, the answer must be negative.

Were one to take literally certain formulations of Sapir, such as those we have quoted above,[25] one might think that his response to (a) is negative, but a closer study of his writings shows that the universality he espoused amounts only to the claim that the subject-predicate distinction is to be found in every language, not in every proposition expressible in a language.

Unlike Sapir, André Martinet gives a positive answer to the second question[26] and in so doing refers us to the 'ergative construction' which allows a language such as Basque to form propositions by successively adding further specifications to a predicate of existence such as *there is*. Where we would say in English

The woman is washing the linen,

the ergative construction would allow us to say the same thing – without any use of the subject-predicate distinction – as follows:

There is washing of the linen by the woman.

But although this ergative construction is very different from the more usual sorts of construction in Indo-European languages, it still belongs entirely to the subject-predicate type, with which it is supposed to contrast. Just as the predicate *is washing* takes at least two arguments: *the woman* and *the linen,* so the predicate of existence *there is* takes only one argument: *washing of the linen by the woman.* Thus the ergative construction is no counter-example to the universality of the subject-

94

predicate construction understood in the second of the two senses we have distinguished.

But we can go further in providing an answer to the question whether a language without any distinction between function and argument, a language employing only impersonal propositions, is possible. Not only is such a language possible but, among formal languages, the *propositional calculus* serves as an example, and were one to bring together all the genuine impersonal verbs in a natural language such as French, German or English one would have a language capable of giving expression to an infinity of different situations. In spite of this, such a language would not be universal, for it would be incapable of giving genuine expression to relations between things and could, at best, *suggest* such relations to an audience through an accumulation of impersonal indications. Thus a language cannot do without the argument-predicate distinction without renouncing the privilege of universality which, as we have seen, is enjoyed by natural languages.

The Different Senses of the Verb 'to be'

The recognition of the irreducibility of impersonal verbs, that is to say: of the existence of essentially unanalysable propositions, is, as we have just seen, the main obstacle which led logicians to renounce the project of reducing every proposition to the schema in which the copula *est* joins together a subject and a predicate. The second factor which led to the demise of this project was the recognition of the ambiguity of the verb *to be;* Frege showed that it had at least four distinct meanings:[27]

(1) It can express existence, as in the propositions *God is.* This seems to be the first sense of the verb *to be* in the Indo-European tradition and it is a sense which has little if any connection with the role of the copula. Indeed Sanskrit, on finding at a relatively late stage that it needed a term to designate the copula, quite arbitrarily chose the verb which signifies existence for this role, whereas ancient Greek originally hesitated between six different verbs:

γίγνεσθαι, ὑπάρχειν,
τυγχάνειν, χυρεῖν,
πέλεσθαι, εἶναι.[28]

It seems, then, that in many Indo-European languages the verb which

95

originally expressed existence and so corresponded to the first sense we have distinguished here, was then re-employed for the other senses, as and when these were conceived of.

(2) It may express the identity of two terms, as in the example used by Frege: 'The morning star is Venus', where *is* signifies *is the same thing as, is identical to.*

(3) It may express the fact that an object belongs to a class, or, as Frege puts it, the fact that an object falls under a concept (*das Fallen eines Gegenstandes unter einen Begriff*). Frege gives as an example 'The morning star is a planet', a proposition which does not, of course, mean that the two terms *morning star* and *planet* are identical, but that the morning star belongs to the class of objects to which the concept planet applies.

(4) To be carefully distinguished from sense (3), is the sense of *to be* which expresses the inclusion of one class in another, or, to borrow Frege's formulation, 'the subordination of one concept to another' (*Unterordnung eines Begriffes unter einen Begriff*). The proposition *man is a mammal* expresses the inclusion of the class of men in the class of mammals. But if I say that Peter is a mammal, the logical nature of the verb *to be* changes completely, since the copula here expresses not inclusion but Peter's belonging to or membership of the class of mammals.

This analysis put an end to several important traditional confusions. The worst of these was the confusion of sense (1) above with senses (3) and (4). The verb for existence on the one hand, and the verb expressing inclusion or membership on the other, separated only with difficulty by the Greeks, became even more mixed up with one another when Priscian translated the Greek term for the *verb of existence, ὑπαρκτικόν ῥῆμα* by *verbum substantivum,* an ambiguous Latin expression suggesting both what today are called *membership* and *inclusion* as well as *existence.*

The danger of such a confusion within any sort of Aristotelian philosophy was diminished by the fact that for such a philosophy an idea has reality only if there corresponds to it some concrete being; that is to say, in more modern terms, to say that an element belongs to a class presupposes the existence of this element, and to say that a class is included in another class presupposes that neither of the two classes is empty.[29] This is put very well in *Le traité de la grammaire française* by Robert Estienne:[30]

The verb called the substantive verb (*substantif*), which is *to be,* signifies neither action nor passion [i.e. what a thing undergoes – Tr.], but it denotes only the being and existence or subsistence of every thing signified by the name it is combined with: for example *I am, you are, he is.* Nevertheless so necessary is it to all actions and passions that we find no verbs into whose analysis it could not enter: for every action or passion requires existence, or subsistence and being.

The confusion of these two senses had been clearly diagnosed before Frege by writers such as Bolzano who, writing about the Cartesian *cogito,* had shown[31] that if *I think* can indeed be expressed in the form *I am thinking,* the word *am* which expresses the copula does not contain the idea of being as it does in the proposition *I am.* It was of importance for Bolzano that the copula *is* 'can be employed even in sentences whose subject does not exist, as for example in: "das Unmögliche ist auch nichts Wirkliches" (the impossible is nothing real)'.

The second important traditional confusion, and the most difficult to eliminate, was the confusion of senses (3) and (4) of the verb *to be,* that is to say, between what is today called membership and inclusion. This distinction was foreign to Schröder in 1890 whilst he was writing his *Vorlesungen über die Algebra der Logik* and is, it seems, almost entirely unknown in most natural languages. It is one of the most fundamental of Frege's discoveries, although it was not until Russell's theory of types a dozen years later that it became possible to appreciate this.[32]

It is only in terms of this distinction that we are able to express formally the difference between a traditional syllogism such as:

Men are mortal
The Andorrans are men
∴ The Andorrans are mortal

and the obvious fallacy, which we have already considered above:[33]

Men are numerous
The Andorrans are men
∴ The Andorrans are numerous.

The apparent parallelism between the two inferences is based on the confusion between membership and inclusion. In the first case we would' today say:

The class of men is included in the class of mortals
The class of Andorrans is included in the class of men
∴ The class of Andorrans is included in the class of mortals

an inference which makes use of the transitivity of inclusion. In the second case, on the other hand, we must say:

The class of men belongs to the class of classes which are numerous
The class of Andorrans is included in the class of men

and from these premisses nothing permits us to conclude that

The class of Andorrans belongs to the class of classes which are numerous.

A third possible confusion, between sense (2) distinguished above (identity) and senses (3) and (4) (membership and inclusion), is also very common in natural languages, although it is easily eliminated. For a simple intuitive criterion is available which can easily be made use of to avoid intellectual confusion: identity is symmetrical whereas neither inclusion nor membership have this property. Thus, for practical purposes, at least, a doubtful case can be decided by turning a sentence round and noting whether symmetry is preserved.[34]

The distinctions employed by Frege, remarkable though they are should by no means be taken to exhaust the relevant possibilites. Although they suffice for contemporary mathematics, at least in the elementary form in which it is (for example) taught, they can be taken much further. Leśniewski[35], for example has developed and refined Frege's distinctions, as we shall now see.

We shall try to situate the distinctions put forward by Leśniewski within the framework of Frege's distinctions.

(1) To express existence, Leśniewski proposes distinguishing between:

(a) ex{b}: there exists at least one individual b, at least one b exists;
(b) sol{b}: there exists at most one individual b, at most one b exists;
(c) ob{A}: there exists exactly (i.e. at least and at most) one individual A, there is exactly one A.

If I say *God exists* the context alone allows us to determine whether the first or the third of these senses is involved: the third sense will only be relevant if the proposition *God exists* is held to exclude polytheism.

(2) In order to express the identity of two terms Leśniewski distinguishes:

(a) $= \{AB\}$: this designates the identity of two individuals, A is the same individual as B and conversely;

(b) $\equiv \{bc\}$: this indicates the mutual inclusion or identity of two classes; identity here does not necessarily imply that there exists an individual which belongs to the two classes; (Leśniewski does not mention classes and talks instead here of an 'equation');

(c) $\bigcirc \{bc\}$: this indicates the coincidence of two classes, such that there exists at least one individual which belongs to the two classes in question (Leśniewski has 'strong existential equality');

(3) Leśnieswki does not distinguish different sorts of membership but retains and makes more precise the term:[36]

$\varepsilon \{Ab\}$: there is exactly one A and this term is either b or the sole b.

(4) Leśniewski distinguishes two forms of inclusion:

(a) $\subset \{bc\}$: weak inclusion, as this is to be found in certain sorts of Boolean algebra, all (individuals, if any, which are) b are c

(b) $\sqsubset \{bc\}$: strict inclusion, as is to be found to a certain extent in Aristotle's logic: any, and at least one, individual which is b is c.[37]

Do Frege's distinctions suffice? Whether it is necessary to follow Leśniewski in detail is a practical question to which only the actual use of the calculus can help provide an answer. Is it, for example, useful to keep the distinction between two forms of inclusion as suggested by Leśniewski? In some cases and for certain elementary problems the distinction is not necessary. It is not required by Boolean algebra which gets on well without it. But if in some contexts no harm comes of ignoring the relation which Leśniewski represents as

$\sqsubseteq \{bc\},$

this is due to the fact that this relation implies the relation

$\subset \{bc\},$

that is to say, if it is true that *every individual b (and there exists at least one such individual) is c,* then I cannot be wrong in asserting simply that *every individual b (whether or not any such exists) is c.* Thus the first proposition may everywhere simply be replaced by the second at the cost of a slight loss in information. But clearly the substitution does not work in the other direction. For although the first proposition implies the second, the second does not imply the first. In most cases it is possible to dispense with the relation expressed by Leśniewski as $\sqsubseteq$; but it is much more difficult to do without $\subset$. Where I choose to replace $\sqsubseteq$ by $\subset$ the only important question is whether the slight loss of information involved has any consequences for the theory I want to construct or the problem to be dealt with.

If such a loss of information is acceptable and if the economy involved is desirable, as is the case with a language such as Boolean algebra, it is *a fortiori* the case for natural languages: on the one hand since, as we have seen, they are not calculi they do not require the same level of precision, and on the other hand, since the resources of signs they have at their disposal are much larger and since also there is the constant possibility of invoking metalinguistic devices where a sign by itself threatens to be inadequate.

The problem is of course somewhat different in the case of the general distinction between membership and inclusion. Failure to recognize this distinction is more serious, since it leads to fallacies, as we have seen. A language which explicitly employed the distinction would no longer run the risk of these fallacies. In the absence of such a guarantee it is only the intuition of the intentional content of inferences, in Indo-European languages at least, which enables us to avoid such errors. The problem is therefore purely economic: are there significant advantages for communication to be obtained by distinguishing between these two senses of the verb *to be?*

All that one can say without being arbitrary is that the confusion of the two senses is not serious provided it is intuition and not the calculus which has the upper hand. This is usually the case when the verb *to be* is employed in the sense of *to exist,* although the danger of misuse is always

100

present. An unclear use of the verb *to be* in Indo-European languages may be the harmful source both of the monism of Parmenides and of the ontological argument, at least as this is put forward by St. Anselm.[38] But these examples belong to the philosophical tradition and experience has shown that the arguments in question have rarely impressed common sense, a proof of the unwillingness of common sense to indulge in an autonomous use of signs uncontrolled by intuition.

The Reduction of the Verb to the Copula-Predicate Form

Although it is important to keep the relations of membership, inclusion and identity distinct from one another, this does not mean that there are not ways of reducing each of these relations to the other. Some sorts of reduction are very familiar in contemporary logic. It is important to mention them here, for these purely logical possibilities delineate a field of *a priori* linguistic possibilities of central importance for anyone whose interests extend beyond noting certain historical evolutions or geographical divergences.

The possibilities of constructing one concept from another can be explained simply and without any formalization in the case of the connection between identity on the one hand and membership and inclusion on the other. That two individuals *A* and *B* are identical signifies that for any class *K,* the membership of *A* in this class implies *B*'s membership of the same class and vice versa. Similarly the identity of two classes signifies that each is included in the other. Thus the different forms of the relation of identity can be constructed from membership, inclusion and certain other functors such as inter-propositional implication and conjunction.

As for membership and inclusion, it should be borne in mind that logicians today can reduce the relation of inclusion to a structure in which the relation of membership occurs. Of these two relations only that of membership appears to be (relatively) basic, and thus it is this relation for which contemporary usage reserves the term *copula*.

If I use the letter *S* to designate the individual Socrates, the letter *m* for the class of mortals and the symbol ε for membership, then the proposition

Socrates is mortal

will be written as

$S \, \varepsilon \, m,$

which signifies that *the individual Socrates belongs to the class of mortals.* But if I want to formalize the proposition

man is mortal

and I use *h* to designate the set of mortals, I may write

$m \subset h$

which signifies that *the class of men is included in the class of mortals.* But I can also dispense with the symbol for inclusion, because *that the class of men is included in that of mortals* signifies that it is true of everything that, *if it is a man then it is mortal,* that is to say:

$(x \, \varepsilon \, h) \supset (x \, \varepsilon \, m)$

where the symbol '$\supset$' is the sign of implication (if ... then ...). Thus the relation of inclusion between two classes can be reduced to an implication between two propositions each of which expresses a relation of membership.

But the indispensability of the relation of class membership is itself relative. It is possible to do without classes and develop what Russell calls a *no-class theory.* Membership of a class can be interpreted as the expression in extension of what a function and one argument express in comprehension.

Socrates is mortal

may be interpreted either as

is mortal (Socrates),

where *is mortal* is the functor and *Socrates* the argument, or as

$S \, \varepsilon \, m.$

Thus every relation of membership in a class can be expressed without the help of the notion of class or the symbol for membership.

And it is this structure which explains how a language whose purpose is communication can perfectly well do without the copula. The desperate attempts of logicians to reduce all verbs to the copula have always run up against the observation of grammarians or simply of sceptics that the copula is by no means universal, that it is foreign to many languages and that even in the Indo-European tradition, which had pushed the development of the copula to its utmost extent, it emerged very late. We have seen that in Indo-European languages the copula was so far from being a basic notion that it came to be expressed by words with other senses, and in particular by words with the meaning of existence or, in other cases, by verbs signifying *standing* or *to have become*.

But it is not enough to note that the copula is dispensable and to explain in this way its absence from many languages. An account must be given of the success enjoyed by the use of the copula once it has come to be introduced into a linguistic system. The explanation is not difficult. We have seen that every verb may be analysed as a function with n arguments; and also that every function with n arguments can be transposed into a function with n-1 arguments provided only that n-1 $\geqslant$ 0. Hence every verb that can be expressed as a function with at least one argument may equally be interpreted as the expression of the membership of an individual in a class.

In spite of an occasional appearance of artificiality, these reductions are nevertheless legitimate. The function with two arguments

Peter loves Paul

can be interpreted as a function with one argument, for example

loves Paul (Peter)

which in its turn can be transformed into the relation of membership

Peter is loving Paul.
(Pierre est aimant Paul)

A function with three arguments, such as

Peter prefers Paul to Jack

can be transformed into a function with only one argument

prefers Paul to Jack (Peter)

which in its turn yields the membership relation

Peter is preferring Paul to Jack.
(Pierre est préférant Paul à Jacques)

The artificiality of such reductions, which has often made them the butt of ironical remarks, is due merely to the fact that the reduction of a function with more than one argument to a function with only one argument or to the membership relation clearly entails that the resources available for analysing the proposition are diminished and hence that there is a loss of information. The function with three arguments

Peter prefers Paul to Jack

is richer in algorithmic possibilities than is the almost grotesquely slight membership relation

Peter belongs to the class of those who prefer Paul to Jack.

But this impoverishment does not affect the logically irreproachable nature of the reduction. And so, on this point, the real historical temptation in logic to reduce all verbs to the copula, the element that had been brought into prominence by the Indo-European tradition, appears largely justified.

There is nothing absurd in the claim of *The Port-Royal Logic* that:

the verb ought not to have any other use than to mark the connection we make in our mind between the two terms of a proposition; but only the verb *to be,* called the substantive (substantif) verb has remained in this simple state.

But one is then obliged to read into the evolution of languages a direction which is not confirmed by philological evidence and suppose that, little by little, men have renounced the simplicity of the verb *to be* and, in order to 'abbreviate their expressions' have progressively added to the copula the meaning of an attribute in such a way that two, not three words, the subject and the verb, suffice to form a proposition.[39] Unfortunately not only is such an interpretation contradicted by the facts of historical philology, it is in part unsatisfactory for logical reasons. For such a reduction of the proposition to the expression of a relation of membership is only possible for verbs that have at least one argument, and so cannot cope with the existence of impersonal propositions, as we have seen.[40]

Can one then say that the invention of the copula in certain languages such as those of the Indo-European family was an 'historical accident'?[41] Certainly, if every invention, even those in logic and mathematics, is held to involve some element of accident. But this cannot mean that the social institution of the copula is purely arbitrary. A society can as little assign any role it likes to signs as it can make a theorem out of any proposition whatsoever. The very structure of the copula explains why many languages, although in themselves excellent systems of communication, do not possess the copula. It also explains why this late invention of Indo-European languages has acquired such an important role and exercised such a seductive influence on so many minds.

It has often been emphasized, correctly, how great an influence the introduction of the copula exercised on the course of Western philosophy.[42] There is a clear parallel between the subject-attribute couple, to which most propositions can be reduced with the help of the copula, and the substance-accident schema into which Western philosophy has been pleased to fit its picture of the world, whether this be because language has marked out the paths followed by different philosophical currents, or because the intellectual schemata have themselves first modelled or marked the structure of language.

The presence of the copula has also influenced the Western intellectual tradition in that it gave prominence to the extension of concepts at the expense of their comprehension or intension.[43] The schema of the copula favours a representation of the world as a set of objects which themselves fall into classes: only classes and objects are needed. This makes possible the abandonment of an alternative which is subtler and deeper (in that it is generalizable and capable of yielding a richer analysis), in which objects are caught up in a finely meshed and infinite network of relations with one another. The commercial societies of the Mediterranean basin in which the Indo-European heritage flourished could doubtless not have done better than to adopt the simplified schema of object and class, a schema which perfectly fitted that representation of objects belonging to a kind without which, even in societies which are technically much more advanced, *commerce* in the modern, economic sense of the word is inconceivable.

The facts of ethnography tend to show that relational schemata are much more diversified and sometimes even logically more developed in those societies which may well be called *feudal* in the sense that relations between individuals do not involve that massive simplification to be found in more advanced societies – and in the sense that the ties of interpersonal dependence are much more complex and strict than those with which we are familiar. The linguistic development of the copula is often unknown in these societies. They have retained a subtlety which our societies have lost. We group in one and the same class of brothers both the person who is the brother of someone of the female sex and the person who is the brother of someone of the male sex. And, as is well known, there are numerous relations distinguished by 'primitive' societies which hold between terms all of which Indo-European societies group together in the single class of cousins.

Traditional Definitions of the Nature of the Verb

Our analysis of the verb leads us to deny any properly logical significance to some traditional characterizations of this grammatical term. Thus it has often been said, following Plato,[44] that the verb is "what expresses actions", where names are applied to "the subjects who perform these actions". The same formulation is to be found in Humboldt, for whom "it is in the nature of verbs ... to express the idea of an action" and "in the nature of names" to designate things (qualities or substances).[45] In the middle of the sixteenth century the *Tretté de la grammère françoèze de Meygret,* the prototype of the French grammars which were to come after it, had defined the verb as 'a part of language signifying action or passion'.[46] Similarly Scaliger, in his *Principes de la langue latine,* tried to show that the distinction between names and verbs corresponded to the distinction between things *in permanentes et fluentes;* that names properly designate what is constant and verbs what is transitory.

It was easy for Arnauld[47] to come up with objections to definitions like these:

there are verbs which signify neither actions nor passions nor what is transient, such as *existit* (it exists), *quiescit* (it rests), *friget* (it is cold), *alget* (it is chilled), *tepet* (it is warm), *calet* (it is hot), *albet* (it is white), *viret* (it is green), *claret* (it is bright), etc.

It is also significant that Plato, only a few lines after writing that the verb expresses an action (πρᾶξις) specified (if that is the word) that it could also express inaction (ἀπραξία) or being (οὐσία). Of the same sort is the definition of the verb put forward by Donatus, which is almost laughable: 'pars orationis ... aut agere aliquid aut pati aut neutrum significans'. But the grammarians of the seventeenth century such as Irson or Chiflet were to employ slightly happier formulations: for them the verb signifies being, acting or suffering (undergoing).

Just what it is that is so artificial in assigning verbs to designate actions, or in the distinction made by Scaliger, emerges when one considers that, as is well-noted by *The Port-Royal Grammar*:[48]

there are words which are not verbs at all which signify actions and passions and even things which are transient;

the reason for this is that from any verb more than one substantive or name can be formed with the help of the relative pronoun, the participle, the infinitive, or some other means: *walk* is certainly a verb, but *the one who walks, the walker, the walk, the fact that Peter walks* are all substantives.

Formulations such as that of Scaliger are not, however, without a certain psychological truth. If we follow the suggestion of Russell and Whitehead quoted above,[49] and represent the world of our experience as a set of objects endowed with certain properties and standing in different relations to one another, then our expression of these properties presupposes that we have isolated the objects to which the properties belong or between which the relations hold. Now psychologists know well that the object-schema applies much more easily to things which are *constant* than to things which are transient or in flux. The psychological tendency to prefer what is constant as an object of perception has its analogue in the logical structure of the function. If the argument designates the object and if the object has been singled out perceptually from amongst what is constant as opposed to what is transitory, then there will be a statistical predominance of arguments designating what is constant, and functors will tend to express the movements and transformations of the object, i.e. in traditional terminology, its actions and passions.

But although none of this may be ignored by the grammarian, it does not properly pertain *pure* or *rational grammar*. Its only basis in logic is this: that if it is true that the arguments of first-order functors (predicates) are necessarily individual objects in view of the theory of types, then – given that the perceiving subject tends to privilege those objects in a perceptual field which possess a certain stability – it will follow that the arguments of first-order predicates will tend to designate individuals which possess a certain stability. And hence the corresponding functors or predicates will as a rule designate the properties of these individuals and their relations. Of course this no longer holds for higher-order predicates or functions: the predicate of a predicate, for example, has as arguments first-order predicates which even if, as arguments, they have a nominal form, have the same meaning-content as a verb corresponding to a first-order function.

If, therefore, what enjoys perceptual stability tends statistically to occupy the role of arguments or, if one prefers, the role of names, then, to the extent that this tendency can be observed, this can only be due to the fact that first-order functions or predicates constitute by themselves a large part of all the functions or predicates of whatever order which are normally made use of in ordinary language. This is the explanation of the fact that Scaliger's point, although without any logical justification, nevertheless corresponds to what is, statistically, a tendency.

This refutation of Scaliger's point is to be found in the *Logische Untersuchungen*,[50] although neither Scaliger nor his formulation are mentioned. Husserl explains why there is a temptation to run together the independence and the dependence of meanings with the independence and dependence of the objects meant.

Confusing the two generates a view according to which a name, as a categorematic expression, would refer to an object which would also be independent, i.e. endowed with that objective independence which perception confers on what is stable; a verb, on the other hand, as a syncategorematic expression, would refer to dependent objects such as qualities or relations which exist only if what they are dependent on exists.

Against the temptation to make use of this identification Husserl repeats in his own way the criticism formulated by *The Port-Royal Logic*, pointing out that

everything that is dependent can be made ... the object of an independent meaning, for example: *redness, figure, likeness, size, unity, being.*

He concluded from these examples that one should never attempt to explain the independence of meanings by referring them to 'objective material moments', since they may also correspond to 'categorial forms'. And, he continues, it is possible to explain how moments which are themselves dependent can be the objects of independent meanings; for it is the intention peculiar to such independent meanings which makes 'objects' of these moments. Following Husserl, then, we must disallow the suggestion of Scaliger, according to which the relation of signifier to signified is that of copy to model. The essence of the signifier is not to copy or picture the object signified, it "consists rather in a certain intention, which can be intentionally 'directed' to anything and everything, to what is independent as much as to what is dependent".

And Husserl concluded that "anything, everything can be objectified as a thing meant", a conclusion which seems problematic only when the expression 'as a thing meant' is restricted to what is effected by the nominal mode of signification alone.[51] There is at least one term where the intention which is appropriate to verbal meanings does not suffice to yield a verb. This is the case when a name designates an individual, i.e. is a grammatical proper name. Frege,[52] who simply strips an Aristotelian point of its narrowly Aristotelian vocabulary,[53] underlines the impossibility of making a proper name play the role of a predicate. For I cannot say of an individual or of any object designated by a nominal term that it *is* Alexander the Great or that it *is* the planet Venus without giving the verb *to be* a meaning very different from that of the copula (for example the meaning of the relation of identity). Thus if it is true that I can always make a name out of a verb, I can only make a verb out of a name where the name is not a proper name.[54]

Attempts have recently been made to base the distinction between name and verb on the parallel distinction between old and new information, the verb designating 'the new information communicated about the object of thought' which is designated by the name.[55] This has the advantage over the traditional definitions criticized above that it seeks the basis of the distinction not in the object itself but in its relation to a subject. But the undoubted truths revealed by these attempts are not always relevant to what we have called pure rational grammar. The psychologist can point out that in non-impersonal sentences where something is said about something else *that about which* something is said often has chronological priority over *that which is said about it* and hence that the most natural step is to name what is familiar in order to connect this with the properties or relations met with subsequently. But it can easily be shown that such considerations are irrelevant to the justification of the essential difference between names and verbs. Consider the case of indicative propositions which function as answers to interrogative propositions introduced by the pronoun *who*. The way in which such questions are posed shows that the new information contained in the response has nothing to do with the verb, which is already completely given as a part of the question.

The new information is expressed, rather, by a name which occupies the place of one of the arguments of the function: it is the communication of this name which makes the proposition a response to the question.

Before leaving this theme it will be useful to look at another distinction sometimes made by grammarians: that between 'nominal sentences' as expressions designating states, and 'verbal sentences' as expressions designating processes.[56] Many languages do in fact display a marked preference for the subject-copula-attribute form in order to express the stability of a certain state. Thus one says

Peter is brown

but

Peter walks/smokes.

In other words, English, like many other languages, tends to reserve the verbal form for the expression of actions or events.

This distinction even has, we think, a certain psychological correctness, as can be seen from the fact that languages often attach very different meanings to verbal and nominal forms which are otherwise very similar. Thus

Pierre agit

designates a precise act (which in English would be reported by

Peter acts

only in the so-called 'dramatic present',) whereas

Pierre est actif (Peter is active)

indicates a permanent property of the subject.

We must conclude, then, that languages have made use of the distinction between forms to express two very different predicates. It is tempting here to invoke the arbitrariness of the linguistic sign: wherever the differences between two forms is sufficiently great or is such that they are opposed to one another in some way, language can profit from the contrast in order to underline a distinction between two senses.

Although class-membership, which is suggested by the subject-copula-attribute form, and functions with one argument, which are suggested by 'verbal sentences', are logically equivalent, their psychological counterparts are not equivalent. To assign an object to a class seems to indicate that the object will remain a member of this class for a certain time at least; it only seems to be psychologically justified to represent a class if its elements are stable and numerous enough to merit our attention. On the other hand, we are more likely to employ a verb if the properties we want to describe are too unusual or singular for us to think of forming a class.

Our perception has its own reasons about which logic knows nothing. Psychologically, it is true that "it is illegitimate to assimilate the nominal form (*the sun is bright*) and the verbal form (*the sun sets*)"[57] and the grammarian cannot ignore distinctions that *pure logical grammar* must ignore. In any case, a distinction such as that between states and processes, to the extent that it has only a psychological basis, is without any rigour. Charles Serrus quotes as an example the sentence *the window opens onto the street*[58], a verbal form, yet one that represents a state and not a process.

Number and Position of the Arguments

The expression of a function raises, finally, the problem of the place of its different arguments. Indeed to use the word *place* here is already to favour one particular answer to the question. To say that

Peter loves Paul

is quite different from saying

Paul loves Peter

for the sense of a proposition is not fixed merely by determining its verb and arguments: it is essential in most cases to determine also the place of its arguments. The exceptions are certain functors such as:

Peter, Paul and Jack love one another,

all of whose arguments are symmetrical when taken in twos, or:

Peter loves Paul and Jack, the one as much as the other,

111

which has a pair of symmetrical arguments, as does

Peter hesitates between talk and work.

There is then a practical problem of communication: how are we to mark the fact that, in a function, one argument has one role and the other argument has a different role? Historically this problem has received at least two different solutions. Some languages have opted for one or the other of the two methods, others have combined them both.

The first solution is to modify the argument itself (for example by adding either a prefix or a suffix) in such a way that this modification

(1) does not hinder identification of the argument, and
(2) simultaneously makes it possible to establish its role.

Thus consider an argument A; it can be assigned the ending *a,* to indicate that it has a certain role with respect to the functor, *e* to indicate a second role, *i* to indicate a third role (if we assume that the functor has three arguments), *o* to indicate a fourth role, and so on. If the verb in question is the verb *prefer* the argument A will be A*a* if it designates the person who prefers, A*e* if it designates what is preferred, And A*i* if it designates what A*e* is preferred to. This is the principle at work in all declensions and one which is also to be found at work, at least in part, in languages such as French, which have no declensions. Frequently in French the third argument of a function is distinguished from the second simply by being preceded by the preposition *à.*

The second historically documented solution makes use of the *position* or, as we have already somewhat over-hastily put it, of the place of the arguments. In traditional algebraic notation the functor expressed by the symbol $>$ takes two arguments which are not interchangeable: the term designating the larger number goes before, that designating the smaller number goes after, the symbol for the functor. The notation devised by Peano and adopted by Russell for the propositional calculus uses the same principle – one need think only of a non-symmetrical connective such as implication – and it is to be found also in natural languages such as English and French. Thus in

Peter loves Paul

the fact that it is Peter who loves and Paul who is loved is marked by the positions of the arguments to the left and right of the verb. An alternative, to be found in Łukasiewicz's notion for the propositional calculus and in the traditional representation of functions, puts the functor at the beginning and distinguishes the arguments by their successive positions after the functor. This utilisation of one-dimensional position is prior to the development of writing which, in the majority of cases, makes use of the way linear succession mimics temporal succession. There is no reason why two and three dimensions should not be used for the places of arguments. Frege has outlined a way of using two dimensions in his *Begriffsschrift*.[59]

The different advantages of the two methods are easily seen. The expressive power of Latin, it is sometimes pointed out, is due to the fact that, since the roles of the arguments are marked by endings, the speaker of Latin can exploit position in order to convey certain nuances:

Petrus Paulam amat (It is Peter who loves Paul);
Paulum Petrus amat (It is Paul whom Peter loves).

In a language where word-position has next to no grammatical function, little effort is required to express what in other languages can only be expressed explicitly, and hence at great length.

Does the grammatical subject, then, have a meaning at the level of what we have called pure grammar? Frege's reply to this question seems to be that the choice of subject has only a psychological importance:

In language, the place occupied by the subject in the sequence of words has the significance of a specially important place, it is where we put that to which we wish especially to direct the attention of the reader.

And further on:

The speaker usually intends the subject to be taken as the main argument; the next in importance often appears as object.[60]

In support of this view he emphasizes the fact that language places at our disposal many different ways of moving any argument we wish to emphasize into the position of the subject; for example, many verbs or predicates have converses (heavier/lighter, give/receive, etc.). But it should be noted that this essentially psychological possibility of emphasizing the argument to which one wishes to direct attention functions properly only in linguistic systems where the role of the argument is marked by its position. Is the privileged term in a Latin sentence that in the nominative case or the object, which stands out because of its position in the sentence?

There is an even simpler and more basic reason for the privilege enjoyed by the subject. In Indo-European languages when a verb takes only one argument this argument is, in almost all cases, the grammatical subject; when it takes two arguments they are normally the subject and direct object;[61] where more than two arguments are involved the language must construct other types of grammatical complements. Thus the subject is the principal argument in a more than merely psychological sense; for the fact that it is the main argument signifies simply that it is the only term that is an argument in nearly all the cases where a function has at least one argument. It is probably even its technical privilege as the main argument that, by drawing attention to the subject, leads to its acquiring a psychological privilege.

But this technical privilege of the subject as principal argument is the reason for yet another privilege. In many natural languages, when a verb takes several arguments normal usage usually allows the same verb to take a smaller number of arguments. Thus *promise,* which would normally take three arguments (a subject, a direct object and an indirect object) – as in:

You promised me this gift

– may occur with only one object:

You promised this gift,

or even without any object and with only the subject as argument

You promised.

In each case although the same verb, *promise*, is involved, its sense does not remain the same, unless the absence of an object is interpreted as an implicit existential quantification:

There exists someone to whom you promised this gift.
There exists something and someone such that you have promised the one to the other.

Such a usage is possible only in a language which tolerates either ambiguity or implicit presuppositions. In either case, as André Martinet has put it, "the subject only differs from an object because it is part of the minimal statement".[62] Thus it is the privilege of the subject that "it could not disappear without eliminating the statement as such".[63] Those arguments, however, which traditional grammarians called *objects* or

114

complements are those which "can disappear without affecting the validity and reciprocal relations of the remaining elements".[64]

It is of course possible to describe the difference traditionally expressed as that between transitive and intransitive verbs as an 'accident of grammar' by emphasizing that "there is no grammatical justification of the difference between *to remind oneself of something* and *to remember something*".[65] There is certainly no logical equivalent of this common distinction and it is no less certain that the class of intransitive propositions, in the ordinary sense of the term, includes the class of propositions whose logical analysis yields functions with only one argument. Hence, for many of our intransitive verbs, the fact that they are intransitive verbs is indeed a matter of pure grammar, though this is not the case for all the members of this class.[66]

One way of making an argument a grammatical subject is provided, as Frege pointed out,[67] by the distinction between active and passive forms. The grammatical arbitrariness apparently introduced by this distinction is in fact made possible by a rigorous framework within which certain arbitrary variations are possible.

We can set out its *a priori* outlines as follows:

(1) Verbs which correspond to functions with only one argument cannot have any passive form;

(2) Verbs which correspond to functions with two arguments (binary relations) can have only one passive form: the two arguments can exchange roles in only one way;

(3) Verbs which correspond to functions with three arguments can have at least two passive forms:[68] if we call the argument to the immediate right of the functor the subject, then there correspond to the active form f (x,y,z) two passive forms f' (y,x,z) and f'' (z,y,x).

(4) Quite generally, a verb which corresponds to a function with n arguments can have n-1 passive forms.[69]

It goes without saying that not all of these pure possibilities are realized in every language; many are not. Whereas English possesses two passive forms for functions with three arguments – a passive sentence with *give* may take as its subject either the gift or its recipient – French makes use of only one passive here and sometimes remedies this weakness by employing antonyms. Thus as well as *donner* and *être donné* (to give, and to be given), French has *recevoir* (to receive).

Is the conclusion to be drawn from this state of affairs that the grammatical form *subject* and the terms for the different complements or objects have no logical significance? Is it logically more satisfactory to call all arguments *complements* and simply provide them with indices in order to distinguish between different arguments?

It should be noted that all binary relations which are not symmetrical can be adequately grasped or understood only when our representation of them is such that one of the arguments is privileged. Indeed, the classical formulation of the theory of relations does just this when, having in mind the classes to which the two terms of a binary relation belong, it speaks of the *domain* as opposed to the *range* of this relation. The grammatical specification of a subject corresponds largely to the perceptual privilege of putting the domain first, which the teaching of logic, if not logic itself, must take into account. If it is impossible simply to identify the term belonging to the domain and the term belonging to the range as grammatical subject and object, this is because the ordinary systems of grammar often maintain this perceptual privilege even in those cases where the symmetry of the relation in question means that it has no basis in logic, as in

Peter is the brother of Paul

If we now consider the distinction made in the grammar of English between direct and indirect objects, we see that the latter term means only that the object is connected with the verb indirectly, that is to say, with the help of the preposition. This suggests the following justification: if we agree to characterize the first argument by the fact that it precedes and the second by the fact that it follows the verb, then in a one-dimensional system the third argument would have to be characterized by an inflection of the argument itself (or by adjoining a preposition), since its position alone does not suffice.[70]

It is interesting to note in the present context the existence of certain verbs in English (or French) to which there corresponds a relation with three arguments: *teach, pay, persuade, steal,* and which are all such that they exploit the *a priori* possibilities made available by the nature of the triadic relation. They can be construed in four ways:
(1) with three arguments: *the teacher teaches grammar to the pupil:*
(2) with two arguments, the second of which designates what is taught, paid, persuaded, stolen: *the teacher teaches grammar;*
(3) with two arguments, the second of which also designates the person with respect to whom the subject acts: *the teacher teaches the pupil;*
(4) with only one argument: *the teacher teaches.*

116

It has often been noted that in French these verbs (*enseigner, payer, persuader, servir, voler*) take two sorts of direct object or complement, though never at the same time. French grammarians usually explain this by referring to a concern, intrinsic to their language, to establish a difference between complements.

If we view the matter from the point of view of communication we may argue as follows: as long as one has a relation with two arguments, then the second complement, whatever it is, may conveniently take direct object position. But if one has three arguments then two solutions are technically possible:

(1) Either one decides, as in Latin, not to give up the mode of construction employed for two arguments: *doceo pueros, doceo grammaticam, doceo pueros grammaticam.* For this solution to be viable it is of course necessary that meaning alone is enough to make clear what the roles of the different arguments are, since the grammatical indications do not do this.

(2) Or one decides, as in French, to drop the mode of construction employed for two arguments in order to ensure that grammatical indications rather than meaning specify the roles of the different arguments. In this case one will introduce a preposition before one of the two objects simply in order to distinguish one from another: *enseigner, voler, servir quelque chose à quelqu'un.* The choice between what is to be the direct complement and what the indirect complement seems to be completely arbitrary. Thus French sometimes inverts the two roles taking care simply not to make use of the same preposition in two co-occurring expressions (a precaution which is necessary if ambiguities like those arising in the case of the Latin double accusative are to be avoided): *payer quelque chose à quelqu'un* or *payer quelqu'un de (or pour) quelque chose; persuader quelque chose à quelqu'un* or *persuader quelqu'un de quelque chose.*

The question of *adverbial complements (compléments circonstanciels)*, is a more delicate problem. First of all, what are the adverbial elements in a proposition? If one takes these to be terms indicating manner, then the function of the adverbial complement turns out to be the same as that of a simple adverb. And whether or not manner is one of the modalities studied by modal logic one will then regard the 'adverbial complement' not as an argument of a function but as a functorial functor that forms a new functor.

In other cases what is understood by *adverbial complements* differs from elements that simply modify the sense of the main verb: they rather determine the spatio-temporal field or setting in which the event reported by the verb occurs. This specification of circumstance (*circonstance*) is here connected with the fact that, at least in most known civilisations, the knowing subject structures the object of knowledge along the lines of the setting or field of the event. The subject's attention isolates an event in order to situate it – sometimes even at a later point in time – within certain spatio-temporal coordinates. Thus between the event perceived and its localisation there is a complex relation, neither simple dependence nor independence, which we describe using the metaphor of a setting or field.

If spatio-temporal circumstances always presented themselves within the field of our knowledge with this quasi-independence relative to the event the only problem for a pure or rational grammar would be to choose between the different technical possibilities for expressing this: a maximum[71] of four coordinates, three for space and one for time, are enough to localize any object or event we want to speak about.

But it is important not to confuse these circumstances or circumstantial specifications (*circonstances* in the proper sense of the term), with the relation to which grammarians often give the name 'adverbial complement' (*complément circonstantiel*). If I say

I am going to Paris

Paris is not the spatio-temporal or setting for my movements. I must interpret the verb *go* as a relation with two arguments and *Paris* is one of these arguments. The same is true of

I live in London

where *London*, too, must be interpreted as an argument.

It must be admitted that no technique whatever can wholly eliminate the element of arbitrariness that is involved as soon as one relies on the cognitive schema formed by the relation between an event and its setting. Indeed this relation itself is somewhat arbitrary. Thus the proposition:

Henry IV died in Paris

may quite naturally be interpreted as a function whose two arguments are *Henry IV* and *Paris*. But one hesitates in the case of

Henry IV was assassinated in Paris.

One might perhaps be tempted to interpret this as a function with only one argument (*Henry IV*), supplemented by an adverbial indication of the place where the assassination took place. Finally, in the case of

Henry IV was assassinated by Ravaillac in Paris in 1610

one is more inclined to an analysis into a function with two arguments (*Henry IV* and *Ravaillac*) that is supplemented by two adverbial specifications, than to an analysis in terms of a function with four arguments (*Henry IV, Ravaillac, 1610, Paris*).

This example illustrates clearly how, for very many adverbial complements, one has a choice between:

(1) interpreting them as the coordinates of a spatio-temporal system of reference such as that suggested by Carnap in his *Logical Syntax of Language*;[72]

(2) interpreting them as genuine arguments.

Thus much prudence is required before any pronouncements are made about the contingency or necessity of grammatical categories. What we have here attempted, for the particular case of the verb, is to trace the outlines of that field of pure, rational grammar within which the contingency of various options makes sense.

Notes

[1] Frege, *Begriffsschrift*, I, §9. Even when dealing with the letter of Frege's text, as here, we retain and make free use of our own vocabulary. Thus we do not hesitate to use the term *functor* although it is quite foreign to Frege.

[2] Cf. ibid.

[3] Unless, that is, the tense of the verb *killed* or *has killed* is considered as an argument of the functor expressed by the root of the verb, which is by no means impossible. Nevertheless, this remark does not detract from the generality of the suggestions here made.

[4] "The Concept of Truth in Formalized Languages", in Tarski, 1956, p.217.

[5] It may be of interest to compare this analysis of the verb *prefer* with that already given in chapter 2, pp. 56–57 above.

[6] We shall need to return to this question later and shall then see that much of what is put forward provisionally here will have to be changed.

[7] Plato, *Sophist*, 262a–263b.

[8] Aristotle, *De interpretatione*, 3, 16a.

⁹ Arnauld and Lancelot, 2nd part, ch. 24, p.171. This leitmotiv of *The Port-Royal Grammar* is taken up again in *The Port-Royal Logic*: "It is easy to see that it [the proposition] must have two terms: the one about which one affirms or denies, that is called the *subject;* and the other that one affirms or denies, that is called the *attribute* or *praedicatum.*" (*La logique ou l'art de penser,* 2nd part, ch.III, p.112.)

¹⁰ Husserl, *Logical Investigations,* V, ch.4, §33, Eng. trans. p.624. This passage seems to have escaped the attention of Charles Serrus who writes in his *Le parallélisme logico-grammatical* (2nd part, ch.4, p.364): "We note the author's prudent silence on the subject of propositions without a subject, which belong to the class of statements but lack the form of predication". In Husserl's case what we have is not a *prudent silence* about impersonal propositions but a brutal denial that they have any sort of existence in their own right.

¹¹ Quoted by A. Martinet, *La linguistique synchronique,* p.212.

¹² Aristotle, *De interpretatione,* 12, 21b.

¹³ *La logique ou l'art de penser,* 2nd part, ch.2, p.107.

¹⁴ Arnauld and Lancelot, second part, ch.19, p.150.

¹⁵ Bolzano, §172, p.250. Bolzano prefers to express the copula by means of the verb *to have,* rather than *to be.* Hence the normal form he employs is 'A *has* b'.

¹⁶ Charles Serrus has shown at length how illusory were the efforts of post-Aristotelian logic to reduce every proposition to the subject-copula-predicate form. We can therefore pass over rapidly ideas that today are familiar and accepted. One defect of the critique of Charles Serrus that needs to be pointed out, however, is that he often tends to confuse genuine impersonal propositions with the following three different cases:

   (a) Sham impersonal propositions, i.e. propositions which, although they have one or more arguments, do not have a genuine grammatical subject, e.g. the Latin locutions

   me paenitet culpae meae
   tui me miseret
   hujus facti me piget
   fratris me pudet (cf. p.162).

Each of these has two arguments, one of which could, logically be interpreted as a subject and which could therefore without much effort be reduced to the form of a predication. In his *Logik* (p.60), Alexander Pfänder defines sham impersonal propositions for languages such as French and German as follows: they are propositions "in which the place of the subject is indeed occupied by the word 'it' but in which it is the following words which then introduce the real subject".

This category of sham impersonal propositions clearly includes expressions beginning with 'il faut' (it is necessary), 'il est permis' (it is permitted), 'il me plaît' (it pleases me), as had already been pointed out by *The Port-Royal Grammar.* When Lancelot and Arnauld suggest interpreting this last expression as signifying: *l'action* or *le mouvement de faire cela me plaît* (the action or movement of doing that pleases me) their analysis on this occasion is not at all artificial or out of place: 'This *il*', they write, with good reason, 'is only a species of pronouns, for *id* (that), which takes the place of the nominative, that is understood or included in the meaning'. p. 149. In our terms, the subject of the verb is itself a propositional argument.

   (b) Propositions in which the subject is included in the verb (cf. Serrus, p.170 and p.395) as in Latin where person – in the absence of a pronoun – is marked by the way a verb is conjugated. But we have seen that a function with n arguments can always be transformed into a function with n-1 arguments.

   (c) Expressions which are not genuinely indicative or those which, although they are categorematic and indicative are nevertheless not categorematic propositional expressions but rather categorematic and nominal, as in the case where, pointing with my finger, I exclaim 'the star' (cf. ibid., p.170, p.396).

120

These confusions somewhat weaken the force of a critique whose fundamental correctness is beyond any doubt.

[17] Lalande, *Vocabulaire de la philosophie*, article *prédicat*.

[18] It is surprising that V. Z. Panfilov (*Grammar and Logic*, p.49) can write that the fact that syllogistic is based on judgments with a subject-predicate structure shows that a proposition within whose content no subject can be distinguished is not a judgment but another special form of thought. Is it necessary to point out that classical syllogistic has no exemplary value here, that it is a complex theory combining two sorts of calculus that today are carefully distinguished. Any variable whatsoever in the calculus of propositions can easily represent an impersonal proposition. Why, then, should we refuse to call such a proposition a judgment? There is nothing to prevent us from arguing as follows on the basis of such judgments:

> if it is raining then it is not snowing;
> it is raining;
> therefore it is not snowing.

[19] *Principia Mathematica*, vol. I, Introduction, ch.2, p.43.

[20] Serrus, 2nd part, ch.2, p.187. The German examples to which Serrus draws attention,
Es regnet, Es donnert,
Es weht, Es lenzt,
Es septembert,
Es weihnachtet sehr,
show very well that these propositions often describe an atmosphere (either in the physical or in the cultural sense). In a language like German the wealth of such impersonal idioms is clearly not unconnected with the position occupied by 'romantic' inspiration in the German tradition.

[21] Quoted by Pfänder, *Logik*, ch.4, p.64.

[22] Ibid., pp.66ff.

[23] Die gemeinte Stelle der umgebenden Welt.

[24] The proposition *a man is taking a walk* implies various spatio-temporal indications such as *here* and *now* just as much as does *it is raining*. Why should these indications form the special subject of *it is raining* when the subject of *a man is taking a walk* remains, presumably, *a man*.

[25] Cf. above p. 90.

[26] *La linguistique synchronique*, pp.212ff. Cf. also Martinet, *Langue et fonction*, (*A functional view of language*, trans. H. und G. Walter) Paris, Denoël, 1970, p.64 and pp.75–78.

[27] Cf. "Concept and Object" in Geach and Black, pp.43ff, 50ff.

[28] According to Meillet and Vendryès *Traité de grammaire comparée des langues classiques*, 1927, pp.537ff, quoted by Serrus, 2nd part, ch.2, p.168.

[29] It is worth noting that Plato, on the other hand, seems to admit that a proposition may express not only the being of what is (οὐσίαν ὄντος) but also the being of what is not (μὴ ὄντος), Plato, *Sophist*, 262c.

[30] Quoted by R. Donzé, *La grammaire générale et raisonnée de Port-Royal*, 2nd part, ch.3, p.106.

[31] Bolzano, §44, p.55.

[32] It should be borne in mind that Frege's article "Concept and Object" appeared in 1892, the theory of types in 1903.

[33] Cf. above p. 52.

[34] A confusion of this sort is nevertheless to be found in a writer like W. von Humboldt who does not hesitate to write in his "Letter to M. Abel Rémusat": "Every judgment may ... be reduced to a mathematical equation. It is this first form of thought that languages clothe in the form that belongs to them ... Instead of saying, 'I find the ideas of the supreme being and

121

of eternity identical' man posits this judgment outside himself and says 'The supreme being is eternal'". "Lettre à M. Abel Rémusat" in: *Werke, V*, p. 261.

35 We draw here on the table of the symbols used by Leśniewski set out by Luschei in *The Logical Systems of Leśniewski*, pp.10f. In each case we give first of all the symbol used by Leśniewski or by his commentator.

36 We shall not here settle the question whether Leśniewski's clarifications do or do not modify the sense of *membership* that has become normal, since Carnap and Frege, in logic and mathematics.

37 It will perhaps be noted that we have omitted the mereological relation of *ingredience* that Leśniewski rightly takes great care rigorously to distinguish both from what we have here called *membership* and from the two forms of *inclusion*. The reason for this is that the relation of ingredience, although it may in certain cases lend itself to some confusion with the last three relations, is rarely expressible by the verb 'to be' alone in its traditional linguistic form. Cf. Luschei, ibid., pp.72ff. [On an 'is of constitution' see D. Wiggins, *Sameness and Substance*, pp.30–31, Blackwell, Oxford, 1980 – Tr.]

38 This at least is Patzig's view; cf. the preface to his edition of Frege, *Funktion, Begriff, Bedeutung*, p.9.

39 *La logique ou l'art de penser*, 2nd part, ch.2, p.107.

40 Bolzano's work illustrated well how logic, though not lacking in serious reasons for attempting to reduce every proposition to the copula-predicate form, soon found itself stuck in an impasse. The very power of the analyses of this author contribute to exploding the two weak points which condemned the whole project from the start:

– the existence of impersonal verbs;
– the fundamental character of relations;

neither of which can be made to fit into the system without depriving it of its most powerful features. Cf. especially Bolzano, §127, pp.173–79.

41 Serrus, 2nd part, ch.4, p.316.

42 Especially Serrus, ibid.

43 Contrary to received opinion, contemporary logic has in fact reacted against this primacy of the extension of a concept. For not only has it – following Frege – clarified the traditional distinction between *intension* and *extension* by aligning these with propositional functions and the sets of their values, it has given a privileged position to *intension* by generalizing, in the way we have described, the notion of function. On the misunderstandings surrounding the notions of *extensional* and *intensional logic* it is interesting to read Carnap's clarifications, cf. *Logical Syntax*, pp.257–60.

44 Plato, *Sophist*, 262a.

45 "Lettre", in *Werke, V*, p. 266.

46 Mounin, *Histoire de la linguistique*, p.119.

47 Arnauld and Lancelot, 2nd part, ch.13, p.125.

48 Ibid.

49 Cf. above p. 92.

50 Husserl, *Logical Investigations*, IV, §8, Eng. trans. p.507.

51 It is difficult to say exactly just what Husserl was getting at here. The passage can be interpreted in two different ways:

(a) Everything can be objectified as a thing meant (*in der Weise der Bedeutung*, in the manner appropriate to meaning); which would mean that anything at all can be made into a name or a verb. In this case we would disagree with Husserl.

(b) Everything can become an object and so correspond to a nominal designation simply in virtue of a nominal meaning-intention. In this case, we could have no objection to Husserl's claim.

52 "Concept and Object", Geach and Black, ed., p.43.

[53] Cf. especially Aristotle, *Categories:* "There is, lastly, a class of things which are neither present in a subject nor predicable of a subject, such as the individual man or the individual horse". (2, 1a) "Substance, in the truest and primary and most definite sense of the word, is that which is neither predicable of a subject nor present in a subject; for instance, the individual man or horse". (5, 1b) "primary substance is neither ... in a subject nor predicated of a subject" (5, 3a). For Aristotle a *first substance* is an *individual*.

[54] It sometimes happens that, for purposes of irony, a verb is formed from a noun. In this case the verb has the meaning of *to behave like, to have the same effects as, to take oneself for*. Cf. Boswell in the Advertisement to the 2nd edition of *The Life of Samuel Johnson:* "Yes, I may add, I have Johnsonised the land; and I trust they will not only talk, but think Johnson".

[55] V. Z. Panfilov, *Grammar and Logic,* 1, p.21. Panfilov expounds and discusses this thesis, ibid., 3, pp.45ff.

[56] It is clear that the word 'nominal' in the traditional expression 'nominal sentence' *(phrase nominale)* is used here in a different sense than the sense it has had previously. For the word implies that the adjective is treated as a name, and so raises problems we do not need to go into here. In the present passage we employ 'nominal sentence' as follows. A sentence is said to be nominal or verbal depending on whether the predicate takes the form of an adjective joined to the subject by a copula or the form of a simple verb. Thus when the subject is not included in the verb or copula, a '*nominal sentence*' must have at least three words, a '*verbal sentence*' at least two.

[57] Serrus, 2nd part, ch.2, p.179.

[58] Ibid., 2nd part, ch.4, p.285; 3rd part, ch.2, p.393.

[59] Frege uses the second dimension in his *Begriffsschrift* and in two different ways:

(1) He uses it first as the basis of a non-linear notation for what is ordinarily expressed in a one-dimensional sequence. Thus where one normally says or writes *if B, then A*, Frege writes

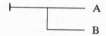

This principle allows him to transcribe propositions of any order of complexity into a two-dimensional space.

(2) He also makes use of the second dimension, as did classical mathematics, as a means of visually mastering a series of propositions that are themselves linear (as in arithmetic) or linearly oriented (as in the *Begriffsschrift*). Frege explains this well in his article "On the scientific justification of a Conceptual Notation": "Such contents ... as they follow from one another are written under one another. If a third follows from two others, we separate the third from the first two with a horizontal stroke, which can be read 'therefore'. In this way, the two-dimensionality of the writing surface is utilized for the sake of perspicuity". (T. W. Bynum, ed., G. Frege, *Conceptual Notation and Related Articles,* Oxford: Clarendon, 1972, p.88.)

As far as this second use of the second dimension is concerned, Frege did not pretend to be, nor was he, much of an innovator. This use of a second dimension is to be found in all advanced sorts of technical operations. It is, for example, the principle of calculation by abacus; it is in particular the foundation of written calculation (where the second dimension makes it possible to follow different lines of reasoning concerned with units, tens, hundreds, etc., which are all carefully aligned vertically for just this purpose). This method spread in Europe from the thirteenth century onwards. One of the advantages of successful formalization is without doubt to bring about that perspicuity *(Übersichtlichkeit)* mentioned by Frege, and which allows mathematical reasoning to master subjects beyond the reach of ordinary reasoning.

It is curious that the first way of using a second dimension has had so little effect. It is one of the rare inventions of Frege not to have had any echo. Frege's successors, Russell especially, gave back to logic its linear arrangement and today no one seems to doubt the advantages of the latter. If we shrink from exploring the possible advantages of a multi-dimensional mode of writing, this is probably due to the fact that temporal succession also governs the appearance in us of our thoughts. Thus a multi-dimensional notation would require us to make such an effort to pass from our thoughts to their written representation and back that we are inclined to regard the effort involved as too great.

The reader may want to point out that Frege's use of the second dimension is not exactly concerned with the position of *arguments* and *functors*. But we have nevertheless taken this opportunity of mentioning the problem of position in its most general form.

60 Frege, *Begriffsschrift*, I, §3, Geach and Black, ed., p.3 and §9, p.14.
61 There are of course numerous exceptions. For example

– verbs with one or more arguments that nevertheless have no grammatical subject: *paenitet, pudet, piget, taedet, ...*
– verbs with several arguments which have no direct object: *disposer de* (dispose of), *pourvoir à* (provide for).

62 *Langue et fonction*, p.79.
63 Martinet, *La linguistique synchronique*, p.230.
64 Ibid.
65 Serrus, 2nd part, ch.4, pp.312f.
66 This does not of course mean that the traditional grammatical notion of *transitivity* is the same as *transitivity* in the theory of relations. A verb which analysis shows to be a function with one argument is grammatically intransitive; as far as the theory of relations is concerned it is clearly neither transitive, nor non-transitive, nor intransitive. These three categories only apply where there are two arguments. In addition, there may correspond to a grammatically transitive verb a binary relation that, logically speaking, is *intransitive* and, conversely, a binary transitive relation may correspond to a grammatically intransitive verb.
67 Cf. Frege, *Begriffsschrift*, I, §19, Geach and Black, p.15 and "Concept and Object", p.49.
68 This 'at least' is intended to take into account a valid point that might be made against what has been said here: a linguistic system might very easily distinguish as passive forms not only the two forms f' (y,x,z) and f'' (z,y,x) but also f''' (y,z,x) and f'''' (z,x,y). This would presuppose that speaker and hearer were aware not only of the particular features of the situation of the first argument or subject, but also of the particular features of the second and third argument. I personally have never come across an example of such a distinction in languages with which I am familiar. This of course does not mean that it is not to be found somewhere. But even if the distinction were not exemplified by any of the linguistic systems that have ever existed, the undeniable possibility of drawing such a distinction should not be neglected at the level of *pure, rational grammar*.
69 Except in the case envisaged in the previous note, where one would take into account not only the argument chosen as the subject but the place of the other arguments. A function with n arguments could then have $(n-1)$ $(n-1)!$ passive forms.
70 The expression 'complément d'attribution' (attributive complement, as in 'He gave them *to his mother*') is not capable of any rigorous definition, as grammarians well know. This expression has its origins, perhaps, in the fact that in French when one has two complements, one designating an object, the other a person, the term designating the object usually plays the role of the direct object, the term designating the person that of the indirect object: *give, attribute*, etc. This fact deserves an explanation, but the latter does not

124

belong to pure grammar; the grammarian must here call on the services of the sociologist, the psychologist and the historian.

71 In general, we have learned to be content with three coordinates, two for space and one for time. Our social space is roughly two-dimensional, although one can easily imagine a society in which it is necessary to specify how high up one lives.

72 Carnap, *Logical Syntax,* pp.315–22.

Chapter Five
Person, Tense, Number

Impersonal and Tenseless Propositions

Languages such as those of logic, mathematics, or indeed the languages of the sciences in general, contain no reference either to the interlocutors or to the time of utterance. This does not mean that time is something that escapes science; on the contrary, no one doubts that it is nearly completely mathematisable. Rather, even when time is mentioned in science one wisely avoids any attempt to attribute the time being talked about in scientific language to the time at which such language is produced. And in those cases where the language of science, draws on what everyday language places at its disposal – because it does not think it useful or possible to develop a formalization of its own – its attention is largely concentrated on the morphological roots of the terms of everyday language. These terms are of course conjugated and made to agree, but the modifications of tense are by and large peripheral. In Carnap's words, in science two sentences with the same wording have the same character "independently of the question of knowing where, when, why and by whom they were uttered".[1] The same is not necessarily true of any two sentences in everyday language. If Peter observes today:

I am taking a walk

Paul may point out tommorow:

Peter took a walk.

Morphologically different though they are, these two propositions nevertheless describe one and the same state of affairs. For, as Carnap says,[2] the structure of a proposition in everyday language, to the extent that words such, as *I, you, today, yesterday, here, there*, are employed, depends not only on the propositions which precede it but also on extra-linguistic circumstances such as the speaker's spatio-temporal position and the possible identity of the interlocutors and what they are talking about. Thus the grammatical verb deserves what has been its traditional appellation, at least since *The Port-Royal Grammar* as: *vox significans affirmationem, cum designatione personae, numeri et temporis.*[3]

Person

It is characteristic of the personal pronouns that, in the words of Roman Jakobson, in them "code and message overlap".[4] They are used to identify certain "protagonists of the narrated event (elements of the code) with certain protagonists of the process of narration[5] (actors of the message)". The subject who says 'I am taking a walk' simultaneously gives his listeners to understand:

– that *it is he who is taking a walk,* that is to say, that he is the agent of the action described;

– and that *it is he who says this,* that is to say, that he is the author of the statement.

Thus in most Indo-European languages:

(1) *Je,* (I) or more generally the first person singular pronoun, whether the subject of the sentence or not, signifies that the person being talked about is *the person talking.*

(2) *Tu,* (you) or more generally the second person singular, signifies that the person being talked about is *the person addressed.*

(3) At least the following two senses of the third person singular are possible:[6]

(a) a restrictive sense in which the pronoun *il* (he) indicates that the person being talked about is neither the person addressed nor the person talking;

(b) a wider sense which covers all those cases which fall under (a) but where every relation – *whether it obtains or not* – between the person being talked about and either the person talking or the person addressed is disregarded.

It is difficult to say, without further enquiry, whether these two uses of the third person singular are equally frequent in languages such as French or English. It is perhaps easier to find examples of the first. A good example of the second would be those (French) statesmen who, observing at the end of their careers the mark they have made, occasionally speak of themselves in the third person. A careful analysis of contemporary texts would reveal many other less exceptional cases. A

127

lawyer presented with the text of a contract in which the third person singular occurs, may sometimes take the 'he' *a contrario* to exclude and sometimes *a fortiori* to imply 'I'.[7]

(4) *Nous* (we) signifies that the person talking (or the persons talking) belong(s) to those being talked about.[8]

(5) *Vous* (you) signifies that the person(s) addressed belong(s) to those being talked about.

(6) Just as we had to distinguish two senses of the third person singular, so also two senses of the third person plural must be distinguished, according as the individuals[9] (two at least) who the pronoun designates are always interpreted restrictively (6a) or not (6b).

The languages of science restrict themselves to the use of the two pronouns corresponding to the general sense of (3) and (6). And it is precisely these two senses which least deserve the description *personal pronoun*. Indeed, does not the expression *personal pronoun* signify that the relevant pronoun in the message communicated designates an individual who is said to be engaged (*I, you/tu*) or not engaged (first sense of *he*) in the very act of communicating this message? The second sense described under (3) and that described under (6), since they presuppose that all such indications are excluded, correspond to pronominal uses to which the adjective *impersonal* might well be applied were it not already employed for another purpose.

Other personal pronouns are possible than those which, restricting ourselves to the Indo-European tradition, we have just analysed. The easiest way to see this is to formalize the terms distinguished so far, taking some of these as basic in order to define the others. Our suggestion here is to retain as basic and undefined the three terms corresponding respectively to the senses analysed under (1) and (2) and the first of the two senses distinguished under (3). We shall designate these E, T and I respectively.[10]

For purposes of abbreviation we shall be less explicit than is theoretically necessary in the way we express the relations between the different personal terms. Thus every time we simply write 'E', the term must be understood as being followed by the indication of a function, so that we should really write

$$E x.f(x,y,z,...n),$$

which stands for a function with n arguments one of which (here 'x') has the privilege of designating the speaker.[11]

128

Likewise, in the interests of simplification, we shall look only at the case where no more than one of the arguments corresponds to a genuinely personal pronoun. Thus one might adopt the convention that the expression

$$E x.f(x, y, z, ... n)$$

is to be the abbreviation of

$$E x\, X y\, X z ... X n.f(x, y, z, ... n)$$

It is clear that there would be no problem in admitting multiple 'personalisations'. The situation is analogous to the well-known phenomenon of multiple quantification in logic. A proposition such as

I prefer you to him

could be written down by representing the three-place predicate

x prefers y to z

as

$$f(x, y, z)$$

and by interpreting the third person *him* in the sense described in 3a. as follows:

$$E x\, T y\, I z.f(x, y, z).$$

Examples like these can easily be dealt with by taking the elementary case as a starting point and this is therefore the only case we shall examine.

If, therefore, we adopt as primitive terms:

(1) E
(2) T
(3a) I,

then the other terms to be found in the Indo-European languages are easily constructed from these three by using the two interpropositional connectives *and* (.) and *or* (v). We propose the following definitions of the terms X, N, V, J and Y which correspond to the senses of the pronouns described in 3b, 4, 5, 6a and 6b respectively:

(3b) $X = Df. E v T v I$
(4) $N = Df. (E.E') v (E.T) v (E.I)$
(5) $V = Df. (T.T') v (T.I)$
(6a) $J = Df. I.I'$
(6b) $Y = Df. X.X'$

The definition of X means that *he,* in its impersonal sense, may equally well designate *I, you/tu* or *he* (where the latter is interpreted to exclude *I* and *you/tu*).

For the other definitions we have had to provide certain terms with indices in order to distinguish E', T', I', X' from E, T, I and X. This is made necessary by the following facts:

(a) Several people may speak together *in the name of* the group they belong to.

(b) It is possible to address several people.

(c) It is possible to speak about several people whether or not they belong to the group of people engaged in speaking with one another.

The definition of N serves to point out that when we say *we* this term may designate either:

(a) me and another me;

(b) you and me;

or

(c) him and me.

Let us briefly consider the first case. When, in performances of *La Marseillaise,* and in accordance with the revolutionary liturgy, the chorus of children begins to sing the verse

Nous entrerons dans la carrière quand nos aînés n'y serons plus...

we might be tempted to interpret this *we (nous)* as *them and me,* a particular case of *him and me* (for, if there are *them and me* then there are *him and me*). Were this the case, each individual singing the word *nous* would designate *himself together with the others.* And each *himself together with the others* would determine the same set of individuals, at least if the privilege *we* accords each *me* – rather than the others within the scope of the *we* – is disregarded. That the sets mentioned every time the pronoun is used coincide easily obscures the unquestionable fact that no member of the choir singing *we* attaches the same sense to the pronouns pronounced. In other words, were one to interpret *we* in the present case as *them and me* the choir would only be able to produce a harmonious sound at the cost of a lack of harmony concerning the sense of the sound; there would be agreement about the extension but not about the intension of the term. It is hardly likely that the relative satisfaction for which the choral *Mitfühlen* is responsible is based on a misunderstanding as banal as this. It seems, rather, that the choral *we* is based on the representation of a plurality of unanimous *me's*. Were the chorus simply the synchronisation of a basic discord it would be difficult to understand why it has been made the very symbol of unanimity.[12]

In the definition of N proposed above it will be noticed that the term E can be factorized.[13]
The definition then becomes

(4) $N = Df. E.(E' \lor T \lor I)$.

In this expression the first definition above

(3b) $X = Df. E \lor T \lor I$

can only be used as a replacement for the expression inside the brackets if the difference marked by the absence of an index is abolished by stipulating that

$N = Df. E.X$

provided that

E is different from X[14]

which might be expressed less simply but more conveniently by writing:

$Nx.f(x,y,z,...n) = Df. Ea.f(a,y,z,...n) . Xb.f(b,y,z,...n)$
$a \neq b$

This way of analysing the first person plural as a disjunction of three distinct conjunctions shows that, if this really is the meaning of *we* in the majority of Indo-European languages, it would equally be possible to decide on a quite different definition of *we*.

1. It might, for example, be the case that *we* designates only one of the three disjuncts, which would give us the following three senses:

$N_1 = Df. E.E'$
$N_2 = Df. E.T$
$N_3 = Df. E.I$

2. It might also be the case that the employment of *we* is restricted to the designation of the disjunction of two of these three terms, which would give us the following three combinations:

$$N_4 = Df. (E.E') v E.T$$
$$N_5 = Df. (E.E') v E.I$$
$$N_6 = Df. (E.T) v E.I$$

Thus we have seven distinct ways of defining *we;* it would now be interesting to know if linguistic systems other than the Indo-European have opted for one or more of these last six senses.

As far as the Indo-European system is concerned – for which, we repeat,

$$N = Df. E.X,$$

provided E and X are distinct – one can guess why this notion has pushed aside the use of other, possible competing forms. It is tempting, since we are here no longer in the domain of logic but in that of the psychology of perception, to follow de Saussure and invoke the need, if a system of two competing terms is to remain stable, for a minimum of contrast between these two terms, that minimum to which they owe their distinctness. Now the six senses listed above are included in the sense of the Indo-European pronoun so that it is always possible to replace one of the former by the latter without any risk of error and merely at the expense of some loss of precision. Thus it seems psychologically difficult, although not logically impossible, for the more inclusive form of *we* to co-exist with the other restricted forms within one and the same linguistic system. This difficulty would of course disappear were the system concerned an artificial language; there is hardly any need to take the reader's sharpness of intellect into account in developing such a language.

If we turn now to the second person plural, we see that the definition implicit in Indo-European languages

$$(5) V = Df. (T.T') v (T.I)$$

may by factorization of T take the form

$$(6) V = Df. T.(T' v I).$$

Apart from this definition, only two others are possible. For the same psychological reason already mentioned in connection with the first person plural, these possibilities are hardly exemplified at all in the Indo-European tradition. It is for the linguists to tell us whether they are to be found elsewhere.[15]

(7) $V_1 = $ Df. $(T.T')$
(8) $V_2 = $ Df. $(T.I)$

Finally, it should be noted that of the two third persons distinguished above, the singular and the plural, the one implies the other:

$I \supset X$
$J \supset Y$.

Thus, a linguistic system may always employ X and Y where I and J are appropriate without risk of error and at the mere expense of some degree of precision. It is difficult to say whether this ever occurs in our Indo-European languages; the legal example mentioned above[16] does however tend to show that languages such as English and French do indeed possess an awareness, even if this is not explicit, of the distinction between the two third persons, both in the singular and in the plural.

We may note that, if there is a logic of person, a logic enabling us to deduce from

We walk

and

You *(vous)* walk

the proposition:

I walk

and

You *(tu)* walk,

it is a logic whose theorems can be obtained, it seems, on the basis of the definitions suggested above. Rather than engage in a tedious enumeration of these theorems we shall merely set out, as examples, the principal theorems concerning the first person plural. They can easily be proved with the help of the definitions above and the rules of the standard propositional calculus:

$N \supset [(E.E') \lor (E.T) \lor (E.I)]$

$[(E.E') \lor (E.T) \lor (E.I)] \supset N$

$[(E.E') \lor (E.T)] \supset N$

$[(E.E') \lor (E.I)] \supset N$

$[(E.T) \lor (E.I)] \supset N$

$(E.E') \supset N$

$(E.T) \supset N$

$(E.I) \supset N$

$N \supset (E.X)$

$(E.X) \supset N$, where X is different from E.

$N \supset E$

$N \supset X$

$(N.V) \supset [E.T.(T' \lor I)]$

$(N.J) \supset (E.I.I')$

$(N.Y) \supset (E.X.X')$

Thus the use of the pronouns possesses a logical structure whose principles are simple enough to lend themselves to formalization. Is it necessary to emphasize that there is no reason to compare the personal pronoun with the reflexive pronoun? The latter, unlike the personal pronoun, involves absolutely no reference to anything external to the content of the discourse in which it occurs. It corresponds to the case where, in a function, one term occurs as argument in different positions. Thus in the case of the verb *kill*, if A occupies both of the two argument-places normally admitted, then I will say, not that *A kills A*, but that *A kills himself*. The fact that one and the same argument crops up at different positions in the function is a feature which, in logical terms, is remarkable enough for languages such as those in the Indo-European family to employ a grammatical form such as the reflexive pronoun in order to draw attention to it.

The main ground for complaint against the Indo-European languages in this connection is that they normally restrict the role of the reflexive pronoun to that of repeating the argument that occupies the subject position. It is true that this restriction leads to a simplification: to remove this restriction on the use of the reflexive pronoun would mean increasing the number of its forms to ensure that it would always be possible to recognize which argument the pronoun corresponds to.

Tense

Mathematics has as little need of the tense of the verb as of person. And, when couched in ordinary language, it employs the present tense for want of an atemporal form: 'The sum of the angles of a triangle *is* equal to the sum of two right angles.' The justification of this use of the present is probably the fact that atemporal truths are those which, at any given moment, belong to the present. Or should one say even more simply that 'this sort of present is the verb taken in and for itself'?[17] Whatever the truth of the matter, the third person present indicative employed in scientific language is as atemporal as it is impersonal. It is only when the mathematician does not use a formalized language that he must use the present indicative. It is useless to ask, in the fashion of some grammarians, whether there are languages that possess atemporal indicative forms; we know that these forms exist. The symbols =, <,>, correspond to what are indubitably verbs which have been deliberately stripped of every temporal inflection, even if, on those occasions when we are obliged to find an oral equivalent for these symbols, this compels us to provide them with a tense. The existence of such verbs contradicts the famous passage in which Aristotle[18] defined the verb as 'that which adds to its own meaning that of time'. We are therefore justified in denying, with Bolzano,[19] that the connection between verb and time is essential.

We cannot, however, follow Bolzano when he attempts to show that the indication of time is to be ascribed not to the verb but to the name:

A proposition of the form 'the object A – has at time t – the attribute b', if its parts are to be clearly indicated, must be expressed in the following way: 'the object A at time t – has – (the attribute) b'. For it does not happen at time t that the attribute b is claimed for the object A; but the object A, inasmuch as it is thought to exist at time t (hence to have this determination) is claimed to have attribute b.[20]

Bolzano's argument here is odd. It seems to accord the object an ontological, or at least epistemological, privilege that is denied its properties (and, we would add, its relations) such that one could not ascribe its properties to an object unless one had previously supplied the object with its temporal determinations. We must admit that we can see absolutely no reason why it should be impossible to attach the temporal indications, in all clarity and distinctness, to the relation between the object and its properties or relations. All that Bolzano shows here is that, instead of attaching temporal indications to the verb, one *can* envisage attaching them to the name.

Before returning to this possibility we must first ask whether tense, as this is expressed in the majority of propositions in natural languages, really does attach to the verb or whether it does not rather attach to the proposition in which the verb occurs as principal member. In other words, should what grammarians call the *tense of the verb* be considered as a functorial functor with one argument which is itself functorial, or as a propositional functor with a propositional argument? Thus in the proposition:

Peter has come

does the tense concern the verb *come* as the grammatical structure of the sentence suggests? In this case the analysis, following Ajdukiewicz, would be

$$\text{Peter} \quad \text{has} \quad \text{come}$$

$$n \qquad \frac{s}{n} \qquad \frac{\frac{s}{n}}{\frac{s}{n}}$$

Of the two fractions under *has come,* the first corresponds to the verb and the second to the tense. Writing this in the correct order we obtain:

$$\frac{\frac{s}{n}}{\frac{s}{n}} \qquad \frac{s}{n} \qquad n$$

Or does the tense in this expression attach to the entire proposition? In this case the analysis would be

$$n \qquad \frac{s}{-n} \qquad \frac{s}{s}$$

the last fraction indicating the tense of the proposition. Writing this in the order prescribed we would then have

$$\frac{s}{s} \qquad \frac{s}{n} \qquad n$$

136

Intuitively it seems much more satisfactory to ascribe tense to the proposition as a whole, although it must be admitted that this is perhaps merely a personal preference and one for which we can provide no serious justification. After all, why should it be impossible to regard *has killed* as a binary functor already possessing its own temporal indications? Why must we wait for it to be *completed* by its arguments in order then to be able to ascribe tense to the proposition as a whole? In the absence of proof of the contrary[21] we shall continue to hold that the two possible ways of linking up the indication of tense, with the verb or with the proposition, have exactly the same extension and are thus equivalent.

The fact that the temporal indication may connect up either with the verb or with the proposition as a whole does not mean that it is impossible to link it up with a name. Bolzano, as we have seen, showed that this was not the case. But consider the curious pronouncement of Charles Serrus:[22] "It is because the verb fundamentally expresses a process that the category of tense belongs to it; and it is because, on the contrary, ideas are static and atemporal, that the category of time is foreign to the name." This assumption that names could only designate ideas clearly does not hold of proper names; there are also transitory phenomena which, in languages like French and English, can only be referred to by giving their spatio-temporal coordinates: *this cloud which is passing by here and now*. Many of the pronouns grammarians call *demonstrative pronouns* are in fact simply names which succeed in designating their objects because they consist entirely of spatio-temporal indications. If it is a fact that our Indo-European languages are nearly always condemned to make use of the verb in order to indicate the tense of the name, it is nevertheless by no means impossible to imagine a language which would have at its disposal a complete system of inflections making possible the clear and distinct designation of *the man I am today, the man that I was yesterday, the man that I will be today,*[23] with the help of a single root and without the help of a verb. The outlines of such a system are to be found even within Indo-European languages, as *The Port-Royal Grammar* points out: the participle, which may easily form the equivalent of a name, sometimes adopts one form for the past and another for the future: *venturus* is *he who will come.*

Not only does nothing prevent us from ascribing indications of tense to names, there are even cases where it is impossible to ascribe such indications to the verb, and which therefore leave only the name as bearer of these indications. If I say that then, in the absence of inflections (which do not exist in a language such as English), the context clearly shows that *the successor of the King* is a name in the future tense and the reference to the future contained within it can clearly not in any way be foisted onto the verb, which is itself in the present or past tense, depending on the interpretation.[24] The way in which the verb, and only very rarely the noun, is provided with temporal inflections in the relatively perfected systems of communication which are the Indo-European languages seems to us to be justified by reasons that are almost entirely of a purely technical nature. These languages have perfected a means of expressing the tense of the name without any need for any genuinely nominal form of inflection: they combine the use of the relative pronouns with those modifications of the verb called *the tenses of the verb*. This is the case in the expression mentioned above, *the man that I am*. These languages, then, are able to do without a morphologically independent nominal tense while retaining the possibility of indicating the tense of the name.

Might there not be an equally elegant method, based on the inverse principle, which would retain independent forms for nominal tense and dispense with independent forms for the tense of the verb, as Bolzano, for example, suggested? It seems nearly certain that such a system is possible, and for the following reason. As we have already had occasion to mention, it is always possible to reduce a function to a relation of membership between a set and its members. Now both members and sets can always be represented by names. It is therefore difficult to see what could prevent us incorporating temporal indications into the name designating the set. Whether or not such a solution could attain the elegant simplicity of the system whereby the Indo-European languages and many others have succeeded in expressing all tense distinctions, nominal as well as propositional, by verbal inflections alone, is, however, open to doubt.

But the existence of verbal tense within a large number of linguistic systems raises many other questions. In particular, given the variety of spatio-temporal coordinates, why choose the temporal coordinate for incorporation into the form of the verb? Why did the spatial coordinates not have this privilege, or at least share it? For together with the *here* of the subject, these coordinates provide a system of reference as solid as the subject's *now*. Thus we might have a verbal expression of *place* as well as the verbal expression of *time* as in indications of tense. But the parallelism goes no further: the unidimensionality of time makes possible a simple definition of an *after* and *before* which provide the basis of the two fundamental tenses, the *past* and the *future*. The pluridimensionality of space (even if one were to restrict oneself to the two-dimensional nature of social space) would require a language to possess as many different *places* as there are directions of the compass. *Here* does not have the advantages of *now:* the latter cuts the line of time and marks the boundary between past and future; but a point on a map, which is what *here* amounts to, does not mark any boundary at all; it is rather the point of departure for an infinite number of points of the compass.[25] The answer to the question *why do verbs express times rather than places?* is, it seems, intimately bound up with the analysis of the structure of the field of our environment.

However, although temporal indications can be given much more easily then those of spatial position, the number of systems capable of indicating tense seems to be considerable. There can be no question of providing an inventory of all of these, particularly in view of the fact that even an inventory of systems that have actually existed is not what should be expected of a pure or rational grammar, since such an inventory could not pretend to be a list of all possible systems. Here, then, we shall simply concentrate on sketching some of the main natural alternatives that suggest themselves whether or not they have in fact been explored by natural or formalized languages.

We found, let us repeat, no semantic difference between the case where the temporal functor is linked to the verbal functor and the case where it is linked to the entire proposition. In any case, even if this assimilation is open to criticisms which have escaped our notice here, it seems to be a fact about Indo-European languages that the only standard way in which the proposition can acquire temporal modifications is via modification of the verb. But if, as we have seen, this yields an indirect method of assigning a temporal indication to nominal expressions, it leaves us in a relatively helpless position if we want to provide with temporal indications not a simple proposition with a *verb* as functor but a so-called *compound* proposition with, for example, a conjunction as functor. If I try to express in the future tense, not proposition *p* or proposition *q*, but the proposition '*p* and *q*', then our Indo-European languages provide me with no temporal inflections for terms, such as conjunctions, other than the verb.

These languages can alleviate the difficulty here which is due to the absence of non-verbal temporal inflections in different ways. For example:

(1) With the help of adverbial modifications, which have no inflected forms. These can be attached to the proposition as a whole.

(2) By moving to the metalanguage, which enables us to regard the future of 'p and q' as equivalent to

it will be true that p and q.

(3) By making use of other intuitively acceptable equivalences such as

$$F(p \text{ and } q) \equiv Fp \text{ and } Fq$$

where 'F' stands for the functor corresponding to the future. This equivalence seems to be as little open to question as the classic theorem concerning the distribution of the universal quantifier:

$$\forall x.(fx \text{ and } gx) \equiv (\forall x.fx \text{ and } \forall x.gx)$$

and it allows us to do without a conjunction in the future tense by substituting for this two verbs in the future tense.

The very existence of these palliatives within Indo-European languages demonstrates at least that a direct expression of the tense of the conjunction might have been conceivable. It would even have been all the more desirable, in view of the fact that the procedure just mentioned – whereby the tense of the complex proposition is distributed amongst its component propositions – can certainly not be applied blindly. And there is every chance that this distribution follows rules every bit as strict and rigorous as those which govern the distribution of the quantifiers. In the languages with which we are acquainted we have not come across any autonomous expression of a temporal functor which can take a compound proposition as a whole. But this is not the case for formalized languages, which today do provide some examples of just this. Thus the first axiom of A. N. Prior's[26] system GH_1 is:

CGCpqCGpGq,

which comprises a temporal functor (G) which takes an implication (Cpq) as its argument, and permits the distribution of this functor over the antecedent and the consequent of this implication.

It is possible to go even further beyond the type of system to be found at work in Indo-European languages by making the temporal functor not a propositional functor with *one* propositional argument or a functorial functor with *one* functorial argument (we hesitated, it will be remembered, between these two interpretations, and are considering them, at least for the time being, as equivalent), but a propositional functor with *two* propositional arguments. This is the case in the system of G. H. von Wright[27] in which the temporal functor, T, which the author suggests reading as *and then,* connects *two propositions,* which may themselves be either simple or compound, so that von Wright can write as a first axiom concerning the distribution of the functor T:

$$(p \lor q) \, T \, (r \lor s) \equiv (pTr) \lor (pTs) \lor (qTr) \lor (qTs).$$

In order to avoid going into the indefinite series of developments possible here we shall restrict our attention to those possible systems which have at least this in common with the natural languages with which we are most familiar, that not only do they envisage hardly any direct expression of modes of temporalisation (as is the case with the systems developed by von Wright), but that in them the integration of temporal indications is founded on the basic distinction between a before and an after, notions which are themselves defined relative to the moment of the act of speaking which we call the *present.*

Indeed it is important to underline one peculiarity of the systems for indicating time as these are to be found in various familiar natural languages, a peculiarity which the very dryness of the term *tense* risks masking from view. That a verb has a tense does not signify purely and simply that the event described in the proposition is assigned a temporal position, vague or precise. If I say that

the people occupied the Bastille on July 14th 1789

it is clearly not due to the date that the proposition is in the past tense. *July 14th 1789* is not specified as being *before today* but as *after the birth of Christ;* it belongs rather to the future of a quite different event. That there is such a thing as *tense,* in the full sense of the word, and as we observe this at work in our language, means that the moment at which the event described takes place is itself related to the moment at which we describe it.[28] In principle there is nothing to prevent us envisaging systems which would drop this reference to the time of utterance and which would specify the different tenses simply by reference to the distance between the event described and some point of origin, the date at which the world is assumed to have been created or, more modestly, *ab urbe condita*. But we happen to know that the majority of historical societies, although they admit equally the two systems of dating, possess a basic form of expression only for the system implying a reference to the present.

But the decision to opt for this sort of reference still leaves a number of traits undetermined. The distinction between a *before* and an *after*, that is to say a *past* and *future*, to which may be added, if required, a *present*, opens up the possibility of other functors which can be obtained by definition. Thus Prior,[29] in his already mentioned system GH_1, proposes forming the past

Pp, i.e. it has been the case that p

and the future

Fp, i.e. it will be the case that p

by taking as primitive, undefined terms

Hp, for: it has always been the case that p

and

Gp, for: it will always be the case that p

and with the help of the following definitions:

F =Df. N G N[30]
P =Df. N H N.

But unless the system is re-adjusted, there is nothing to prevent us from reversing the procedure invented by Prior,[31] that is, we might define the functors G and H by taking F and P as undefined primitives and by using the definitions:

G =Df. N F N
H =Df. N P N.

Although these different possibilities are implicit in the world around us, they are exploited by no known language.

Another possibility which is hardly ever taken advantage of or which is exploited only in an indirect fashion, is that of specifying the distance between the present and the later or earlier event. Prior[32] and his pupils have invented systems along these lines which combine the advantages of fruitful results and very simple methods. If we take P as our only primitive, an expression such as

$$P \, n \, p$$

indicates that the event designated by p occurred or was the case n units of time ago;

$$P \, o \, p$$

indicates that it is present;

$$P \, (-n) \, p$$

that it will occur in n units of time;

$$\Pi \, n \, P \, n \, p$$

(where Π is the symbol of the universal quantifier), that it has always been the case that p and will always be the case that p.

It is not that our societies do not have at their disposal ways of quantifying time which are as rigorous as that sketched by Prior. Rather, they normally reserve these for systems of absolute dating, as in the case of calendars, a system of temporal reference established either in a unidirectional way relative to an origin or bidirectionally relative to a privileged event (B.C. and A.D.). Such a system, as has already been pointed out, exists alongside the system of temporal reference based on the present. The reason for this does not seem to be too difficult to understand. It is natural enough for us to subordinate all consideration of events external to our everyday activities to the present in which these are carried out, but the calender is a system of quantification which is an established social institution and it is difficult to see how it could function if it had to be refashioned anew at each moment. Even if one did this one could only improvise a much simpler system.

In addition, the wealth of distinctions explored by Prior are not to be found, with a few exceptions, in the tense systems of natural languages. At most one can sometimes make out certain efforts to mark how far something lies in the past or in the future, degrees of priority and posteriority, so that there is not only a past and a future but a more-or-less-past and a more-or-less-future. This is the basis in French of the distinction between the *passé simple,* designating the completed act, and the *passé composé,* designating the act whose effects continue into

143

the present. *The Port-Royal Grammar*[33] goes so far as to give a genuinely measurable criterion for the distinction: the French simple past, we are told,

is not properly said except of a time which was at least one whole day removed from the time at which we speak; for one does indeed say in French *j'écrivis hier* [I wrote yesterday] but one does not say *j'écrivis ce matin* [I wrote this morning] nor *j'écrivis cette nuit* [I wrote tonight], but rather *j'ai écrit ce matin, j'ai écrit cette nuit.*

"Our language is so exact regarding the propriety of expressions that it allows no exceptions to this rule", is their optimistic conclusion. They observe that "the future can also admit of the same distinctions" and note the existence in Greek of a paolo-post future "which marks that the thing is about to happen, or that one ought almost to consider it as done", unlike the ordinary future which "just points out that the thing will happen".

The confusion between different tenses as these are found in natural languages is increased by the fact that, although many languages agree in distinguishing *before, after* and *during,* apparently no language clearly determines what should and should not fall under these terms. Matters would be quite simple if the event, property or relation expressed by the proposition had only an instantaneous existence. In that case every event or state, in virtue of its punctual nature, would necessarily be prior to, simultaneous with or posterior to, every other event which is also by definition punctual; here there would be the least possible degree of ambiguity. But when I announce in the present tense a certain present state of affairs, the latter, which is given as being present, has a certain thickness, a beginning and an end; and these can only be determined by taking into account not only the objective features of this state of affairs but also the manner in which the subject organizes his experience of it.

Thus when I say of two events that the one is prior to the other, the term *prior,* although an apparently straightforward term referring to a single, simple dimension, does not explicitly indicate whether the event said to be prior to the other event finished or merely began before the second event began or finished. It will be noticed that, depending on the sense chosen, the *relation* which we shall call the relation of *precedence* or *priority,* although it is always transitive, is sometimes non-symmetrical and sometimes asymmetrical, that it is sometimes reflexive, sometimes non-reflexive and sometimes irreflexive. A rigorous definition of *past, present* and *future* would therefore have to be preceded by a choice of a set of conventions. And it is not surprising that natural languages do not make this choice. It has often been noticed that in a language like French or English the present may express, quite independently of its atemporal use, a habitual state *(he is intelligent)*, a situation that lasts for a period of time *(il dort)*, an instantaneous act (he stands up, he decides – in the 'dramatic' present). In each case the present expands or contracts to fit the event.

Yet other sorts of temporal indication are possible. A somewhat subtler system grafts onto the basic distinction *past, present, future* (defined, respectively, by their priority to, simultaneity with and posteriority to the time of utterance), complementary relations of precedence, simultaneity and posteriority defined relative to an event which has been previously recognized as prior or posterior. As is well known, some languages, such as French, exploit some but not all of these possibilities. Arnauld and Lancelot[34] suggest a name for these: 'tenses compound in meaning'. *The Port-Royal Grammar* points out three such tenses in French: apart from the *pluperfect,* which designates what is past with respect to another thing that is also past, and the *future perfect,* which indicates will be past in relation to the future, there is the *preterite imperfect.* This uses the imperfect and the past, whether simple or compound, *(composé,* i.e. the present perfect) to indicate what was present with respect to the past. To quote the example and the commentary of *The Port-Royal Grammar:*

when I say ... 'I was supping when he entered' the action of supping is indeed past with regard to the time at which I speak, but I indicate it as present with respect to the thing of which I speak.

Arnauld and Lancelot pointed out that, at least in French, there exists an unexploited possibility "of adding a fourth compound tense, that which would mark the future in relation to the present", i.e. would designate what will be present with respect to the future. A desire for symmetry, pointed out by Roland Donzé[35], made them add that there would thus be "as many compound future tenses as compound present tenses". The preoccupation with completeness should have led them to mention two other possibilities which are not made use of: the indication of what was future with respect to the past and of what will be future with respect to the future.

But it is easy to understand why our languages leave *empty places* here and possess neither a *less-than-perfect* nor a *future posterior.* The use of

145

the past perfect and of the future perfect suffice to express the temporal relation (and its converse) between two events in the past or two events in the future. A term designating a future event with respect to the past or to the future is missing because *at any given moment* we possess a means of expressing the future which has no equivalent amongst means available for expressing the past. The one-dimensional nature of speech and its correspondence (albeit very relative) with the uni-dimensionality of the time of narrated events are such that, for any two states of affairs asserted in two successive propositions the verbs of which are in the same tense, the interpretation preferred, in the absence of any indication to the contrary, is always that the event narrated second is the second event to occur.

Gender and Number

There is little to be said about gender.[36] The method of indicating the class to which a name or the subject of a verb belongs by means of the morphology of the name and verb alone was in itself a happy invention. For the use of these classes to be intellectually advantageous it is in addition necessary that their extension is not arbitrarily restricted, that is to say, their extension should correspond to an intension that is not only precise but also possesses some interesting properties. In this respect a distinction such as that between what is animate and what is inanimate (as employed in certain languages such as Algonquin as the basis of the opposition between genders) seems considerably superior to the distinction between masculine and feminine which can only be made to cover the variety of objects we experience if we employ metaphors, that is to say, intellectual deception.[37] This distinction between animate and inanimate does indeed today play a fundamental role in our ordinary way of thinking. It alone would make it possible to outlaw by purely grammatical rules the propositions already mentioned:

The table loves Peter
Peter seduces the table

in the face of which even the distinctions of the theory of types are powerless.

The distinctions, however, on which the use of the genders in most Indo-European languages – but not English – rest, no longer correspond to anything which is in any way precise, whatever sense attached to them in the original social contexts and whatever sorts of experience they corresponded to in the past.[38] In particular, the distinction made in French between masculine and feminine gender appears to be, in the present state of society and of our scientific knowledge, quite as arbitrary as the distinction made in Navaho between *round objects* and *long objects*[39] or, in certain Bantu tribes, between ten or even twenty genders,[40] and is in any case much more arbitrary than the Chinese distinction which is based on the main directions in space.[41]

If, after Esperanto and Volapük, someone could be found who was willing to create a completely new language, free of the historical defects to which gender so often gives rise, he would have the option of simply abandoning every sort of gender distinction. But he might also retain the principle and reform the different gender categories in such a way that they designate, for example, the major semantic categories that language-use invites us to distinguish within a category such as that of name. He might, for example, return to the distinction *animate/ inanimate;* he might also add some distinctions inspired by the rules of type theory making it impossible to confuse proper names, common nouns used to refer to individuals and common nouns used to refer to the properties of individuals, so that one could distinguish quite generally between the different terms of the first three or four type levels, i.e. the most basic and usual terms.[42]

Here it is not enough to say, as does Couturat,[43] that gender, unlike "truly logical categories such as number and tense", is a "contingent or accidental category". The *principle* of gender, to adopt Couturat's own somewhat clumsy term, is not in any way less *logical* than the principle of tense or number. It is only the application of the principle in most of the languages known to us which is open to question.

The problem of the grammatical expression of number presents itself in terms which differ somewhat from those of the problem of gender in that the study of number cannot be separated from the more general problem of quantification. Indeed, what is called *number* in grammar is a way of expressing a type of quantification concerning what the name or one of the arguments of the verb designates by means of a simple modification of this name and of this verb. But a linguistic system employing number by no means necessarily renounces other forms of quantification, in particular quantification by means of adverbial expressions. The evolution of languages tends to show that the role of the sort of quantification which is integrated with the name or the verb, what we call number, is slowly diminishing, at least in many languages, in favour of such unintegrated forms of quantification.

The trial disappeared from Indo-European languages a long time ago. In the evolution of classical Greek we find the steady disappearance of the dual.[44] Since then the Indo-European languages have in genereal been content with the simple opposition between the singular – designating unity or totality – and the plural – designating plurality or totality. If the ambiguity of this usage, due to the double expression of totality *(man is mortal, men are mortal)* creates no particular problems, this is because our languages possess additional, appropriate quantifiers *(all, always, some, sometimes, at least, at most,* and in particular the series of whole numbers) which have not only made the dual and the trial superfluous, but also leave little useful scope for the surviving forms of singular and plural.[45]

The plural form in the Indo-European languages has the striking peculiarity that, unlike gender, it attaches itself not only to names but also to verbs and that this plural form of the verb indicates not, as one might expect, the plurality of the processes expressed by the verb, but that of one of its arguments, the subject.[46] Thus in such languages there is *properly speaking no plural of the verb,* no ending indicating a plural event or plural state of affairs expressed by the proposition. From the point of view of pure or rational grammar such details do of course appear to be quite arbitrary, even if habit has long since eliminated any possible feeling of arbitrariness.

The different quantifier expressions in languages, adjectival, adverbial and pronominal, as well as those invented by logicians during this century, show just how wide is the range of choice for someone who wants to set up a system of communication. Besides, it has been known since Frege and Russell that one quantifier suffices for nearly every form of quantification. With the help of the existential quantifier *(for at least one)* or of the universal quantifier *(for all)* it is possible to construct the other, as well as the series of natural numbers. The first problem that poses itself, then, in an investigation of the modes of quantification a language possesses, is that of establishing whether the language possesses an expression which is equivalent to one of these two quantifiers.[47] Once this has been determined, the second step is to establish what supplementary modes of quantification have been adopted for purposes of economy.

For although the mathematician may regard it as a matter of honour to reduce to a minimum the number of undefined primitive terms, even if this then increases the length of what he demonstrates with their help, the same attitude would be ridiculous where the aim is to develop a system of communication. Certainly, the aim should be to avoid multiplying gratuitously the number of terms. But the presence of a term which is logically superfluous is more than justified if it leads to economy of expression. Besides, neither mathematicians nor logicians disdain economies of this sort: they simply introduce them independently of the axioms, by means of definitions.

Categories Between Number and Gender Foreign to Indo-European Languages

Finally, a word of warning about a certain interpretation of the suggestions put forward in this chapter relating to person, tense, gender and number. We have relied on categories to be found in the grammars of Indo-European languages since it seemed natural to take as a starting point for our reflections materials and concepts which are familiar both to the reader and to the author. There is of course no doubt that, although we are able to locate individual variations within each of these categories, we could have found still more basic sorts of variation which would call into question the very existence of these categories and, in return, would bring to light other, possibly unfamiliar categories.

One example must suffice. In certain communities, linguistic forms may vary, according to the sex, and sometimes according to the status, either of the speaker or even of his interlocutor. Thus Boas pointed out the existence in some Eskimo dialects of variations in the pronunciation of certain phonemes that depend on the sex of the speaker. Similarly Sapir,[48] in his studies of the Yana Indians in the North of California, pointed out that certain forms (the language of the men) signify that the speaker is a man and that his interlocutor is a man, whereas, other forms (the language of the women) signify that either the speaker or the interlocutor is a woman (inclusive *or*). Similarly Korean and Malayan indicate the position of the speaker in the social hierarchy, whereas Nahuatl indicates the position of the interlocutor.

With respect to these and analogous cases, the Indo-European author or reader is tempted to pose the following question: do such linguistic practices pertain to *person* or to *gender?* Should we be puzzled by such forms, just as zoologists were puzzled by the ornithorhyncus? We ought, rather, to recognize that what we have here is a novel form for which our Indo-European tradition has provided no name – for the simple reason that it seems never to have explored these linguistic possibilities.

Notes

[1] Carnap, *Logical Syntax,* ch.3.

[2] Ibid.

[3] We shall ignore the questionable aspects of applying the expression *vox significans affirmationem* to the verb.

[4] Roman Jakobson, "Shifters, Verbal Categories and the Russian Verb", §1.5.

[5] Ibid., §2.11.

[6] On reflection one sees that many meanings of *it* other than those we have mentioned are also possible. Thus in particular it would be necessary to apply the analysis to the. phenomenon of *case,* where the study of this or that natural language would soon force us to allow for possibilities that are not mentioned here. At the moment it would be tiresome to seek to set out all the different combinatorial possibilities.

[7] All the usual French grammars with which we are familiar specify that the first person designates 'the person who speaks', the second person 'the person one speaks to', the third person 'the person or thing one speaks about'. They seem therefore to claim that the sense of the third person pronoun in French is that which we have described under 3(b). Arnauld and Lancelot, on the other hand, mention on two occasions that the meaning of the French third person is the meaning we have described under 3(a). Chapter 7 of the 2nd part of *The Port-Royal Grammar* points out that the pronouns of the third person replace the names of things or the names of persons other than the person who is speaking or being spoken to. Chapter 14 then explains that the third person is used where "the subject of the proposition is neither oneself nor the person being spoken to".

Roland Donzé, who draws attention to this divergence of opinion between *The Port-Royal Grammar* and the grammars used today, concludes that the former avoids "an error that is very common today; for it is obvious that the third person cannot be defined as the person one is talking about, since one speaks about oneself in the first and about the person one is speaking to in the second person". The explanations we have given show that there can be no question of an *error* here, but rather of two different interpretations. For contrary to what Donzé says, there is nothing to prevent us from defining the third person as the person being spoken about. If we do this then the cases in which it is possible to use the first person and the second person will be included in the set of cases in which the use of the third person is possible.

[8] In order to be complete it would be necessary carefully to distinguish at least two senses of the first-person plural, on the one hand a *distributive* sense such that from

We are taking a walk

I may infer

I am taking a walk;

and, on the other hand a *collective* sense, such that from

We have killed 30,000 enemies

I may not infer

I have killed 30,000 enemies.

For although each person takes a walk, each person has not killed 30,000 enemies. The use of *we* that we are attempting to formalize in this chapter corresponds strictly to the first of these two senses and the distinctions we shall establish below (pp. 130–131) all strictly fall within the scope of the first sense.

We really need, then, another term for the collective *we* and it would be necessary to characterize its use either by axioms or by definitions; it would also be necessary to connect the two *we*'s with one another by using axioms like:

$$N' \supset N''$$

where N' would correspond to the distributive sense and N'' to the collective sense.

If we were to continue to observe such strict requirements we would have to do the same for the plural forms of the second person that exist in languages such as French or German.

[9] We ignore here the possibility of a dual, a trial, etc., in order to concentrate on the plural as this is to be found in present-day Indo-European languages.

[10] Guided by mnemonic considerations, we have taken the first letter of the Latin terms *ego, tu, is.*

[11] Thus if we take as an example the first definition given on p. 130 above, we find that when written out in full, this definition (3b) would run as follows:

$$Xx.f(x,y,z,...n) = \text{Df. } Ex.f(x,y,z,...n) \lor Tx.f(x,y,z,...n) \lor Ix.f(x,y,z,...n).$$

[12] Our analysis does not pretend to exhaust all the features of this choral situation. If it is true that *each* of the children singing *Nous entrerons dans la carrière* ... may individually aspire to this fate, it suffices for him to dream of sharing it with the others, in step with the others, for one to move from the *distributive* to the *collective* sense of *we* (to use the terminology introduced in note 8 above). And the satisfaction bound up with the choral *Mitfühlen* depends largely and in most cases on the fact that the collective *we* has a force or power that *I* does not possess; we need think only of our example: 'We have killed 30,000 enemies'. But this is another problem and we have decided to concentrate on the analysis of the distributive *we*.

[13] The distributivity of interpropositional conjunction relative to disjunction makes possible this factorization.

[14] We here ignore the peculiar case of the so-called 'royal "we"'.

[15] Some of these possible ways of defining 'we' and 'you' are mentioned by R. Jakobson, who discusses how they are exploited within Russian ("Shifters, Verbal Categories and the Russian Verb", §3).

[16] P. 128.

[17] Bréal, *Essai de sémantique*, p.339, quoted by Serrus, part 2, ch.2, p.164.

[18] *De interpretatione*, 3, 16b.

[19] Bolzano, §127, p.177.

[20] Ibid. It will be observed that Bolzano's way of putting the problem is a little different from

the way it would be put today. The difference is due to the fact that, as we have already had occasion to point out, the normal form of a judgment for Bolzano is: *(object) A has (property) b,* and so it is the copula *has,* and not what we have called the verb, that, according to him contains no temporal indication. Nevertheless we think that this difference does not really affect the point at issue.

21 The simplest way of refuting the hypothesis we provisionally advance here would be to provide an example in which the difference between the two is strikingly obvious.

22 Serrus, part 3, ch.2, p.417.

23 "Nothing prevents us imagining a concept like 'my father' ", writes André Martinet, "as referring to the past. We then say, for example, 'my late father'. We speak of an ex-president, of former times, of an elapsed period of time, of a horse that had to be put down. In other words, to express the 'past' we make use of names, and nouns, of lexical and semantic procedures. For verbs, on the other hand, morphological procedures are popular. It is of course easy to think of a language in which the past would be expressed by means of one and the same particle for persons, things, processes and states". (*La linguistique synchronique,* pp.206f.)

24 Here we must deal with a possible mistake. If, in the sentence given, 'the successor of the King' is a name in the future, it is not because this expression is synonymous with the relative clause 'he who will succeed the King', which contains a verb in the future. For in the sentence

I have met the successor of the King

'the successor of the King' is of course a name in the present; what is referred to is the present successor of the King. It is certain that the absence of nominal tenses in our languages has led to the development of a form of blindness in us that encourages all sorts of confusion.

25 Some languages do have *places* (just as ours have *tenses)* corresponding to the different points on the compass. It will be noticed that the most economical system of places would certainly be that which adopts the principle of Cartesian coordinates.

26 Cf. A. N. Prior, *Time and Modality, Papers on Time and Tense,* as well as the article "Postulates for Tense Logic". In this article Prior groups together for purposes of clarification and comparison some of the systems he had investigated previously, in particular those which we allude to here.

27 "Quelque remarques sur la logique du temps et les systèmes modales" *(sic), Scientia,* Nov.-Dec. 1967, pp.1–8.

28 This particular feature runs the risk of letting in various antinomies in certain cases. The use of the present tense of the indicative combined with the use of the first person makes it possible to obtain the antinomy of the liar in its most compact form. For if every tense (past, present or future) involves a reference to the moment of speaking, in the case of the *present tense* this reference is an identification. It is this identification which makes possible the imperceptible transition from the language being spoken to the metalanguage: to say 'I lie' is to say that the person who says this, lies at the moment he says it.

29 "Postulates for Tense Logic", p.1.

30 N of course represents negation. One can already see intuitively that *it will be the case that p* has the same sense as *it will not always be the case that not-p.*

31 This possibilitiy is mentioned by Prior himself in *Papers on Time and Tense,* pp.88–97.

32 Ibid., pp.3f.

33 Arnauld and Lancelot, 2nd part, ch.15, p.133.

34 Ibid., p.134.

35 Donzé, 2nd part, ch.3, p.123.

36 At least in Indo-European languages, the grammatical category of gender hardly concerns verbs at all (except in their nominal forms, in particular the participle), but rather names,

152

nouns, pronouns and adjectives. Nevertheless it is enough for our purposes that there is no *a priori* obstacle to verbs being modified in a way which depends on the gender of their arguments in the same way as they are modified for number. There may even be some advantage in incorporating gender not only into names but also into the verb. Arnauld and Lancelot (2nd part, ch.14, pp.130f) point out that oriental languages often give to the same person of the verb two different endings depending on which sex the proposition refers to. And they add that "this is often useful to prevent equivocation". The presence of a gender common to both names and verbs in semitic languages is also pointed out by A. Martinet (*La linguistique synchronique*, p.208), whilst B. L. Whorf (*Language, Thought and Reality*, p.70) relates that in Navaho special endings are added to verbs, and not to the subject, according to the category this subject belongs to. Bloomfield and Jakobson draw attention to an analogous phenomenon in Algonquin (cf. Jakobson, "Shifters, ...", §2.2). Notice that in all these cases the specification of the gender of the verb (i.e. of the functor) depends not on the functor itself but on the membership of one of its arguments in a certain class. There is nothing to prevent a linguistic system distinguishing between different inflections of the functor depending on whether the functor itself belongs to this or that class of functors rather than on whether an individual belongs to a certain class of individuals or, more generally, an argument-name belongs to a certain class of names. This principle might serve to integrate type considerations and grammar.

[37] The triple distinction *masculine, feminine, neuter,* to the extent that it incorporates the previous two distinctions, would be more stable than the binary distinction *masculine, feminine.* Nowadays English adheres more closely to this triple distinction than does German ('das Weib', etc.) – a great help to the learner of English, who no longer needs to burden his memory with distinctions for which he can see no justification.

[38] Let us not hesitate to call them remnants or survivals, in spite of the fact that the use of such concepts is nowadays often criticized. One often reads on this point that before explaining a social fact as a remnant of some previous state, it is first of all necessary to explain why it is that what survives does survive – as though the inertia of certain social phenomena were not an observable fact, like the inertia of certain biological or even physical phenomena. The objection we have described is right about one thing: the degree of inertia is itself variable, depending on the nature of the phenomena in question. The survival of a use of words is of a very different sort from the survival of a pyramid. It is true that explanations appealing to the notion of survival have often been used, wrongly, as though this notion could explain everything. But the irony with which explanations of this sort are nowadays often received does not constitute a refutation. It is not a question of knowing whether a form of explanation is new or not, but whether a particular explanation of this form is true or false.

[39] Cf. Whorf, *Language, Thought and Reality*, p.69.

[40] We do not want to say here that the distinctions made in Bantu are arbitrary relative to the state of Bantu societies and to the state of knowledge in these societies, but that they appear to be relative when compared to the present state of scientific knowledge and of society. Whether these distinctions are arbitrary from the point of view of the Bantu (as our distinction between masculine and feminine is indisputably arbitrary from the point of view of our society) is a question we must leave to the specialists to settle.

[41] If it is true that Chinese has ways of indicating that objects belong to different spatial directions, can one still speak here of *genders?* Would it not be more exact to talk of *places,* as we did above. Is the reason that the familiar term *gender* is preferred not simply that, unlike *tenses, places* are hardly to be found at all in the Indo-European tradition (for the reasons we have mentioned)?

[42] There can be no question of incorporating all the rules of type theory into grammar since this would involve admitting an infinity of genders. In any case what was said above in chapter 2 may lead one to guess what sort of difficulties a grammatical distinction between terms of

different types would lead to. Would these difficulties be compensated for by any real advantages? One might, for example, lay down by a grammatical rule that the verb *eat* takes as its first argument only terms of one genus (*animate individual*) and as its second argument either terms of the same genus or terms belonging to another genus (*animate individual* or *inanimate individual*) to the exclusion of every other genus. If the morphology of verbs authorized them to have a genus, this might for example consist in an indication of the type-level of the predicate represented by the verb.

43 *Bulletin de la société française de philosophie*, 1912, p.59.
44 "The dual is to be found regularly in Plato; it is rare in Demosthenes and has disappeared by the time of Menander" (Meillet, op.cit., p.58).
45 In the Indo-European family, Lithuanian has kept the dual. Outside this family a dual is to be found in Koryak, a trial in many languages or dialects of Melanesia, Indonesia and Australia, a quadral in at least one Polynesian language (cf. Hjelmslev, *Prolégomènes à une théorie du langage*, p.72 trans. p. 53 and *Le langage*, p.148).
46 Cf. Martinet, *La linguistique synchronique*, p.208.
47 This seems to be the case in the languages with which we are familiar.
48 *Selected Writings in Language, Culture, and Personality*, pp.179–180, and esp. pp.206–212. Cf. also Bloomfield, *Language*, pp.45–46.

Chapter Six
The Moods

And here Alice began to get rather sleepy, and went on saying to herself, in a dreamy sort of way, 'Do cats eat bats?' and sometimes 'Do bats eat cats?' for, you see, as she couldn't answer either question, it didn't much matter which way she put it... She generally gave herself very good advice, (though she very seldom followed it) and sometimes she scolded herself so severely as to bring tears into her eyes; and once she remembered trying to box her own ears for having cheated herself in a game of croquet she was playing against herself.

Lewis Carroll, *Alice in Wonderland,* ch.1

The Fundamental Status of the Non-Indicative Moods: Optative, Imperative, and Related Moods

It would be impossible to establish any parallel between what grammarians call *mood* and what they call *person, tense, gender* and *number.* But we must not forget the qualification introduced in chapter III; everything we have discussed since then applies fully and without qualification only to what grammarians call the *indicative* mood. We have concentrated so far on this mood alone purely for reasons of simplicity. It is appropriate to deal with mood at *this* point in our argument because *mood* (French: *mode*) does not seem to *modify* the nature of the *name,* which is the subject of the next chapter, in the way that it affects the nature of the verb and of the proposition, which have been the topics of previous chapters. When a name refers to an object this reference can be incorporated into a statement, an order or a wish; in the indicative, the imperative or the optative mood the designation *this dog* remains the same.

It is a historical fact that the indicative enjoys a very privileged position in the modern languages belonging to the Indo-European tradition. We have already pointed out that it was difficult not to connect the privileged position of the indicative with that privilege enjoyed by the theoretical attitude which was imposed by the intellectual revolution begun by the Greeks. So central has the indicative become that it has ended up by obliterating the other moods, to such an extent that even in popular usage the distinction between them is unclear and philosophers often treat the non-indicative moods as supplementary moods obtained from the principal mood by transformation. In the fifth century B.C. an author such as Protagoras could still, according to Diogenes Laertius, range propositions into entreaties, questions, orders, answers, without according primacy to any one type over the others. But this is no longer the case in *The Port-Royal Grammar*[1] whose authors do not hesitate to write:

I have said that the *principal* use of the verb is to signify affirmation, because we shall show later that it is also used to signify other movements of the soul such as *to desire, to pray, to command*, etc.

This text is revealing in that what emerges are the beginnings of an attempt to reduce the non-indicative moods to the indicative, to wit, to varieties of indicators of subjective states. This attempt can be followed throughout the entire rationalist tradition in grammar: had not such ancient grammarians as Apollonius, Priscian and Theodore Gaza[2] already defined the moods as *inclinations* or *affections of the soul*? It is only a small step from here to the interpretations of the inflections of mood as mere indications of such inclinations.

It was all the more easy to take this step in view of the fact that it was possible to make use of an ontological (and no longer merely historical) privilege enjoyed by the indicative. For it is always possible to express indirectly in the indicative whatever is directly expressed in any other mood. There is, as Husserl points out, an "alteration of attitude which makes it possible at any time to give expression to wishing and wish, asking and question, or the like, not immediately but mediately, after the fashion of a judgment".[3] It belongs to the very nature of the indicative that one can always move from propositions such as *what are you doing? do that!, may he ...*, to the corresponding propositions: *I am asking you what you are doing, I order you* or *beg you to do that, I want him to ...* In each of these cases the order, the entreaty or the wish lose the form of their direct formulation in order to constitute the content of a judgment. The content of a judgment – that is to say, what it indicates – is a question, an order, an entreaty or a wish, and the judgment is true if and only if the said question, order, entreaty or wish occurs or is real.

There is, then, in most languages a fundamental ambiguity, clearly described by Husserl, in terms such as *expression of a wish, of an order,* etc. The following are generally not kept strictly apart:

(1) The direct expression of a wish, order, etc.
(2) The judgment stating that one is expressing or has expressed this wish, order, etc.

This confusion is clearly not the result of some accident. The source of possible confusion is built into the very structure of these acts (indication or statement wish, order, ...). It is not only philosophers who have exploited this confusion, although thanks to their interest in ontology it was to lead them directly to a psychologistic interpretation of mood. Most grammarians of the eighteenth century, for example the collaborators of the *Encyclopédie,* held that the moods had no logical significance but were in some sense merely indicators of psychological states. Above all, however, the possibility of this confusion has, if not inspired, then at least supported the slow and progressive tendency towards the elimination of the non-indicative moods from our use of language, a tendency which has by no means yet come to an end but is silently at work in all modern languages.

This ontological privilege of the indicative by virtue of which it can indirectly express the content which is directly presented in other moods does not at all justify the reduction of all these other moods to the indicative. The fact that it is possible to indicate or mention that one is asking a question does not go any way towards showing that questions do not form a basic mood of their own. A question is not itself a psychological state and even if one wanted to reduce it to such a state one would not succeed. For a question is quite distinct from the simple indication of ignorance or curiosity to which one might be tempted to reduce it. If an order were not something very different from the communication of someone's will and a wish very different from the communication of a desire, how could we distinguish an entreaty or a request from each of these cases?[4] *Orders, entreaties, wishes* are in reality acts, individual or social, which are structurally just as basic and original as indicative assertion or judgment, and hence as little capable of being reduced to the latter as they are capable of being reduced to one another.

It is therefore, we must admit, worrying to find Chomsky apparently congratulating himself on finding in earlier writers instances of analysis in terms of deep structure in which "imperatives and interrogatives are analysed as, in effect, elliptical transforms of underlying expressions with such supplementary terms as *I order you ... or I request ...*".[5] Can one really say that 'venez me trouver' (*come and fetch me*) really has the deep structure of 'je vous ordonne (prie) de me venir trouver' (*I order you to come and fetch me*)? There is no doubt the two expressions have the same sense, that they are equivalent and that one can always be used instead of the other. But this does not authorize us to consider one (the indicative proposition) as the *deep structure* of the other (the imperative proposition), a view which in our opinion arises from the most artificial reductionism.

Curiously, logico-grammatical rationalism, like modern psychologism, seems on this point to have been a victim of illusions that are deeply rooted in the Western tradition to which they both belong. The prejudice that has granted to indication (assertion) and the indicative mood an exorbitant privilege compared to the other moods has given rise to these two different reactions. The dream of a certain logical rationalism which would like the entire domain of *logos* to belong to the domain of theoretical consciousness turns out to stem from the same source as the myth of the reduction of intersubjective relations to simple psychic states and their communication.

The *indicative, interrogative* and *imperative* have their own *sui generis* structures that neither logic nor grammar have the right to misrepresent. Grammar, psychology and Western science generally have all worked together to push aside the irreducibility of these structures. Mathematics is and remains the science of the indicative. One of the great merits of Husserl and his disciples is to have begun to direct the attention of Western thinkers to the seriousness of this failure to recognize these structures. After Husserl a writer like Leśniewski, although he continues to develop a logic within the bounds of the indicative mood, at least seems to be aware of the limits of indicative structures. Not until the beginning of the second half of the century did logicians begin to think about translating this awareness and recognition into the form of calculi for autonomous non-indicative logics.[6]

If we ignore the conditional, the subjunctive, the infinitive and the participle,[7] which are not moods in the sense in which we shall use the word, then in most modern Western languages we really find, apart from the indicative, only two verbal moods – the interrogative and the imperative.[8] It is true that certain forms for expressing mood survive that are not verbal forms. The Stoics, especially, had pointed out that the vocative is really a mood, in spite of the fact that its morphology makes it look like a case: for it does not signify that a name occupies a certain position within the proposition but determines (and this is the role of an authentic mood) a relation – to be called *address* (or 'appellative') – between two interlocutors. Nor is an exclamation reducible to the structure of its content (which it may borrow from other moods) but essentially involves a reference to the situation and behaviour of a single speaker. That the vocative and the 'exclamative' have survived the general decline of the moods in the Indo-European tradition is due to the facts about human life with which these structures are bound up. As with all moods, an exclamation and an address may in principle be made the object of an indicative judgment, but it is difficult to see how the spontaneity these acts presuppose could survive their being expressed indirectly in this way.[9]

There is in Indo-European languages a mood whose expression successfully blends with the expression of the indicative and does so without any metalinguistic detour; this is the mood that, following Austin, might be called the *performative*:[10]

I baptise you in the name of ...
In virtue of the powers vested in me, I make you ...
The President of the Republic promulgates the law the content of which follows:
I promise to ...
I declare three no trumps ...[11]

Sentences such as these, though expressed in the indicative mood, do not amount to statements about any pre-existing or even co-existing fact. These 'declarations' usually *create* the very fact they appear to *state*.[12] To consider them as statements would be to confuse each act with a report of the act. That these sentences are not indicative (i.e. assertive) sentences is shown by the fact that, although a baptism, a naming, a promulgation, may be valid or invalid, although a promise may be licit or illicit, sincere or 'false', although a call at cards may or may not be a bluff, nevertheless the propositions with which the performance of these acts is bound up are never either true or false. Thus even if it were to turn out to be the case that no language had ever established a morphological distinction between *indicative* and *performative* we would nevertheless be obliged rigorously to maintain this distinction in pure grammar.

On the other hand, there are, as is well known, autonomous forms of expression of the *optative* in many languages and, within the Indo-European tradition, such forms of expression could still be found in Ancient Greek and Sanskrit. However, the processes of rationalisation in Western societies and the privilege accorded to economic relations has rendered even the expression of a wish out of date; in the eyes of *homo oeconomicus* the wish is a relic of magical behaviour which should be replaced by rational behaviour. And the fact that it is impossible to rid the 'rational' mentality of all wishes, that wishes turn out to contain a rational element or basis, is held to be due to the fact that it may be useful to communicate to others the object of one's desires. But then in behaviour of this sort there is no longer any spontaneity to be preserved at the level of expression; indirect expression in the indicative mood will suffice. Thus it is not surprising that the optative has nearly disappeared from the Indo-European tradition and that we make do with being able to say to others: 'I want ...'.

In order to avoid all risk of fallacious assimilations we should point out that the category of wishes (*souhait*) or desires (*désir*) is, in addition, quite different from those of indicative assertion, order, entreaty or advice we have mentioned above. These last examples as well as cases such as that of advising are essentially social acts, that is to say, they only exist as such if they are expressed and directed to another person.[12] Alone on his island, Robinson could not address any indicative assertion to anyone (except God) nor any entreaty or order.[13] But there was nothing to prevent him from wishing away to his heart's content. An unexpressed wish remains a wish; although this does not mean that wish and desire are identical, even if it is sometimes difficult (in societies such as ours that are so marked by the rationalisation of intersubjectivity) to distinguish between the expression of a wish and the communication of a desire. St. Anthony, beset with temptations and, like Robinson, isolated in lonely silence, did perhaps not wish for what he desired.

A mood which differs from the optative yet has a similar structure is what the ancient grammarians sometimes call the *concessive* mood. It is remarkable that Arnauld and Lancelot,[14] in spite of their usual reductionist inclinations, carefully distinguish this mood both from the optative and from other moods. The concessive mood, they explain, corresponds to a situation in which "we are content with granting a thing, although absolutely speaking we do not will it; as when Terence says: *profundat, perdat, pereat: let him expend, let him lose, let him perish*".

They immediately add that "men could have been able to invent an inflection in order to indicate this mental experience". The fact that no such inflection has been invented does not, of course, authorize us to confuse this mood with wishes, for one accepts precisely what one does not wish, nor with orders or even permissions, for the simple reason that an order or a permission relates two individuals, the person who gives this order or permission, and the recipient, whereas the concessive mood may well concern only one person, as when we resign ourselves to the occurrence of some unknown event. But even where what we agree to accept is the activity of another person, the examples chosen by Arnauld and Lancelot show well that it is very often the activity of a *third person*. In this respect the concessive is closer to the optative than to the imperative.

Both the optative and the concessive must be distinguished from yet another mood, the expression of regret – even where, as in European languages, such expressions often seem paradoxically to adopt the form of a wish:

Would to God he had done otherwise!

– which can also be expressed as:

If only he had acted differently!

This sort of regret must be carefully distinguished from wishes relating to events whose outcome is not yet known:

Please God he has done what you suggested!

or

If only he has done what you suggested!

Those non-indicative moods which have retained their own independent forms of expression – the interrogative and the imperative – have normally absorbed other moods. This process of absorption has nevertheless followed a definite pattern in which certain criteria are at work. It was made possible by the fact that the moods absorbed were – at least as far as their essential structural features were concerned – isomorphic to the moods that actually absorbed them.

Thus the imperative was able to assimilate at least four other quite different moods. For our current use of the imperative embraces not only the order, the only act suggested by the word's etymology, but often also:

(1) *The precative mood:* the entreaty or request is so different from the order that, although it does involve a relation of subordination between two subjects, the subordination is the converse of that involved in an order. Sanskrit had an inflected form for the precative mood but this soon disappeared, almost without trace.[15]

(2) *The hortative mood:* the spectator shouting *run!* to the athlete would be no more than a figure of fun were he to imagine that he was thereby ordering the athlete to beat some record. It is also clear that if it were in the athlete's power to beat the record, he would not stand in need of any requests or entreaties that he might beat it. Exhortation is a mood with a structure of its own.

(3) *The advisory mood:* in order to give someone advice we nowadays sometimes make use of a statement in the indicative mood (*I advise you to* ...), sometimes of a form of words in the conditional (*In your position I would* ...), and sometimes of the imperative. The fact that there is no longer any independent mood for the expression of advice should not blind us to the irreducible structure of this act.

(4) *Invitations* (*l'invitatif*): the invitation to dinner I address to a friend can clearly not be assimilated either to the imperative I might employ in a moment of haughtiness or the precative form to which courtesy might move me; nor can I be said to be giving my friend permission to eat with me.

If the imperative, the precative, the hortative, the advisory and the 'invitative'[16] are today in effect run together in a single mood, this confusion, abritrary though it is, has only been made possible by the presence within each of these moods of a structure which in part they all share. We cannot pretend to be able to isolate this common structure here, but we should like to bring out some of its features by considering some specific points:

(a) At least four of these moods involve more than the first person singular: only those who, like Alice in Wonderland, agree to 'pretend to be two people'[17] can address requests or advice to themselves. And when they do so they must address themselves in the second person: "'I advise you', says Alice to herself".[18] Exhortation, however, is not necessarily a social act of communication: it is possible to exhort oneself. Someone

162

who encourages himself by saying 'Allons-y' or: 'And here we go!' gives expression to a genuine first person singular by using the first person plural (the only first person our imperative puts at his disposal).[19]

(b) These five moods have in common that, although they allow the first person plural this then has a quite special structure. Although this structure is equally complex in each of the five cases, it is not certain that the structure is identical in each case. What, for example, does an order in the first person plural signify, when addressed by an officer to his men? Is the imperative *chargeons!* (*let's charge!*) not equivalent to the conjunction of an imperative in the second person plural (*chargez!*) and an indicative sentence in the first person singular (*I shall charge*)? It is, however, not at all certain that an analysis of the hortative *chargeons!* yields the same conclusions. For it is very likely that the isomorphism between the *imperative, hortative, precative* and *advisory* moods, although it suffices to justify their assimilation at one level, disappears once the analysis is pushed a little further.

(c) Insofar as all these moods, except the hortative,[20] differ from most other moods in that they aim to get another person to behave in a certain way, it is difficult to see how the person addressed can avoid being named or at least indirectly mentioned within the relevant speech act. The indicative, on the other hand, can always be impersonal in the sense that it need not necessarily mention the person addressed. Similarly, given an indicative proposition that does not make any reference to the person the speech act is addressed to, e.g.

It is raining

or

Peter is taller than Paul,

one can always ask:

Is it raining?
Is Peter taller than Paul?

or formulate a wish:

May it rain! (Puisse-t-il pleuvoir!)
May Peter be taller than Paul! (Puisse Pierre être plus grand que Paul!)[21]

But I can never take this indicative proposition and form a proposition

163

which would correspond to any of our four moods. This provides us with the explanation of the fact that some languages that lack inflections of person in the indicative nevertheless display them when the imperative is used.[22]

d) The past tense, in all forms, is foreign to these five moods: advice, an order, a request, an exhortation, or an invitation concern only the present or the future.[23]

These four remarks allow us to oppose these five moods not only to the indicative but also to the optative, for which

(1) the first person singular is conceivable;

(2) the first person plural does not differ markedly in its behaviour from the way it behaves in the indicative;

(3) the person *in whose presence I may express a wish* is not necessarily mentioned in the content of the wish;

(4) a past tense form is also conceivable: the structure of the relation between the event and the knowledge the subject may come to have of it is such that, as we have seen, I may wish that such an event had occurred in the past.

There are, on the other hand, other features which bring the imperative, the precative, the hortative, the advisory and the mood of invitation closer to the optative and increase their common distance from the indicative. It has already been pointed out that a theorem of the calculus of propositions such as

if *p*, then *p* or *q*

would be out of place in a logic of the imperative. To mention a classic example, my intuition prevents me from deducing from

Post this letter

the complex imperative proposition

Post this letter or burn it.

Now this impossibility, which has no equivalent in the case of the indicative mood, is common to the optative and to all four moods which have been absorbed by the imperative.

Can one speak, as do some authors, of a permissive mood which is distinct from the imperatives? The imperatives we come across in grammars are so constructed that they can be employed to express not only orders but also prohibitions (simply by adjoining a negation); for *to forbid* is *to order not to.* On the other hand, it is strange that it is in general grammatically impossible to employ the imperative for the direct expression of permission and this is true even though *to permit* is just *not to forbid,* that is to say *not to order not to.* Thus it is that permission can be expressed in most languages only by resorting to the indicative i.e. by making use of just that formula we have already discussed: *I permit you to ...*

In our opinion, the distinction between orders and permissions is artificial, unless one also intends to distinguish between orders and prohibitions. Orders, permissions and prohibitions all belong to the same mood *in this sense:* that the relation between the person who prohibits, orders or permits and the person to whom these are addressed always remain exactly the same. Nothing therefore justifies a distinction. If the Indo-European languages have not developed any means of expressing permission on the basis of the imperative, it is probably for the following simple reasons. What one permits is what one does not prohibit, and the existential situation of subordination, which gives both orders and permissions their sense, is such that the person who takes the initiative and is the source of imperatives (where this includes both orders and permissions), will naturally convert his desires into orders, whereas the permissions he might give would be merely the negatives of his desires.

The Special Case of the Interrogative

From James Harris' *Hermes*[24] to Eric Buyssens' essay on *Les Langages et le Discours*[25] grammarians have in general agreed that the lot of the interrogative mood is a special one. The other non-indicative moods we have looked at so far, from the imperative to the optative, have in common that they express an intention to act on persons or things or at least a regret that matters – things or persons – did not turn out in accordance with our desires. In different ways these moods, to use Harris' naive expression, "publish volitions". The interrogative and the moods that are to be found in its domain involve, again in Harris' words, the need "to have some perception informed", just as indicative assertions "publish some Perception either of the Senses or of the Intellect".

If we speak here of the domain of the interrogative this is because, by virtue of a similarity of structure, the latter has been allowed to absorb the mood of uncertainty or doubt, which we could call the *dubitative* mood. We can make up for the effect of the lack of a grammatical expression of the dubitative mood by using, in addition to the indirect indicative statement which is available for this as for every mood,

I doubt that ...
I don't know whether ...
I don't know who ..., etc.,

a straightforwardly interrogative form of words:

Is he good?
Is he naughty?

The structure common to the interrogative and dubitative moods shows itself in two ways. The first concerns the true-false distinction which, as we have seen, is characteristic of the indicative. It seems to be, if not inexact, at least not enough to say that – like a performance, an order, a request or exhortation – neither a question nor a dubitative sentence can be true or false. For interrogative and dubitative sentences are what they are only because they bear on a matter which is essentially such that it is expected to be the object of an assertion. In this sense, although the question *itself* does not fall within the scope of the principle of the excluded middle, the assertion it demands, to which it refers and which is its real *raison d'être,* does fall within the scope of this principle. Some logicians, with the aim of establishing an interrogative or erotetic logic, have taken this feature of questions as their starting point in order to extend to this area the advantages of extensionality which, in the domain of indicative propositions, made it possible to establish the calculus of propositions with the greatest possible degree of simplicity.

Thus the two groups (a) the imperative, together with those moods that are closely related to it, and (b) the interrogative and the dubitative, are not equidistant from the true/false opposition. Were it not for this distinction one would be tempted to propose the following axiom as one common to all the non-indicative moods: since their truth-values drop out of consideration, one might admit the equivalences of any two orders, any two entreaties, any two questions, so that, for each of these moods one might assume:

$$a \equiv b$$

an equivalence suggested by the passage from Lewis Carroll which

provides this chapter with its motto: 'Do cats eat bats? Do bats eat cats?'
But we can do better than this axiom, which would only have the effect of
uselessly over-burdening our calculi. For if we were to disengage the
notion of *equivalence* from the narrowly extensional value it has in
standard (indicative) propositional logic, in order to base it either on
certain features of intension or even on a new form of extensionality we
might perhaps want to assert – but only for the interrogative and the
dubitative moods – the equivalence of any proposition and its negative.
The question

Is it good?

can be considered as equivalent to the question

Is it not good?

even if usage, in many languages, has sought to provide each of these
questions with distinctive nuances. Languages may, for example, use
these equivalent forms to allow the person putting a question to indicate
to those he is addressing what his own answer is, or at least the answer he
expects.

The second trait which clearly displays the similarity of structure
between interrogative and dubitative propositions is that they both fall
into two classes depending on whether the interrogation or doubt
concerns the truth-falsity either of the whole proposition or simply of this
or that part of the proposition, to wit, its functor, or – as is perhaps more
often the case – its arguments. We are thus led naturally to distinguish
what, in the case of questions, Carnap calls yes-no questions such as

Does Mary love Peter?

from what he calls wh-questions,[26] that is to say questions traditionally
introduced by an interrogative pronoun, adjective or adverb, such as:

Who does Mary love?
Who loves Peter?[27]
What is the relation between Mary and Peter?

For if, generally speaking, an indicative proposition can be represented
as a function with n arguments:

$$f(x, y, z, \ldots n)$$

questions and doubts may concern either the whole of the expression or one or more of the terms $f, x, y, z, \ldots n,$ [28] whether functor[29] or arguments.

What is definitely excluded, however, is the possibility that the question (or the doubt) should bear simultaneously on the entire expression and on one of the arguments or on the functor, that the question be at one and the same time a yes-no question and a wh-question. It has already been pointed out that expressions such as

Has Peter met who? (as a purported interrogative)

or even

I don't know whether Peter has met who? (as a purported dubitative)

are not grammatically well-formed in any language. The reason for this is that when interrogation or doubt apply to the entire expression they must raise the issue of the truth-value of the proposition, although this proposition, if it contains an interrogative pronoun, adjective or adverb, just cannot have a truth-value until the reply corresponding to the interrogative word is forthcoming. We have here, then, an *a priori* impossibility.[30]

At least in the case of questions, the essential distinction between these two types, noted by Carnap, is more or less explicitly recognized within natural language. This does not mean that a large number of our questions are not, as they stand, largely ambiguous. Let us merely look at the case where a question bears on one of the arguments of the proposition. The question

Who does Mary love?

may have at least four different meanings:

(1) The question may presuppose that it is certain that Mary loves *at least* one person, in which case the question points to several possible replies. For example, *Peter,* or *Peter, Jack and Susan,* or even *humanity as a whole.* But it excludes the reply *no one.* Such a reply would simply show that the question was badly put. Bolzano, who takes as an example of just such a use of *who* the question

Who caused God?[31]

suggests calling the question *impossible, imaginary* or *absurd.* For such a 'question' combines in one and the same expression the *assertion* that the relevant someone or something exists and the *question* proper, which concerns the identity of the thing or person. If the question is not to be absurd, then the assertion it contains must already be true. This enabled Bolzano to suggest calling a question *true* or *false* according as to whether it indicates *correctly* or *incorrectly* "our desire to be instructed about the subject of the question"[32] – a suggestion that breaks with the usage customary in the Aristotelian tradition.

(2) The question may presuppose that one knows quite well that Mary loves one and only one person. This type of question exists in many natural languages. In English it generally has the form

Who is the person that Mary loves?

Such a question points to an infinite number of possible replies: 'Peter', 'Jack', 'John'; but it excludes both replies in the plural and the reply 'no one'. Here our *question* combines the *assertion* that there exists at least and at most *one* person loved by Mary with the *question* proper which concerns the identity of this person.

(3) The question may simply presuppose that Mary may love at most one person. Those who ask

Who does Mary love?

or

Who is the person that Mary loves?

may in certain cases not hesitate to admit that it is not at all certain that Mary *loves,* but that *if* she loves then there can be only one person that she loves; in this case 'loves' constitutes a function – i.e. its value may be undefined for certain arguments but it can never take two values for any single argument – thus we can call this the *functional* use of 'who'.[33] If it is not to be absurd the question requires answers such as *no one, Peter* or *Jack* but excludes plural answers.

(4) But the question may also, strictly speaking, contain no presupposed assertion, so that it is always possible to reply *no one, Peter,* or *everyone*. This is the most general sense of 'who', the widest sense, although it is not necessarily the most widespread sense of the word.

These distinctions which we have drawn concerning 'who' now allow us to understand why there may exist another type of question not mentioned by Carnap and which we have so far passed over in silence. For one might be tempted to think that there are only differences of nuance between the four questions:

Does Mary love Peter?
Is it Mary who loves Peter?
Is it Peter that Mary loves?
Is what Mary feels for Peter love?

that they are not merely different ways of putting one and the same question, although in the first case the question concerns the entire proposition, in the second and third the arguments, and in the fourth the functor itself. In favour of assimilating all four cases is the fact that a reply to any of the four questions immediately provides an answer to each of the other questions.

In spite of appearances, however, these four questions, which are to be met with in everyday contexts, are examples of four quite different sorts of question. In order to disentangle the maze in which these differences are hidden it is enough to invoke the distinctions we drew in our discussion of 'who'. The difference between wh-questions and the present cases is that here the argument or functor is given: what the speaker asks for is confirmation or rejection of its role as argument or functor. Let us analyse only one example of the various possible distinctions. The difference between.

Who is it that Mary loves?

and

Is it Peter that Mary loves?

needs no commentary; yet the second of these two questions also differs in its turn from

Does Mary love Peter?

since it may presuppose, just like the first of these two questions, that there is *at most* one person that Mary loves and *at least* one such person, the question being, in the first case, who this person is and, in the second case, whether it is really Peter. Thus the positive answer to

Is it Peter that Mary loves?

170

does not merely mean that Mary loves Peter, as does a positive answer to

Does Mary love Peter?

but also implicitly excludes the possibility, which the last question leaves open, that Peter is merely *one of the people* that Mary loves.

The grammatical features of the interrogative we have here briefly described all seem to have their equivalents in the case of the dubitative mood. There, too, we would have to distinguish three types of proposition depending on whether the ignorance or doubt concerns (1) the entire proposition:

I don't know whether Mary loves Peter.

(2) This or that argument or the functor of the proposition – which has been left indeterminate:

I don't know who loves Peter.

(3) This or that argument or functor of the proposition – which is given but put into doubt:

I don't know whether it is Peter that loves Mary.

In the second and third case we would have to make just those additional distinctions we were led to in our analysis of the interrogative. We have preferred to concentrate on the example of the interrogative simply because the interrogative forms of words have survived in a clearer form in modern languages or have acquired a sharper outline, and so are the more familiar of the two.

Some of our remarks might give the impression that the replacement of one mood by another can only come about if one structure can be assimilated by the other, in which case the structures would have to be very similar if not identical. Although this is indeed very probably the main factor which has made possible the historical impoverishment of many moods, though it does not justify it, it may also happen that the substitution of one mood for another has no other aim than that of masking the structure of the original mood. The two false questions such as

Would you give me ...?
May I have ...?

conceal a request when addressed to an equal; they hide the brutality of an order when addressed to a servant. In

Is it not hideous?

the question serves to modify the dogmatism of a harsh judgment. Here the transition from one mood to another actually presupposes a fundamental structural difference and would be impossible without it.

The Distinction Between Moods and Modalities

Finally, we must emphasize how important it is not to confuse, as do some authors, the grammatical moods with what in logic are traditionally called the modalities: necessity, impossibility, contingence, possibility. If I say

It is necessary that p

where p represents a (normal, indicative) proposition, the proposition as a whole is just as much an *objectifying act,* to use Husserl's term once more, as is the simple proposition p.[34] The modalities all belong to the indicative; in this respect they have nothing to do with the moods. Thus we must strictly distinguish a dubitative proposition, whose content would be expressed in the indicative mood by p, from each of the three following propositions:

It is possible that p
It is contingent that p
It is possible that p and it is contingent that p.[35]

It is no less true that the evolution characteristic of modern societies is, paradoxically, making man increasingly blind to such essential distinctions. The assertion of a possibility often seems to us to be strictly equivalent to the expression of a doubt: nevertheless, there lies between the two the rigid boundary of objectifying acts.[36]

This very blindness of modern man in the face of the radically distinct structures of the different moods is not without interest for the historian and sociologist. To overlook this is to overlook one of the fundamental features of modern societies, a feature so fundamental that many have

172

become incapable of returning to these moods in order to become aware of them. Precative, hortative, advisory, dubitative[37] – these moods have perhaps never found complete grammatical expression in any language. But it is certain that, from Sanskrit to modern Western languages, there has been a gradual impoverishment of the original forms of their expression. One should perhaps see in the process of simplification involved in this evolution one of the signs of that slow process of rationalisation, the beginnings of which were described by Mauss and whose final phase has been described by Max Weber. But this rationalisation, which in the case of the indicative has meant an enrichment and development of the system of communication, may also, as we have seen, involve a betrayal of authentic rationality.

Notes

[1] Arnauld and Lancelot, 2nd part, ch.13, p.123.
[2] Cf. Serrus, 2nd part, ch.2, p.164 and Donzé, 2nd part, ch.3, pp.112–115, who gives this characteristic quotation from Priscian: "Modi sunt diversae inclinationes animi, varios ejus affectus demonstrantes".
[3] *Formal and Transcendental Logic,* Preparatory Considerations, p.24.
[4] Cf. Adolf Reinach, *Zur Phänomenologie des Rechts,* ch.1, pp.37ff.
[5] Chomsky, *Cartesian Linguistics,* p.46.
[6] The most developed of such logics so far seems to be interrogative or erotetic logic. Cf. A. and M. Prior, 1955, and G. Stahl, 1963.
[7] The conditional is a form of the indicative; we shall return to the other three later.
[8] It is of little importance that grammarians do not generally describe an interrogative form of words as a *mood.*
[9] This is true above all of exclamations and is much less true of the category of appellatives or address. Indeed the spread of telecommunications seems to have favoured the replacement of the vocative by indications or statements of an appeal. For since the person addressed cannot see who is calling him in communication of this sort a statement has the advantage over the vocative that it contains a designation of the caller. This is the reason for the replacement of the vocative by formulae such as (*this is*) *a calling b.*
[10] Cf. especially Austin, *How to Do Things With Words,* 1962 and "Performative-Constative" in J. Searle, ed., *The Philosophy of Language,* Oxford: Oxford University Press, 1971, pp.13–22. We have somewhat modified Austin's distinction between performative and constative. For although, following Austin, we distinguish between the performative and the indicative which is constative, we also distinguish just as carefully between the former and every form of the imperative, the precative, etc.; he sometimes mentions as examples of performatives:

    I order you to …
    I beg you to …
    I request you to …

As defined by Austin the performative is, therefore, in our terms, a category which brings together a whole series of moods having nothing in common but the fact that they differ essentially from the indicative, making no further distinctions within this range.

11 These examples are taken from Austin, except the third, which we have taken from G. Kalinowski, 1974, p.64. [Cf. Reinach, op. cit., pp. 165 ff. – Tr.]

12 Cf. Reinach, op.cit., ch.1, pp.37ff. [An account in English of Reinach's work on the structure of acts of promising, ordering etc. is given by B. Smith in: B. Smith, ed., *Parts and Moments. Studies in Logic and Formal Ontology,* Munich: Philosophia Verlag, 1982, pp.297–303. – Tr.]

13 Marx's irony on the subject of Robinsonades loses its point when the structures to be investigated are *a priori* structures for which the method of imaginative variation is perfectly suitable.

14 Arnauld and Lancelot, 2nd part, ch.16, p.137.

15 Even those grammarians and logicians who distinguish between *oratio precativa* and *oratio imperativa* as two fundamental moods have sometimes been pushed by reductionism to want to reduce the *oratio optativa* to the first of these. It is easy to see what it is that suggests such an assimilation. But it is none the less inadmissible. A request or entreaty necessarily requires two people, a wish only one. In this respect the structure of an entreaty is much closer to that of an order than that of a wish.

16 Our claim is not that, when the history of language began, these moods were all quite distinct from one another. Here a Robinsonade would indeed be improper. The ontological distinctness of these moods does not imply that they have ever been historically distinguished.

17 Lewis Carroll, *Alice in Wonderland,* ch.1.

18 Ibid.

19 Cf. Jakobson, 1957, §3.4 who points out that in Russian it is the existence of a first person singular that serves to distinguish the hortative from the imperative.

20 Jakobson points out (ibid.) that in Russian "in the imperative the addressee is always implied, whether he is in the singular or the plural and whether there is or is not any participation on the part of the speaker, whereas the hortative implies the addressee and/or the speaker".

21 That the content of the wish obtained in this way is ridiculous is another matter.

22 Cf. especially Panfilov, *Grammar and Logic,* p.66.

23 Although ontologically impossible, a morphologically past imperative is to be found in some languages; but in such cases the grammatical *tense* has lost its properly temporal character. This is indeed the case in Ancient Greek: "The reasons leading a speaker to use a present imperative or an aorist imperative had nothing to do with time." (J. Humbert, *Syntaxe grecque,* 3rd ed., Paris: Klincksieck, 1960, ch.7, p.177.)

24 Quoted by Chomsky, *Cartesian Linguistics,* pp.31f.

25 Pp.74ff.

26 Carnap, *Logical Syntax,* p.296. The term 'W-Fragen' or 'wh-questions' derives from the initial letter(s) of interrogative pronouns, adjectives and adverbs in German and English: *wer/who, was/what, wo/where, wann/when.*

27 In French 'Qui aime Pierre?' is ambiguous and may mean either 'Whom does Peter love?' or 'Who loves Peter?'

28 Some grammarians, for reasons of clarity, disallow questions that concern several arguments. But questions of this sort are all the same *a priori* possible. K. A. Wachowicz (1974, p.159) gives the following example. "Imagine a situation in which different tasks are to be distributed amongst different individuals; if, after long discussion, some measure of agreement has been reached but the matter has not been completely settled or is not completely clear for those present, one of the participants may perhaps ask the question: 'Who is doing what, finally?'".

29 Although we did not succeed in distinguishing between the case where tense concerns the

174

proposition as a whole and the case where it concerns only the verb (pp. 135–136), neither doubts nor questions present any comparable problems. The difference between

Does Susan love Peter?

and

What is the relation between Susan and Peter?

requires no explanation, even if it is true that the answer to the second question generally provides the materials for an answer to the first question.

30 We take this explanation, which the facts seem to require, from Wachowicz (op.cit., pp.164f): "A sentence containing a wh-word, which is a free variable, is comparable to an open formula in logic. One cannot assign a truth-value to an open formula without first assigning an interpretation to the free variable". In this passage, which comes at the end of her article, the author shows how the circumstantial explanations of this phenomenon put forward by linguists for this or that language must give way to the *a priori* impossibility to which, following Wachowicz, we have pointed.

31 Bolzano, §145, p.193.

32 Ibid., §22, p.25.

33 It will be noted that the previous use (no.2) already described an *application*.

34 [On *objectifying acts* cf. Husserl, *Logical Investigation* V, §§32–43. Objectifying acts that have a propositionally articulated content, Husserl argues, may be existence-positing or existence non-positing (*setzend* or *nicht-setzend*) and in particular they may contain existence-positing or non-positing names. This distinction is discussed in the next chapter; , cf. especially pp. 180ff. The term *positing* (*setzend*, *positionnel*) has been used in the present translation first of all because it is used by Findlay in his translation of the *Logical Investigations* and then also in order to mark the fact that the complex theory behind the term should not be too quickly equated with more superficial accounts of related notions like 'presupposition', etc. Although Husserl distinguishes between the use of a positing name and the assertion of existence which can be obtained by modifying this use – between the use of a term that involves taking some object to exist, and the assertion that this object exists, – this distinction has been overlooked in the present chapter and elsewhere, for reasons of simplicity. – Tr.]

35 Some writers occasionally call what is simultaneously possible and contingent *bilaterally possible*.

36 As common as the confusion of the dubitative mood with the modality of the possible is the confusion of the imperative with the norm *it is obligatory*. If we do not insist here on this distinction this is because we have gone into the matter at some length elsewhere.

37 This enumeration does not of course pretend to be exhaustive. We do not think that the list of possible moods could come to an end. There are some basic moods – for example, *blessings, curses, incantations,* –which we have not even mentioned, even though they have left some traces in our contemporary rationalized languages. If it is difficult to see how these are basic moods in their own right, this is because

(1) they correspond to attitudes which may be thought to be in the process of disappearing; in any case, they have no *rational* interest (in the modern sense of this term).

(2) They are in general more or less isomorphic with other moods such as the imperative or the optative, and this of course facilitates their absorption by the latter.

We have not mentioned the mood that corresponds to *thanking,* which is still alive and flourishing or, at least, which would be flourishing were it not that, in a manner very characteristic of the evolution of our societies, it is increasingly being replaced by the indicative expression of *acknowledgement of gratitude.*

Chapter Seven
The Name

'Edwin and Morcar, the earls of Mercia and Northumbria, declared
for him, and even Stigand, the patriotic archbishop of Canterbury
found it advisable ---'
'Found *what?*' said the Duck.
'Found *it*', the mouse replied rather crossly: 'of course you know
what "it" means'.
'I know what "it" means well enough, when *I* find a thing', said the
Duck: 'it's generally a frog or a worm. The question, is what did the
archbishop find?'

Lewis Carroll, *Alice in Wonderland*, ch. 3

What we Shall Understand by 'Name'

We have treated the *name* or *substantive* as a categorematic term, that is
to say, as a self-sufficient expression. In this we have followed Husserl
and so have deviated considerably from the usage of most grammarians.
In particular, the sense of the word *substantive* to which we shall adhere
here resembles what some grammarians have sometimes suggested
calling a substantive name (*nom substantif,* also *noun substantive*) and
which they opposed, within the class of nominal forms, to the adjectival
name (or, *noun adjective*).[1] For these writers meant by the term
substantive name names "which stand alone in an utterance without
having any need of another name" in order to designate their object, in
other words, those that already constitute a categorematic expression,
whilst they reserved the term *adjectival names* for those nominal terms
which "must be connected with other names in an utterance" in order to
make a complete meaning.

We shall follow Husserl in calling only members of the first of these two
classes of terms *names* or *substantives*. And we shall observe the principle
behind the distinction very strictly; we shall say that *Napoleon, this man,*

176

a scholar are substantives or names, whereas we shall refuse to apply these terms either to *human* or to *scholar*. (But notice that in French we would call *la science* but not *science* a name, although the English word *science* may be a name.) Grammarians, in contrast, seem to have been attracted by a very different usage of the term *name* or *substantive* or *noun*. What they in general call a substantive is not necessarily a categorematic expression. Husserl is clearly alluding to this traditional sense of the term in the following sentences:[2]

It is not, therefore, a mere *noun,* perhaps even coupled with an attributive or relative clause, that makes a full name: we must also add a definite or indefinite article, which has a most important semantic function. *The horse, a bunch of flowers, a house built of sandstone, the opening of the Reichstag,* also expressions like *that the Reichstag has been opened* are names.

Thus one can say, moving from the traditional sense to that suggested here, that one and the same grammatical 'substantive' or 'noun' such as *scholar* (and, in French, *homme*) may help to form several different names: *this scholar, every scholar* are two names designating two quite distinct objects; *the scholar* (or *the man*), *a scholar* (or *a man*) are also two names, but we would be right to criticize these names for their ambiguity unless the context tells us more exactly what they designate. One can imagine a language which would have as many grammatically independent 'nouns' as it had 'names', which would have a 'noun' for *this man* and another for *every man*. But we know that most languages have not adopted this solution: it has not, in any case, been the Indo-European solution. Very likely it has been rejected because of a desire not to multiply terms.

The Indo-European solution has been to construct the innumerable names that a language requires in order to designate the innumerable objects of all possible experience by using terms which, by themselves, do not have a complete sense but which designate an *object* – in the most general sense of this term – when completed by this or that determiner. Thus European languages have come to possess a whole arsenal of determiners without which they would be obliged either to create as many grammatical substantives as there are objects to be designated, or to go to the other extreme and make do with a limited number of referents to go with their poor vocabulary; examples of such determiners are the demonstrative and possessive adjectives as well as indefinite adjectives

177

(i.e. quantifier expressions) and the article. The brevity of the article makes it very convenient. But this is balanced by its ambiguity in a language like French, in which it is difficult to distinguish the singular sense of the article from the universal or generic sense (a problem which arises in a somewhat different way in English: 'l'homme' may be taken to refer to one man or to man in general, whereas 'man' requires a generic reading and 'the man' a singular reading),

Names of Individuals (1): Proper Names

Having clarified what sense we shall attach to the term *name* we shall first concentrate on names standing for individuals and only then move on to the analysis of other cases. Within the class of names of individuals the following categories can be distinguished.

(1) *Proper names,* which we shall define as names that designate at most one individual. Although we have no reason for avoiding the traditional grammatical term *proper name,* it should be clear that as we use the term it designates a broader category than was usual in traditional grammar, and for two reasons.

First, *Immanuel Kant* is of course a proper name, whether this category is understood in the traditional way or not. But

the philosopher who was born in 1724, taught at the University of Königsberg and died in 1804

is also, as we use the term, a *proper-name* – provided it is admitted that Kant did not have a colleague at the University of Königsberg who taught the same subject and came into the world and died at the same time as Kant. We know, of course, that this name designates the same individual referred to above by his Christian name together with his family name – again, provided the reader will grant the assumption that the Kant family did not contain a pair of Immanuels.

Secondly, our definition of *proper name* has been so constructed as to make possible, within this category, a further distinction, due to Husserl, between positing and non-positing (*setzende* and *nicht-setzende*) acts, that is to say, between acts implying the existence of their objects, for example acts of memory, and those, such as day-dreaming or the entertaining of propositions, which do not imply that their objects exist. Thus our definition leads to a distinction between two sorts of proper name:

(a) *Non-positing proper names,* which simply designate at most one individual without guaranteeing that they designate at least one individual.

(b) *Positing proper names,* which designate one and only one individual.

Cursory inspection of natural and formalized languages will very soon reveal that one sort of proper name is much more frequent than the other. In the languages we are familiar with, non-positing proper names have left hardly any trace at all. But this does not allow us to ignore them; our analysis is after all concerned explicitly with pure possibilities. The non-positing proper name, although much rarer than the positing proper name, belongs to a much simpler type than the latter and, although infrequent, is much easier to define. In order to obtain a non-positing name from a positing name it suffices to cancel from the assertions implied by the relevant act the assertion that there exists at least one object corresponding to the referring term. In general, the proper names to be found in ordinary language and which are also found in some formalized languages are positing proper names, that is, they imply the existence of the object designated.

This does not mean that every object designated by a positing proper name enjoys, or at least has enjoyed, an existence in accordance with the physical and social norms which we normally use in agreeing to recognize that an object exists or has existed. *Bécassine* or *Croquignol* are proper names designating persons, *Clocher-les-Bécasses* the proper name of a locality. The designations effected by these expressions involve positing acts. But I do not, of course, believe that the heroes of the *Aventures de Bécassine* or the adventures of the *Pieds-Nickelés* really lived in the spatio-temporal world to which I belong, nor would I dream of looking up the place concerned in an atlas. The fact that they correspond to positing acts means that they are proper names which refer to one and only one object, that there is only one *Bécassine* and one *Clocher-les-Bécasses* and that this remains the case whatever the existential status of these objects is. But these examples have one disadvantage; the fact that they will be readily conceded to enjoy the existence that belongs to a social myth may easily lead to confusion. Let us therefore imagine as an example the proper name

the famous numismatist who was born on December 17, 1823 in the very room in which I am now writing.

Now I have never before thought that any sort of scholar, numismatist or not, could have been born in this house – a house which was in any case built less than ten years ago and the date above was one I chose completely at random. Thus what I know makes it certain that no numismatist, eminent or not, was born in 1823 in the room in which I am now writing. The name I have invented is nevertheless to be regarded as a positing name; that is to say, it will be held to imply the assertion that this birth occurred on the given date; the assertion is simply false.

These considerations will only seem trivial to the reader who fails to see their connection with certain long since classic discussions in logic. *Principia Mathematica*[3] has made us familiar with what are there called *descriptions,* and which have more or less the sense of, for example, *he who* ... or *the such and such* ... Whitehead and Russell consider the example of the designation *the son of B* and point out that it implies both that B really has a son and that this son is B's only son. The same is true if I speak of *the author of 'Atala'.* On the other hand, if I consider the set of whole numbers nothing prevents me from speaking about 'the square root of sixteen'; similarly, if I consider the set of regular polyhedrons, I may use the name 'the regular pentrahedron'.[4] But these expressions do not designate any genuine object, for they do not satisfy at least one of the following two conditions that are customarily expressed in logic as follows:

$$\exists x f x$$

that is to say, there exists at least one object for which the function holds;

$$\forall xy[(fx.fy) \supset (x=y)]$$

that is to say, if the function takes both x and y as arguments, then x and y are identical.

An expression like 'the regular pentahedron' does not satisfy the first of these conditions because there is no polyhedron that could be so designated; the expression 'the square root of sixteen' does not satisfy the second condition because the number 16 has two square roots. There is, however, someone who wrote *Atala;* and if someone wrote *Atala* then this author is no other than Chateaubriand.

Of these two conditions, only the second is common to both positing and non-positing proper names. The first is, as we have seen, the mark of positing proper names. Thus the name *the author of 'Atala',* whether it is considered, as it normally is, as a positing name or as a non-positing name, will always be a name which implies no error. As to 'the square root of 16', whether taken as a positing or as a non-positing name, it does not meet the requirement to which it pretends in virtue of its form as a proper name. Because of this it may be described as *erroneous*[5] because it implies an error or a falsehood. The name 'the regular pentahedron' is erroneous[5] only if – as in current usage – it pretends to the status of a positing name.

The passages Husserl devotes to these types of nominal expression in the *Logical Investigations*[6] have, except for differences of style and formalization, almost exactly the same content as the text of *Principia Mathematica* already mentioned. Husserl takes as his examples names such as 'Prince Henry', 'the statue of Roland in the market-place' and points out that

someone who uses these names in their normal sense in genuine discourse 'knows' that Prince Henry is a real, and not a mythic, person, that a statue of Roland does stand in the market place. ...the objects named certainly confront him differently from imaginary objects,

and, Husserl adds, it is not enough simply to say that these objects appear to him as existent, this is just what this person expresses when talking about such objects.

The difference between Husserl and Russell is that the former did not get any further than describing positing proper names in such a way that we become aware of their paradoxical status, whereas the latter succeeds in going beyond a simple description of the paradox. The paradox of positing proper names is, Husserl tells us, that they

intend and name objects as *actually existent,* without thereby being more than mere names, without, in other words, counting as full assertions.[7]

In very simplified terms, we might say that the proper name is a name which has the properties not of a name, but of an assertion. Whitehead and Russell remove all traces of paradox from this state of affairs with the introduction of their iota-operator. For what is the meaning of the proposition

The person who was born on December 17, 1823 in this room in which I am working was a great numismatist?

We note, to begin with, that this proposition comprises a function or predicate

was a great numismatist

whose only argument place is here occupied by the proper name

The person who was born on December 17, 1823 in the room in which I am working

This proposition can be analysed into the conjunction of three elementary propositions:

Someone who was born on December 17, 1823 in this room in which I am now working.
There are not two different persons born in this room on this date.
The person in question was a great numismatist.[8]

If, therefore, the entire proposition is false, this means, in accordance with De Morgan's laws, that at least one of the propositions in the conjunction into which the entire proposition can be analysed is false:

(a) either the person concerned was not born in this room on that date;
(b) or at least two different people were born in this room on that date;
(c) or the person who was in fact born in this room on that date had no gifts as a numismatist.

Names of Individuals (2): Definite Common Names

A name may designate not a unique individual but all the individuals in a determinate class. It is here that it becomes even more important to distinguish, with Husserl, between "two different sorts of names and nominal acts, *those that give what they name the status of an existent,* and those that do *not* do this".[9] For not only is this distinction essentially possible, but usage itself also generally distinguishes implicitly between two sorts of definite common name, according to whether the name does or does not imply that the set of individuals designated contains at least one member. The name *the French*, in its ordinary use, is an existence-positing name, for it does not require the extra presupposition *if at least some Frenchman exists*. On the other hand, the nominal expression

every man capable of swimming 100 metres in less than 52 seconds

can only be a positing expression if I assume that someone is capable of such a feat. Even more obviously, if I name

sixteen-legged calves

while admitting that no such monster has ever existed, or simply without knowing whether this is the case, the expression is indeed a name, but a non-positing name.[10]

It is well-known that the confusion between positing and non-positing definite common names is at the root of certain sophisms. Aristotle's philosophical realism made him accept as concepts only positing names. Modern logic, on the contrary, tends increasingly to discard the positing character of concepts,[11] – amongst other reasons because of the importance of the role that the notion of the empty set can play in mathematics. This choice is a matter of convention and intellectual convenience, although it must be clear what the conventions are; depending on whether the subject of my proposition *every man capable* ... is or is not an existence-positing expression, I may or may not deduce that *some man is* ...

Thus every proposition containing at least one argument that is a common name that is held to be a positing name, for example,

every inhabitant of the Department of Lot-et-Garonne is mortal

can be analysed as a conjunction of two elementary propositions:

there is at least one inhabitant of the Department of Lot-et-Garonne;
every person, if he lives in Lot-et Garonne, is mortal;

so that the negation of such a proposition would mean that at least one of these two elementary propositions is false. And the proposition

the inhabitants of Utopia are mortal

is false if either

(1) there exists no inhabitant of Utopia;

or

(2) there is at least one inhabitant of Utopia who is immortal.

Names of Individuals (3): Indefinite Names

Just as there are definite common names, whether positing or non-positing, so too there are indefinite common names. These differ from all other sorts of names which determine the object they designate, in that they either do not suffice to determine the precise object they designate or they do not designate any precise object at all. Thus the majority of writers on the topic are wrong to run together under the label *indefinite descriptions* two very different classes of expressions:

(a) In the proposition

I met a man who was wearing glasses

the nominal expression

a man who was wearing glasses

is indefinite in the sense that it designates imprecisely an object that is itself precise. The indefinite character of the name is here the gap between the very definite character of the object referred to and the indeterminate or imprecise way in which it is referred to.[12] The fact that someone wears glasses is too broad or general a characterization for me to be able to identify the individual I met.

(b) In the proposition

One doesn't expect to meet a human being in the desert

the name *a human being* is also indefinite but it is a different sort of indefinite name. The speaker is not designating something definite in an imprecise fashion here: it is the object, as well as the referring expression, that is indeterminate.

What we have here is once again the distinction between positing and non-positing names. In

I met a man who was wearing glasses,

the indefinite name

a man who was wearing glasses

is a positing name; that is to say, it implied the existence of such an individual. In our last example, on the other hand, the fact that the name

a human being

is a non-positing name may not be apparent as a result of our knowledge

184

that human beings exist. But the sentential context in which we deliberately inserted the name clearly indicates that it does not imply the existence of a determinate human being.[13]

It is all the more important to underline the distinction between these two sorts of indefinite name since the distinction is not very common in contemporary logic, for reasons that are not difficult to guess. The aim of logic is, as we have seen, to substitute operations on signs that designate, for reasonings or inferences concerning designated objects. As long as logic is concerned with the signs used to designate, it need not concern itself with the question whether these are precise or not, nor with the question whether such imprecision is a matter of inadequate designation or of some radical indeterminacy in the object designated. Nevertheless in certain cases it may be logically important to distinguish between the imprecise designation of a determinate object and the case where it is the object itself that is indeterminate; the first type of designation, unlike the second, indicates that there exists at least one individual corresponding to the designation. Thus it is not surprising to find in works of logic that, when indefinite names are referred to, they are positing names.[14]

But these considerations, although they justify the preferences of logic insofar as it is a calculus of operations on signs, are not relevant to a grammar understood as a system of communication. It is not enough for such a grammar simply to choose among possible designations those that lend themselves to operations. Such a grammar can only avoid betraying its universal character by endeavouring to associate a distinct mode of designation with each of the distinct objects capable of being designated.

Participle, Adjective and Relative Clause

Before moving on to consider categories of names that do not designate individuals, we shall look briefly at some special grammatical constructions employed in most Indo-European languages that function as names designating individuals: participles, adjectives and relative clauses.

Of participles *The Port-Royal Grammar* says somewhat loosely that they are 'real names'. We cannot accept this in view of the definition we gave above of the term 'name'. But although participles alone cannot be said always to form names – just as grammatical 'substantives' do not always form names – it is nevertheless true that, like 'substantives', they *may* form names or *contribute to* the formation of a name. We have seen, for example, that the Latin participle *venturus* may designate *he who is to come,* the unique individual whose arrival is awaited. With respect to what we have called a name the participle is here in exactly the same position as the 'substantive': although it does not constitute a name by itself, it provides one of the main elements contributing to the constitution of a name. It is this possibility of forming a name from a proposition that justifies the very existence of participles: the participle is, we may say, one of the means of nominalising a proposition that is available to a speaker.[15] This explains why it is not a mood, any more than the infinitive or the subjunctive are moods, in the sense in which we said that the indicative, the imperative or the optative were genuine moods.

The functions of the adjective are closely related to those of participles, with which it is often confused. Its most obvious function is that of forming names. In

the pretty girl we have just passed·

the adjective *pretty* does not form a name by itself, but allows us to narrow down the scope of *the girl we have just passed* so that we can pick out one and only one girl who answers to this description. In other words, it allows us to form a positing proper name. This is what grammarians often call an 'epithet' or 'attributive adjective'. But the great advantage of an adjective is that it can also be used to express a functor. For in order to obtain the equivalent of a verb from an adjective it is enough to combine it with the copula *is*. In

the girl is pretty

is pretty represents a functor with only one argument place. Between what we have called adjectives and verbs there is, we may say, a structural connection such that

a verb, which is the expression of a predicate, may, thanks to its participial form, play the role of an adjective and so help to form a name;

an adjective, which may help to form a name, may also represent a predicate by addition of the copula.

In the participle and the adjective Indo-European languages possess two rival means of producing the same result. In a sense, therefore, one of these is superfluous. It is remarkable that languages so often profit from this *logical* redundance by introducing a distinction that is only of perceptual or psychological significance. As has often been pointed out, the verbal form lends itself more readily to the expression of what we perceive as actions or events, where the adjectival form lends itself to the expression of what we perceive as states. Thus the expressions

le soleil brille

and

le soleil est brillant,

although they have the same logical structure, have two different meanings:

(1) *le soleil brille* may be used to express the fact that, for example, at the moment of speaking the sun is shining.

(2) *le soleil est brillant* may be used to express a state or feature of the sun, its brilliance, a state the sun continues to be in even when hidden behind very dense clouds.

The use of the adjective is particularly frequent in cases of functions that take only one argument. In this sense one may say that an adjective expresses a determinate class or set. Functions with only one argument play a central role in the formation of adjectives for purely statistical reasons:

the first such reason is that, as we have seen, every function with more than one argument can be reduced to a function with a single argument; thus there is no logical obstacle to forming an adjective from any given function;

the second reason is that adjectives may have complements. An adjective such as *intermediate,* which corresponds to a functor with three arguments, will take two complements: *intermediate between A and B.*

In many Indo-European languages, when the adjectives correspond to functors with two arguments and when the relation expressed by such functors is *symmetrical,* then it is possible simply to connect the two names designating the arguments with the conjunction *and:*

Peter and Jack are brothers
These two dogs are the same size.

It is a weakness of this construction that it does not allow for any distinction between this case and the very different case in which a predicate with only one argument is applied equally to different subjects:

Peter and Jack are dark-haired
These two oak trees are green.

Thus those languages that contain this construction misleadingly assimilate two different situations which have no logical connection with one another.

The relative form, too, may owe its justification to the fact that it makes possible a certain nominalisation of the proposition. For as Arnauld and Lancelot write, [16]

What is unique to the relative pronoun ... is that the proposition into which it enters (and which may be called *subordinate*) can be part of the subject or of the predicate of another proposition.

In such a case the essential or characteristic trait of the relative construction, as Bolzano pointed out, [17] is that the terms it connects are a name and a proposition.

However there are certain features of the use of the relative not taken into account by these remarks. These remarks describe what, in Chapter 3, [18] we called the *non-restrictive* use of the relative, as opposed to its restrictive use. For in its restrictive use the first argument of the relative, its antecedent, is not a genuine name but rather what grammarians call a 'common name or noun', and the result of the operation is itself a common name. In addition, as we have seen, the second argument of the relative form – whether restrictive or non-restrictive – is not exactly a proposition but a propositional functor with one nominal argument.

Turning to the expression *he who*, equivalents of which are to be found in many languages, we may analyse this as a nominal functor whose only argument is itself a propositional functor with a nominal argument. This we may represent, using Bar-Hillel's method, as:

$$\frac{n}{\left[\dfrac{s}{(n)}\right]}$$

Seen in this way, *he who* may be regarded as a basic functor, although many Indo-European languages *(is qui, celui qui)* seem to have formed it from *who* taken in its non-restrictive sense. Although we have in effect treated the non-restrictive *who* as a nominal functor with two arguments, one of which is nominal and the other functorial, of the following sort:

$$\cfrac{n}{(n)\ \left[\cfrac{s}{(n)}\right]}$$

our discussion of the notation for functors with several arguments[19] tends to show that we might equally well regard this descriptive *who* as a functorial functor with a nominal argument of the following type:

$$\cfrac{\cfrac{n}{\left[\cfrac{s}{(n)}\right]}}{(n)}$$

Thus, once this functor is furnished with its nominal argument (for example, *is* in Latin, *celui* in French), we end up with what is effectively the same notation for *he who* as before.

However, even if, as seems to be the case, the expression *he who* has in many languages been formed from the non-restrictive *who,* it is the restrictive use of *who* to which *he who* is most akin. In particular, both *he who* and the restrictive use of *who* exhibit the same ambiguities. In English *he who* and *the man who* refer sometimes to

the person who is the only being satisfying the following conditions ...

(this sense of *he who* corresponds to the use of the iota operator in the logic of descriptions, as has been already mentioned), and sometimes to:

every being who satisfies the following conditions

with or without the guarantee that there exists at least one such being. The non-restrictive use of *who* is narrower and less ambiguous, for its role is above all that of taking various propositions all of which have arguments in common in order to form a single proposition. In the example mentioned by Husserl[20]

The Minister, who is now arriving, will take the decision,

the entire proposition is equivalent to the conjunction of (1) and (2):

(1) The Minister is now arriving
(2) The Minister will take the decision,

the subordination being made possible by the presence of the same argument, *the Minister,* in the two propositions. In the example given in *The Port-Royal Grammar,* [21]

God, who is invisible, created the world, which is visible,

the entire proposition is equivalent to the conjunction of three propositions:

(1) God is invisible
(2) God created the world
(3) The world is visible

the double subordination being made possible by the presence of an argument common to the first and second proposition (*God*) and of an argument common to the second and third proposition (*the world*).

Names of Properties or Relations – Names of Classes

Names are not used only to designate individuals or pluralities of individuals. A name may also be used to designate a property or a relation. This process of nominalising a predicate is described in almost the same terms in Campanella's *Philosophia rationalis,* in Husserl's *Logische Untersuchungen,* and in textbooks of modern logic. Let us agree with Husserl[22] that 'an adjective is, so to speak, predestined to function predicatively, and, as a consequence, attributively', that its 'original unmodified meaning' is its predicative role, as in the example *this tree is green.* Then we may say that the adjective may be stripped of the function it has when it is attributed to a name designating an individual and may 'itself be nominalised, i.e. become a name'.

If I say

green is a colour

the term *green* no longer has the same sense as in

this tree is green,

for what is intended is no longer simply, for example, 'a dependent moment in the make-up of a concrete object'. Thus if an adjective, which in general corresponds to a verb with only one argument place, or any verb, can be modified or transformed so as to yield a name or names, the latter will be able to function as arguments within other functions.

If the modification of the kernel form of an adjectival kernel content (of the kernel itself) yields syntactical material of nominal type then such determinately constructed names can enter into every syntactical function which requires names for its syntactical materials in accordance with the formal meaning-laws.

It is a common-place in modern logic that, although the study of predicates applying to individuals – i.e. predicates whose argument places are occupied by names standing for individuals – is primary, there is nothing to prevent us from considering these predicates in turn as objects to be designated by names. These names will occupy the argument-places in predicates of a new type, which are sometimes called *predicates of predicates,* for just this reason. These, in their turn, may be nominalised to become arguments in functions of a higher level. Thus if I say, for example,

Peter is superior to Jack[23]

the predicate *is superior,* a predicate taking two arguments which are themselves names designating individuals, may be nominalised. But the name *superiority* formed in this way may now occupy an argument place in a proposition such as

Superiority is transitive.

Is transitive is here a predicate of a predicate (but one taking only one argument place) and may itself be nominalised, as when I speak of *transitivity* in general. Thus every adjectival or verbal form may be employed grammatically not only as the functor of a function with the required number of nominal arguments but, in addition, once it has been nominalised, as a nominal argument of a higher-order function. What we have in such cases is, therefore, not an example of the "frequent confusion of the roles of adjectives and names",[24] which it would of course be perfectly legitimate to condemn, but a *permanent* possibility of transforming adjectives (and verbs) into names, a possibility founded in the very nature of adjectives and verbs.

It is not only adjectives and verbs that can be nominalised but quite generally any functor. For example, the propositional functor with one propositional argument, *not*, can be nominalised to yield *negation;* similarly the propositional functors with two propositional arguments that are dealt with in the classical propositional calculus: *and, or* (in the sense of *at least one*), *or* (*at most one*), *or* (*at least one and at most one*), *if* and *if and only if*, give rise to the names: *conjunction, inclusive disjunction, incompatibility, exclusive* or *strict disjunction, implication* and *equivalence*.

The objects designated by these names also have properties of their own. Thus we can say:

Conjunction is symmetrical
Implication is transitive
Conjunction and disjunction are distributive with respect to one another.

In this way we obtain predicates (taking one argument in the first two cases, two arguments in the last case), which in their turn may be the objects of further nominalisations, allowing us to speak of

Symmetry
Transitivity
Distributivity[25]

The predicate-nominalisations we have been looking at concern what has traditionally been called the comprehension of the predicate. This type of nominalisation should be carefully distinguished from that variety of nominalisation that concerns the extension of a predicate, i.e. not the predicate itself, nor the *individuals* satisfying the predicate but *the set of these individuals*. For, as has been known at least since Peano, it is necessary to distinguish carefully between *all the individuals of a set* and *the set of these individuals*. Ordinary language all too readily confuses the following three distinct nominalisations:

(1) *Men* is a name designating all men; I may connect this name with the predicate *are mortal* in the proposition

Men are mortal.

(2) If, on the other hand, we take the predicate *to be a man*, this may,

192

as we have seen, be nominalised. We obtain in this way *the property of being a man*. And it would be absurd to say of this property, or of *humanity* when defined in this manner, that it is *mortal*.[26]

(3) Finally, I may take the extension, rather than the comprehension, of the predicate *to be a man* and designate *the set of all men*. Of such a set I may say that it is *very large,* although I cannot say the same of *men,* without changing entirely the meaning of the predicate in question. The name of a set or class is the result of a distinct sort of nominalisation.

Names of States of Affairs

It is possible to nominalise not only a functor or the set corresponding to its extension, but also the content of an entire proposition. Given the proposition

Peter is superior to Jack

I may nominalise not only the predicate *is superior to,* which would yield the name *superiority,* but *the very fact that Peter is superior to Jack.* And who would deny that the name *that Peter is superior to Jack* is a name very different from *superiority,* that it designates a *fact* which is quite distinction from the *relation* designated by the latter name? One may say that the term *that* or *the fact that*[27] is a functor that forms the name of a state of affairs. This is the point of the text of Husserl's that has already been quoted,[28] in which the expression *that the Reichstag is open* is recognized as a name.

Husserl indeed devoted a great deal of attention to this type of nominalisation,[29] attempting to show that, in the proposition

That rain has at last set in will delight the farmers,

one cannot say that the statement *rain has at last set in* is the subject of *will delight*. But *that rain has at last set in*

is a name in exactly the same sense as all other nominal expressions of facts ...; just as other names name other entities [*anderes*], things,[30] properties, etc., so it just names (or presents) a state of affairs, in this particular case an empirical fact.[31]

Thus the distinctive character of the expression *that* is shown in the distance it establishes between the statement corresponding to a certain state of affairs and the name designating this same state of affairs. Although this name presupposes the *possibility* of such a prior statement, it can only become a name thanks to a radical transformation of the intentional direction which is a feature of the statement-form. The possibility of such a transformation of the content of a judgment into a nominal expression is, says Husserl, rooted in *a priori* fashion in the nature of things, just

as there is an *a priori* possibility, resting on the ideal essence of geometrical figures, that 'one' can turn them about in space, distort them into certain other figures, etc.

This is the explanation of the fact that, whereas there are many names (all proper names) which, as we have seen, cannot be transformed into predicates, *that* always makes possible the formation of a name from the content of any proposition.[32]

Grammarians are by no means unaware of such nominalisations. N. Ruwet writes[33]:

A nominalisation is essentially the conversion of a sentence into a noun or noun phrase, and it can always be described by means of a transformation that embeds a transformed version of a constituent sentence in the position of a noun or noun phrase in a matrix sentence.

The same author points out the equivalence between, on the one hand, the subject clauses of the sort considered by Husserl and the object clauses (completive or that-clauses) of a language such as English or French and, on the other hand, 'subject and object noun phrases'. A language such as English is lucky in possessing a special type of nominalisation: the possibility of adding the -ing ending to a verb. This form of words may lead to confusion because of its ambiguity: it is easy to confuse the simple nominalisation of the predicate dealt with above with the following very different cases, where it is the content of a statement that is nominalised. For the English form of words allows us to write both

-ing is (logically) symmetrical[34]

and

proving that theorem was difficult.[35]

In the latter case, the fact that the verb *to prove* lacks an explicit subject should not mask the fact that what we have here is an equivalent of the term *that:* the absence of such a subject means only that *whoever the subject might be* the proposition is true, and hence that the subject is arbitrary.

French, on the other hand, makes do with two other forms of nominalisation that also exist in English. The expression *the fact that* (*le fait que*), or simply *that,* has the advantage over all other forms of nominalisation that it can be used whatever the number of the arguments of the function expressed in any given proposition. One can also obtain an equivalent nominalisation by using the infinitive. This type of nominalisation is indeed the justification for the existence of the basic form of the infinitive, which is not a verbal *mood,* but the nominal form corresponding to the propositional form of the statement. It should be emphasized that the infinitive is a nominal form corresponding to the propositional form of the statement and not a nominal form of the verb or the predicate. For if, as we have seen, it is possible to say

Superiority is transitive

usage does not allow us to say:

To be superior is transitive

Certain confusions may readily arise here in connection with verbs that correspond to functions with only one argument, e.g. *to lie, to die.* In such cases it is often difficult to see what the difference is between *a lie* or *death* understood as nominalisations of the verb, and *to lie* or *to die* understood as the nominal forms corresponding to the propositional form of a statement whose only argument may be filled by an arbitrary term: *that one lies* or *that one dies.* On reflection, however, it becomes evident that, for example, shame is not a property of a lie nor sadness of death. What is shameful is *that one lies;* what is sad is *that one dies.*

This point emerges even more clearly if we consider the example of Husserl's quoted above. We have seen that in the proposition

Green is a colour,

the term *green* is a nominalisation of the verb or predicate *is green.* But this nominalisation of the predicate *to be green* has nothing in common with the nominalisation normally expressed by the infinitive *to be green* and which is in fact the nominalisation corresponding to the statement *x is green* (where x is the object in question or any object determined by the context). Thus, as will readily be admitted, one can write neither

To be green is a colour

nor

Being green (*le fait d'être vert*) is a colour.

And even if we make explicit the object which is supposed to be green, we still cannot say

The fact that this tree is green is a colour.

On the other hand, I may say

To be green constitutes a natural advantage for an arboreal animal[36]

in the same sense in which one can say that:

The fact that an arboreal animal is green constitutes a natural advantage for it

whereas it would be impossible to say that

Green constitutes a natural advantage

in the way we would say of it that *it is a colour.*

Where the function takes at least two arguments all possibility of confusion disappears. But our use of the infinitive is such – and here we come up against the limits of its use[37] – as to presuppose that the subject of the verb in the unmodified proposition is the same as the principal name in the proposition in which the subject – after nominalisation – comes to occupy an argument place. Thus if I agree *to die for the fatherland* or *to lie to save my life* then I agree that *I* shall die or lie. In a context in which there is no reference to any determinate individual the subject presupposed by such an infinitive is *one, everyone, anyone.*

Another classic way of obtaining a nominalisation is to use an abstract name. Depending on whether it does or does not take complements (and, in English, determiners) such an abstract name expresses, as we have seen, either a simple nominalisation of a verb or predicate, as in

Superiority (La supériorité)

or the nominalisation of the content of a statement, as in

The superiority (la supériorité) of Peter to Jack.

The second of these two names cannot be interpreted simply as a particular case of the first, as though what we have were a concept with a narrow extension and a richer comprehension than in the first case. This is shown by the fact that the properties of the object designated by the first name cannot all be properties of the object designated by the second name. I cannot say of *the superiority of Peter to Jack* that it is transitive. In spite of the shared kernel of meaning the word *superiority* does not play the same role in the two cases.

Compared with the use of the infinitive the use of such an abstract noun has both a disadvantage and an advantage. The advantage is that it is not subject to the restriction to which, as we have just seen, the use of the infinitive is subject: the subject of the statement that provides the materials for nominalisation may become a complement of the abstract name. The disadvantage, at least in a language such as French or Latin, is that very often there is no way of distinguishing between the different complements of the abstract name, i.e. the different arguments taken by the function. This is the source of the famous ambiguities mentioned in all the grammars: is *Peter's curse* something of which Peter is the author, or is he the object of the curse? In Latin, writes Benveniste,

the function of the genitive clearly results from a transposition of a verb phrase into a noun phrase: the genitive is the case that, in a two-noun construction, transposes by itself the functions that are carried by the nominative or accusative in a construction with a finite verb.[38]

The Subjunctive as the Nominalisation of a State of Affairs

The fullest, and hence most clumsy, way of nominalising a proposition, (i.e. what corresponds to a state of affairs) is the *that-* or *the fact that-* construction. Now it should be noted that in French this construction normally involves a transition from the indicative, which is a feature of the original statement, to the subjunctive. Might the function of the subjunctive – which is by no means a *mood* in the sense we have given to this term – not be to express the radical modification of intentional directedness described by Husserl? It would be what a grammarian such as Charles Bally in his *Linguistique générale et linguistique française*[39] called a 'functional transposition'. The original statement, instead of preserving its independence as an indicative judgment, gives way to a nominal phrase subordinated to a new function in which it occupies the position of an argument.

From this perspective it is, we think, at last possible to introduce some order into the extraordinary difficulties grammarians have always found themselves in when confronted with different forms of the subjunctive. For if we group together all the moods distinct from the indicative under the traditional heading of *oratio ordinativa* (discourse essentially connected with behaviour), and if we oppose this to *oratio enunciativa,* as the domain of the indicative, then we must admit that in most of its uses the subjunctive is a case of *oratio enunciativa* and, far from being a distinct mood, is in fact a part of the indicative mood itself.

It is today often felt to be surprising that the grammarians of the Renaissance did not employ the morphological criteria that are now used in order to identify the subjunctive, and that they relied on criteria that were really semantic. Robert Estienne, for example, in his *Traicté de la grammaire françoise* [40] defines his terms as follows:

When one speaks with cause or condition and there are two moods or manners joined together to make a complete (*parfaicte*) sentence, as when I say

Quand je l'auray dict (When I shall have said it)

the sentence is not complete unless I add something such as

tu le sçauras (you will know it)

or something of this sort.

Thus to the astonishment of the modern reader Estienne gives as an example of the subjunctive the future perfect (*futur antérieur*), somewhat as we quoted various sentences as being in the optative mood above, although this mood has no morphology of its own in French or English.

Might it not be the case that the surest way of justifying the use of the subjunctive (in French) – in contrast to the overprudent approach of most grammarians – is to begin by defining the *deep structure* or, more modestly, the *ideal type* of the subjunctive? It would then remain for the grammarian, in his role as both psychologist and sociologist, to explain to us the respects in which the different historical forms of the subjunctive deviate from this type. The classical grammarians, who were much less preoccupied with sticking to the immediate morphological facts than are contemporary grammarians, came very close to successfully formulating such an ideal type. Thus Arnauld and Lancelot[41] distinguish within the category of *oratio enunciativa* between 'simple affirmations' such as *he loves, he loved* and 'modified' or 'conditioned affirmations' such as *quoiqu'il aimât* (although he loved); they then add "it is from these latter sorts of inflections that grammarians have made their *mood* which is called the *subjunctive*".

Two sorts of considerations prevent us from accepting such a simple schema. The first is that a proposition may be subordinated to another proposition – or rather a propositional expression of a state of affairs may be nominalised so that it functions as an argument within another proposition – without it being the case that this subordinate proposition is any the less true or, let us rather say, without the state of affairs referred to by the name being any the less real. Thus in languages such as French it is often difficult to distinguish the case where

le fait que Pierre soit venu (the fact that Peter has come)

is a positing name, from the case where it is a non-positing name (where there is no implication that Peter has come). In the second case we would say in French

je doute que Pierre soit venu (I doubt whether Peter has come)

whereas we would say

je sais que Pierre est venu (I know that Peter has come).

This leads to occasional differences in the use of the subjunctive depending on whether the sentence is positive or negative and, especially, on whether it is indicative or interrogative:

tu es sûr qu'il est arrivé (you are sure that he has arrived)
tu n'es pas sûr qu'il soit arrivé (you are not sure about whether he has arrived)
es-tu sûr qu'il soit arrivé? (are you sure about whether he has arrived?).

The indicative in the first example signifies that the name formed by the that-clause is a positing name; that is to say the state of affairs that he has arrived is real. Thus we are tempted to analyse this first proposition as a conjunction of the following sort:

Tu es sûr qu'il soit arrivé et il est arrivé (you are sure about whether he has arrived and he has arrived).

– a conjunction for which of course we can find no equivalents in the case of the second and third examples.[42]

In other words, our suggestion is to interpret the indicative in such a that-clause as the result of the joint operation of two rules whose effects cancel each other out:

(1) The rule that the clause designating a state of affairs is subordinate to a *main* clause which itself expresses another state of affairs leads us to express it in the subjunctive.

(2) The rule that if the state of affairs normally expressed by the subjunctive is in addition implicitly affirmed to be a real state of affairs (i.e. to be capable of giving rise to an independent affirmation), this will be marked by the indicative mood.

There is a second consideration that must be added to Arnauld's schema if we want to bring the ideal type and the morphology of the subjunctive more closely together. Usage does not distinguish between the non-positing name that designates a state of affairs in an indicative sentence and such a name in a sentence in the *oratio ordinativa* mood. Consider, again, our examples:

tu n'es pas sûr qu'il soit arrivé (you are not sure about whether he has arrived)

es-tu sûr qu'il soit arrivé? (are you sure about whether he has arrived?).

Now since a non-indicative proposition may easily contain a positing name – and so may contain a genuine implicit assertion, in spite of its non-indicative morphology – there is no reason to be surprised at finding precisely the same interplay between subjunctive and indicative in *oratio ordinativa* that we have just analysed within *oratio enunciativa:*

Sais-tu que Pierre est venu? (Did you know that Peter has come?)

Penses-tu que Pierre soit venu? (Do you think Peter may have come?)

So far we have encountered nothing that is in any way logically questionable. Names, we have seen, have more than an exclusively indicative use, and since a positing name implies an assertion of existence – the existence of an individual, in the case of names of individuals; the reality or obtaining of a state of affairs in the present case – it is convenient to make use of the assertive mood, the indicative, for this assertion of existence. The subjunctive, on the other hand, indicates simply that the name is obtained by nominalising sentences and sentence-parts corresponding to states of affairs and objects that are *capable* of forming the subject matter of assertions, without it being the case that any such assertion would be present.

Usage gives rise to error when the fact that names formed with the subjunctive, which are morphologically identical with propositions that neither are nor contain assertions, leads grammarians to conceive of the subjunctive as some sort of vague, subjective indicative that one can use wherever one wants to express something that is not a simple assertion. Thus it is not uncommon to find the morphological subjunctive being used to express moods such as the optative or the imperative. Yet the order expressed by

Qu'il vienne! (Let him come!)

is not a name, whereas the same expression in

J'ordonne qu'il vienne. (I order him to come.)

is a name. In French, however, the mere fact that in each case

qu'il vienne

is not an assertion suffices to justify grouping them together as far as many people are concerned.

Quotation Marks

In addition to the designation of a state of affairs by means of the expression *that* and the nominalisation of a predicate, we must distinguish a form of nominalisation effected by means of the functor called *quotation marks*. Using the method suggested by Ajdukiwiecz we may begin by giving the form of these three types of nominalisation so that the differences between them are as clear as possible.

(1) The name of a state of affairs introduced by *that* or *the fact that* is a name in just the same respects as a proper name designating a singular object, the only difference being that its content may form the matter either of a statement or of a purely nominal designation. We may therefore represent the name introduced by *that* as

$$\frac{n}{s} \quad s$$

– provided it is admitted that *s* may represent not only an already existent statement but any content that *can* be asserted.

(2) The nominalisation of a predicate can be analysed, as we have seen, as the employment of a nominal functor with a functional argument, since this sort of nominalisation consists in making a name from a verb or predicate, i.e. from a functor. Thus a name such as *green* may be represented as follows:

$$\frac{\dfrac{n}{s}}{n} \quad \frac{s}{n}$$

where $\frac{s}{n}$ represents the one-argument predicate *is green* and $\frac{s}{n}$ the functor that transforms this predicate into a name.

(3) As we shall shortly see, the nominalisation that is effected with the help of quotation marks may in certain cases consist in forming a name from a proposition. This we might represent as follows:

$$\frac{n}{s}\ s$$

But let us look first at the general meaning of quotation marks and, once again, take Husserl as our guide.[43] Quotation marks are the functor which allows us to make a name from any element of discourse whatsoever – whether categorematic or syncategorematic:

'if' is a particle;
'and' is a dependent meaning;
'the earth is round' is a proposition.[44]

"The words certainly occupy the subject-position", writes Husserl, "but their meaning is plainly not the same as that which they have in an ordinary context". What the quotation marks bring about is a "meaning-transformation"; they enable us to take any group of expressions in a sentence and make out of these a name that may occupy any argument place in a categorematic whole.

The phenomenon described by Husserl, as he himself points out, is no other than that described as *suppositio materialis* by the scholastics. This *suppositio,* says Husserl, consists in the fact that "every expression ... can occur as its own name, that is to say it names itself as a grammatical phenomenon". But, Husserl points out, if I say

'the earth is round' is a proposition

it is not the state of affairs that the earth is round that is a proposition, for

202

it is quite clearly not a proposition; what *is* a proposition is the proposition 'the earth is round'; and I cannot say of this that it is a proposition unless I name it. And it is just such a process of nominalisation that the quotation marks indicate.

Husserl is perhaps here *pedagogically* wrong to bring together the nominalisation of a statement and the nominalization of a syncategorematic expression when he continues:

> If we say *'and' is a conjunction* it is not the moment of meaning normally corresponding to the word *'and'* that is put into the position of subject ... In this abnormal meaning 'and' is not really syncategorematic, but a categorematic expression: it names itself as a word.

But the example of *and* differs from that of a complete proposition in that, unlike the latter, it leaves no room for any ambiguity.

The nominalisation effected by quotation marks may be applied to any set of expressions and so it is impossible to specify a unique type of formalization to capture such a functor within the system developed by Ajdukiewicz: the only constant feature in formalizations of this functor is that the numerator of the fraction must be n. As to the denominator, it may be represented either by s or by n, depending on whether the quotation marks flank a sentence or a name, or it may itself be represented by a fraction, if what is enclosed by quotation marks is a functor ($\frac{s}{ss}$ in the case of *and*), or it may also have to be represented in some quite different way.[45]

There are at most two cases in which uses of quotation marks may easily lead to ambiguity. The first case arises when the quotation marks apply to a categorematic proposition and the structure of the quotation-functor risks being confused with the structure of what we have called the functor *that*. It is important to see that the quotation-functor here forms a name that designates a proposition, whereas the name formed by the functor *that* designates not a proposition but a state of affairs – which may also (this is, we would say, a parallel possibility) be expressed by a proposition.

If I say that *Peter's death distresses me* it is not the *proposition 'Peter is dead'* that distresses me, but rather *the fact that Peter is dead;* or, to return to Husserl's example, it is not the proposition 'the rain has set in at last' that will please the farmers, but the fact that this is how things stand, the fact *that the rain has finally set in*. It is then imperative to distinguish between the state of affairs that can be the objective correlate of a 'judgmental intention'[46] as well as the object of a designation, from the proposition expressing this state of affairs, a proposition which – thanks to the existence of quotation-marks – can in its turn be named. Judging about judgments, says Husserl[47]

differs from judging about states of affairs; having a presentation of or naming a judgment is likewise different from having a presentation of, or naming some state of affairs ...

The second case where the use of quotations may easily lead to confusion is the case where what is flanked by quotation marks itself expresses a functor. The difficulty then is to distinguish between the name formed by the quotations and the name formed by the nominalisation of the functor itself. It is sometimes a delicate matter to distinguish between the two, and language, both ordinary language and that of the logicians, all too easily confuses

'is superior' – with superiority;
'if' – with implication;
'and' – with conjunction, etc.

But clearly one ought not to say

'is superior' (or 'if') is transitive,

or

'and' is symmetrical,

but rather that 'is superior' is the expression of the functor marking superiority, that 'if' is the expression of the functor marking implication, that 'and' the expression of the functor marking conjunction, and so on. The fact that one or other of the given functors is transitive or symmetrical does not lessen the absurdity of saying that its expression is itself transitive or symmetrical. *Transitivity* and *symmetry* are properties that we see *a priori* to be such that they can be applied to relations but, as we also see *a priori*, not to expressions – whether the expressions refer to individuals, properties or relations at whatever level.

Finally it may be noted that the use of the quotation-functor does not oblige us to settle the question whether an expression that is named in this way must be understood – to use a traditional distinction that has lost none of its value – as a *logical supposition,* as in the example:

'2 + 2 = 4' is a true proposition,

or as a *linguistic supposition,* as in the example:

'2 + 2 = 4' is made up of five symbols.

In each case the predication concerns the same expression, even if in certain cases one may be obliged to distinguish rigorously between the expression's form and its content. Thus there is nothing to prevent me writing

'2 + 2 = 4' is a true proposition and is made up of five symbols.

The Confusion Between a Proposition, its Name, the State of Affairs it Asserts, and the Name of this State of Affairs

The confusion between a proposition, its name, the state of affairs it asserts, and the name of this state of affairs is one of the major inadequacies of contemporary logic. The failure to recognize the following double distinction often leads people to pass from any one of these four possibilities to any one of the others:

(1) The distinction between any expression and its name;

(2) The distinction between a state of affairs on the one hand and, on the other hand, the proposition stating this state of affairs or the name designating it.

As to the first of these distinctions, it must be admitted that when logicians insist on the difference between an object and its name their remarks begin by being so crude and yet so basic that they take on a comic note. Thus Carnap writes:[48]

If a sentence (in writing) refers to a thing – my writing-table, for instance – then in this sentence a designation of the thing must occupy the position of the subject; one cannot simply place the thing itself, namely the writing-table, upon the paper.

And Tarski,[49] too, warns us that

the fundamental conventions regarding the use of any language require that in any utterance we make about an object it is the name of the object which must be employed and not the object itself.

J. Rosser[50] writes

It is generally agreed about statements that a statement about Smith must contain a name of that thing rather than the thing itself.

In cases such as this we have no difficulty in distinguishing between what designates and what is designated. We do not confuse the two meanings of the expression 'Paris' – to use Carnap's example[51] – in:

Paris is a town

and

'Paris' is bi-syllabic

in spite of the identity of sound. Here the first occurrence of the sound designates a town and forms the name of a town; the second occurrence designates a name and forms the name of a name.

But when what is designated is itself a linguistic expression, that is, when we can no longer rely on the existential status of the object designated to distinguish it from what designates it, then the risk of confusion is indeed great. The name formed by *Paris* pronounced out loud or written on paper is easily distinguished from the town of stone and earth; but it is just this sort of obvious criterion that is lacking when I want to distinguish between a word (or a group of words) and its name. Where the expression to be named is syncategorematic I will probably have no difficulty in distinguishing between its name, which as a name is of course categorematic, and the expression itself. Everyone can see the difference between the two meanings of the same sound 'and' in the two expressions:

Peter and Jack

and

the conjunction 'and'.

On the other hand, when the expression designated is itself a categorematic expression then it does indeed become difficult to

206

distinguish between, for example, some proposition p and the name of this proposition 'p', and to avoid confusion of names with names of names. For in such cases no criterion such as that provided by the syncategoreme-categoreme opposition is available.

Now confusions of this sort are not merely an accidental feature of various linguistic systems. They have their basis, as Husserl has shown,[52] in a possibility written into the very form of all expression, the possibility that "the verbal expression functions with modified meaning as a 'proper name' of its original meaning". This modification, "having *a priori* universality, conditions a large class of equivocations in *general grammar*", equivocations which, since they are bound up with modifications of the verbal act of meaning "extend far beyond the peculiarities of individual languages".

'Paris' is the name of Paris;
"The weather is fine" is the name of the proposition 'the weather is fine'.

It should also be noted that if, thanks to quotation marks, our languages have, at least in their written form, the means of distinguishing between the name of a name and a name, as well as between a proposition and its name, this way of drawing these distinctions disappears at the level of spoken language: quotation marks, at least in Indo-European languages, cannot be pronounced. This indicates that this somewhat refined semantic distinction evolved at a later date and only in the context of the more elaborated form of language – the written form.

At the beginning of his *Grundgesetze der Arithmetik*[53] Frege points out that his reader will be astonished by the frequent use he makes of quotation marks but that he wants thereby to distinguish the cases where he speaks of the sign itself from those cases where he speaks of its meaning. One may, he continues, criticize this usage as pedantic, but if one starts neglecting to express these distinctions in order not to burden the sense of what one says with what is self-evident, it is all too easy to lose one's way once one ceases to be aware of the initial, deliberately accepted[54] imprecision in the course of an argument. But logicians and mathematicians do not always have Frege's scruples. They observe that "for the greater part of logic one can be rather careless about the use of quotation marks without getting into any difficulty"[55] – a fact that explains the frequency with which quotation marks are neglected and the general tolerance of this.[56]

We need spend little time on the distinction between a state of affairs and the proposition stating it, as we shall be obliged to go into the matter in some detail in the next chapter. It may be enough to point out here that this distinction is perhaps even more difficult to make than the distinction we have just examined and for an equally fundamental reason. For what Tarski expresses by saying:[57]

the sentence 'snow is white' is true
if and only if snow is white

is that one can always establish an equivalence between the reality of a state of affairs and the sentence stating this state of affairs. This is, as we shall see, a quite general characteristic of the predicates *is, is not, is true, is false* – which Husserl[58] suggested calling 'modifying predicates' and which he opposed to 'determining predicates'. The latter, like most familiar verbs, simply express 'properties of the apparent subjects'. In the case of the four modifying predicates, however, it is not enough to say that the first two take as a subject a name designating a state of affairs, the last two a name designating a proposition, sentence or statement. Rather, these predicates stand in a double relation to one another, such that an equivalence can be formed between the proposition formed by *is* (or by *is not*) and the name of the state of affairs on the one hand, and, on the other hand, between the proposition formed by *is true* (or by *is false*) and the name of the proposition stating this same state of affairs. This equivalence is indeed the source of all confusion in this area.

Notes

[1] The traditional opposition between *noms substantifs* and *noms adjectifs* (between substantive and adjectival nouns or names) has two very different but equally interesting senses, which are sometimes unfortunately mixed up with one another and marked by the same expressions.

(a) The substantive nouns designate what Aristotelian philosophy regarded as the first substances, i.e. individuals; the adjectival nouns stand for accidents or, as we would say today, properties and relations that only exist because these individuals exist. Although closely bound up with its Aristotelian origins, this distinction has found almost universal acceptance today, for it corresponds to the modern distinction between arguments and predicates.

(b) The substantive nouns correspond to categorematic nominal expressions, the adjectival nouns correspond to nominal syncategorematic expressions. This is the distinction to be met with in our text.

These two possible senses of the opposition between substantive and adjectival names are distinguished by Lancelot and Arnauld (2nd part, ch.2, pp.69f) from whom we have quoted freely above. Nevertheless it is only today that the developments due to the theory of types make it possible properly to grasp the difference between the two senses. Let us consider the example from *The Port-Royal Grammar* of the word 'red'. The expression may seem to be an adjectival name in both senses we have distinguished and this is indeed the source of the confusion of the two distinctions. Nowadays, however, it has become much easier to distinguish, without any risk of confusion, between on the one hand

– 'this red rose', the name of an individual and 'red' or 'the colour red', the name of that quality which belongs to this individual; and on the other hand

– 'this red rose', which is a categorematic term, and the syncategorematic term 'red'.

The quite remarkable analysis of *The Port-Royal Grammar* is the best that could be done before Frege and Russell.

2 Husserl, *Logical Investigations*, V, §34, Eng. trans. p.625.

3 Whitehead and Russell, *Principia Mathematica*, vol.I, pp.30ff.

4 We take this example from Bolzano, whose remarkable analyses of the subject we are dealing with here paved the way for the analyses of Husserl and Russell. Cf. Bolzano, esp. §70, "Reale und imaginäre Vorstellungen". Bolzano's analyses are themselves not without connection with certain analyses of Leibniz, in particular Book II of the *Nouveaux Essais*.

5 Here a delicate terminological problem presents itself. How should a name that implies a false assertion be described? To call it a 'false name' ('nom faux') would conflict with the tradition that reserves the terms 'true' and 'false' for propositions. Nor can one say that it is a sham name (faux nom), for it is a genuine name (ein echter, richtiger Name). Bolzano, discussing a related point (§70), p.94) suggests the German term 'imaginär' ('imaginary') because the object designated does not exist outside our representation of it, although his suggestion is heavily qualified. But in this passage Bolzano deals only with examples such as 'the regular pentahedron', which certainly correspond to no object. He does not consider expressions such as 'the square root of sixteen' which it would be difficult to describe as *imaginary*. Thus, for want of a better alternative, we shall suggest the term 'erroneous' (erroné).

6 Husserl, *Logical Investigations*, V, §34, Eng. trans. pp.624–27.

7 Ibid., Eng. trans. p.625.

8 It would serve no purpose to introduce the symbols used in logic to say the same thing.

9 Husserl, *Logical Investigations*, V, §34, Eng. trans. p.626.

10 Some writers in English use 'noun' for non-positing and 'name' for positing nominal terms. Thus E. Luschei writes: "I call *name* only any constant that names at least one individual". (1962, p.6.) The names defined in this way are then split up into *unshared names* (what we have called *proper names*) and *shared names* (what we have called *positing common names*).

11 It should nevertheless be noted that a writer as important as Leśniewski does not share at all this tendency which we have perhaps somewhat over-hastily described as 'contemporary'.

12 It is obvious that this precision or exactness is unconnected with the fact that the name here is singular: for if I say 'I met some people', the people I mean, although there are several of them, are no less determinate than the objects in our example in the text.

13 Although nothing prevents us from replacing the indefinite name 'a human being' in our text by a perfectly definite name, for example by a proper name.

14 This is especially true of Leśniewski; cf. Luschei, ibid., p.11. As well as the symbol for a proper name Id[B] and for a definite positing name Kl[b] we are introduced to an indefinite positing name cl[b] the object of which is an '(individual) collection of (at least one individual which is) b; (individual) collection of (one or more individuals which are) b; (collective) composite (resp. aggregate, set, manifold) of (one or more) b'.

15 It is more exact, in the case of the participle, to speak of 'nominalisation of the proposition'

209

rather than 'nominalisation of the verb'; for it is a complete proposition and not the predicate expressed by the verb that is nominalised in this way. This is true even if the verb has no complement, i.e. if the function expressed by the verb only has one argument. In 'a weeping man' it is not 'to weep' but 'he weeps' that is nominalised by the participle.

16 Arnauld and Lancelot, 2nd part, ch.9, p.99.

17 Bolzano, §58, p.74. The reference to Bolzano here involves a slight misrepresentation of his ideas. For Bolzano is not exactly thinking of *name* and *proposition* but of their correlates, which he calls respectively *Vorstellung* and *Satz*. What is remarkable in Bolzano is that on the basis of his analysis of 'who' one can see him very largely anticipating the generalized notion of *functor* (see esp. pp.72–74). On the other hand he seems not yet to see that from the same term 'who' one can obtain different functors.

18 Pp. 80–81.

19 Pp. 82–83.

20 Husserl, *Logical Investigations*, V, §35, Eng. trans. p.628.

21 Arnauld and Lancelot, 2nd part, ch.9. The question is also taken up in *La logique ou l'art de penser* (2nd part, ch.1, p.103) with only slightly different examples: 'God, *who is good*', 'the world, *which is visible*'.

22 Husserl, *Logical Investigations*, IV, §11, Eng. trans. pp.515f. [Translation slightly modified. By 'dependent moment' here and elsewhere Husserl means an individual property or relation – a 'particularized property' – that is dependent on something else. – Tr.]

23 It is of little importance how 'superior' is to be understood; with respect to intelligence, strength, moral value...

24 Serrus, part 3, ch.2, p.410. Thus not only is there no cause for surprise about what is supposed to be the *confusion* of adjective with name, but it is not possible to go on to say, as does Serrus, that 'The only marked difference is between these and the verb.' For in fact here adjective and verb share the same fate: both can be nominalised.

25 We may wonder whether, in two of the examples mentioned in the text:

Superiority is transitive

and

Implication is transitive,

the transitivity is in each case of the same sort.

In order to appreciate the full scope of the question let us add a third example: one may say of two predicates of individuals such as *is triangular* and *is trilateral* that they are equivalent. This relation of equivalence is itself a second-order binary predicate, since its arguments correspond to first-order predicates. Now we may say of this equivalence relation that it, too, is transitive. But this transitivity itself refers to a monadic third-order predicate, since it has a second-order argument.

On the other hand, when we talked of the transitivity of superiority, the predicate we wanted to designate was a second-order predicate, since its argument was only a first-order argument.

In short, the term *transitivity* may cover two different names according to whether we are talking about the transitivity of the superiority of one individual to another individual or the transitivity of the equivalence of two predicates that have individuals as their arguments.

The case of the transitivity of implication differs from both of the preceding cases since the arguments of an implication are names neither of individuals nor of predicates but of propositions. The two sorts of transitivity we have just compared had in common at least the fact that transitivity there applied to propositional functors with nominal arguments (to what are normally called *predicators*), whereas the *transitivity of implication* involves a

210

propositional functor with arguments that are themselves propositional, in other words what is normally called a connective.

Thus for the three uses of 'transitive' in our examples we have found three different concepts. We could only succeed in giving a definition of *transitivity* that would be capable of capturing these three uses, such as

the functor X with two arguments is transitive iff for any *a*, *b*, and *c*, if X*ab* and X*bc* then X*ac*,

if we allow that X is any arbitrary binary functor and *a*, *b*, and *c* are any arguments whatsoever (and it is not necessary to specify the level or sort of the arguments provided they are all of the same sort and level).

[26] We do sometimes say this, but then, whether we realize it or not, what we have is a case of metonymy based on a failure to recognize the levels of the predicate.

[27] We employ the term 'the fact that...' only hesitantly since it has the disadvantage that it implies the truth of the clause with which it combines, whereas the functor *that* is normally followed by clauses where this implication does not hold: *I fear that..., I doubt that..., I deny that...*, etc.

[28] P. 177.

[29] Husserl, *Logical Investigations*, V, §36, Eng. trans., pp.631–35.

[30] Here 'things' should almost certainly be understood to mean 'individuals'.

[31] Although here we do really have a fact (the rain has set in) this existence-positing character is not to be found in every case.

[32] *The Port-Royal Logic* (2nd part, ch.1, pp.103f.) contains a remarkable analysis of what we have called the functor *that*, although it is expressed in language that is less adroit than that of Husserl.

[33] Ruwet, *Introduction to Generative Grammar*, ch.4, p.172.

[34] This example is taken from Luschei, *The Logical Systems of Leśniewski*, ch.1, p.8.

[35] This example is taken from Chomsky, *Syntactic Structures*, 5, p.41.

[36] If, for example, we admit that this natural camouflage permits it to approach its prey or escape its enemies.

[37] Limits that do not apply to Latin because of its infinitive proposition.

[38] N. Ruwet, who quotes this text (*Introduction*, ch.4, p.187), adds in brackets after 'of a verb phrase': 'Chomsky would say "of a sentence"'. For it is important, as we have seen, to distinguish clearly between a nominalisation of a statement and a nominalisation of the verb or predicate.

[39] 3rd edition, 1950.

[40] Quoted by R. Donzé, 2nd part, ch.3, p.113.

[41] Arnauld and Lancelot, 2nd part, ch.16, p.136. It seems that the honour of having drawn this distinction so clearly must go to Arnauld, since Lancelot, in his *Nouvelle méthode pour apprendre facilement et en peu de temps la langue espagnole* did not locate this distinction within the *oratio enunciativa* but collected within the subjunctive all the "tenses which do not affirm the thing simply and directly, as do the Indicatives, but by modification or dependence: either because they express some condition, some possibility, some desire or something of this sort" (quoted by Donzé, ibid., p.116). This definition of Lancelot's is, at first glance, much closer to the morphological subjunctive than Arnauld's definition. But it turns out to be unable to provide a satisfying basis, of the kind that is provided by Arnauld's definition, for the logician who wants to disentangle the fundamental reasons for the complexity of usage.

[42] All the same, it would be wrong to represent French grammar as more 'logical' than it is. Not only does it allow one to say in certain cases:

Tu n'es pas sûr qu'il est arrivé
Es-tu sûr qu'il est arrivé?

but it even disallows:

Tu crois qu'il soit arrivé

even though the verb *croire* takes a non-positing (non-factive) complement and it would be
more normal to construe it in the same way as *douter* ('je doute qu'il soit arrivé).

43 Husserl, *Logical Investigations*, IV, §11, Eng. trans. pp.513–16. Husserl should not be
regarded as a pioneer in the study of quotation marks. What he has to say on this subject was
largely anticipated by Frege and, well before Frege, by Bolzano. It was Frege and Bolzano
who paved the way. (Cf. Bolzano, §58, p.89).

44 These are Husserl's own examples.

45 There are even cases where the denominator cannot be formalized; for example, when I
speak about the symbol '∞' specifying neither its meaning nor the semantic category of the
term it symbolizes, or when I speak about the phoneme 'a' or the cabbalistic word
'abracadabra'.

46 Husserl, *Logical Investigations*, V, §36, Eng. trans. p.633.

47 Ibid., V, §33, Eng. trans. p.623.

48 Carnap, *Logical Syntax*, IV, p.154.

49 "The Semantic Conception of Truth and the Foundations of Semantics", p.16. The
quotation from Tarski presents only one problem: the term 'convention'; is the fact that
these conventions are so fundamental not due to their being something quite different from
conventions?

50 *Logic for Mathematicians*, 1953, ch.3, p.50.

51 Carnap, *Logical Syntax*, IV, p.153.

52 Husserl, *Logical Investigations*, IV, §11, Eng. trans. p.515.

53 Introduction (Olms edition, p.4).

54 The confusion is increased by the fact that it is not enough to distinguish an expression from
its name. One must also distinguish between an expression as a single historical occurrence
("as a single spatio-temporally determined thing", writes Carnap, ibid., p.154) and the
expression as a form that keeps its identity through the different occasions on which it may
be expressed. To take Carnap's example, the Lord's Prayer refers us to an expression in this
second sense; here the prayer I have in mind is that taught by Jesus, which I consider
independently of its millions of repetitions. If I mention the Lord's Prayer that Jack
repeated yesterday, then the term is being used in the first of the two senses. Carnap
(loc.cit.) sets out a list of the different possible designations of such expressions.

55 Rosser, *Logic for Mathematicians*, ch.3, p.51.

56 We too stand in great need of just such forbearance in the present work.

57 "The Semantic Conception of Truth", p.15.

58 Husserl, *Logical Investigations*, IV, §11, Eng. trans. p.514f.

Chapter Eight
Negation and Conjunction

Coordination and Subordination

We shall concentrate on interpropositional conjunctions, in spite of the fact that what is called *coordination* is a variety of conjunction in which not only may two propositions be connected but also, equally often, two similar propositional parts. It is well known that even conjunctions which do not appear to conjoin propositions can be shown to function as interpropositional conjunctions. If I say that

Molière was born and died in Paris

the conjunction connects the two verbs simply in order to avoid repetition of the other elements in the proposition. It is an abbreviated way of saying

Molière was born in Paris and Molière died in Paris.

Similarly, that variety of conjunction which forms a new class from two classes and which is to be found both in ordinary language *(and, or)* and in Boolean algebra (intersection, union), can also be reduced to an interpropositional conjunction, once it is admitted that class-membership is merely the extensional counterpart of what, in intensional terms, is the possession of a predicate. If Peter belongs to the class formed by the intersection of the class of stupid individuals and the class of naughty individuals, if, in other words, he is *stupid-and-naughty,* I may equally well say:

Peter is stupid and Peter is naughty.

The aim of our reduction is not to deny the grammatical interest of non-propositional conjunctions. The logician is, as we have already pointed out, occasionally justified in adopting a reductionist attitude, for his main concern is to set out a system as economically as possible. Such an attitude would be much more difficult to justify in the case of a system whose main purpose is communication. In such a system all abbreviations are welcome, even when these make it necessary to lengthen the system's vocabulary.

In the same way, we shall quickly pass over the traditional grammatical distinction between two sorts of conjunction, *subordination* and *coordination*. From the point of view of logical grammar this distinction is extremely fragile. It is tempting to claim that any genuine conjunction can be expressed either as a coordination or as a subordination. It makes little difference whether I say

p although q

or

q; however p.

The difference between the two is purely psychological. In the first case I emphasize the relation between the two propositions; in the second case the two propositions themselves.

But it would be wrong to forget those cases where there are not two possible versions of the same conjunction, in particular those conjunctions which the *calculus of propositions* has, over the last 100 years, shown us how to analyse. It is worth bearing in mind that a logician who, for pedagogical purposes, tries to find equivalents of the interpropositional conjunctions in ordinary language sometimes finds examples of coordination such as *and, or,* and sometimes examples of subordination, such as *if.* If necessary it would be possible to create a conjunction or a conjunctive locution which would express *and* and *or* by subordination. For do we not occasionally say, admittedly with a certain lack of precision,

p en même temps que q (p at the same time as q)[1]

instead of

p and q.

It would not, on the other hand, be by any means easy to form a coordinative conjunction equivalent to *if* which would simply follow the order of temporal succession:

p; * q.

In

if p, then q

p does not figure as a claim I can assert; for it is possible that my complex

214

proposition is true even though *p* itself is not true.

In order to obtain subordinative conjunction of the sort required there are only three possible solutions. Two of these can be observed at work in the conjunction *or*, which in this respect completely resembles the conjunction *if*, for it is as impossible to assert *p* in

p or *q*

as it was before in *if p then q*. In *if* and *or* the two propositions are *subordinated* to one another. The three solutions are:

(1) To split the conjunction into two parts, so that each conjoined proposition and not only the first is preceded by a sign. Thus one often says in French:

ou bien *p*, ou bien *q* (either *p*, or *q*).

The only difference between *if* and *or* would then be that since *if* is not symmetrical it would require two different symbols whereas one symbol suffices for *ou* (*or*). The same solution is usual in Indo-European languages for connectives such as '*ni... ni...*', ('*neither... nor...*'). This symmetry to be found at the level of expression in French is not present in certain languages. Thus in the English *either... or...* and *neither ... nor* and in the German *entweder... oder...* and *weder... noch* we have a dissymmetry at the level of expression which would really only be justified if the concepts were not symmetrical. As far as pure grammar is concerned the Latin *nec... nec...* seems the more satisfactory option, unless we interpret the apparently dissymmetrical forms of words in German and English as a way of putting the symbol for the connective at the head of the two propositions and the second term as a way of simply marking the separation between the two propositions.

(2) To prohibit any pause or punctuation between '*p*' and '** q*', so that it is impossible for the listener first to hear *p* or the reader first to read '*p*' and only then '**q*'. This is the solution sometimes accepted for

p or *q*

an expression which is only intelligible if I do not have time to assert *p* before perceiving *or q*.

(3) To place the symbol which expresses the connective not before the second proposition but before the first proposition. This is the way the symbolism suggested by Łukasiewicz for the *propositional calculus* works.

These three solutions to the problem of expressing *if...* are all to be found in English and French. Thus one can say

(1) If *p*, then *q*
(2) *q* if *p* (this time without any pause)
(3) if *p*, *q*.

It then becomes difficult to see why *if* is supposed to mark subordination whilst *or* marks coordination. One sometimes reads in grammars that conjunctions expressing coordination differ from those expressing subordination in that they connect terms 'of the same sort'. This should not of course be taken to imply symmetry. It seems likely that it is due to the symmetry of *or* that the two propositions in *p or q* seem to be of the same sort; and it is because *if* is not symmetrical that *p* and *q* in *p if q* do not appear to us to be of the same sort. But there are conjunctions expressing coordination which are not at all symmetrical (*because, therefore*) and conjunctions (or conjunctive locutions) expressing subordination which are (*when, just as*).[2]

Grammarians also had another logical criterion for distinguishing coordination and subordination, although they have made as little use of it as they have of the first criterion, at least as little systematic use. For it is possible to regard two propositions as coordinated if each remains true independently of its connection with the other. On this interpretation *and* would be the conjunction *par excellence* for

p and q implies *p*

and

p and q implies *q*.

Subordinate propositions would then be complex propositions which assert only the subordination of their parts but do not allow any separate assertion of either of the parts, as with

if *p*, then *q*.

Or would then have to be grouped together with the conjunctions of subordination and *because* with conjunctions of coordination since

p because *q*

seems to imply the assertion of *p* and the assertion of *q*.

216

There has been, then, no lack of criteria available with the help of which the distinction between coordination and subordination could have been put on a firm logical footing. But in the languages we are familiar with these criteria have not been made use of. The distinction has instead been given a psychological basis; there is subordination when, for one reason or another, the attention required by one proposition differs from that required by the proposition with which it is connected. In

p because *q*

p is the centre of attention and requires *q* as its justification. *Just as* is felt to mark subordination, in spite of the fact that it is symmetrical, because one of the propositions it conjoins is related unilaterally to the other; it is the psychological dissymmetry which, overriding the logical symmetry, justifies the subordination. It is probable that this psychological dissymmetry is in some way connected with an awareness of the logical criteria we have mentioned, namely

(1) symmetry
(2) truth of the constituent propositions.

But although these criteria have a role here, they are not invoked *as* criteria in order to establish a disjunction.

The interplay of the conjunctions of coordination and subordination serves as a way of taking into account the limits of our attention. Coordinations endow a message with what Claudel, in order to describe the breaks in his own verse, called 'intelligible mouthfuls'. They allow the attention to halt for a pause at the point where two sentences connect in order better to grasp the meaning they have as a whole without neglecting the connection between them. The conjunctions of subordination ensure that the sentence is a sentence, for they guarantee within the total proposition the connection between the constituent propositions. Too exclusive a recourse to coordination would involve a segmentation that would tire the attention; subordination alone would rapidly overwhelm the attention.

We shall now present at least provisionally, as a merely utopian conception, a solution to the problem presented by the opposition of coordination and subordination. The distinction between the two can be founded on the basis of a logical criterion, one of the two mentioned. We would then have a case of a coordinative conjunction if and only if the

217

complex proposition implied the truth of each of its 'constituent propositions'. Only conjunctions which permit this detachment would involve coordination. There are in fact three families of conjunctions which allow this detachment:

(1) *And,* as well as other conjunctions with the same logical content but which involve a different psychological emphasis. In particular *but,* and the conjunction *now,* (French *or*) uses of which imply the assertion of the two propositions they coordinate.

(2) *Therefore* as well as its equivalents such as *hence, thus.* If we say

p therefore *q*

this means

(a) *p;*
(b) if *p* then *q;*
(c) the two previous propositions allow me to assert *q.*

Therefore is an elliptical equivalent of what logicians call the *rule of detachment.* Thus

p therefore *q*

implies the truth of each of the two connected propositions. This can also be expressed as:

p therefore q implies p and q

and allows us to consider *therefore* as a particular case of *and.*

(3) *Because* and its equivalents (e.g. *en effet*). If we say *p because q* this means

(a) if *q* then *p;*
(b) *q;*
(c) the two previous propositions allow me to assert *p.*

p because q is therefore another elliptical equivalent of the *rule of detachment.* It, too, can be considered a particular case of *and* since it, too, implies *p and q.*

In our utopian formulation all conjunctions other than *and* and analogous terms on the one hand, and *therefore* and *because* on the other hand, would have the form of subordinations whether or not they were

218

symmetrical. Thus the moments at which our attention would be invited to pause would correspond only to those moments at which any slackening in our attention would not prevent the parts of the relevant proposition from having a sense; for even if the relation expressed by *and, therefore* or *because* ceases to fall within the span of my attention the mere succession of *p, q* would still be significant as a series of assertions. The least fragile system of discourse would indeed have slackenings of attention coincide precisely with the privileged points at which interruptions in what is being said are made possible by the presence of connections which authorize logical detachment.

It has been known for a long time that it is possible to reduce every proposition of the calculus of propositions to a conjunctive normal form. Is this not a guarantee that the segmentation of discourse into elements connected by *and,* or by particular forms of *and,* can always be easily carried out? But then the propositional calculus is not rich enough to capture with any sort of completeness the conjunctions of ordinary language and, strictly speaking, one has no right to apply conclusions derived from it to the latter. Yet not only does what we call the propositional calculus form at the very least the rough framework for ordinary language, it is also interesting to note that it too lends itself naturally to just those interruptions and pauses whose logico-psychological convenience has just been pointed out – and so, at the very least, it cannot be said to obstruct these.

We can now begin to see that our utopian considerations do in fact correspond in outline to the way things really are. It is quite true that the use of the conditional which Indo-European languages make available to us allows us to prolong – *artificially,* we shall say – the development of an implication and ignore or pass over even the most marked interruptions; with the appropriate verbal form indicating to the interlocutor that what is being said falls within the scope of the assumption. But if we ignore this often very felicitous technique, what remains is just ordinary language as described in our utopian formulation. In ordinary language the really marked interruptions correspond to those *ands, therefores* and *becauses* which, especially in the case of *and,* we very often do not express at all. The *ifs* and the *ors,* and all genuine subordinations in just the sense in which these have been defined above, are the very substance of all our paragraphs and expositions.

Negation and the Conjunctions
Applied to States of Affairs and Propositions

The study of conjunctions took a major step forward with the elaboration of the calculus of propositions. Nevertheless, the calculus of propositions has been responsible for what are perhaps new misunderstandings about conjunctions which are not easily removed. These difficulties are of two main sorts.

(1) The great merit of the calculus of propositions is that it provides a system of conjunctions (if we take the word 'system' in the broad sense made necessary by Scheffer's discovery that this system can be reduced to one term)[3] which provides an adequate first step in a foundation for mathematics. But this adequacy does not extend to other sorts of reasoning and it seems that even within the body of mathematics the use of the calculus of propositions involves certain simplifications and over-simplifications, although it is possible to explain why these do not involve any disturbing logical consequences.

(2) As its name suggests, the calculus of propositions has been implicated from the very beginning in a misunderstanding which at least some of its originators do not seem to have noticed and which it is difficult (and indeed pointless) to keep in mind when using the calculus, even when one is aware of the possibility of misunderstanding.

For what does the word 'proposition' in 'calculus of propositions' mean? Does it designate simply the theorems of the calculus? This would have the curious consequence that every logico-mathematical theorem established on the basis of nothing more than a calculus would have to be regarded as having the form of a proposition. In fact the expression 'calculus of propositions' can designate only the set of rules which permit certain combinations of propositions, combinations which together with variables for *elementary* or *atomic* propositions and connectives yield the (tautological) forms of *compound* propositions. But when we write

Cpq, that is: if p then q

Apq, that is: p or q

or

Kpq, that is: p and q

do the terms 'p' and 'q' really represent propositions or are they in fact names designating *states of affairs*, states of affairs which could doubtless be expressed by independent propositions provided we decide to ignore the conjunctions which link them here?

This latter interpretation is the one suggested by Husserl. He mentions the case where in the antecedent of some hypothetical or causal proposition we say *'if* or *since* S is *p'*, and the case of the second or subsequent member of a disjunction 'or S is *p'*, and he points out that

in each case the state of affairs – *not* the *judgment* – is our object in a different sense, and is accordingly presented in the light of modified meanings, from what it is for the judgment whose full objective correlate it is.[4]

Thus what logicians sometimes call a 'constituent proposition', represented by the letters *p, q* or *r,* is improperly so called. It is not a proposition at all but

objective in much the same sense as a thing caught in a single-rayed act of perception, imagination or representation – although a state of affairs is of course no thing, and cannot be perceived, imagined or represented in the stricter, narrower sense of these words.

May the propositional calculus not mask the fact that, to quote Husserl again:[5] between terms which function as names of states of affairs on the one hand, and "the propositions corresponding to the same states of affairs" on the other hand, "there is, from the point of view of their intentional essence, a difference which is governed by the ideal relations of laws"? Thus if I say that there is at the same time both the state of affairs *p* and the state of affairs *q,*[6]
or that

it is the case both that *p* and that *q*

or that

the fact *p* and the fact *q* are both real,

then the intentional direction of my judgment is quite different from the case where I would say that

'*p*' is true and '*q*' is true

or that

it is true both that *p* and that *q*

or

the proposition p and the proposition q are both true.

In both series the functor establishes in every case a conjunction of terms, is a functor with two arguments. Now if we follow Husserl's interpretation and terminology we will be led to say that a functor cannot admit propositions as arguments but only names. And in each of the cases we have distinguished we find two names. But in the first series of formulations the names designate what we have called states of affairs, whereas in the second series they express propositions. If names of objects are represented by capital letters, propositions by lower-case letters, and the names of linguistic expressions by quotation marks flanking the corresponding expressions, and if we represent 'and' by a K preceding the two conjoined terms, then we can symbolize the first series of propositions by

K P Q

and the second by

K "p" "q"

with K expressing the co-existence of two states of affairs in the first case, and the conjunction of two true propositions in the second case.

Husserl was not chiefly concerned with the calculus of propositions for, as the quotations above indicate, he mentions besides disjunctive and hypothetical propositions also the case of causal propositions. What he has to say nevertheless applies to the calculus of propositions as a special case. The distinction we have just made "does not of course mean that the corresponding acts are totally foreign to one another". On the contrary, Husserl continues,[7]

the matter of the proposition is partially identical to that of the nominal act, it is the same state of affairs which is intended. Hence the great similarity between the acts is not accidental but founded on the meanings involved.

What Husserl says about the conjunction *because*[8] can be extended, *mutatis mutandis,* to any connective belonging to the calculus of propositions: if I say "'because S is p', the *because* may refer us to or point back to a judgment to the effect that S is p; but in the assertion of the causal proposition itself this judgment is not carried out; S is not *said* to be *p*". Rather the representation of the *fact that* S is *p*, founds the thesis of the consequent. This thesis then, implies, not only that one can assert S is *p* but also that S is *p* even though the proposition itself is not asserted.

Let us now try to make clearer the 'great similarity' Husserl speaks of between the proposition expressing a state of affairs and expressions used to designate the state of affairs. This similarity can be defined as follows: if the nominal act designates a state of affaires P such that

P is real

then and only then can I say, using "*p*" as the name of the proposition which expresses this fact, that

"*p*" is true.

In other words, the two propositions are equivalent; and it is this which explains the classical confusion of the assertion that 'the being of the state of affairs conditions the being of another state of affairs'[9] with the assertion that the antecedent proposition (that which asserts the obtaining of one state of affairs) conditions the proposition which is its consequence.

Thus the calculus of propositions, at least in many of its presentations, is dangerously ambiguous. Only with difficulty can one distinguish between the propositions

it is raining and '*it is raining' is true*

or between the propositions

it is not raining and '*it is raining' is not true*.

All the functors made use of in the propositional calculus can have two senses – and two senses which are such that in many cases it is important to be able to pass from one to the other. Is negation, for example, negation of the reality of a fact or negation of the truth of a proposition? 'Does it matter'? someone is likely to wonder vaguely. For if the move from the one to the other is so easy, since the two terms are, though not identical, certainly equivalent, then the risk of error is, at least in most restricted uses of the calculus of propositions, strictly zero.

Is there any *need,* that is to say, to distinguish between a calculus of propositions and what, for want of a better word, we must call a calculus of names of states of affairs,[10] a calculus whose functors would have truth-tables equivalent to those made use of in the propositional calculus with

223

one exception: in all columns except the last (right-most column), the 'T' of the truth-tables for the propositional calculus would be replaced by 'R' (for 'real') and each 'F' by 'I' (for 'irreal'). The table for negation then becomes:

P	Not P
R	F
I	T

Here P is the name not of a proposition but of a state of affairs, whilst Not P expresses a proposition which consists in the negation of a state of affairs and which might be expressed as

There is no P.

In other words, negation here is not what it is in the propositional calculus, a propositional functor with a propositional argument, but rather a propositional functor which takes a nominal argument. Similarly, the table for conjunction would be

P	Q	K P Q
R	R	T
R	I	F
I	R	F
I	I	F

The binary connectives of this calculus of names of states of affairs are not propositional functors with two propositional arguments but propositional functors taking two nominal arguments, each of which designates states of affairs.[11]

It is as just such a calculus of names of states of affairs and not as a calculus of propositions that Frege conceived of his *Begriffsschrift*. In order to avoid the confusion of state of affairs and corresponding judgment he introduced the subtle notation which has since been neglected by his successors.

Frege, of course, represents any judgment whatsoever as

$$\vdash\!\!\!-\!\!\!-\ A$$

in which both the vertical and the horizontal strokes have a precise function.[12]

224

(1) The horizontal stroke indicates the content of the judgment. This Frege suggests reading as *the fact or circumstance that (der Umstand, daß)*. Hence

———— A

is not yet a judgment but a "mere combination of ideas" (*Vorstellungen*) which is such that "the author is not expressing his recognition or non-recognition of its truth". That the latter can be preceded by the horizontal stroke in this way is due to the fact that what A represents *can* be the object of a judgment. Frege expresses this by saying that this content is *beurteilbar*. Not every representation is *beurteilbar;* the representation (*Vorstellung*) of a house, to use Frege's own example, is not *beurteilbar*. The fact that there is a house – which is absolutely distinct from the representation of a house – is, however, *beurteilbar*. We can then say that the horizontal stroke applies only to the designation of those quite special objects which are states of affairs.

(2) The vertical stroke is what transforms the simple designation of a state of affairs into a judgment asserting this state of affairs; it captures the moment of assertive force. Frege calls it the judgment-stroke (*Urteilsstrich*) and the horizontal stroke he calls the content stroke. Thus Frege gives as an example of an object that is *beurteilbar* the fact of mutual attraction between the poles of a magnet to which there corresponds the possible judgment:

The poles of the magnet attract one another.

Frege also expresses the same idea in a different way. Imagine, he says, a language which, instead of expressing events with the help of propositions, names them using names which then become subjects of the one single predicate: 'is a fact'. Thus instead of saying *Archimedes perished during the siege of Syracuse* one could say *The death of Archimedes during the siege of Syracuse is a fact*. "Such a language", Frege concludes, "is our *Begriffsschrift* and the sign|——— is its common predicate for all judgments".

Frege is careful to present each of the functors he introduces as what, in our terminology, we would call functors with nominal arguments. Negation attaches not to the proposition but to the content: "Es haftet also die Verneinung am Inhalte." It must be considered as "a mark of that which is *beurteilbar*".[13] The symbol of negation expresses "the fact that the content does not obtain [literally: *occur*]".[14]

Let us look at the way Frege introduces the binary connective which is so fundamental in his system, that of implication.

If A and B stand for contents which are *beurteilbar,* there are the following four possibilities:
1. A is asserted and B is asserted.
2. A is asserted and B is denied.
3. A is denied and B is asserted.
4. A is denied and B is denied.

therefore signifies the judgment that the third possibility does not obtain, but one of the three other possibilities does obtain.[15]

What exactly does this mean? Certainly not that one of these possibilities is realized. *B implies A* means that
(1) Either it is possible to assert A and to assert B.
(2) Or it is possible to assert A and to deny B.
(3) Or it is possible to deny A and to deny B.
It does not mean that
(1) Either A is asserted and B is asserted.
(2) Or A is asserted and B is denied.
(3) Or A is denied and B is denied.
Recent editions of the *Begriffsschrift* contain Husserl's notes on his copy of the work. Husserl dispels the ambiguity we have been looking at as follows:

Let us take the judgment 'if B is, then A is'. We have here four possibilities:

B is not
— then A can be
— then A cannot be

B is
— then only A can be
— but A cannot not be

This formulation is to be preferred to Frege's own, and is closer to what Frege actually thinks. For the primitive terms of the *Begriffsschrift* are not true or false propositions but names of states of affairs which, as such, exist or do not exist. When Frege gives a proposition consisting of a connective and two terms, A and B, these two terms represent, as Frege always points out, the circumstance that (*der Umstand, daß*).

This similarity, if not identity, of views between Husserl and Frege – in spite of quite different terminologies – can be considered as the completion of investigations begun by Bolzano who, in a different terminology again, made considerable advances in this area.[16] Frege's distinction between the circumstance or state of affairs and the judgment takes up a distinction – between *Satz* and *Urteil* – about which Bolzano wrote a great deal. Every judgment contains a *Satz* which conforms or does not conform to the truth. Judgment is the assertion of a *Satz* such that the judgment is true when the asserted *Satz* conforms to the truth and false where this is not the case. There is, writes Bolzano, "an essential difference between a real judgment and the simple thinking or representing of a *Satz*".[17] And he gives the following example: I may think the *Satz* that there exist races of pygmies, without judging that such races exist.

Frege would certainly have been inclined to strip of their metaphysical connotations, or at least tone down, Bolzano's developments of these ideas to the effect that there exist an infinite number of *Sätze an sich*, distinct from *Sätze* which are actually uttered, expressed or merely thought. But when one looks at the detail of the analyses one notes that there is almost complete agreement between Frege and Bolzano. Let us look at two examples, implication and negation, which are central to Frege's system.

(1) Bolzano considers a judgment in the form of an implication:[18]

If A is, then B is

and explains that the *Sätze* which are the antecedent and the consequent are not judgments. The judgment concerns only the fact "that the *Satz* that B is follows from the truth of the *Satz* that A is".

(2) Bolzano also paves the way directly for Frege's use of negation. The negation which belongs to a negative judgment concerns, he says, the *Satz,* not the *Urteil,* and so a negation of the *Satz* is conceivable, independently of any judgment. The negation of the *Satz A,* for which Bolzano writes "Neg. A" is "the *Satz* that A is false".[19]

In a sense all that remained for Frege to do was to draw the consequences these analyses had for the symbolism which was to become the *Begriffsschrift*. Bolzano's analysis of implication, which we have quoted above, is taken over almost directly in Frege's conceptual notation. And as to negation, Bolzano's idea that it attaches to a content whether or not this has the form of a judgment leads Frege to affix the symbol which corresponds to negation to the *content stroke* which stands to the right of the vertical *judgment stroke*.

The terminological differences between Frege and Bolzano are extremely slight and are easily identifiable. For if, as we have seen, Frege seems to prefer the expression '*der Umstand, daß*', he nevertheless occasionally mentions as a synonym Bolzano's '*der Satz, daß*'.[20]

It is also interesting to note that Peirce was to come to a similar conclusion, although by a very different route, and even though his terminology is also quite different. He opposed the *proposition* (which he also called a *dicent*) to the *assertion*, more or less in the same way as Bolzano and Frege oppose *Satz* to *Urteil*. "A *dicent*", he writes in 1905, "is not an assertion but a sign capable of being asserted". But an assertion, on the other hand, implies a *dicent*. Unlike the proposition, "the act of assertion is not a pure act of signification"; and he concludes with a formula expressing his philosophy which, although it is so very different from that of Bolzano, does not contradict the latter at all:

the act of assertion is the exhibition of the fact that one subjects oneself to the penalties visited on a liar if the proposition asserted is not true.[21]

On the other hand, one of the central differences between Frege's system and that of *Principia Mathematica* is that the latter is not presented as a calculus of propositions built up from names of states of affairs, but as a calculus of propositions built up from elementary propositions. It is an interesting question whether the preservation of Frege's system was not connected with its extraordinary symbolism which makes it possible to distinguish between proposition and state of affairs much more clearly than does the symbolism of Whitehead and Russell or of all subsequent systems. For it is not enough merely to borrow Frege's symbol⊢——and use it before every independently asserted proposition. Is the full significance of Frege's symbolism really preserved if this symbol is, as Whitehead and Russell put it, simply used "for distinguishing a complete proposition, which we assert, from any subordinate propositions contained in it but not asserted"?[22]

228

The *complex* proposition (the expression now acquires its full meaning) is presented in *Principia Mathematica* as an "aggregation of propositions" or, more exactly, as a "function with propositions as arguments",[23] no longer are the arguments nominal. About negation, also called the *contradictory function*, they write:

The Contradictory Function with argument p, where p is any proposition, is the proposition which is the contradictory of p, that is, the proposition asserting that p is not true.

Here $\sim p$, or not-p, signifies the negation of a proposition and not, as for Frege, the non-obtaining of a state of affairs. Similarly,

The Logical Sum... is the proposition asserting p or q disjunctively, that is, asserting that at least one of the two p and q is true,

and the logical product is "the proposition ... asserting that both p and q are true".

As for *implication*, a term hallowed by usage and introduced, it seems, by Russell and Whitehead, the very expression continues to support the misunderstanding it encourages. *Implication* is an expression which combines much more easily with propositions that with states of affairs. The examples in *Principia Mathematica* are clearly to be understood in this way.

'Socrates is a man' implies 'Socrates is mortal'.[24]

The traditional way of teaching the calculus of propositions follows by and large Russell and not Frege. In the Warsaw School, for example, Łukasiewicz in his *Elements of Mathematical Logic* interprets negation as a propositional functor with a propositional argument and the binary connectives of the calculus of propositions as functors with two propositional arguments.[25] In the Göttingen School Hilbert and Ackermann speak of an 'Aussagenkalkül' just as we have been speaking of a calculus of propositions, in which there are complex propositions and constituent propositions; for "sentences can be connected in a definite manner to form new sentences".[26]

The slide from the *calculus of names of states of affairs* to the *calculus of propositions*[27] in the proper sense of the word was suggested by the invention of truth-tables. For as we have seen, these owe their striking pedagogic simplicity to the form of presentation which is now traditional in which the elementary terms represent propositions.

Once the equivalence is admitted between

'P is a fact'	and	'"p" is true'
'Not P is a fact'	and	'"p" is false'
'P and Q is a fact'	and	'"p" is true and "q" is true'

and, more generally, for every connective:[28]

| 'P * Q is a fact' | and | '"p" is true * "q" is true' |

and once it is recognized that 'every time two propositions are seen to be equivalent one of them may be substituted for the other in every formula with which we are concerned', then the confusion at the edges of the theory of propositions finds its justification. The more so if one is of the opinion that, as *Principia Mathematica* tells us, mathematics is a matter of extensions rather than intensions. It is enough for two propositions to have the same extension for us to be justified, within certain limits, in taking one for the other.

If, now, we broaden the field of our attention, leaving aside the calculus of propositions, to return to consideration of a language whose *raison d'être* is communication, the problem which arises – which we shall outline rather than seek to solve – is that of knowing if, in such a system, any advantage would be gained by distinguishing the two sorts of negation: the negation of a fact and the negation of a proposition. For example, if we keep *not* for the negation of a fact

It is not raining

we may introduce Neg for the negation of a proposition, thereby avoiding the somewhat cumbersome form 'It is not true that it is raining', and write:

Neg it is raining.

Might it not be a good thing to introduce two forms for every conjunction employed in Indo-European languages in order to distinguish on every occasion conjunctions of facts such as

I am wet because it is raining

(the intension or comprehension of which is quite clearly not: 'The proposition "I am wet" is true because the proposition "it is raining" is true'), from conjunctions of propositions such as,

$x = 2$ since $x + 2 = 4$

(on the assumption that I already believe that $x + 2 = 4$)?

But is it not slightly absurd to think that such distinctions could be of interest in ordinary language or provide the latter with a degree of precision lacking even in the calculus of propositions, at least in its classical form? On the other hand, perhaps ordinary language has or ought to have certain aims that the calculus of propositions within its self-imposed limits does not and should not have. One example would be the aim of taking into account the intension or comprehension of terms and not only their extension. In the majority of cases, it is true, natural languages are completely incapable of distinguishing the two possible uses of their conjunctions. Nevertheless some languages do possess conjunctions for both roles, which may indicate the presence of just such a distinction.

There is, for example, the contrast between *because* and *since*, or between *parce que* and *puisque* in French, equivalents of which are to be found in other languages. It is only very rarely that it is possible to say

I am wet since it is raining (*puisque*),

and one is unlikely to say

$x = 2$ parceque $x + 2 = 4$ (*because*)

whereas

$x = 2$ since $x + 2 = 4$

is perfectly possible. Usage here distinguishes between an expression indicating that one state of affairs is the cause of another and an expression indicating that one proposition is the reason for another. (Is not the same distinction responsible for one difference between the French *car* and *en effet*?)

Thus, the distinction between conjunctions of facts and conjunctions of propositions can only be observed in certain surface phenomena of Indo-European languages; it is not sufficiently thematised to represent more than merely nuances of meaning.

Extensionally Defined Conjunctions and Strict Conjunctions

The confusion masked by our everyday use of conjunctions is not only due to the fact that the distinction between conjunctions of facts and conjunctions of propositions is not really thematised. It is also due to inadequate recognition of another distinction, that between conjunctions defined simply by their truth-values, as is done by truth-tables for the calculus of propositions, and, on the other hand, conjunctions founded on an internal connection between propositions.

Implication provides a striking example of what happens when the two types of conjunction are confused. Our ordinary reasonings, which consist largely in our connecting the various facts we recognize with a series of *therefores,* rely on a species of implication which has been held to be captured by the notion of implication of the calculus of propositions. But the link between the two is very loose. For the connection of two facts A and B by *if* excludes only the case where the antecedent state of affairs is real and the second state of affairs is not real. Thus if it is raining I may justifiably claim

If two and two are four then it is raining

and when it is not raining I may truly say

If two and two are four then it is not raining.

We can ignore all complications due to the role of time here and which might be thought to be at the root of what is so paradoxical about such sentences. Material implication allows us to write further:

If two and two are four then water is composed of oxygen and hydrogen.

The natural reaction to this claim is that there appears to be absolutely no reason for drawing any conclusion whatsoever about the composition of water from the observation that two and two are four. Thus sentences like this, although allowed by the rules of the calculus of propositions, are somehow out of place in ordinary language.

The fact that the conjunction *if* in the Indo-European tradition may have at least two distinct senses was fully grasped by the logicians of the *Megarian School.*[29] There was a lively polemic between the supporters of the interpretation put forward by Philo, which corresponds to the use of implication in the modern calculus of propositions, and the partisans of

232

the interpretation put forward by Diodorus Cronus which is more satisfactory in that it takes into account the intensionality requirements mentioned above. So lively was this debate, Callimachus writes in an epigram, that even the crows on the roof-tops would caw about it.

Nor did the distinction between the two senses of implication escape Frege, who recognized the distinction between assertoric connections on the one hand and apodictic connections on the other. But, explained Frege, if I term a proposition apodictic, necessary, then

I am giving a hint as to my grounds for judgment. But this does not affect the conceptual content of the judgment; and therefore the apodictic form of a judgment has not for our purposes any significance.[30]

This question, of course, attracted renewed interest when C. I. Lewis pointed out that implication in Russell's system does not at all mean that the implied term is the logical consequence of the antecedent term. Now this notion of logical consequence does indeed seem to be basic to the language of the sciences. Where does this leave a logic which does not capture it? It was considerations of this sort which led Lewis and his successors in the domain of modal logic to extend the vocabulary of the *calculus of propositions* and, in particular, to add a symbol for *strict implication* to the symbol for ordinary *material* implication. Strict implication applies to those cases where implication does not correspond only to certain truth-values (those indicated by truth-tables) but expresses a logical connection between antedecent and consequent propositions such that the second really is the consequence of the first.

The problem presented by *strict implication* was further complicated by the fact that C. I. Lewis, following Russell, interpreted *material implication* as an implication between propositions and not between states of affairs; he then went on to interpret *strict implication* as another form of implication between propositions.[31] Now it seems that there is a difference between *strict* and *material implication* both at the level of states of affairs and at the level of propositions. Thus by combining the distinction between conjunctions of facts and conjunctions of propositions and the distinction between those that express only truth-relations with those that also express a logical connection, we obtain, for every conjunction, four different possibilities. For the reason we have given above, the difference between these four possibilities is most easily seen in the case of implication:

(1) *Material Implication of Facts.*
Example:

If it rains, he will nevertheless go for a walk.

It would clearly be absurd to interpret this proposition as meaning: *If it is true that it is raining, then it is nevertheless true that he will go for a walk.* In addition, the rain does not provide any reason which explains why he will go for a walk; and the expression 'nevertheless' in our example serves to underline this absence of any mention of reasons and to indicate the presence of contrary reasons.

(2) *Strict Implication of Facts.*
This may be based on a relation of causality or identity between two phenomena. For example:

If there are traces of footprints, then this is because someone has passed by here;
if there is water, then there is hydrogen.

(3) *Material Implication of Propositions.*
Example:

If it is true that $2+2 = 4$, then it is true that H_2O is the chemical formula of water.

Here we do indeed have two propositions, but it is evident that we cannot *deduce* the second from the first, in the ordinary sense of the word.

(4) *Strict Implication of Propositions.*
Example:

If it is true that $x+2 = 4$, then $x = 2$.

This possibility of distinguishing similarly four alternatives for negation and the binary connectives, has found expression in contemporary logic where systems have been created which correspond to these different possible alternatives.

(1) Thus in Frege's system, as we have seen, the connectives and negation are understood in the material sense, and concern states of affairs. One could also interpret Russell's system in the same way, at the cost of betraying his intentions.

234

(2) Lewis' system of strict implication is a system which has room both for strict connectives and material connectives, where both concern states of affairs. The idea of ignoring Lewis's intentions in this way and of taking strict implication to be an implication between states of affairs[32] was put forward by Carnap.[33]

(3) The system sketched by Carnap in his *Introduction to Semantics* for what he calls 'radical semantic concepts'[34] employs – this time quite deliberately – material connectives to connect propositions.

(4) The system sketched by Carnap in the same work for what he calls 'L–concepts'[35] embraces simultaneously strict connectives and material connectives, both of which concern propositions.

The relations between these four systems are such that it would be possible to construct each of the systems in such a way that one could establish a bi-univocal correspondence first between the theorems of the first and those of the third system; then between the theorems of the second and those of the fourth system. Any two theorems which stand in such a relation to one another would be equivalent. This equivalence explains why the confusion of systems (1) with (3) (particularly in the writings of Russell) or that of system (2) with (4) (for example in Lewis) has become entrenched. If we now compare, respectively, system (1) with system (2), or system (3) with system (4), then since (2) is a development of (1), and (4) a development of (3), it follows that the set of theorems of (1) and that of the theorems of (3) are included, respectively, in the set of the theorems of (2) and in that of the theorems of (4). But systems (2) and (4) must not only count amongst their theorems all the theorems of systems (1) and (3) as well as the theorems which involve only strict connectives, but in addition all theorems involving both strict and material connectives at the same time.

Carnap is very clear about the relation between what we are here calling system (4) and system (3), that is to say between what he calls the system employing L-concepts and the system which involves only 'radical concepts'.[36] The fact that he speaks of an *inclusion* of the L-concepts in the corresponding radical concepts does not by any means signify that the *inclusion* we have just pointed out of the set of theorems of system (3) in the set of theorems in system (4) is ruled out. Carnap has in mind the *inclusion of concepts,* whereas we have in mind *inclusion of systems.* What he calls inclusion is very clearly expressed in the first four postulates on which he bases his system for the L-concepts and which we may set out as follows:[37]

235

P1. If a proposition is L-true it is true.
P2. If a proposition is L-false it is false.
P3. If a proposition L-implies another proposition, then it implies this other proposition.
P4. If two propositions are L-disjoint one with another, they are disjoint.[38]

If we now return to our consideration of ordinary language, the question is whether the latter can have any interest in following these logical suggestions. Should it possess such a four-fold system for negation and each of the conjunctions? We have already seen that the idea of distinguishing between conjunctions according as they apply to states of affairs or to propositions is not totally foreign to natural languages. May we draw identical conclusions with respect to the distinction between those connectives we have, perhaps clumsily, called material and those we have called strict connectives?

This problem has in fact no real analogy with the previous problem. In the majority of cases, as Russell has well explained,[39] the distinction between material and strict implication, although an exact distinction, may safely be neglected: the main logical interest of implication is that it allows us to move from a recognition of the truth of the proposition p on the one hand and of the proposition $p \supset q$ on the other hand, to a recognition of the truth of the proposition q, a proposition of whose truth we were hitherto ignorant. $p \supset q$ is thus the bridge which allows us to pass to the truth of q provided we have been able to establish the truth of p. This means that there are two cases in which the proposition $p \supset q$ loses all intellectual interest.

(a) The case where proposition p is recognized to be false; for since this means that $p \supset q$ must be recognized to be true, it provides us with no information about the truth of q.

(b) The case where the truth of proposition q is already recognized; for then I cannot possibly have any more need of $p \supset q$ in order to establish the truth of q.

The nature of material implication is such that I can admit $p \supset q$ when I know:

either that p is false
or that q is true.

But if this 'extensional' reason is the only reason which allows me to write

236

$p \supset q$, then this proposition becomes useless or superfluous. The only case where $p \supset q$ can have cognitive value is where recognition of the truth of this proposition is based neither on recognition of the falsity of p nor on prior discovery of the truth of q, in other words, where the reason which makes me allow that $p \supset q$ is true is not purely extensional. In this case $p \supset q$ corresponds to a strict implication.

Although the divergence between material implication and strict implication was the first such difference to attract attention, an analogous divergence can be found in the case of the other conjunctions. Thus Tarski points out that the proposition

2 x 2 = 5 or New York is a large city

which is undoubtedly true if *or* has the meaning of disjunction in the propositional calculus, will in ordinary language normally be considered false, if not meaningless.[40] Similarly, Tarski added, if one of our friends, when asked about the date of his departure, were to reply that he was leaving today, tomorrow or the day after tomorrow, where he knew very well that he has definitely decided to leave today, would we not regard him as a liar? From the point of view of the propositional calculus, however, if he leaves today, then he leaves today or he leaves tomorrow or he leaves the day after tomorrow.

A disjunction has cognitive value, is worth mentioning, only if we are not already in possession of some stronger truth. In the mouth of the person who knows that p, the proposition p *or* q is pragmatically a lie, in that it lets the listener assume that the speaker only takes the trouble to state p *or* q because he does not know whether p. This is why the *or* of ordinary language contains in general, apart from the simple assertion that forms disjunction within the propositional calculus (i.e. that at least one of two propositions is true), the additional assertion that the author of the statement does not know which of the two propositions p or q is true. Here again language has no interest in distinguishing two terms, one corresponding to what we call strict disjunction, the other to what we call material disjunction, for the simple practical reason that material disjunctions which are not also strict disjunctions have no role in ordinary language.

This leads us to conclude that, within a linguistic system like our natural languages, the distinction between strict and material conjunctions may be much more easily neglected than the distinction between conjunctions of facts and conjunctions of propositions. That such a distinction corresponds to a distinction *in re* does not by itself mean that it is useful to introduce it into a language, otherwise the distinction we have been looking at would be linguistically marked. It would also be necessary for the practical conditions of the exercise of language to provide the speaker with the reasons for taking it into account. Thus the reasons justifying the structure of a given language are not all to be found at the level of semantics. The last word on the explanation of the discrepancy between ordinary conjunctions and those of the calculus of propositions must be left to pragmatics.

Remarks and Warnings

Some remarks and words of warning are in order after what has been said about conjunctions. First, what we have said about *because* and *therefore*[41] should not lead us to conclude that these conjunctions of coordination have no equivalent amongst the conjunctions of subordination. On the contrary, if we leave aside for the time being the distinction between conjunctions of fact and conjunctions of propositions, the expressions

p; for q	$(p;$ car $q)$
p; as q	$(p;$ en effet $q)$
p, because q	$(p,$ parceque $q)$
p, since q	$(p,$ puisque $q)$
q; therefore p	$(q;$ donc $p)$

appear to be so nearly equivalent to one another because they all authorize the detachment of p provided both q and $q \supset p$ are recognized. It is easy to convince oneself that we cannot pick out cases of strict and cases of material implication from these five locutions. In each, as we have already suggested, the implication involved is material *because* it is strict. The distinction between the use of conjunctions which concern facts (*for, because*) and the use of conjunctions which concern propositions (*en effet, therefore, since*) seems much more promising.

We have not dealt with the concessive conjunctions and the calculus of propositions ignores them almost completely. One of them, nevertheless has a truth-table:

p	q	
T	T	T
T	F	T
F	T	F
F	F	F

For if the complex proposition here takes the same truth values as its first component, this means that this proposition is exclusively a function of its first term and that its value is independent of that of the second term. This possibility is just what English and French express with the concessive form of words: *p whatever q*, (*p* quelque soit *q*).

It is easy to understand why the calculus of propositions ignores a connective like this, which says that *p* is true but refuses to take account of the truth of *q*. It is a redundant expression that one can simply replace by *p*. In the calculus such a connective is utterly useless; for what purpose could be served by emphasizing that indeterminate terms are indeterminate? Within a calculus there are no ways of expressing ignorance but only a way of being silent.

This is not true, however, of a system whose purpose is communication. Let us leave aside the case where *p whatever q* expresses a temporal nuance, i.e. underlines the supra-temporal value of a proposition in opposition to the possible variations of transient states, as when we say

two and two are four, whether it is raining or not.

I may have a certain pedagogical interest in indicating that, if I am not certain about the truth of some proposition, this uncertainty does not affect the certainty I have about some other proposition. One may be led to say something about the limits of one's knowledge – for example by giving hints (to use Frege's term). It is for this reason that concessive conjunctions have their role within language.

A conjunction such as *although* even plays a considerable role in the practical exercise of rationality; it consists in the subtle interplay of hints and allusions just mentioned. *p although q* means all of:

(1) *q* is true.
(2) One should not think that, since *q* is true, one can also admit: $q \supset \sim p$ and hence detach $\sim p$, (alternatively, one should not think that $\sim p$ *because q*).
(3) On the contrary, *p* is also true.

239

These warnings, winks almost, to the interlocutor, have an indisputable function in the communication of thought.

The aim of our last remark is to show, by reference to an example, that one cannot make any adequate judgments about the form conjunctions have in this or that language without reference to the structure they illustrate. We shall take the example of the conjunction *or,* a conjunction which is often very difficult to define in Indo-European languages. This is because this one term often hides three different meanings which it is today easy to distinguish clearly for anyone who is familiar with truth-tables.

p	q	p or q at least one	p or q at most one	p or q at most and at least one
T	T	T	F	F
T	F	T	T	T
F	T	T	T	T
F	F	F	T	F

Ordinary language provides numerous examples of these three meanings, which are all equally possible although, as we shall see, they are not equally frequent.

(1) If I say, that to perform a certain function, it is necessary to have a bachelor's degree or a degree in law, it is evident that my *or* does not exclude from the number of candidates those who have both degrees. This is what is called the 'inclusive or' and is to be found in the algebra of classes (union) as well as in the algebra of propositions (disjunction).

(2) It is much more difficult to find in ordinary language examples of the second use. Those one can construct have something artificial about them. I might say that the moral of La Fontaine's fable *Le Savetier et le Financier* can be put as follows: *one can't be rich and enjoy peace of mind at the same time, it's either one or the other.* The *or,* here, does not mean at all that it is impossible to be neither the one nor the other. La Fontaine's other fables show that one could very well be neither rich nor happy and thus his fable does not signify that poverty brings peace of mind, but only that wealth and peace of mind are incompatible: one may be rich or enjoy peace of mind, but only one of these at most. (This sense of 'or' is also that of the Sheffer-stroke in logic, on which Nicod based his system for the propositional calculus.)

(3) In the famous words of the rebellious silk workers from Lyon:

To live by working or to die by fighting!

It is evident that if one has decided to make at least one or the other one's goal, this decision also shows that one can only obtain one at most of these goals. One cannot combine the advantages of the two attitudes. What we have here is what is generally called an *alternative*.

It would certainly not be without interest to survey systematically the different meanings of *or* in some text or other in order to compare their relative frequency of occurrence. And such an analysis would also have to allow for those cases where the context does not allow us to determine the sense intended by the author. Without wanting to provide any such analysis – which might deal not merely with some author but also, if based on a well-chosen statistical sample, with an entire language, whose physiognomy could thereby be described – it seems to us to be more or less certain that the second of these uses of *or,* at least in the languages with which we are familiar, is much rarer than the other two. It has already been pointed out that a language like Latin has one term for the first use *(vel)* and another for the third use *(aut),* but Latin does not possess a term for the second use. Languages such as French, German and English which suffer from the lack of such a morphological distinction compensate for this either by appeal to context or by emphasizing the word *or,* when it is used in the third sense, by a variety of means including gesture, inflection of the voice, repetition of the word *or,* etc. But in these languages the second use of *or* is so rare that it may even seem somewhat improper to call it a use of *or,* and examples of its use are, as we have seen, difficult to construct without getting too far away from the ordinary practice of language.

The reasons for this lack of a distinct expression for this second possible use of 'or' are very simple. Why introduce an autonomous term for what can be expressed almost equally simply by using another term? For

at most one of *p* or *q*

is equivalent to:

at least one of not *p* or not *q,*

since it means that at least one of the two propositions is false. The simplicity with which one can express 'or (at most one)' by using 'or (at least one)' combined with negation is certainly the reason for the rarity of this term in language. And this in spite of the privileged position Sheffer's functor 'or (at most one)' enjoys in logic, a privilege to which a system devoted almost entirely to communication is nearly completely insensible.[42]

On the other hand, the relation between the first and the third use is such that

(1) The first sense of *or* cannot be formed directly from the third.

(2) The third sense of *or* can be formed from the first by using *and;* for

p or q (at least one and at most one)

says the same as:

$[p$ or q (at least one)$]$ and $[$not p or not q (at least one)$]$

or the same as:

$(p$ and not $q)$ or (not p and $q)$ [at least one].

But composite forms such as these are so cumbersome that it is advantageous to abbreviate them by creating a new form. And so it is understandable that Latin employed simultaneously *vel* and *aut,* without feeling any need for a further term. On this one point, then, we need not hesitate to say that Latin is a system of communication that is *better constructed* than the majority of living Indo-European languages.[43]

To the reader who is shocked by this introduction of a value-judgment, an expression of preference, we would point out, at least provisionally, that only such a value-judgment can help us to understand certain aspects of the evolution of languages. During recent years a new conjunction has appeared, first in English and then, after a suitable delay, in French – the 'and/or' or 'et/ou' – which is always used in the sense of 'or (at least one)'. This new conjunction is increasingly making its way into commercial contracts. Those who adopt this usage are, often without knowing it, being influenced by logical discoveries of the last century. How many legal misunderstandings, indeed how many trials, have been due to the fact that the interlocutor did not always know, when the speaker said 'or', exactly what the speaker meant; was the speaker himself clear about what he meant? These facts led to the tardy creation of a new term, since it could not be furnished by ordinary language. The first to feel the need for this improvement (how should it be described, if not so?) of our language were those for whom language is precisely a technical means of agreement, namely lawyers. Thus logic has not merely helped to transform the metalanguage of mathematics. It has also, by introducing itself into the law, shown that our languages, which are ensembles of more or less happy solutions to different technical problems, can show themselves to be responsive to improved solutions in spite of the weight of history.

Notes

1. It is of course then necessary to strip 'en même temps que' of all properly temporal meaning.
2. One may, it seems, accept the implication

$$\forall ab[(a \text{ when } b) \supset (b \text{ when } a)].$$

For example:

Jules jumped when John ran

is equivalent to

John ran when Jules jumped.

3. It should be borne in mind that Sheffer showed in 1913 that each of the two connectives 'neither... nor...' and 'or (at most one)' suffice to obtain all the other binary connectives as well as negation. But the axiomatic simplification to which the use of this method leads is largely unrelated to that practical simplicity (especially brevity of expression) which is desirable in a system of communication.
4. Husserl, *Logical Investigations*, V, §33; Eng. trans., pp.622f.
5. Ibid., §36; Eng. trans. p.633.
6. Here again we have an expression, 'simultaneously', that must be stripped of all temporal meaning.
7. *Logical Investigations*, V, §36; Eng. trans., p.633f.
8. Ibid., Eng. trans., pp.633ff.
9. Ibid., Eng. trans., p.634.
10. It is only reluctantly that we employ this expression. Its main defect is that, like other related expressions such as 'the fact that', its ordinary usage often presupposes that the state of affairs or fact in question is indeed real, whereas in our use of these terms here, the state of affairs or fact is not necessarily posited as real but is often merely assumed, supposed or entertained. In

I doubt whether she loves him

'whether she loves him' can only be regarded as a name of a state of affairs if this expression ceases to carry any existence-positing force.
11. In any case, from within the perspective here adopted, the very expression we have so frequently used – 'propositional functor with two propositional arguments' – is not exactly adequate to what we have just formalized as

$$K \text{ "}p\text{" "}q\text{" (cf. p. 222).}$$

since the arguments of the functor are not propositions but, as the quotation marks indicate, *names* of propositions.

If one follows Husserl and claims that the arguments of every functor are names, then in order not to have to reform the (Warsaw School) terminology we have here been using without all too many scruples, a measure of clarification must be introduced. What we have called 'functors with propositional arguments' and 'functors with functorial arguments' are not functors whose arguments are themselves propositions (in the first case) or functors (in the second case). They are, rather, functors whose arguments are, respectively, the *names* of propositions and the *names* of functors.

The ingenious system developed by Ajdukiewicz in order to verify the grammaticality of expressions has, then, the serious defect that propositions on the one hand and the names of the states of affairs stated by these propositions on the other hand are represented in the same way. This encourages the confusion of very different semantic categories.

12 Frege, *Begriffsschrift*, I, p.1ff.

13 Ibid., §4: "Ich halte es daher für angemessener, die Verneinung als ein Merkmal eines *beurteilbaren Inhalts* anzusehen." [Cf. Husserl, *Logical Investigations*, VI, §39, Eng. trans., p.770: "The differences between *is* and *is not* are differences of intentional matter" and not differences in act qualities such as judging, assuming, positing or non-positing. Cf. also V, §40, Eng. trans., p.647 – Tr.]

14 Ibid., p.10: "der Umstand..., daß der Inhalt nicht stattfinde".

15 Ibid., p.5.

16 Bolzano, *Wissenschaftslehre*, especially §19, pp.20–23 and §34, pp.43–44.

17 Ibid., §34, p.43.

18 Ibid., p.44.

19 Ibid., §141: "Sätze, in welchen von anderen Sätzen gehandelt wird" – p.188.

20 Frege, *Begriffsschrift*, I, §2, p.2.

21 Quoted by Ogden and Richards in *The Meaning of Meaning*, Appendix D, p.284.

22 *Principia Mathematica*, 2nd ed., vol.I, ch.1, p.8.

23 Ibid., p.6.

24 Matters are made worse in *Principia Mathematica* by vacillations in the use of words. As Carnap has pointed out, the word 'proposition' is employed sometimes to designate the state of affairs a proposition states, and sometimes this proposition itself, and this often within the space of a few lines. One reads in one and the same paragraph (Vol. I, Introduction, ch.6, p.44): "what we call a 'proposition' (in the sense in which this is distinguished from the phrase expressing it)..." and "the fact that propositions are 'incomplete symbols'..." (quoted by Carnap, *Introduction to Semantics*, Appendix, p.235).

25 Cf. p.23: "the functor N is a sentence-forming functor of one sentential argument" and, p.25: "The symbol is thus a sentence-forming functor of two sentential arguments".

26 Hilbert and Ackermann, *Grundzüge der theoretischen Logik*, ch.1, p.3 (Eng. trans., p.3): "Sentences *(Aussagen)* can be combined in a definite manner to form new sentences. For example, from the two sentences '2 is less than 3' and 'snow is black' one can construct the new sentence '2 is less than 3 *and* snow is black'".

27 We prefer to keep to the terminological opposition of 'proposition' to 'state of affairs' such as is to be found in Wittgenstein (who speaks of '*Satz*' and '*Sachverhalt*'), rather than follow the usage becoming standard in Anglo-Saxon terminology which opposes 'sentence' to 'proposition'; the former corresponds to our 'proposition', the latter to our 'state of affairs'. Carnap, who defends the sentence-proposition distinction (*Introduction to Semantics*, pp.253ff) mentions Lewis and Langford as precedents ("the proposition is the same with the fact that") and Quine ("propositions, not in the sense of sentences, but in the sense of what sentences may be taken to symbolize") and other writers such as A. A. Bennett and C. A. Baylis ("Propositions are usually expressed by sentences"). 'Proposition', understood in this way, seems to us to convey something much more dangerous than 'state of affairs'.

28 We must recognize that it is wrong to treat the connective * as though it were the same functor in

P * Q is a fact

and in

    'p' is true * *'q'* is true.

The functor is different in each case, since the nature of the arguments changes.

[29] Cf. J. Łukasiewicz, "On the History of the Logic of Propositions", in *Polish Logic 1920–1939*, pp.72ff and I. M. Bocheński, *Ancient Formal Logic*, pp.89ff. According to Bocheński, the Stoics, following the Megarian School, distinguished four possible senses of *if* (apart from its meaning in *if and only if*). The meaning on which Diodorus insisted is not exactly the sense taken up by C. I. Lewis, but this meaning had already been identified and belonged to the four meanings distinguished by the Megarian School. It is to Peirce and then Łukasiewicz that we owe the recent discovery of the astonishing analyses of the Megarian School which historians (even Prantl) had shown themselves unable to understand. In order to get an idea of the comparative weakness of the analyses accepted during the period between the Stoics and Frege one only has to read what writers as important as Arnauld and Nicole say about conditionals (*La logique ou l'art de penser*, ch.9, pp.134ff). One reads here that the contradictory of

    If you eat forbidden fruit you will die

is

    Although you eat (quoique vous mangiez) forbidden fruit you will not die.

Yet having declared that 'the propositions considered as the negatives and contradictories of conditionals are only those in which the condition is denied', Arnauld would have had to reject the version that today would be suggested by the calculus of propositions, namely:

    You will eat forbidden fruit and you will not die

in order to put in its place:

    It is possible that you eat (mangiez) forbidden fruit and that you do not die (mouriez).

[30] Frege, *Begriffsschrift*, I, §4, p.4: "So gebe ich dadurch einen Wink über meine Urteilsgründe. *Da aber hierdurch der begriffliche Inhalt des Urteils nicht berührt wird, so hat die Form des apodiktischen Urteils für uns keine Bedeutung.*"

[31] On this point, however, Carnap has shown himself to be a faithful disciple of Frege:

It is important to note the *fundamentally different nature of implication and the consequence-relation.* Materially expressed: the consequence relation is a relation between sentences; *implication is not a relation between sentences.* [Whether, for example, Russell's opinion that it is a relation between propositions is erroneous or not, depends upon what is to be understood by a "proposition". If we are going to speak at all of 'that which is designated by a sentence', then implication is a relation between what is so designated; but the consequence-relation is not.] 'A⊃B' – as opposed to the syntactic sentence "B" is a consequence of 'A" – means, not something about the sentence 'A' and 'B', but, with the help of these sentences and of the junction-symbol '⊃', something about the objects to which 'A' and 'B' refer. (Carnap, *Logical Syntax*, pp.254ff.)

The only point on which Carnap is unfaithful to his teacher Frege, in our opinion, is when he writes "with the help of these sentences". As far as Frege is concerned, *even here* we do not have sentences, but *states of affairs,* which can only be stated in sentences (propositions), because they are *beurteilbar.*

[32] As an elementary example, we may mention that Lewis's system does not simply replace the

consideration of material implication by strict implication but envisages relations (of implication) between strict implication between two terms and material implication between the same two terms.

33 *Introduction to Semantics*, p.66.

34 Ibid., B, §9, pp.33–40.

35 Ibid., C, §14, pp.60–78. 'L' here is the initial letter of the word 'logic'; it signifies that the rationality of these concepts is founded on their intension and not on mere truth-values; they might be described, using a term taken from Lewis, as strict concepts.

36 Ibid., pp.63f.

37 On the meaning of the symbol L see note 35 above. We have transposed rather than reproduced what Carnap says in order to avoid new symbols and the need for new explanations.

38 We do not want to imply, in our references to the system constructed by Carnap for L-concepts, that this system presents no difficulties. The main difficulty is due to postulates 14 and 15 which can be transposed as follows:

- If a proposition is L-true, then it is L-implied by every proposition.
- If a proposition is L-false, then it L-implies every proposition.

Carnap recognizes that these postulates will not easily be accepted by everyone, but he justifies their adoption as follows:

(1) What is at issue is a matter of convention not truth, and the adoption of *this* convention leads to simplifications.

(2) These postulates also fit our conception of L-implication, for a proposition L-implies another proposition if and only if it is impossible for logical reasons that the first be true and the second false.

We shall not discuss the first of these reasons, although it ought to be taken into account. As to the second, we note that Carnap's definition of L-implication means that this departs somewhat from ordinary deduction. Let us consider an example:

'two and two are four' L-implies 'the sum of the angles of a triangle is equivalent to two right angles',

since it is impossible, *for purely logical reasons,* for the first of these propositions to be true and the second false. Now one clearly cannot *deduce* (in the traditional sense of the word) the second proposition from the first; and so one cannot say it is the consequence of the first. If we want to get back to the intuitive sense of *consequence* we simply cannot admit all the postulates with which Carnap underpins his use of L-concepts. In particular, we shall have to abandon postulates 14 and 15, whatever practical advantages they have. The question whether these postulates must be replaced by new postulates not mentioned by Carnap remains completely open: cf. ibid., pp.64ff.

39 Whitehead and Russell, *Principia Mathematica*, Vol.I, ch.1, pp.20ff.

40 *Introduction to Logic*, Part 1, II, pp.22ff.

41 P. 218.

42 Cf. note 3, above.

43 However, the Latin use of *vel* and *aut* should not be made out to be more rigorous than it really was. This is shown by the fact that the first text that, to our knowledge, establishes a perfectly explicit distinction between the three senses of *or* is a Latin text reported in the *Digest* and there attributed to Proculus, a Roman jurist of the first century A. D. in which the writer gives the three following examples of the three meanings of *or:*

(1) (at least one): *"Omne animal aut facit aut patitur:* nullum est enim quod nec faciat nec patiatur: at potest simul et facere et pati".

(2) (at most one): "*Aut sedet aut ambulat.* Nam ut nemo potest utrumque simul facere, ita aliquis potest neutrum: veluti is qui accumbit".

(3) (at least one and at most one): "*Aut dies aut nox est:* quorum posito altero necesse est tolli alterum: item sublato altero poni alterum".

It is revealing that, for each of these three senses here, Proculus uses *aut* and never mentions *vel*. (*Digestum Novum seu Pandectarum juris civilis tomus tertius,* Coloniae Allobrogum, Excudebat Stephanus Gamonetus, MDCXII, pp.1832–33.)

Chapter Nine
Adverbs and That-Clauses

The Two Possible Expressions of Modality

Why discuss adverbs and propositions containing that-clauses together, since their juxtaposition only gives rise to misunderstandings? Precisely *because* these misunderstandings are so frequent, particularly in the Indo-European tradition, it will be useful to begin by trying to isolate them.

We can begin with the observation that many languages can give one and the same modal nuance to a particular propositional content, either by making the verb which expresses this propositional content the argument of an adverb:

Peter has certainly wounded John

or by making the propositional content the argument of another proposition:

It is certain that Peter has wounded John.

In our first example the adverb 'certainly' is a functor which takes as its argument (this is, indeed, the etymology of the word 'adverb') the *verb* 'has wounded', which is itself a predicate with two arguments, to form the quite distinct two-place predicate 'has certainly wounded'. It is therefore a functorial functor with a functorial argument, which we shall represent, following the method of Ajdukiewicz as:

$$\frac{\dfrac{s}{nn}}{\dfrac{s}{nn}}$$

In our second example, on the other hand, the principal functor 'It is certain that' can be seen to take as its argument the proposition 'Peter has wounded John' in order to make a new proposition. It is thus a propositional functor with one propositional argument, which we should henceforth write as:[1]

$$\frac{s}{s}$$

Confusion arises when one tries to make a semantic distinction correspond to this syntactic distinction, for this is by no means always possible or easy in natural languages, nor even in some formal languages. If we follow the sense rather than the letter of the grammatical construction, we must recognize that, whether expressed by the adverb 'certainly' or by the proposition 'it is certain that', the *certainty* involved attaches to the whole proposition 'Peter has wounded John' and not at all to the predicator 'has wounded'. This is the source of the temptation to give the same representation for both examples.

Thus, in connection with the two propositions:

Peter is seriously ill

and:

Peter is certainly ill,

Hubert Hubien[2] has noted that the analysis suggested by traditional grammar led to a failure to recognize their essentially different structures. For in the first case the seriousness is that of the illness, and I would express something quite different were I to say

It is serious that Peter is ill (It is a serious matter that Peter is ill).

There is no sort of implication between these two propositions: that Peter is seriously ill is of no import to someone who is indifferent to Peter; and even if his illness is not very serious as an illness it may well be serious as far as his professional activities are concerned. In short, the adverb 'seriously' takes as its argument the functor 'is ill', whilst, if sense is taken into account, the argument of both the adverb 'certainly' and of the proposition 'it is certain that' is the proposition 'Peter is ill'.

Interchangeability of uses of the two grammatical forms is sometimes justified by the fact that they are taken in the same way, although there is no need to go as far as Hubien, for whom

Peter is often ill

necessarily means

249

It often happens that Peter is ill.

But a quite different interpretation is possible, along the lines of

Peter is often-ill

where 'is often-ill' can be translated as 'is a valetudinarian'. In this precise case the two grammatical structures, different though they are, correspond to equivalent situations because of the very nature of what we call *frequency* and *illness: Peter is a valetudinarian if and only if it often happens that he is ill.*

The possibility of confusing the adverbial and the completive proposition arises whenever there is an equivalence between the two constructions and is at the origin of the difficulties met with in the post-Aristotelian tradition which centre on the distinction between *de dicto* and *de re* modalities. This is not the place to recall the reasons, bound up with the expression of his philosophical system, which led Aristotle to accord a privileged place amongst all conceivable modalities only to *necessary, impossible, possible* and *contingent.*[3] It is enough to note merely that this particular choice in fact concerned in each case a modality where there is only a slight difference between the completive expression:

It is necessary that A is B
It is possible that A is B

and the adverbial expression

A is necessarily B
A is possibly B.

In the Aristotelian context these difficulties involved in the expression of necessity and possibility were further complicated by the fact that the Stagirite proposed analysing a simple categorical proposition as the inherence of a predicate in a subject. But given a modalised categorical proposition, would the modality attach to the predicate or to the relation of inherence marked by the copula, or to the whole proposition? Aristotle himself did not raise this question explicitly and so is led to give what amount to quite different answers in different contexts. And historians have given divergent interpretations of his thought on this point because they referred to different texts. Thus if one concentrates on chapter 12 of *De Interpretatione* one is led to the conclusion that the modality modifies the whole proposition,[4] whereas J. M. Bocheński, on the basis of chapter 13 of Book I of the *Prior Analytics,* was able to show that modality attaches not to the proposition but to the predicate or, in certain cases, to the subject, and to single out the merit of Theophrastus's innovation in making the whole proposition the argument of the modal functor.[5]

Theophrastus's idea was not immediately successful. In the twelfth century Abelard[6] mentions the interpretation according to which the modal proposition takes as its argument the sense of another proposition, but he does not accept this interpretation as a solution.

In the expression

Possibile est Socratem currere

the modality (here *possibility*) would be the predicate to which would correspond as its subject the proposition

Socrates currit.

An anonymous author[7] at the end of the same century went so far as to express his rejection of such an interpretation by writing that the expression

Socratem currere est possibile,

– in which the simple inversion of word order underlines that it is the infinitive proposition of which possibility is predicated – is *eo ipso* not a modal proposition. For this author, as for Abelard, modality affects the copula, that is, the instrument of 'composition' and can no more be a predicate than it can be the subject in a modal proposition.

This tradition of reflection on the nature of the modal functor resulted in the distinction between *de re* and *de dicto* modalities in the work of Albertus Magnus, William of Sherwood, Peter of Spain and Thomas Aquinas. Classic though the distinction has become, it has never established itself in any completely univocal manner. It remains tied, as it was for its inventors, to certain features of Aristotelian logic, a fact which in part diminishes its interest today.

Thus according to St. Thomas[8]

That Socrates runs is possible (Socratem currere est possibile)

is a *de dicto* modal proposition, since the dictum (*that Socrates runs*) is the subject of which the mode (*possibile*) is the predicate; whilst

For Socrates it is possible to run (Socratem possibile est currere)

is a modal proposition *de re,* since it treats not at all of *the possibility that Socrates runs,* but of the *possibility of running* as this concerns Socrates.

For St. Thomas,[9] as the context shows, the aim was to set out the theory of modalities on the basis of the then traditional classification of propositions into *universal, particular* and *singular,* by specifying that a *de dicto* modal proposition could only be singular, since its subject was always a single proposition, whereas any sort of quantification might apply to a *de re* proposition:

> For every man it is possible to run
> For any man it is possible to run
> For Socrates it is possible to run.

Although little more than historical interest attaches nowadays to the project of expounding the modalities on the basis of Aristotelian logic as a whole, the distinction between the two ways of expressing modality retains the merit of posing an important question. Is the real argument of the modal functor – the object it modifies – the proposition as a whole, or the predicate alone?

This question retains its pertinence even if the considerable evolution of the meaning of the word *predicate* in contemporary logic is taken into account. The fact that, since Frege, the *copula* is no longer separated from the predicate itself, and that the latter – or rather the *predicator –* is distinguished not only from the *subject* of traditional grammar but also from all the complements or objects which form the arguments of the relation expressed by the verb, does nothing to change matters. If I say, in the context of the theory of universal gravitation,

> Body A necessarily attracts body B,

this can only be interpreted as a *de dicto* modal proposition if the *necessity* applies to the proposition

> Body A attracts body B;

in order to interpret it as a *de re* modal proposition it requires, in Aristotelian terms, the form

> Body A is attracting-necessarily-body-B,

so that the modality concerns the *predicate* (in the Aristotelian sense);

252

whereas in post-Fregean terms we need only consider the adverb as concerning the predicator 'attracts'. The step from Aristotle to Frege makes no fundamental difference to the sense of the question.

In any case if one reads contemporary writers on the subject one finds that of the two possible interpretations of modality – or at least of *necessary* and *possible* – logicians have clearly opted for *de dicto* modality and have decided to treat the modal functor as a propositional functor with a propositional argument, rather than as a functorial functor with a functorial argument. As Rescher puts it:[10]

When... a proposition is itself made subject to some further qualification of such a kind that the entire resulting complex is itself once again a proposition, then this qualification is said to represent a *modality* to which the original proposition is subjected.

But there is no need to be overly impressed by this contemporary approach.

The possibility of treating modality as a functorial functor does find an echo in certain logical systems. Thus, following C. I. Lewis, the majority of contemporary logicians introduce – usually by means of a definition – an equivalence between the expression

$$p \rightarrow q$$

where the symbol $\rightarrow$ expresses *strict* or *necessary* implication and the expression

$$\Box(p \supset q)$$

where the symbol $\Box$ expresses the necessity of the implication which follows. In other words it is recognized that the modality of *necessity* may be considered either as a functorial functor or as a propositional functor.

The favour currently enjoyed by the propositional interpretation of modality amongst logicians is due not to grammatical reasons but to advantages and difficulties which are purely logical and, what is more important, which are inseparable from those specific sorts of modality which, for different reasons, are currently receiving more attention than others from logicians. Thus it is now quite possible to construct modal systems where *strict implication* is the primitive term on the basis of which the propositional functor of necessity is defined. But it is significant that:
(1) The definitions of propositional necessity on the basis of strict implication or of another related connective such as strict incompati-

bility ($p//q$) make it impossible to set out the clear relation between *definiens* and *definiendum* that is exhibited by the equivalence above. Consider, for example, the definitions suggested by Meredith and Ishimoto respectively:

$$\Box\alpha = \text{Df.} (\alpha \rightarrow \alpha) \rightarrow \alpha$$
$$\Box\alpha = \text{Df.} (\alpha/\alpha)//(\alpha/\alpha)$$

(2) Such definitions do not allow one to construct, on the basis of strict implication (or incompatibility), a system equivalent to every system which can be constructed on the basis of propositional necessity (or possibility). This equivalence works only for certain systems: on Meredith's definition it no longer works for systems weaker than S4; on Ishimoto's it apparently does not work for those weaker than S3.[11]

So little is the current preference for a propositional interpretation of modality due to grammatical necessities that in the not too distant past logicians opted for an alternative analysis. We can illustrate this by looking at the adverbial expression of comparison: 'more ... than', which allows of two interpretations, functorial and propositional. For in the proposition

Peter is more stupid than Paul

'more ... than' may be analysed as a functorial functor with a functorial argument. Taking as argument the predicate (with one nominal argument of its own) 'is stupid', it yields a predicate with two arguments 'is more stupid than'. But in the same proposition 'more ... than' may also be analysed as a propositional functor with two propositional arguments in the sense that, taking as arguments the two propositions 'Peter is stupid' and 'Paul is stupid' it yields the new proposition

Peter is more stupid than is Paul.

This sort of propositional interpretation of 'more ... than' can be seen at work more or less explicitly in certain languages such as Latin,[12] where it expresses a comparison between two individuals. But much more important is the fact that it alone captures the way comparisons are made, not about two individuals with respect to one property, but about one individual with respect to two properties:

Peter is more stupid than naughty,

that is to say:

Peter is more stupid than he is naughty.

However it should be noted that, apart from some isolated attempts, such as that of G. H. von Wright,[13] the functorial interpretation of 'more ... than' has prevailed in the logico-mathematical tradition. The development of the *theory of relations* in the wake of De Morgan, Schröder and Russell has in a sense confirmed the mathematical use of > and < in the functorial interpretation which this usage so well exemplifies.

Definition of the Adverb

Wherever an adverb can be analysed as a functorial functor with a functorial argument, its argument may not always by a simple *verb,* as its etymology suggests. For in Indo-European languages the argument of what is called as adverb may itself be either an adverb or an adjective. An adverb can be applied naturally to an adjective because adjective and copula together make up an intransitive verb: the adverb 'very' takes as argument the adjective 'stupid' to form the new attributive adjective 'very stupid' in the same way in which, in another context, it takes as argument the intransitive verb 'is stupid' to form the new intransitive verb 'is very stupid'. And we have already looked, in chapter 3, at an example given by Ajdukiewicz where an adverb takes an adverb as its argument.

It might therefore seem tempting to give a definition of *adverb* capable of subsuming all the different situations to which, as we have seen, traditional grammar has applied the term, by defining it as a functor which forms a functor of the same type as that which it takes as an argument. This would certainly avoid the inconvenience of Ajdukiewicz's method that a notation can only be assigned to any adverb whatsoever provided its context is already familiar. Thus what is ordinarily regarded as one and the same adverb: 'always', will be represented as

$$\frac{\dfrac{s}{n}}{\dfrac{s}{n}}$$

if the argument is a propositional functor with one nominal argument (*run always*); as

$$\frac{\dfrac{s}{nn}}{\dfrac{s}{nn}}$$

if its argument is a propositional functor with two nominal arguments (*love always*); as

$$\frac{\dfrac{s}{nnn}}{\dfrac{s}{nnn}}$$

if its argument is a propositional functor with three nominal arguments (*hesitate always between some object and some other object*); as

$$\frac{\dfrac{s}{nss}}{\dfrac{s}{nss}}$$

if its argument is a propositional functor with three arguments, one of which is nominal and the others propositional (*hesitate always between doing this and doing that*), and so on.

But a procedure of this generality, even if it can deal with most adverbs, cannot deal with the case we have met with above (*more ... than*), where the functor which is the argument of the adverb *(is stupid)* has one argument less than the resulting functor *(is more stupid than)*. Here the adverb must be represented by Ajdukiewicz's method, which has the advantage of immediately making apparent the dissimilarity between the numerator and the denominator:

$$\frac{\dfrac{s}{nn}}{\dfrac{s}{n}}$$

We have no other alternative but to give an even more general definition of an adverb as *a functorial functor with a functorial argument*.

This means recognizing that negation may also have adverbial status. For although logicians have traditionally viewed negation as something which concerns the proposition as a whole, or rather the state of affairs expressed by the proposition, our Indo-European grammars, as we have seen, by often joining it directly to the verb suggest that it is a functorial functor with a functorial argument rather than a propositional functor. In the expression

Jack does not move

I can consider the negation as that functor which takes the predicator *moves* to form the new predicator *does not move* (= *is immobile*) or, equally well, as a propositional functor the argument of which is *the fact that Jack moves*. It is therefore not surprising that traditional grammar should have classified negation as an adverb; particularly since by doing so it allows for the practice of those mathematicians who, instead of applying negation to an equation as a whole, do not hesitate to strike through the equality sign as if the argument of negation were the functor '$=$'.[14]

The adverb, then, may be considered as a category or set of categories with a structure of its own. This was not the case for *The Port-Royal Grammar*[15] which describes the adverb as an abbreviation used only for 'signifying in a single word what would only be otherwise indicated by a preposition and a noun'. If in certain cases the adverb just amounts to a preposition and a noun, we do not think that we can conclude from this, like Dumarsais,[16] that it is simply 'a word that abbreviates'. Rather, it is our prepositions which must themselves be considered as functors which, taking a noun as argument, form an adverb.[17] In addition, the type of noun taken as an argument must be specified; not any type of noun will do. That *sapienter* can be analysed as *cum sapientia*, as Arnauld and Lancelot point out, is made possible by the fact that *sapientia* is a substantive formed by nominalising a first-order predicate: *such and such an individual is wise*.

The Specific Nature of the Completive Construction

The reasons for the distinction between adverbial and completive modes of expression are not only logical. Although it is often possible to find two equivalent expressions, one adverbial, the other completive, for one and the same content, this possibility is not due to a general law. In particular, it is difficult to find an adverbial equivalent for the whole range of completive propositions in which the arguments of the principal functor are partly propositional and partly nominal:

x knows that...

x prefers to... rather than to...

But in the case of the completive proposition it is important to beware of a harmful confusion – all too easily suggested by the equivalence we have put forward – between what the medievals called *modality de dicto* and what we have called a *propositional functor with propositional arguments*. For the term *dictum* is not unambiguous: even when the temptation of understanding it as an already affirmed proposition is avoided, there is a risk of interpreting a modal *de dicto* as a proposition which concerns an affirmation. Thus Robert Blanché writes that a statement of modality, in so far as it 'dominates the *dictum* as a whole... belongs to a different level... from the latter... because it says something about it, treats it as its subject-matter';[18] also, according to Blanché, such a statement would belong to the meta-language. Thus the *de dicto* modality, he says, can only be regarded as a part of the calculus at the risk of 'failing to appreciate the hierarchy of languages'. But the expression of *de dicto* modality seems to be no more meta-linguistic than the expression of classical propositional negation. For does not the latter concern the *dictum* as a whole? We are, therefore, justified in considering *de dicto* modality as something which, like negation according to Bolzano and Frege, does not attach to the proposition – a form of words we sometimes employed insofar as it is a limited abuse of language which can be tolerated within certain limits – but to its content. Here again it is not an *assertion* which is modified, but a *fact* or *state of affairs* which is capable of being the object of an assertion.

The situation is analogous to the situation we met with in the discussion in the last chapter of negation and the connectives of the propositional calculus. There is good reason to distinguish in the expression of modality between the cases where the argument is a genuine *proposition,* for example where one affirms the necessity of an algebraic equation, and those cases where this argument is a simple *state of affairs* which may be necessary without it being the case that one could also speak of the necessity of the assertion of the same content. The vagaries of terminology are such that it seems possible that in the work of certain authors the *de dicto/de re* distinction has acquired just this latter sense. Whether or not this is in fact the case, the important thing is to avoid confusing this second distinction between modalisation of the state of affairs and modalisation of the proposition with the first distinction – which was our starting point – between the functorial and propositional expressions of modality.

The Case where the Distinction Between the Two Expressions of Modality is no Longer Possible

Finally it should be noted that this distinction between the functorial and propositional expression of modality disappears, as a matter of *essence,* in those cases where the argument of the modality is an impersonal proposition, that is to say, where analysis fails to distinguish any argument of the predicator whatsoever. In *it is raining,* since the separation of subject and verb is merely a grammatical artifice and there is no argument which is really distinct from the predicator, there is no way to characterize independently the application of the modality to the functor and its application to the proposition. The two applications are indistinguishable, so that it is impossible to maintain the distinction illustrated above by means of examples such as

Peter is seriously ill

and

Peter is certainly ill.

But what, it might be objected, of expressions like

It's raining a lot
Certainly it's raining,

where the distinction we have been arguing ought not to exist, *can* be made out although the only possible argument of the modality is the propositional content as a whole? Is it not necessary to distinguish the second expression, where the modality concerns *the fact that it is raining,* from the first in which it is not this fact which can increase or decrease but rather the *volume of rain?*

259

This objection rests on a confusion of the distinction between functorial and propositional modality with a very different distinction. For it is important to note that only the first four of the traditional sorts of adverbs, of place, of time, of quantity, of manner, of affirmation, of negation, etc., concern what might be called the *modalities of being* of the propositional content:

> It's raining here
> It's raining now
> It's raining a little
> It's raining heavily.

In the case of the remaining families of adverbs, the modality is a matter of the relations of knowledge or of assertion to this content:

> It's certainly raining
> It's probably raining.

This distinction between what can summarily be called *objective* and *subjective* modality can be made even when the possibility of distinguishing between functorial and propositional modality has disappeared.

Confusion of these two distinctions is somewhat encouraged by the fact that subjective modality is more easily expressed in propositional fashion, whereas objective modality may, it seems, be expressed equally well in propositional or functorial fashion. It is because *certitude* is a *subjective modality* that, in spite of appearances,

> Peter is certainly ill

is more naturally interpreted as a propositional modality, whereas in the case of *seriousness,* whether I adopt the functorial mode of expression:

> Peter is seriously ill,

or the propositional mode of expression:

> It is serious that Peter is ill;

in both cases we are dealing with an *objective modality*. In the first case what is serious is (the nature of) the illness which Peter has; in the second case what is serious is, as we have seen, the circumstance *that Peter is ill* as a whole.

Notes

[1] It should be emphasized once and for all that the use of 'propositional argument' in what follows designates not exactly a proposition but a state of affairs capable of being the objective correlate of a proposition. Thus, for purposes of brevity, 'proposition' and its derivatives will be used in a way which was criticized in the last chapter.
   [The French expression 'proposition complétive' has occasionally been translated as 'completive proposition', but only when its meaning is: *a proposition containing a 'that'-clause as one of its arguments.* – Tr.]

[2] "Philosophie analytique et linguistique moderne", in *Dialectica*, vol.22, fasc.2, Lausanne, 1968, p.114.

[3] Cf. J.-L. Gardies, *Essai sur la logique des modalités*, 1969, p.13.

[4] Cf. W. and M. Kneale, *The Development of Logic*, 1968, p.83.

[5] J. M. Bocheński, *A History of Formal Logic*, pp.101–3.

[6] Abelard, Dialectica, ed. L. M. de Rijk, 1956, p.195. In this passage Abelard attributes an interpretation like this one to an author he calls 'Magister noster' and who may be, according to his modern editor, William of Champeaux.

[7] '... hec est modalis: *"possibile est Socratem currere"*, hec tamen non: *"Socratem currere est possibile"*, quia in propositione modali modus nec subicutur vel predicatur, sed determinat compositionem'. L. M. de Rijk, *Logica modernorum*, 1967, vol. II, part 2, p.390.

[8] Cf. W. and M. Kneale, *op. cit.*, p.236 and Bocheński, *op. cit,* pp.182ff.

[9] If indeed St. Thomas is the author of the treatise *De modalibus*, something which is by no means certain.

[10] N. Rescher, *Topics in Philosophical Logic*, 1968, p.24.

[11] Cf. G. E. Hughes and M. J. Cresswell, *An Introduction to Modal Logic*, London, Methuen and Co., 1974, pp.295, 297 and Robert Feys, *Modal Logics,* Louvain: E. Nauwelaerts, Paris: Gauthier-Villars, 1965, p.90.

[12] Where the following two constructions are both possible:

   Petrus major est Paulo
   Petrus major est quam Paulus (est).

[13] Cf. in particular von Wright, *The Logic of Preference*, 1963.

[14] It should not be concluded from this that the adverbial treatment of negation will always yield the same logical results as its propositional treatment. If negation is treated as an adverb then, as C. L. Hamblin notes, the proposition

   John does not read all the books

must be taken to mean that he does not read any books. Cf. *Montague Grammar*, edited by Barbara Partee, p.256.

[15] Arnauld and Lancelot, Second part, chapter 12, p.121.

[16] Cited by Chomsky, *Cartesian Linguistics*, p.46. In the particular case of the adverb it is surprising to note the interest shown by Chomsky in the analyses of Arnault and Dumarsais and the tolerance he shows in his descriptions of these analyses. The way certain classical grammarians dodge the issues posed by adverbs seems to be characteristic of a particular form of grammatical rationalism, which is naively attached to the reduction of basic categories at all costs.

[17] As is done, for example, by Richard Montague, *Formal Philosophy*, p.250.

[18] *La logique et son histoire d'Aristote à Russell*, 1970, p.77. It should however be pointed out that certain medieval authors did carefully underline the distinction between dictum and

261

proposition. Thus the author of the *Tractatus Anagnini* was careful to specify, around 1200, that one can say:

(1) loquendo de rebus: "omnis fenix est animal";
(2) loquendo de propositionibus: "vera est ista:
    'omnis fenix est animal'";
(3) loquendo de dictis: "verum est omnem fenicem esse animal".

L. M. de Rijk, *Logica modernorum*, vol.II, part 2, p.238.

Chapter Ten
Aspects of Aspect

Aspectualizers and Grammar

In this chapter we shall not attempt to determine what the grammatical notion of 'aspect' involves nor the justification for using this term. The word is employed in what follows, in a deliberately approximate fashion, to refer to the study of certain verbal forms, *aspectualizers*, that are said to have an aspectual or temporal value, such as *to begin to, to cease to, to continue to, venir de* (to have just), *to be going to*.

In addition, we shall consider only the uses of these verbs in French and English, although it seems likely that some of our conclusions can be extended to other languages. Such a procedure may, of course, simply provide further opportunities for ironical reflections on our pretentions to set out the elements of a pure, rational grammar.

But examples from French and English will provide us with no more than a foothold and a starting point. There can be no question here of providing a theory that is capable of dealing with the range and variety of uses of such expressions in French or English. Indeed, our aim in what follows only makes sense on the assumption that such a theory is impossible in languages such as English or French. Expressions like those to be studied in this chapter may fit situations of very different kinds, depending on the syntactic and semantic contexts. To mention only one example, to which we shall have occasion to return, what grammarian would dare to condemn *cesser de commencer à (cease to begin to)* as ungrammatical in French? All we can hope to do is to clarify certain possible a *priori* conditions on the grammaticality and agrammaticality of this sort of expression. This is our justification for speaking here of a rational grammar, however empirical our point of departure is.

The present chapter makes use of certain semantic procedures not employed elsewhere in this book and which have been studied in detail elsewhere.[1] In an expression such as

Peter is beginning to dig his garden*

we have, in principle, two different possible ways of giving a grammatical analysis of *is beginning to.*

(1) We may treat it as a *functorial functor with one argument* that is itself *functorial;* the functor *is beginning to* takes the functor *dig* as its argument to form the new functor *is beginning to dig.* It will be seen that, to the extent that *dig* is a functor with two nominal arguments (*Peter* and *his garden*), *is beginning to dig* will itself be a functor with two nominal arguments. Had the argument of *is beginning to* been a functor with a single nominal argument (such as *work* or *dig* taken as an intransitive verb) or had it been a functor without a nominal argument (as in impersonal sentences), the new functors so formed (*begins to work, it is beginning to rain*) would itself have taken the same number of nominal arguments (in these two cases 1 or 0) as its functor-argument.

(2) We may also treat *begin to* as a propositional functor with two arguments, one of which is nominal, the other propositional. On this analysis *Peter* is the nominal argument of *is beginning to* whereas *Peter digs his garden* is its propositional argument. When combined with the functor *is beginning to,* these two arguments immediately form a proposition, the global proposition with which we started. If we opt for this analysis rather than the first analysis we must take care to ensure that the nominal argument (here *Peter*) of *is beginning to* (at least when it has a nominal argument) is at the same time the first nominal argument of the functor (here *digs*) that forms the proposition (here *Peter digs his garden*) that is the propositional argument of *is beginning to.*

For reasons that are in the first place at least of a logical nature, and to facilitate the analysis of aspectualizers carried out below, we opt for the second type of analysis. In other words, we shall treat *begin to, cease to, continue to, be in the course of, to be going to* as functors that take a name and a proposition as arguments and that have the additional peculiarity that, if this proposition-argument is not impersonal, its subject must be identical with the name-argument. But now this last grammatical requirement itself allows us to ignore, logically speaking, the subject of *is beginning* and concentrate on the clause. For in our example *what is beginning* is that *Peter digs his garden.* There is thus nothing to prevent us from transposing our expressions so as to obtain impersonal sentences

It begins to be the case that Peter digs his garden
It is ceasing to be the case...
It continues to be the case...

(Il est en train de se faire que…)
It has just been the case that…
It is going to be the case that…

that resemble the classic forms of modal propositions (*It is necessary that*), deontic propositions (*It is obligatory that*), or temporal propositions (*It will be the case that*). From now on we shall consider our group of aspectualizers only as transposed in this way.

Before it is possible to construct a model of the group of expressions under study, we must introduce an important distinction that concerns their proposition-argument. In a language such as French, this proposition-argument may correspond to two very different situations.

(1) If I say that *Peter is working* or that *Peter is beginning to work,* the truth of these sentences implies, in the first case, that Peter is actually working at *each of the instants* during which he is working; in the second case, that Peter is actually working at *each of the instants* of a certain length of time from the instant at which he begins to work.

(2) If, on the other hand, I say that *Peter is dying, that he is covering a certain distance,* or that *he is beginning to cover this distance,* the truth of the first two sentences clearly does not imply that Peter dies or covers the distance in question at *each of the instants* of a certain length of time from the instant at which he begins to cover this distance.

It seems to us to be impossible to deal with these two uses that in French (and in many other languages) are combined or confused with one another, in terms of a single model. For in the first case the truth of the proposition-argument for a determinate space and time can be analysed in terms of the truth of the same proposition at each of the instants of this temporal stretch. (Peter has *worked for two hours*). In the second case, on the other hand, such an analysis is impossible. If I say that *Peter took two hours to die,* he did not die at any of the instants of this temporal stretch, not even the last one, although it is true that he *passed away* (which is not at all the same thing) at this last instant. In the first case it is possible to quantify over the instants of time (*Peter worked at each instant of these two hours*). In the second case it is possible to quantify only over those collections of instants that are periods of time (*There was a period of two hours that Peter took to die*).

At least in French and English the confusion is complicated by the fact that there is an ambiguous use *not only* of the aspectualizers with which we are here concerned *to be engaged in, to begin to, but also* of expressions

265

that serve as the propositional argument of such aspectualizers. Thus the verb *die* refers sometimes to that passage from life to death that is often said to be instantaneous and to which only the first sort of quantification applies and sometimes to that transition characteristic of all except so-called 'sudden deaths', which is sometimes described as an 'agony' and whose occurrence is bound up with a temporal stretch the instants of which are held to be inseparable.

The problems we face are of course very considerably simplified if we limit ourselves to those propositions whose truth over a particular stretch of time (a period which in the limit case can be reduced to a single instant) can be considered equivalent to their truth at each instant (even, when, in the limit case, the instant is unique) of this stretch. A limitation of this sort seems to us to be a prerequisite of their semantic verification. It also means of course that the gap between our analysis and a language such as French or English increases. In order to reduce this gap it would be necessary to construct a second model for those propositions whose truth concerns not instants of time but sets of instants and to combine these two models. But such an ambitious programme belongs to the distant future. Here we shall stay within the self-imposed limits just indicated.

The first step is to grant that the aspectualizers with which we are concerned involve a conception of time that can be characterized by a relation of *priority* (*anteriority*) between instants, a relation that is clearly irreflexive and transitive and hence asymmetrical. If the symbols $\sim, ., \supset$ designate respectively the connectives of negation, conjunction (and) and implication (if ... then) and if $t, t', t'', \ldots$ are variables for instants, $\forall$ the universal quantifier (whatever) and if *ant* expresses the relation of priority between the two terms following it then we shall say

$$\forall t \sim \text{ant}\, t\, t$$
$$\forall t\, t'\, t'' \left[(\text{ant}\, t\, t' . \text{ant}\, t'\, t'') \supset \text{ant}\, t\, t'' \right]$$
$$\forall t\, t' (\text{ant}\, t\, t' \supset \sim \text{ant}\, t'\, t)$$

There seems to be little doubt that the first two of these properties and so also the third, which follows from them, can be regarded as features of the ordinary representation of time presupposed by expressions such as *begin, cease, continue*. But as soon as we turn to *connectedness* which can be translated by the formula

$$\forall t\, t' (\text{ant}\, t\, t' \lor \text{ant}\, t'\, t \lor t = t')$$

266

where the symbol ∨ stands for the connective of disjunction (or) and = expresses identity (between two instants), it is by no means evident that this relation invariably captures the relationship of *priority* between instants. For to say of any two instants, past, present or future, that one of them must be anterior (prior) to the other or vice versa unless they are identical is tantamount to adopting a strictly linear conception of time. On this view temporal instants in the past as well as in the future are ordered along a single line. One might, however, be tempted by an alternative. The unilinearity of the past, the source of the necessity with which every completed event is immediately endowed and which makes it henceforth impossible for such an event to have been other than it was, may be opposed to the plurilinearity of the future, the source of the future's lack of determination. To make this distinction is to admit *connectedness* only in the past. In what follows we shall ignore this restriction of connectedness to the past because such restrictions are based on a confusion between the *future* and the *possible*.[2] If I say that it is possible that it will rain tomorrow, I assert the existence of *at least* one rainy tomorrow amongst the different possible tomorrows. If, on the other hand, I go so far as to say that *it will rain tomorrow,* I assert that the real tomorrow, which is of course unique, will be rainy, without making any reference to the set of possible tomorrows. In French the use of the future allows a clear distinction between

Il pleuvra demain (It will rain tomorrow – the indicative mood)

and

Il est possible qu'il pleuve demain (It is possible that it rains tomorrow – clause in the subjunctive)

and

Il est nécessaire qu'il pleuve demain (It is necessary that it rains tomorrow – clause in the subjunctive)

This grammatical distinction seems to presuppose the *unilinearity* of both future time and past time and hence the unlimited *connectedness* of the relation of *anteriority,* in spite of the legitimate doubts about this point that we have just mentioned.

The *density* of time gives rise to further doubts. Time is dense if between any two distinct instants there always exists a third

$\forall t\, t'\, [\text{ant}\, t\, t' \supset \exists\, t''\, (\text{ant}\, t\, t''\,.\, \text{ant}\, t''\, t')]$

where $\exists$ is the existential quantifier (for at least one). If we add this property, then we attribute to the succession of instants the same properties as the rational numbers. Now it seems that within a language such as French, we find two distinct ways of representing time and two different uses of language:

(1) There is first the common habit of taking the succession of temporal instants to be not only *dense* but *continuous* like the real numbers. Thus, if we take *density,* which is the only property that interests us here, it is as easy to determine the existence of a third instant between any two distinct instants as it is to determine a third point between two distinct points on a line, however close they are to one another.

(2) But it is also often the case that the succession of the moments of social time, in particular that of different days

Monday, Tuesday, Wednesday...
the first, the second, the third... of the month
yesterday, today, tomorrow...

is treated in such a way that between two successive days there is no room for any temporal instant.

Thus at the level of the spoken language we find two competing uses, one admitting and one rejecting the *density* of time, both of which we must take into account.

What is it to *begin, to cease* and to *continue* to do something? Let us begin by concentrating on this question. We may use t_0 as a constant designating the present instant. The proposition

At t_0 Peter begins to F^3

which, as we have seen, can be transposed as follows

At t_0 it begins to be the case that Peter F-s

can be analysed as the conjunction of the following two assertions

(1) During a certain period of time immediately prior to t_0 Peter does not F
(2) At t_0 and during a certain period of time immediately subsequent to t_0, Peter F-s.

268

Similarly, the proposition

At t_0 Peter ceases to F

can be analysed as the conjunction of the following two propositions

(1) During a certain period of time immediately prior to t_0 Peter F-s.
(2) At t_0 and during a certain period of time immediately subsequent to t_0 Peter does not F

Finally the proposition

At t_0 Peter continues to F

may be analysed as the conjunction of the first of these two assertions with the second of the two assertions that, as we have seen, characterize the proposition

At t_0 Peter begins to F

It will be noted that this conjunction may also be reduced to the simple proposition

During a certain period of time that begins before t_0 and that finishes after t_0 Peter F-s.

What we have said so far about the three verbs *begin, cease, continue* is in part open to the criticism of arbitrariness. The most we can pretend to do here is to describe the most frequent meaning exhibited by uses of these verbs. But it goes without saying that in French or English, for example, these meanings are by no means definitely fixed or, to be more exact, usage jumps from one meaning to the other without this being at all obvious. To give just one example of a possible meaning not captured by our description, it may be the case that

At t_0 Peter continues to F

remains true even if, during a particular period of time following on immediately from t_0 Peter does not F, provided he F-s at t_0 and for a period of time immediately prior to t_0. Nevertheless, it remains the case that we can only give a model of the way language works by fixing more or less arbitrarily the features to be retained by the model, even if we subsequently become aware of uncertainties about the way a language really works and modify our model.

In spite of this our descriptions of *begin to, cease to, continue to* can be expressed in the language of *first-order predicate calculus with identity*. We quantify over instants of time and the two-place predicate $f(tx)$, or ftx for short, means that x F-s at t. We may note here, without pursuing the matter, that the transposition we have noted from

x begins to F

to

It begins to be the case that x F-s

could with equal, if not greater justification be rendered as a predicate with one argument, ft. For we would not know what to do with the second argument if we had to express that *it is beginning to rain*.
The proposition

At t_0 x begins to F

can be expressed in the language of the first order predicate calculus with identity by the conjunction of the following

(1) $\exists t \{\text{ant } t\, t_0.\ \forall t'\ \{[(\text{ant } t\, t' \vee t = t').\ \text{ant } t'\, t_0] \supset \sim ft'\, x \}\}$

(2) $\exists t'' \{\ \text{ant } t_0\, t''.\ \forall t'''\ \{[(\text{ant } t_0\, t''' \vee t_0 = t''').\ (\text{ant } t'''\, t'' \vee t''' = t'')] \supset ft'''\, x\}\}$

It goes without saying that in order to represent

At t_0 x ceases to F

all we need to do is to replace, in the above two conjuncts, "$\sim ft'\, x$" and "$ft'''\, x$" by "$ft'\, x$" and "$\sim ft'''\, x$" and that in order to express

At t_0 x continues to F

we need only replace, in the first conjunct, "$\sim ft'\, x$" by "$ft'\, x$".
The transpositions we have just carried out make quite clear the logical equivalence between *begin to* and *cease to not*. It will also be seen that the description we have chosen to give of *continue to* would fit certain uses of *to be engaged in* equally well so that we may treat these two expressions as synonymous, without, however, deluding ourselves that this decision avoids clashing with various concrete usages. We have merely singled out and privileged a description common to the two expressions, a de-

scription picked out from two sets of descriptions which, in concrete linguistic reality, are not at all identical but merely secants.[4]

The transposition suggested of *begin to, cease to* etc. provides us with our first method of checking the grammaticality of certain combinations of expressions. Thus to begin with the most elementary cases, expressions such as

At t x begins and ceases to F
At t x begins and continues to F
At t x begins and continues to not F

can be seen immediately to be agrammatical and we find the justification for this in the fact that once transposed into the language of the predicate calculus, they yield contradictory expressions. The way in which we defined *begin to, cease to, continue to* and *continue to not* makes each pair of these expressions logically incompatible provided we add to the axioms and rules of the predicate calculus, the theorems establishing the properties of irreflexiveness, transitivity, connectedness and the relation of priority between instants. Asymmetry, it will be remembered, can be deduced from the first two properties and we have no need to assume *density* here, which shows that these incompatibilities remain incompatibilities whichever of the two conceptions of time we distinguished are applied.

The vocabulary we have employed also allows us to express the future and past of a verb provided we do not seek to distinguish between different types of past tense *(present perfect, simple past)*. Thus the expressions

x will F
x has F-ed

may be re-written as

$\exists t (\text{ant } t_0 \, t . f t x)$
$\exists t (\text{ant } t \, t_0 . f t x)$

If, now, we combine this way of re-writing the tenses of verbs with the transposition just described, the agrammaticality of expressions such as

x begins to F and *x* will never F
x ceases to F and *x* has never F-ed
x was F-ing when he began to F

will be justified by reference to the same logical basis as before.

The translation of these expressions into the predicate calculus shows that they are contradictory without assuming the *density* of time. If, however, we look at expressions that are related to those of the latter sort, such as

x ceases to F and has never been engaged in F-ing
x begins to F and *x* will never be engaged in F-ing

we find that the very same method indicates that the density of time must be presupposed if they are to be shown to be contradictory.

This method of transposition provides a means of assigning to completive expressions (such as *x begins to F*), which are clearly not directly expressible in the language of the *calculus of predicates,* equivalent expressions formed from the usual predicates with nominal arguments (such as *t is prior to t'* or *x* F-s) which are easily expressed in this language. And since this reduction of the one sort of expression to the other can be repeated indefinitely, we have a criterion for deciding whether the apparently tricky class of expressions such as *begin to begin, continue to continue, begin to continue,* in which the completive proposition occurs twice, is in fact grammatical.

Having stressed the possibility of translating aspectualizers into the language of the calculus of predicates we want now to deal in some detail with an alternative approach. This alternative yields exactly the same results as the first, but employs different methods. It provides a good illustration of the possibilities for investigating modality by semantic methods that have been opened up by work inspired by writers such as Carnap in the last two decades. The possibility of re-writing aspectualizers already mentioned so as to obtain, without any loss of sense, impersonal propositions such as

It is beginning to be the case that *x* F-s

suggests that they have some similarity with the classical modal propositions and this suggests immediately that the semantic treatment of modal propositions can be applied to the expressions we are interested in.

Aspectualizers and the Semantics of Modal Propositions

In order to provide a semantics we face a choice between using simple linear schemes which have the advantage of directly illustrating the linearity of time and sequences of tableaux in which each tableau represents an instant or a set of successive instants, the left-hand column containing propositions that are true at that instant or set of instances and the right-handed column propositions that are false at that instant or set of instances. For reasons of convenience that need not concern us, we shall opt for the second type of schema.

This means that we shall analyse expressions such as

At $t_0 x$ begins to F

not as a conjunction of two propositions, one concerning the immediate past which excludes the present, the other concerning the immediate future and including the present, but as the conjunction of three propositions concerning

a certain period belonging to the immediate past
the present instant
a certain period belonging to the immediate future

respectively, where, of course, both past and future exclude the present instant. Thus, to the proposition under consideration we assign a sequence of three tableaux. In the centre tableau, which represents the instant t_0, we write the two propositions *x begins to F* and *x* F-s in the *true* column; in the left-hand tableau, which represents a period immediately prior to t_0, we write in the *false* column the proposition *x* F-s (without which there would, of course, be no beginning at t_0); finally, in the right-hand tableau, which represents a period immediately subsequent to t_0, we write in the *true* column the proposition *x* F-s.

in some period immediately prior to t_0		At t_0		in some period immediately sub- sequent to t_0	
true	false	true	false	true	false
		1. *x* begins to F			
	2. *x* F-s	2. *x* F-s		2. *x* F-s	

In order to see why the expression

At t_0 x begins and ceases to F

is agrammatical, it suffices to observe that the truth of the second conjunct of this conjunction would make it necessary to write the proposition xF-s in the *false* column of the centre tableau. The assertion of the conjunction would then involve the contradictory claim that the proposition x F-s is at the present instant both true and false.

In order to see why the expression

At $t_0 x$ begins and continues to F

is agrammatical it suffices to note that the truth of the second conjunct of this conjunction would force us to accept that there is a period of time immediately prior to t_0 for which x F-s is true. It is true that we have no guarantee that this period immediately prior to t_0 is identical with the period, itself immediately prior to t_0, for which the truth at t_0 of x *begins to F* led us to admit the falsity of x F-s. But if it is true that the two periods immediately prior to t_0 that are required by the double admission at t_0 of the truth of x *begins to F* and of x *continues to F* are not necessarily identical, the fact that they are both immediately prior to t_0 implies that necessarily the one is included in the other so that the period determined by this inclusion, which is itself immediately prior to t_0, will be such that the proposition x F-s would be both true and false over this period.

Analogous arguments, that it would be tiresome to set out here, can be used to establish all the other incompatibilities between the 4 terms *begin to, cease to, continue to, continue not to* taken in pairs. Now it goes without saying that, although our desire to stay as close as possible to the data with which experience presents us has meant that we have so far proceeded by making use of a simple argument, it is easy to reduce this argument to a set of rules which guarantee that the level of rigour we have attained is that of a purely formal procedure.

The tableau that corresponds to the proposition x *begins to F* can be used to show why x *begins to F* and x *will never F* is agrammatical. For the second conjunct amounts to the claim that for every period after t_0 the proposition x F-s is to be written in the *false* column. Now the period immediately subsequent to t_0 for which the truth at t_0 of x *begins to F* had forced us to accept the truth of x F-s is clearly included in the immediate, infinitely prolonged future for which x *will never F* has just forced us to accept the falsity of x F-s.

274

The expression

   x was engaged in F-ing when he began to F

would force us to assume the existence of an instant t prior to the present instant t_0. The tableau corresponding to this instant t which would stand to the left of the tableau for t_0 would have on its left a tableau corresponding to a certain period immediately prior to t. In this last tableau the truth at t_0 of x *was engaged in F-ing* or, if one prefers, the truth at t of x *is engaged in F-ing* would oblige us to put x F-s in the *true* column.

in some period immediately prior to t		At some instant t prior to t_0		At t_0	
true	false	true	false	true	false
3. x F–s		2. x is engaged in F-ing		1. x was engaged in F-ing	

   Of course we have omitted all implications that play no role in our argument; thus we have not written x F-s in the *true* column of t, nor have we set out a tableau for some period immediately subsequent to t for which x F-s would again go into the *true* column. For, in order to complete the demonstration by showing why the initial expression is agrammatical, it suffices to note that the subordinate clause of our proposition would oblige us to write x *begins to F* in the *true* column of t, which would imply to the left of tableau t a period immediately prior to t for which x F-s is false; this period will necessarily overlap with the other period immediately preceding t for which we were obliged to grant that x F-s is true.

   So far, it will be observed, we have not found it necessary to take into account the density of time. In other words, the reasons we have given for the agrammaticality of various expressions hold good whether time is represented as an infinitely divisible stretch, similar to the geometrical line, or, for example, as a sequence of days, similar to that of the whole numbers. However, the proposition

   x ceases to F and has never engaged in F-ing

is a contradiction if one rejects the density of time.

For if the density of time is rejected then for a sequence such as the following, this proposition will be true.

in every period prior to yesterday		yesterday		today		tomorrow	
true	false	true	false	true	false	true	false
				x ceases to F			
	x F-s	x F-s			x F-s		x F-s

According to our model, the proposition *x ceases to F* is true today since:
(1) for a certain period of time immediately prior to today, namely *yesterday, x* F-s;
(2) today and for a certain period of time immediately prior to today, namely, *tomorrow, x does not F*.
Periods of time, it will be noted, can be reduced to punctual entities such as *yesterday* and *tomorrow*. As for the proposition

x has never been engaged in F-ing

it is also true, that is to say, its negation

It has been the case that *x* has been engaged in F-ing

is false, since the only past moment at which *x* F-ed, namely yesterday, was not preceded by nor indeed followed by, any other moment at which *x* also F-ed. We must therefore conclude that our initial proposition may be true, may have a sense.

If, now, we admit the density of time the tableau which, in our model above, represented *today* will henceforth designate the instant t_0 at which *x* ceases to F.

But if we take the tableau which represented *yesterday* to stand for some instant prior to t_0 at which the proposition *x* F-s is still true, this instant, however close it is to t_0, must be distinct from it so that the density of time makes it necessary to admit other instants before and after t_0 at which *x* F-s is also true since it only begins to be false at t_0. For it to be the case that x ceases to F at t_0, then, it is necessary that x has previously been engaged in F-ing and this is the explanation of the agrammaticality of the expression we started out with.

If we now apply this semantics to the study of expressions in which an aspectualizer occurs twice, we find a first group of such expressions:

x begins to begin to
x begins to cease to
x continues to begin to
x continues to cease to

whose agrammaticality can be determined without invoking the *density* of time. Consider the first of these expressions. If *x begins today to begin to F* then it must be the case that

x begins to F today, which implies that *x F-s today*,
and *tomorrow x begins to F* which implies that *x does not F today*.

The group of expressions

x ceases to cease to
x ceases to begin to
x begins to continue to

differs from the four previous cases in that this group of expressions is only contradictory if one admits the density of time. The first of these three expressions, for example, is true in the following model:

the day before yesterday		yesterday		today		tomorrow	
true	false	true	false	true	false	true	false
				x ceases to cease to F			
					x ceases to F		
		x ceases to F			x ceases to F		x ceases to F
x F-s			x F-s		x F-s		

Here the truth today of *x ceases to cease to F* is justified by the fact that the proposition *x ceases to F* is true yesterday and false today and tomorrow. The truth yesterday of *x ceases to F* is justified by the fact that the proposition *x* F-s is true the day before yesterday and false yesterday and today. The falsity today and tomorrow of *x ceases to F* is based on the sole fact that the proposition *x* F-s is false yesterday and tomorrow respectively.

But if we admit the density of time the tableau which, in our model, stood for *today* will henceforth designate the instant t_0 at which *x ceases to cease to F*. And if we read the tableau that represented *yesterday* as referring to some instant prior to t_0 at which the proposition *x ceases to F* is still true, this instant, however close it is to t_0, must be distinct from t_0. Thus the density of time implies that after this instant and before t_0 other instants at which the proposition *x ceases to F* is also true, since it only begins to be false at t_0. It is therefore, necessary, if *x ceases to cease to F* that it had previously been *engaged in ceasing to F*. There is no need to continue our analysis since we had determined at the start that 'to be engaged in' and 'continue' are synonymous and had recognized the contradiction inherent in the expression 'continue to cease' to which our analysis had led us.

Matters are quite different in the case of the two expressions:

x ceases to continue
x continues to continue

both of which can be true even if one admits the *density* of time. The first of the two expressions corresponds to the instant at which the subject, having F-ed for a certain period, (which, if time is not dense, must contain at least two distinct instants) F-s a last time: then *x* still does not cease to F but it ceases to continue to F. Hence, if time is dense, the only difference between *cease* and *cease to continue* is that, in the first case, at the present moment *x* no longer F-s, in the second case it still F-s. In the first case the immediate past *during* which *x still F-s* is an interval *open on the right-hand side* whereas it is closed in the second case. In order for it to be true that *today x continues to continue to F* it suffices that *yesterday, today and tomorrow x continues to F,* a condition which is, for example, satisfied if *the day before yesterday, yesterday, today, tomorrow and the day after tomorrow x F-s.*

It would be over-simple to conclude that we have shown that the three

278

groups of duplicated aspectualizers which we have distinguished are such that

(1) the duplications in the first group are agrammatical;
(2) the duplications in the second group may give rise to certain *ambiguities* in usage, traces of which should be found in natural languages; and
(3) the duplications in the third group will always be accepted as grammatical.

These syntactio-semantic conclusions which, it should be borne in mind, are dependent on the *relatively arbitrary* fashion in which we initially fixed the sense of *continue to* etc. can be modified by pragmatic considerations which we should not lose sight of.

Let us take as an example the last duplicated expression we examined.

x continues to continue to F

The first thing to note is that the implication

If x continues to continue to F, then x continues to F

can only be true because, were it false, i.e. if its antecedent were true and its consequent false, the truth of this antecedent would imply the truth at t_0 of the proposition x *continues to F*, which is the consequent whose falsity we have just assumed. On the other hand, the implication that is the converse of the last implication

If x continues to F, then x continues to continue to F

can be falsified by the following model

the day before yesterday		yesterday		today		tomorrow	
true	false	true	false	true	false	true	false
				x con- tinues to F	x con- tinues to con- tinue to F		
			x con- tinues to F	x F-s		x F-s	
	x F-s	x F-s					

279

but can only be falsified in this manner if the *density* of time is rejected. In other words, if we admit the *density* of time, we must regard the two expressions

    x continues to F
    x continues to continue to F

as logically equivalent.

But although the simple expression and the duplicated expression are equivalent, the double aspectualizer may easily appear to be absurd. It is not any sort of semantic absurdity that is involved, such as the contradictions yielded by the double aspectualizers in the first of our three groups, but a *pragmatic uselessness* like that exemplified by sequences of modalities in the system of modal logic S5, where $\square\square p$ (*it is necessary that it is necessary that p*) is equivalent to $\square p$ (*it is necessary that p*). It may, therefore, be felt that the equivalence just noted between a simple and a duplicated aspectualizer should lead us to consider such duplication as agrammatical. For the exploration of the semantic basis of agrammaticality should not make us forget the possibility of a pragmatic basis for agrammaticality.

The methods employed so far also make possible an analysis of

    x has just F-ed
    x is going to F

The first expression is ambiguous and we shall concentrate on that meaning of the expression that corresponds to the following conjunction of three assertions:

(1) at a moment t, just prior to the present moment t_0 x F-s;
(2) during a certain period, immediately prior to t x does not F; and
(3) during the period immediately subsequent to t and immediately prior to the present t_0 x does not F.

Let us agree, finally, that the meaning of *x is going to F* will be symmetrical in the future to that of *x has just F-ed* in the past.

One apparent difficulty presented by our description is connected with the inexactness of the notion 'just prior to' employed above. The extension of *being just prior to* can only be fixed by the context in which it occurs. It may vary from a few seconds to some thousands of years. Consider the difference between the case where I say at 12.01 that *the midday bell has just rung* and the case where the contemporary palaeontologist assures us that, as far as the different geological eras are concerned, *homo sapiens has just made its appearance on earth.* In order to give a precise meaning to 'have just', it would be necessary to determine *for every particular context* the maximal distance admitted between t and t_0 which justifies the use of the expression.

It will be observed that our description tends to allow that expressions such as

x has just F-ed, F-s and is going to F
x is going to have just F-ed

are *in principle* grammatical even when time is *dense.* We add the qualification 'in principle', because, in fact, whether or not an expression is grammatical depends on the verb we subtitute for the variable F. The combination of *have just* and *going to* with *begin* and *cease,* as described above, means that we must recognize the grammaticality of

x has just begun to
x has just ceased to
x is going to begin to
x is going to cease to

whilst the expressions

x has just continued
x is going to continue

can only be recognized as grammatical if the density of time is rejected.

Our analyses make one or two final remarks necessary. We have described certain expressions as *agrammatical* which are merely contradictory and which language avoids simply for the reason that such a contradiction prevents them from corresponding to any real situation, whereas in the logical tradition, they would normally be considered to be grammatically well-formed. It seems, then, that we are here ignoring the distinction which has been established at least since Husserl's *Logical Investigations* and which we expounded in Chapter One, between absurdity (*Widersinn*) and nonsense (*Unsinn*). If what is agrammatical belongs to the domain of nonsense, it must be a mistake to treat expressions belonging to the domain of absurdity as *agrammatical.* For absurd expressions such as

p and not -*p*

are well-formed expressions in the eyes of the logician.

We have no hesitation in deviating from traditional usage, first, because, as we saw in Chapter One the boundary between the domains of *grammar* and of *logic* is not something that can be settled by any self-evident criterion; secondly, because, in most languages, no one can determine exactly where grammar stops and logic begins. Where the boundaries are unclear our choice of where to draw a boundary can be based largely on what uses we want to make of languages.

A language used for purposes of calculation, such as logic, must treat logically contradictory expressions as grammatical if only because any other alternative would restrict the uses of logic. To mention just one example, the most readily accessible, the very possibility of reductio proofs[5] clearly presupposes that language can contain contradictory expressions which must therefore be grammatical.

But matters are different in the case of natural languages which, because of their ambiguities are not suitable for purposes of calculation and capable at most of being used to communicate arguments. It is because the purpose of such languages is above all communication, or, more generally, expression, that these languages should not state *what cannot be true*. Once again, then, pragmatic and not syntactic or semantic reasons make it possible for natural languages to contain at the level of grammar structures which, in languages whose purpose is calculation, must play a logical role only.[6]

Notes

* [The main verb in sentences such as *Pierre commence à becher son jardin* is occasionally translated in what follows by the English progressive form: *Peter is beginning to dig his garden* because the use of the simple present in English is restricted to such contexts as the 'dramatic present'. But the reader should bear in mind that what is under discussion in this chapter is aspect insofar as it is expressed by aspectualizers such as *is beginning to (commence à)* and *not* the use of the progressive form – *is digging, is beginning to dig* – to express aspect. The French aspectualizers *commencer à, cesser de, continuer à, venir de, aller* all correspond roughly to at least one English aspectualizer, whether this is used in the simple or the progressive form. But *en train de* is translated either by the continuous form of a verb which is not an aspectualizer or by *engaged in* – Tr.]

1 J.-L. Gardies, *Essai sur la Logique des Modalités,* Paris: P.U.F., 1979

2 On the representation of the *future* and the *possible,* see my *Essai sur la Logique des Modalités* – reference in last footnote – book I, chapters 1 and 2 and book II, chapter 3.

3 To F, of course means here to satisfy the predicate *f.*

4 Let us give an example of one sense of *to be engaged in (être en train de)* which *continue to* does not have. We have seen that if we say that *Pierre est mort en deux heures de temps*

282

(Peter took two hours to die) Peter's *dying* is not related to any of the instants that go to make up the two hour period, but is related to the totality of these instants. The form of words *être en train de* (be engaged in) is a means of passing from the action as related in this way to a totality of instants – what some grammarians call an *accomplishment* – to the action as related to each instant of this totality. Thus if *Pierre est mort en deux heures de temps* we cannot say that he died at each instant during these two hours. Rather: *At each instant during the two hours he was (engaged in) dying.* There is no corresponding use of *continuer de* (continue to).

Yet another sense of *être en train de* not possessed by *continuer de:* if I say that *Pierre était en train de travailler quand il a été interrompu* (Peter was engaged in working when he was interrupted) *was engaged in* clearly does not imply any continuation of the action subsequent to the moment at which Peter was interrupted.

5   This easily understood example has the disadvantage that it seems open to an objection – the existence of intuitionist logic. But it would be easy to show that intuitionist logic itself, even if it rejects reasoning by the absurd, nevertheless presupposes the grammaticality of contradictory expressions. Otherwise it would be necessary to define in intuitionist logic the grammaticality of

not (p and not -p)

which is a theorem in Heyting's logic, in such a way that the grammaticality of this expression did not presuppose that of

p and not -p.

6   This chapter originally appeared as "Éléments pour une grammaire pure de l'aspect" in *Modèles Linguistiques*, vol. III, 1981, 112–134.

Chapter Eleven
Conclusion

The other project was a scheme for entirely abolishing all words whatsoever; ... since words are only names for *things,* it would be more convenient for all men to carry about them such things as are necessary to express the particular business they are to discourse on.

Jonathan Swift, *Gulliver's Travels,* Part III, ch.5.

The Technical Schema of Communication

Let us now retrace the course of our argument in order to mark the main differences between it and other, closely related projects.

(1) We have not tried to set out the ideal grammar of a language whose goal is precisely defined terms and rigorous rules for their combination. On this point our aim differs from Carnap's attempt to construct the grammar of a language adapted to the use of science.

(2) Nor has our aim been that of the grammarian: that of providing a formal analysis of languages with which we are familiar, a logico-mathematical framework which will account as exhaustively as possible for the data provided by observation. Such aims are legitimate and, as we have seen, have an interest of their own. But our aim has been to provide the outlines of an inventory of the grammatical forms shaped by the very structure of communication, to show why some are necessary, and to give some idea of the wealth of other possibilities. Although we have by no means ignored facts of usage and the preoccupation with finding ideal solutions to grammatical problems, these have not been central to our concerns.

Our intention was to study the grammar of a certain type of language, which, though historically the most influential, is certainly not the only conceivable type of language. Two sorts of language have been deliberately ignored:

(a) The term 'language' is often applied, as we have seen, to systems of signs which, although they are rule-governed, have no meaning. We have often had to take into account the grammar of expressions without meaning, but this has always been incidental to our principal aim.

(b) The term 'language' is often used of systems of expression to which the distinction between signs and what they mean or signify does indeed apply, but where the relation between the two, insofar as they are related in any adequate manner, tends to be no more than a simple one-to-one correspondence. The best example is provided by musical notation, and is worth looking at in some detail.

Just as it is important to distinguish the fact that it is raining (independently of any naming of this fact) from my assertion 'it is raining', so, too, the symbols of the score I have in front of me are not to be confused with the passage of Mozart's music which is being played for me or which I remember. But the correspondence between signs and sounds here has nothing to do with that between a fact and the report of a fact. The articulation of the correspondence between sign and sound has been refined by centuries of musical theory and practice:

– to the form of each symbol (semibreve, minim, crotchet, quaver) there corresponds the duration of a different sound;

– to their position in the stave there corresponds a different tone quality.

Thus there is a genuine isomorphism between the printed score and the piece that is played, say, on a piano, in spite of the heterogeneity of the material support in each case. Yet one looks in vain for any such isomorphism in the languages we have been looking at. The correspondence between spoken language and phonetic writing-systems is indeed constructed in the same way as the correspondence between melodies and scores. But one qualification is needed here: our phonetic writing-systems are not the work of theoreticians whose aim was to provide a perfect correspondence between signs and sounds, and the weight of history has often overridden technical preoccupations. Thus the difference between musical notation and phonetic writing systems is simply the difference between a perfect and an imperfect system.

Another example of a 'language' (if this is here the correct term) which rests on an isomorphism between signs and what they signify is that of maps in geography. For the term 'language' is often used in such a way that the mere distinction between sign and object and the fact that the sign has been introduced to designate the object enable one to speak of a *language* which *represents* objects. But caution is needed here. The relation between a spoken and a written sentence is quite different from that between a sentence, whether written or spoken, and the corresponding state of affairs or even the perception the sentence expresses. That we frequently use the verbs *signify* and *symbolize* for both relations demonstrates only that they should be avoided. A famous example of the confusion is provided by Aristotle's assertion[1] that 'spoken words are the symbols of mental experiences and written words are the symbols of spoken words'. The language with which we have here been primarily concerned, however, is that which means or signifies *objects* or *states of affairs* and not that which simply takes another material support in order to form a structural equivalent of the object *signified* or *meant*.

A very simple assumption has guided what has been said so far: that language is, by and large, an instrument of communication and that it is in terms of this function that the main features of grammar have to be explained. It is necessary to go into this simple assumption here, since, where it has surfaced previously, certain criticisms have certainly occurred to the reader, criticisms coming from different quarters which we must now examine.

Even if we ignore the conceptual notations of logic and mathematics, whose main purpose is not communication but calculation, we find that our ordinary uses of natural languages exhibit many other functions than that of rational communication. Some of these functions we have already looked at, particularly in our examination of the *moods* of the verb, for although they are inconspicuous and easily overlooked within the indicative mood, they show up very clearly in the optative or performative moods. The following functions have been distinguished:

(1) A *conative* function, whose importance was emphasized in particular by K. Bühler and then by R. Jakobson.[2] It is in virtue of this function that we can bring a situation into being; this function is often to be found in performative uses of language.

(2) An *expressive* (or as it is sometimes called, an *emotive*) function. We often speak in order to 'get something off our chest' without any wish to provide someone with information. Poetical uses of language rely in part on this function, and the autistic use made of language by children, old people, dreamers, simpletons, or those who are simply absorbed in their own thoughts, relies on just this function.

(3) A *magical or incantatory* function by means of which we try to act

286

directly on the external world without making use of any transmission of information. Although grammatical imperatives are often employed to carry out this function it should not be equated simply with an order addressed to things.

(4) A *phatic* function, observed in particular by Malinowksi[3] in 'primitive languages', but which can be seen at work in many familiar situations, e.g. in society dinner conversations where it is not 'what is said that matters so much as that something is said'[4] or in those exchanges on the telephone which serve essentially to verify that the line is working ('Hello. Can you hear me?') or to attract the interlocutor's attention or to make sure that one does not lose his attention;[5] or all those situations in which the speaker may have no interest in communicating anything at all but seeks simply to fill a space in a conversation by making use of 'this caressing or reassuring quality of speech in general'.[6]

(5) A *distinctive* function, well described by Sapir: a social group, for example a group of people who are or were at the same school, a gang of thieves, the members of a club, a salon, even (as Proust pointed out) a pair of lovers, 'tends to develop peculiarities of speech which have the symbolic function of somehow distinguishing the group from the larger group into which its members might be too completely absorbed'.[7]

The goal or functions of language listed here are functions of the same sort as the function of communication. But there is a further, more serious point. Might it not be the case that some of these aims, which have so far perhaps been somewhat neglected, are prior to those upon which our attention has been concentrated? It has been said that both in the life of an individual and in the evolution of societies the autistic or incantatory use of language largely precedes its use as a means of conveying information. "A long rational education is needed", writes K. Vossler,[8] "to convince people that language is made for speaking, that is to say, made only for the purpose of reasonable communication with our fellow men". Might it not be the case that to explain language by reference to communication is to get things the wrong way round and to invoke what language turns into in order to give a bad rationalisation of what it is?

In order to answer this objection it is necessary to distinguish between *communication* and *information,* the latter being defined as *communication which is strictly indicative.* When considering language as a means of communication we took great care not to reduce it merely to a means of transmitting information; we took every precaution to preserve the independence of the non-indicative moods, performatives, imperatives, optatives, etc. To consider just one example: an order is a communicative act, even though, as we have seen, it cannot be reduced to the mere communication of a desire or a wish. If one wants to treat communication as the essential function of language it is important not to begin by reducing it, as André Martinet sometimes seems to do, to the simple "transmission of experience from one person to another".[9] If this reduction is avoided then much of what linguists have called the *conative function* of language turns out to belong to the domain of what we can justifiably call communication.

We must nevertheless recognize that not *all* the linguistic functions we have distinguished can be grouped under the concept of communication if the concept is not to be deprived of all sense. In addition, as André Martinet has emphasized, linguistic functions which are not communicative normally require a communicative framework. Even when communication is furthest from our minds we behave "as if it were necessary to make others understand us".[10] Let us consider the case of the phatic or expressive functions. The reason why the exercise of these functions cannot simply be replaced by mere noise is that the participants in, say, salon conversation indulge in a "comedy of communication"[11]: the garrulous bores who inundate us with suggestions to which we do not even listen enjoy the fact that they have found "a victim with whom they can pretend to communicate".[12] The role of communication in what we have called the *distinctive* function of language is even clearer; here there is no longer any question of comedy; we are concerned with the satisfaction of communicating within the small group for which we reserve messages that are at once indicative of our privacy and intimacy and yet incommunicable to others.

It is not, then, enough to recognize that communication is 'the primary function of language'; for until this expression has been clarified it means nothing at all. If communication is not only one of many linguistic functions or goals, then this is because the exercise of other functions presupposes communication. Without communication there would be no phatic function, no expressive function and no distinctive function; but man has been able to develop systems of signs which have communication as their only function. Thus the function of communication is the only aim or goal in the absence of which language would lack all other aims. This is why all non-communicative functions "presuppose a use of language whose modalities are determined by the communicative uses to which they are put".[13]

Language can therefore justifiably be regarded as a technique for communicating. This function is only slightly less evident than is the technical function of a tool, and for the following reason: the material existence of a tool makes it relatively easy to grasp what sort of purpose it has. On the other hand, *language*, the instrument we employ in *speech* acts, exists only – to use Saussure's distinction – as a *virtual* system, and this makes it correspondingly difficult to perceive. This apart, the fact that language may involve other functions than the technical functions of communication does not set it apart from any other sort of instrument. For one can brandish an axe or spear for other reasons than to cut or pierce something; such brandishings may serve as a means of self-expression or of self-affirmation in a dance or parade or even as the expression of a threat. Clearly, too, that important part of a tool, which we call its decorative aspect not only does not serve but may even impede any technical purpose.

It is nevertheless possible to study a technique or a tool by taking into account the 'ideal type' of the technical aims involved. For, as Max Weber has shown, the interpretation of a group of dispositions as the means of carrying out a particular aim provides the historian and sociologist with a very simple and reliable framework within which to get results. This framework can be developed by taking into account additional considerations of a different sort in a way which enables one to understand why an institution has deviated from the basic *ideal type*. Indeed, it is in the study of techniques of different sorts that the method of ideal types is most necessary, so necessary that historians often forget to make explicit what seems to them to be self-evident in such cases.

Were I to write a history of a certain sort of boat, the general explanatory schema, implicit because it is so basic, would rely on a whole series of physical characteristics: weights, comparative properties of solids and fluids, Archimedes' principle, etc. It is because of these facts that the boat is constructed either of a material whose specific weight is less than that of water or consists of a hollowed-out shell.

The horizontal form traditionally taken by boats can only be understood if the clash between two conflicting requirements is explicitly taken into account:

– the advantage gained by ensuring that a vessel has a maximum capacity, a requirement best satisfied by a circular form;

– the necessity of streamlining the vessel in such a way as to facilitate its movement.

Once we have an ideal type of this sort, then this can be the basis of other, supplementary considerations. For it would be wrong to ignore the fact that the explanation of the form of ships can never simply be a matter of technical considerations; the fact that what is responsible for the variations to be found in the forms of boats around the world is not simply differences in the elements or in the materials available; or the fact that a history of the ways technical innovations spread which accorded due importance to the routes taken and natural obstacles responsible for the varying degrees of expansion would not tell us everything about the nature of the instruments invented.

We will be able properly to understand the sense of such instruments in for example their magical, religious or simply symbolic uses only if we connect the empirical knowledge we possess about these with the model of their technical function, itself considered within the context of the means available to man. The reason for this connection is not only that it illuminates what is being explained, but rather – as Weber has amply demonstrated in his methodological writings – that it throws into relief what cannot be explained in this way, i.e. what must be explained in a different manner. The study of the technical function of a tool, over and beyond its positive advantages, is thus the indispensable negative preliminary to a study of all the other hidden functions and meanings it has; it is what gives a sense to the technical notions of invention and transmission.

That grammar may in part be regarded as a technique, signifies that grammar does not make sense without some reference to norms. The history of tools and techniques is, indeed, *normative,* in the following quite precise sense: although it has no business praising the excellence or denigrating the defects of the technical solutions it deals with, it can nevertheless only understand the structure of these solutions by reference to the problems posed. In most cases it can only make sense of the success and spread of one solution at the expense of another by referring to their relative adequacy. There is, therefore, something extremely naïve in the boast, more than a century old, that grammar should concern itself with "the search for laws which have no normative elements",[14] with "separating scientific linguistics from normative grammar".[15] The progress achieved in the experimental sciences seems in this respect to have so impressed those concerned with the discipline of grammar that they are able to dream of eliminating from their subject-matter everything except facts which are dealt with in the classical inductive manner. The elimination of value-judgments has seemed to some to be a scientific ideal; yet by its very nature grammar is such that it is impossible to study "the positive science of the facts of language"[16] unless these are viewed against the background of the technical problems to which these 'facts' often announce themselves as the solution.

It can now be seen that the term 'grammar' normally hides two different sorts of grammars which are often unfortunately confused because of the admittedly very close links between them. One sort of grammar explains how different known languages have come to be the way they are, and therefore, as we have just seen, involves comparing solutions with the demands of the situation to which the solutions are a response. This sort of grammar, which can be called descriptive must therefore already involve normative considerations. And just as the history of techniques – which is only possible if the historical solutions are compared with problems and obstacles encountered, i.e. if normative considerations are brought in – must be complemented by a normative methodology of techniques, so too descriptive grammar must be complemented by normative grammar.[17] In grammar, as in engineering, no amount of irony can rob expressions such as 'proper use', 'correct employment' of their sense.

It should not be thought that the above involves a failure to appreciate that a part of what grammarians call 'correct usage' is technically purely gratuitous and simply due to tradition. Our point is only that the nature of grammar is such that value judgments about usage are entirely justified. Contemporary grammarians are plagued by feelings of guilt that have robbed them of any inclination to lay down the law and this makes them happy to run the risk of being thought 'lax' because then at least they cannot be accused of being 'purists'. Their guilty conscience has its roots, at least in part, in an unjustified analogy with experimental science. But the role of the grammarian as judge is only open to the criticism that it betrays a 'metaphysical', 'substantialist', 'ontological'[18] or, let us say, an incorrect attitude where technical necessity and the weight of tradition are confused and what is simply the best solution or merely one possible solution is presented as necessary.[19]

This last remark justifies one aspect of the position argued for in this book that may have seemed paradoxical and might easily give rise to a criticism of the following sort: in what has been said so far there is no knowing whether what is being put forward is an ideal grammar quite different from the inferior grammars we are already familiar with or

291

whether, on the contrary, the aim has been to isolate a sort of grammatical skeleton and show that this is the basis of all grammars. Grammatical rationalism has often been the object of criticism of this sort. Its adversaries have often been able to show how it wavers between two tendencies, 'each being used to justify the other', in turn: 'the universality of fact and the necessity of law'.[20] But this oscillation, we would claim, is perfectly normal; far from undermining our thesis it tends rather to confirm it. For it is a peculiarity of certain technical solutions that where they are, as a matter of fact, universal or widespread, this always points to the excellence of their advantages as instruments.

But our refusal to admit the parallel between experimental science and linguistics, popular though this has been since the nineteenth century, is itself justifiable only if this parallel is in fact based on a naïve view of experimental science. Carnap has quite correctly pointed out that the use made by the physicist of physical laws is such that if someone were to try and apply these laws *a priori* to the objects of everyday experience such as stones and trees he would fail utterly. For these laws apply not to the objects of everyday experience but to objects that have been simplified through idealization, for example to the ideally straight pendulum or level of the physicist; "it is only with the help of the laws relating to these constructed forms, that he [the physicist] is then in a position to analyse into suitable elements the complex behaviour of real bodies."[21] Pure grammar is not very far removed from the pure physics of the lever or pendulum; it is only by virtue of this initial movement away from the world of real bodies that physics is finally able to deal with the latter. And there is nothing paradoxical in the claim that, as Carnap puts it: "the structure of a given language such as German or of certain classes of languages or even of some language within a language can best be studied and explained by comparing it with a constructed language as a system of reference".[22] The advantage which Carnap mentions is even more obvious if comparison is made not simply with some *artificially constructed* language, which is what the quotation may suggest, but with a language constructed to meet certain requirements, precisely those requirements the languages under study have to meet.

It is only if one agrees with Husserl that it is after all possible to find "*a priori* laws of the combination and transformation of meanings, laws which must be more or less revealed in every developed language, both in its theory of grammatical forms and in a related class of grammatical incompatibilities",[23] and if, secondly, one is successful in establishing

292

such laws, that one can account for "contingent linguistic habits" and go on to distinguish between the different "matters of mere fact concerning language, which develop in one way in one speech-community and in another way in another". In terms of a distinction dear to Chomsky, the recognition of the "surface structures of a language" presupposes prior recognition of the 'deep structures' common to different linguistic systems. There is, therefore, nothing astonishing about the apparent discovery by generative grammar of a sort of common fund of universal structures, arrived at by comparing linguistic systems as different from one another as the Amerindian languages on the one hand and the Indo-European languages on the other. Even less surprising should be the psychological observation that "the speaker of a language knows many things that he has not learnt".[24] What is astonishing, however, is that the grammarians of historically existing languages have needed more than a century to get used to no longer being dazzled by history and to give up preaching the false gospel that "languages could differ from one another in completely unlimited and unforeseeable ways".[25]

The Linguistic *A Priori*

There is one respect, however, in which Chomsky, or at least some of those linguists who claim to be influenced by him, do not seem to be completely free of certain traditional prejudices. After showing the deep similarity between the tendencies of *The Port-Royal Grammar* and *Generative Grammar,* Nicholas Ruwet[26] attempts to qualify this similarity by emphasizing the latter's originality compared to the former: *The Port-Royal Grammar* defined deep structure directly "without first analysing the surface structures"; to this extent, Ruwet informs us, it suffered from the limitations inherent in every conception which takes as its starting point mental processes and simply postulates these *a priori.* Chomsky and his collaborators, in contrast, are said to have begun by analysing surface structures and to have proceeded from there to the point where they have discovered deep structures, a discovery which is only supposed to have been possible via a systematisation of results obtained in part through the initial analysis. For someone who sees generative grammar in this light the universalist conclusion – which was already to be found in *The Port-Royal Grammar* – is put on a much sounder basis: it is obtained *a posteriori,* and does not rest on any initial postulate.

We do not know the extent to which these remarks would command the agreement of Chomsky himself. But he has, it may be noted, been careful to reject the reproach of *apriorism* which has been directed against 'philosophical grammar',[27] showing that if the latter merits reproach, the weaknesses that need to be criticized are more likely to be "exactly the opposite of those imputed to it by modern critics". Philosophical grammar has restricted itself to an approach which has been too narrowly descriptive because of its timidity in the face of the charge of apriorism. It has indeed tried to pick out common structures behind the different sorts of examples. But "what is missing is a theory of linguistic structure that is articulated with sufficient precision and is sufficiently rich to bear the burden of justification". Chomsky here certainly does not reject the possibility of building up to this theory of linguistic structure on the basis of analysis of surface structures; but his point seems to be that he would have no objection to the alternative approach.

It has to be recognized that the idea that to reason *a priori* is "to be unfaithful to the spirit of the positive method"[28] is widespread even amongst philosophers; that to proceed by "'reasoned speculation' is to fail completely to recognize... 'the demands of science' and to construct a grammar 'in a scholastic spirit'; that it belongs to genuine science to 'ignore everything except the classification of facts so that in this way laws emerge'". Genuine science, it is held, can explain only with statistics, comparison and analogy; and only by confronting different vocabularies and grammars is it possible to give a new sense to the question of general grammar. "A general grammar", Charles Serrus continues,[29] "cannot be constructed as a non-Euclidean space is constructed. It must be made to result from the observation and interpretation of facts". There are, indeed, many who take it to be obvious that there are more reasons for taking seriously "an inductively based general grammar" than "a pure grammar derived from the *a priori* requirements of mind in general"[30] and that, in Bloomfield's phrase, "the only useful generalizations about language are inductive generalizations".[31]

The comparison with non-Euclidean geometries certainly goes much too far. The time will perhaps come when the pure grammar corresponding to ordinary rationality will be sufficiently highly elaborated for grammarians to think about developing alternative pure grammars corresponding to no known semantic field. But it should not be

294

forgotten that the innovation that non-Euclidean geometries represent presupposed the existence of a fully worked out system of geometry – the Euclidean system – and, in particular, a by no means definitive, but provisionally adequate account of its axiomatic basis. It is the parallel between pure grammar and Euclidean geometry which stands out most strikingly. But then, may not the interpersonal network of communication constitute a set of determinations as solid in the face of intellectual probing as that pure space to whose determination Euclid has attached his name, a set of determinations sufficient, perhaps, to constitute the object of a science of nature as essentially *a priori* as geometry or the arithmetic of whole numbers?

Nevertheless we do not wish to assert that the *a priori* status of grammar could be completely aligned with that of *a priori* sciences preceding it in time such as those we have mentioned. There are essential differences between grammar and geometry. The first of these differences lies in the fact that geometry can consider the structure of space independently of any consideration of the knowing or acting subject. Only that very special branch of geometry which is the theory of perspective accords a role to the knowing subject, for perspective is the foundation only of *visual* space. Indeed it is the genius of the Greek creators of perspective to have inserted this geometry of visual space into the geometry of pure space by putting the knowing subject into the latter and founding the properties of visual space on those of this reconstituted pure space. If it is true that perspective is the only example of an *a priori* discipline involving some consideration of the subject on which the Greeks succeeded in conferring definite scientific status, it is as a member of the family of such disciplines that the nature of grammar must be sought. The much earlier success of perspective is due to the fact that consideration of the subject had led to determinations which appear to be extremely simple: the two extremities of the object seen, together with the apex formed by the eye of the seeing subject, delimit an angle which decreases the more distant is the object.

Consideration of the grammatical subject is much more difficult. Nowhere in the scientific capital accumulated by the Western tradition does one find any related *a priori* science which might be used to help construct the science of grammar, an already constituted science into which it would have been enough to introduce the subject, just as the theory of perspective was introduced into geometry. And we must admit that we cannot see what such a science could have been; for there is no

295

pure communicative space independent of communicating subjects.

There is another difficulty. As long as this pure grammar remains only sketched in outline, the boundary between those matters of grammar which do and those which do not belong to it will remain uncertain. Geometry succeeded relatively quickly in separating what belongs to the realm of geometry proper from everything in the)X̂«T% which is foreign to the pure space of which it presents itself as the science. But the corresponding rupture in the sphere of grammar is a much more delicate matter. The difficulty is certainly not that of distinguishing purely grammatical properties from those which are properly historical but rather of making the indispensable distinction between the requirements of pure grammar and those of psychology.

Seen in this light the analyses put forward here leave much to be desired. For it will certainly have been noticed that these analyses have appealed to two sorts of consideration. There has been:

(1) The appeal to basic and irreducible intuitions. Any explanation may, unless it is circular, arrive at a point at which the explanatory term itself appears to be intuitively given and so inexplicable. We consider that it is one of the tasks of analysis to delay this appeal to a basic intuition as long as possible. But however long the delaying process be, it is difficult to see how explanation could, finally, avoid coming up against its own limit.

(2) The appeal to the technical aspects of communicative situations. Consideration of these aspects has often allowed us to avoid recourse to 'phenomenological intuition' which is, of course, always only all too easy – or, rather, to postpone this step a little longer. But the appeal to such considerations brings with it a difficulty of its own. For, at least in the present state of psychology, they can only with difficulty be distinguished from psychological considerations and this leaves us open to the reproach of first expelling psychology and then letting it in by the back door. The problem here is both difficult and extremely serious and it seems better to recognize that we have no satisfactory solution available. As is well known, this is precisely the problem that lies at the centre of Husserl's own work; and the anti-psychologism of the *Logical Investigations* was to undergo a certain evolution.

But no matter what difficulties arise in determining the status of grammar, we do not think that it is possible honestly to deny the *a priori* nature of pure grammar. Is it not, therefore, somewhat artificial to seek at all costs to regard as the main features of the universal grammar only what is yielded *a posteriori* by the empirical study of grammar? It is true

296

that, if pure or rational grammar is indeed *a priori* then the *a posteriori* approach will also be able to find in experience traces of this *a priori*. But has anyone ever praised the first geometers for not going beyond the stage of experimental discovery of the elementary theorems of geometry? For it is evident that the very fact that Euclidean geometry agrees with our perceptual space means that purely experimental knowledge of this sort of geometry is always possible. The formula which makes it possible to calculate the area of a triangle could easily have been established by comparing the measurements of different sorts of triangles; and Galileo did not forbid himself to evaluate the surface of a cycloid by purely experimental means. But approaches such as these are not, we think, the most promising guarantees of the scientific nature of either geometry or grammar.

For to adopt this sort of approach is to condemn oneself to complicated explanations of what can be explained simply. In the course of praising the advantages of such a quasi-experimental method over the *a priori* approach of *The Port-Royal Grammar,* Nicolas Ruwet[32] considers the examples.

Pierre aime beaucoup Marie avec passion (Peter loves Mary a lot with passion)

Pierre a bien travaillé avec ardeur (Peter worked well with zeal)

Pierre a été terriblement battu avec sauvagerie (Peter has been beaten terribly with great savageness)

and observes "that all these sentences, that contain both an adverb and a prepositional phrase which is an adverb of manner, are ungrammatical", adding that "there are perhaps semantic reasons for this, but it is difficult to isolate them *a priori*".[33] Ruwet therefore suggests that, taking the ungrammaticality of these sentences and the grammaticality of certain other sentences as our basis, we construct a hypothetical schema capable of excluding the first and generating the second. In this way, he says, "one is quite naturally led to bring together in one equivalence class all the elements that cannot co-occur, namely the adverbs ... and prepositional phrases of the type *avec* + NP". All this we can do, he says, "without having recourse to semantic presuppositons".

Now there is no major objection to this attitude. It is difficult to see how an approach of this sort could fail, but that this is the case is due to reasons which are not available to Ruwet. For the attitude underlying such an approach, the success of which is not in question, is both arbitrary and futile:

(1) It is arbitrary: for who is to say that the three sentences in the example are ungrammatical and the others, which we have not quoted, are grammatical? Will one be obliged to verify the observation by means of a questionnaire? Or is Ruwet simply appealing to the knowledge everyone has of the *traditional* rules governing language? Can he be quite sure that he is not appealing to an intuitive awareness of the very rule he is aiming to formulate? One might just as well seek to establish the truth of *two and two are four* by appeal to universal agreement.

(2) It is futile: for such an approach will never yield the *why* of the matter but only the *how:* yet only the former can justify the latter. Thus it is not surprising that Ruwet's analysis brings him up against another problem: "one is led to ask oneself why the structure of a simple sentence normally only admits a single 'manner'-constituent at most; this is indeed a fact, the necessity of which does not immediately spring to mind".[34] Indeed it does not, and yet it is with this necessity that analysis should begin.

For if I mention two different ways in which a verb is modified, I must inevitably find myself in one of the following four situations:

(a) Either the *manner* in the one case is different from that in the other case, for, as can easily be imagined, there are several different sorts of *manner* in Indo-European languages. On this interpretation the co-occurrence of two adverbs of manner presents no problems whatsoever. It is possible to say

Pierre a travaillé longuement et intensivement (Peter has worked intensively for a long time)

because the meanings of the adverbs are not connected; one can work intensively for a short period of time.

(b) Or the manners belong in each case to the same area of meaning, but the adverbs are incompatible. It is easy to see that the reason why the adverb *beaucoup* (a lot) cannot be combined with *nullement* (not at all) is purely logical.

(c) Or the manner belongs in each case to the same area of meaning but the two adverbs express two degrees of manner such that one at least implies the other. Thus to combine *un peu* (a little) with *beaucoup* (a lot) would be redundant since *a little* is implied by *a lot*.[35]

(d) Or, finally, we have the case of an adverb which modifies another

298

adverb, as in the case of *very,* and co-occurrence of this sort presents no problems.

What we have here is, in our opinion, a set of rules which has its *a priori* basis in the nature of communication. It is therefore not surprising that such rules are rediscovered by grammarians as a result of empirical investigation; the opposite would be, to say the least, disturbing. But the view that they must be rediscovered in this way is not only naïve, it may also be harmful. For what is really of interest is to see how different historically existing linguistic systems deal with the grammatical *a priori,* the way they interpret it, and even the way they may finally betray it, something they are quite capable of doing: the defects of a system may not suffice to prevent its being viable.[36] What is important to the grammarian is precisely the distance between the pure and the empirical grammar; and this can only be grasped if one has a clear notion of the structures of pure grammar.

It would be a mistake to read into such a pure grammar any sort of postulation of a human mind with a single identical structure. This traditional claim is made today within the context of a certain sort of rationalism and seems to us, at least at present, to involve a variety of psychologism (and as we have seen, rationalism can in some cases easily combine with psychologism). It is not that we are in a position to refute such a hypothesis; it is enough that the hypothesis is not required. Whether or not we shall one day be able to provide with a serious anthropological grounding what at the present time is pure hypothesis, we have already, in the situation of the knowing subject who acts and communicates with other subjects, all that is needed to provide pure grammar with its foundations. The latter is as little evidence of some universal psychological structure as is the relative universality of arithmetic. If these two sciences do illustrate some universal psychological structure it is the structure of that relation between consciousness and the object on which number is founded or the structure of that relation between consciousness and objects as well as other subjects in which communication consists, and it is this that marks out the outlines of grammatical necessity.

Pure grammar is not, we claim, founded on the identity of an anthropological psyche but on the identity of a field of grammatical accomplishments, and it is because of this that we rarely find absolutely fixed forms. Such forms are only to be found in certain cases, for example where the field of grammatical accomplishments is so narrow that there is room for only one solution. But in most cases several solutions are possible which may, it should be noted, be of unequal value. It is for this reason that it is difficult to accept without any reservations what Carnap calls the principle of tolerance:[37] "In logic there are no morals. Everyone is at liberty to build up his own logic, i.e. his own form of language, as he wishes. All that is required of him is that, if he wishes to discuss it, he must state his methods clearly, and give syntactical rules instead of philosophical arguments".

As soon as the aim of syntactic rules is not only to distinguish between those arrangements of symbols which are and those which are not allowed, but also to lead to arrangements which make up the means of expression we call *discourse,* these rules must satisfy quite precise technical requirements. In this technical domain there is no room for morality – but norms cannot be excluded. The technique of communication does not always tell us exactly what to do. More often than not what we are told has the form of a disjunction: we are told of a range of things that we *can* do. But this involves tracing the boundary between what is possible and what is impossible. And once a goal has been introduced, the awareness of what is possible and of what is impossible, i.e. of means and of obstacles, will obviously take on a normative character. Contrary to Carnap's claims, one cannot say without exaggeration that "we have in every respect complete liberty with respect to forms of language".[38] The fact that there are usually several possible solutions does not mean that "before us lies the boundless ocean of unlimited possibilities".[39]

The Structure of Discourse and the Structure of Thought

Perhaps there is, after all, some justification for the frequently criticized attitude of grammarians who think that custom is not the only authority in matters of grammar. We seem, in this study, to be harking back to Roger Bacon's single grammar, common to all natural languages, a substance underlying their accidental variations; back to the old grammatical logicism of Port-Royal in the seventeenth century, or of the *Encyclopédie* a century later, of the *idéologues* in the ninteenth century and of Couturat at the beginning of the twentieth; to the thesis of the quasi-innateness of language which Chomsky has identified in early

German Romanticism, in the work of August Wilhelm Schlegel and Wilhelm von Humboldt. There is no need to deny the resemblance: for is it not the case that the advances in grammatical analysis due to phenomenologists, logicians and linguists are beginning to justify an ambition which seemed derisory only as long as adequate tools were not available?

This does not mean that it is necessary to embrace certain classical illusions peculiar to grammatical rationalism, such as that which leads rationalism to base itself on the claim that there is a parallelism between forms of thought and forms of discourse, as though speech were merely a translation of the affections of the soul. The Aristotelian claim that spoken words are the 'immediate signs' of 'states of the soul',[40] one repeated by such classic authors as Lancelot and Arnauld for whom to speak is to 'explain',[41] 'signify',[42] or 'make known'[43] *our thoughts* by means of signs which we have invented in order to "indicate what goes on in the mind",[44] seems to have encouraged the belief that words, at least in their rational aspect, are no more than shadows or traces of the mind. It is as if the undeniably "intimate relation between thought and its verbal expression" of which Couturat speaks[45] could not be anything but the relation of identity or, at least, an equivalence relation. This conception finds almost perfect expression in the following text of Donaldson's:

We find in the internal mechanism of language the exact counterpart of the mental phenomena which writers on psychology have so carefully collected and classified. We find that the structure of human speech is the perfect reflex or image of what we know of the organization of the mind: the same description, the same arrangement of particulars, the same nomenclature would apply to both, and we might turn a treatise on the philosophy of mind into one on the philosophy of language, by merely supposing that everything said in the former of the thoughts as subjective is said again in the latter of the words as objective.[46]

This sort of rationalism is far removed from that espoused in the present work. Grammar is not an instrument of thought but an instrument of communication. If, therefore, it displays a rational structure, this is not the structure of thought but of communication. The ambiguity here has unfortunately been increasingly fostered by the development of algebras which are indeed instruments, if not of thought, then at least of calculation, that is to say, of quasi-thought, and which are – somewhat improperly, as we have seen – unhesitatingly called *languages*. It is thus important to understand why the fit between thought and logic is much closer than that between thought and grammar.

On the other hand it would be dangerous to confuse the immense distance separating thought and discourse with the distance there may be between logic and grammar. Is logic, especially in the algebraic form it now tends to adopt, still really an 'art of thinking', to use the expression from the subtitle of *The Port-Royal Logic?* Is it not the case that logic is not the art of thinking but the art of organizing thought so that it can be controlled, i.e. of ordering thought so as to take into account that linearity to which expression in time is subject and to which pure thought, before it is even capable of being formulated, is by no means subject? In this respect logic, as the art of the *logos,* i.e. as the science of the verifiable and communicable forms of thought, is itself at some considerable distance from pure thought, a point often overlooked by those who denounce *logico-grammatical parallelism.*

It is true that, vague though they are, such formulations as the following are unexceptionable: "grammar does not constitute a canon for thought", „the law-governed nature of thought is one thing, that of discourse another thing".[47] But our agreement cannot extend to inferences from these claims such as: "it is not true that there is a pure grammar subjacent to empirical grammars"; it is not as if the commitment to such a pure grammar must be accompanied by a commitment to the existence of "unchanging forms of mind"[48] as its indispensable corollary. Although we have no objection to our position being assimilated to the traditional current of grammatical rationalism, this does not imply that we can accept all the details of the different historical attempts to rationalize grammar. Indeed, it seems that a sketch of pure grammar has only recently been made possible by writings such as those of Frege and Husserl. Finally, it should be noted that it is of course erroneous to think that the refutation either of some contemporary attempt at logico-grammatical rationalization or of some long-past attempt automatically amounts to a refutation of every such attempt.

A work such as that by Charles Serrus is very characteristic of this last-mentioned attitude. Although the author discusses Husserl's theses at great length and is far from ignorant of contemporary developments in logic, his refutation of grammatical rationalism leads the reader to assume that the essential feature of the latter is "the reduction of different grammatical attitudes to a basic form" and that this reduction could only be inspired by the "belief that all logic turns only on the law of identity".[49] This is an allusion to certain efforts to reduce every grammatical proposition to a predicative form and then subsequently to identify the main copula with the sign for equality as this is found in mathematical equations. The artificiality of such a reduction no longer needs underlining, for it is evident not only that "when one reduces problems of grammar to the relations between substance and atrribute one is the dupe of a relatively late interpretation of the nominal phrase due to the influence of Aristotelian logic"[50] and, in particular, that to assimilate the equality-sign to the third person of the present indicative is to be the victim of confusions denounced with the utmost clarity by Frege.

Logic and its Mathematical Heritage

It is true that logic today is still concerned with preoccupations bequeathed by its founders. Not only was it developed by mathematicians, but by mathematicians concerned to find an intuitively satisfying solution to the problem of the foundations of mathematics. In this sense logic has indeed been the hand-maid of classical mathematics and it still bears the marks of its period of slavery. Frege, certainly, saw very clearly that a genuine grasp of the forms of thought had, as such, an "importance extending beyond the domain of mathematics".[51] The same conviction is to be found in Russell's writings. But in each case the very titles of their works demonstrate that their main concern is to assure the foundations of mathematics. Each thought it possible and interesting to extend the rigorous analysis of deductive reasoning their work had finally made possible "to regions of thought not ordinarily supposed to be amenable to mathematical treatment", but this extension was, to use the expression of Whitehead and Russell,[52] a 'subsidiary aspect'.

Its initial subjection to mathematics in the modern period led logic to concentrate its analyses on the relations to which mathematics makes reference, that is to say, first and foremost to binary relations or, more exactly, to a particular sort of binary relations, those which take two *individuals* as their arguments. Even triadic and tetradic relations do not really become important, as *Principia Mathematica*[53] points out, until one begins to study geometry. For geometry makes do not only with binary relation such as that expressed by the sign for equality but may also make use of triadic relations such as *between* (A is between B and C) or even tetradic relations such as *equidistance* (the points A and B are at the same distance from one another as are the points C and D).[54]

303

But what is really striking about these examples of relations in mathematics is that the arguments of all the relations mentioned belong to one and the same semantic field; they all represent individuals, and individuals belonging to a very restricted group, for example, points on a surface. Thus the subordination of logic to mathematics diverted attention from the study of what is by far the larger group of relations in which the names corresponding to the arguments designate objects belonging to very different semantic categories – a field of study which would have been much more delicate and tricky and more deceptive in its results than investigation of the simpler sort of relation.

Principia Mathematica gives an excellent example of this point,[55] the binary function *A believes p,* in which the first argument is a name designating an individual and the second argument is a name designating what we have called a *fact that.* This function can be contrasted with the function *A knows p* which, although its arguments are the same as those in the previous case, is quite different. Here there is a connection between the function *A knows p* and the proposition *p* (i.e. the proposition asserting the fact designated by the name which is the second argument of the function), namely: the truth of the proposition *A knows p* implies the truth of *p* (an implication which is not reversible). The truth-values of *A believes p,* however, as Whitehead and Russell point out, may differ whatever the truth-value of the proposition *p.* I can equally well believe that a state of affairs obtains which does not obtain as believe that a state of affairs does not obtain which does in fact obtain. I can refuse to believe that what in fact obtains does obtain, as well as believe that what does not obtain obtains. Now, as *Principia Mathematica* nicely puts it, there can be no question of excluding such functions from our investigations; but the functions in which the work is centrally interested are those where the truth-value of the function can be determined by the values of the different arguments. And this, the authors say, is bound up with the extensional nature of mathematics.[56]

The connection between contemporary logic and mathematics is a double one: on the one hand, as we have seen, it came into being to serve mathematics; but, on the other hand, it too aspires to that formal rigour exemplified precisely by mathematics, the science for which it seeks to provide foundation. Now if the aim of logic is to be mathematical in this sense then there is no reason why it should burden itself with the consideration of functions which do not easily lend themselves to treatment in terms of a calculus, or rather, which cannot be shown, or

304

simply *cannot yet* be shown, to lend themselves to such treatment. It is for reasons such as these that sentences containing *that*-clauses *(completive propositions)* are more or less absent from logic. Such propositions correspond to situations in which the arguments of the function (i.e. the subject and the complements of the 'main verb') belong to very different categories (on the one hand individuals of a certain type, persons, on the other hand *facts that*), categories so different that they seem, to date at least, to make impossible any representation of the corresponding functions in terms of the familiar calculi.

De Morgan complained that the logic he had been taught was incapable of allowing the deduction of the proposition *The head of the horse is the head of a mammal* from the proposition *The horse is a mammal,* although the transition seems perfectly natural. But contemporary logic does not allow the deduction of the truth of the proposition *p* from that of the proposition *A knows p,* in spite of the fact that inferences of this sort are the foundation of all steps in science, for it is evident that we cannot admit the truth of a proposition unless we admit first that our knowledge of the fact stated by the proposition implies the truth of the proposition stating the fact.[57]

Whether or not completive propositions concern the foundations of mathematics, and whether or not these propositions permit of algebraic treatment and so will allow us to imagine what the relevant operations are, these questions lose much of their undeniable logical interest when our aim is simply to set out a system which makes communication possible. Our activities as human beings confront us with situations which we can only describe with the help of functions whose arguments do not have that semantic uniformity which provides arithmetic and geometry with those astonishing rational possibilities which science has striven to catalogue for nearly three thousand years: *we explain, we relate, we refuse, we promise,...* But the fact that these functions do not lend themselves to any of those miracles we call *operations* does not mean that they cannot be described.

The Structure of Discourse and the Structure of its Object

We would like, finally, to distinguish our position from yet another form of rationalism about grammar, that which seeks the basis of grammatical structure not in thought nor in the expression this finds in discourse but in the states of affairs asserted and mentioned by the latter. For if, as Aristotle put the matter, spoken words are 'the immediate signs' of mental experiences,[58] do not the latter refer in their turn to "things of which our experiences are the images"? And should we not therefore expect to find within discourse the structure of things rather than the structure of thought, which functions merely as an intermediate relay-stage in the act of *meaning?* What is simply the mention of a possibility in Aristotle receives a precise formulation in Wittgenstein's *Tractatus:* if the propositional sign is the sign with which we express our thought should we not organize this expression in such a way that the elements of the propositional sign correspond to the *objects* of our thought?[59]

The semantic relation involves what are really three distinct terms: not only the symbol and the thought it expresses but also the object the symbol designates or the state of affairs it describes and of which the thought that finds its expression in the symbol is the representation. It is this three-termed schema, already present in the analyses of Aristotle, which is, at least implicitly, the basis for the criticisms Bolzano makes of Kant and above all of Hegel.[60] In *The Meaning of Meaning*[61] C. K. Ogden and I. A. Richards suggested representing this with the help of a diagram containing a triangle in which each of the three terms would correspond to an apex of the triangle. Only two of the sides of this triangle are marked in, that standing for the relation of symbol to thought and that standing for the relation of thought to object; the third side, however, is marked only as a dotted line, for the relation between symbol and object in the process of symbolization is not direct but must necessarily make use of the intermediate relation of representation. It is nevertheless the case that this third relation, between symbol and object, is the important one, the only relation we may call *true* or *false;* the relation symbol-representation being at most *correct* or *incorrect* and the relation representation-object *adequate* or *inadequate.*[62] Now if only the relation between symbol and object is true or false should the justification of the structure of the symbol not be sought in the structure of the object?

The temptation is an old one and one to which philosophers have regularly yielded from St. Bonaventura at least until Wittgenstein. In order to demonstrate that God is not nameable the Seraphic Doctor relied in particular on the fact that a name must have a certain likeness to the object and share a certain proportion (*proportionem et similitudinem aliquam ... ad nominatum*). The project of constructing at least an

306

artificial language whose structure would reproduce that of the facts was espoused by Russell after the success of *Principia Mathematica*. A logically correct symbolism must, he thought, arrive at "a certain fundamental identity of structure between a fact and the symbol for it", such that "the complexity of the symbol corresponds very closely to the complexity of the facts symbolized"; thus there would be "one word and no more for every simple object"; what is non-simple would be expressed by a "combination of words derived from the words for the simple things that enter in"; a language analytically constructed in this way would reveal, by virtue of its construction, the logical structure of the facts which would be the object of the assertion.[63]

It was Wittgenstein who was to exploit to the full this thesis of the parallelism between the organization of discourse and the structure of facts, and to draw all the consequences from it, including the most extreme. As the states of affairs, the totality of which is the world, are combinations of objects, so, too, propositions asserting states of affairs form, together with their constituent names, combinations with the same structure. A proposition is, first of all, a fact in the world like that other fact, the state of affairs which it represents. And as Russell points out in his Introduction to the *Tractatus,* one of the key problems Wittgenstein set himself was that of determining what extra condition a fact must satisfy in order to be the symbol of another fact. "If a fact is to be a picture, it must have something in common with what it depicts".[64] This common element is what Wittgenstein calls form and is defined as the possibility of establishing between the elements of the fact-picture the same relations as those to be found between the elements of the fact which it pictures. And it is true that the value of the mode of articulation of what we call *pictures* or *images,* paintings, maps, musical scores, etc., even of certain diagrammatic representations and conceptual notations used in science, lies in the faithfulness with which they reproduce – whatever the scales and sign material employed – the mode of articulation of the objects represented.[65]

As Wittgenstein points out:[66] "At first sight a proposition – one set out on the printed page, for example – does not seem to be a picture of the reality with which it is concerned". But he adds: "neither do written notes seem at first sight to be a picture of a piece of music, nor our phonetic notation (the alphabet) to be a picture of our speech". There is no doubt that, as we have seen,[67] musical notation turns out on examination to be a (nearly perfect) picture of what it seeks to represent and phonetic notation an imperfect picture, in precisely the sense Wittgenstein gives to the word 'picture'. But in the case of those sorts of language which have been the object of our investigations, nothing justifies the assimilation of the relation of *meaning* to the very special relation between a picture and its object. It is for this reason that it is advisable to distinguish sharply between *meaningful languages* and *mimetic languages* (for which the term 'notations' should perhaps be reserved), whether these notations are "the result of a deliberate effort by generations of scholars to bring their symbols into simple correspondence with the things they designate",[68] or whether such transposition – as is the case with our writing-systems – has taken a route which is intellectually much more obscure and contingent.

The failure to recognize the need to distinguish the two types of language is to be observed not only in authors who, like Wittgenstein, thought they had discovered a similarity between discourse and its object, but also, strangely, in just those philosophers who reject this thesis. Thus Gilbert Ryle, criticizing Wittgenstein and others, writes:[69] "I do not see how, save in a small class of specially-chosen cases a fact or state of affairs can be deemed, in its structure, like or unlike a sentence, a gesture, or a diagram. For a fact is not a collection – even an ordered collection – of bits in the way in which a sentence statement is an arranged collection of noises, or a map an arranged collection of scratches". This objection makes the mistake of putting the propositions of meaningful languages, natural and formalized, on the same level with geographical maps, which employ one of the most developed examples of mimetic languages. And in this case it is by no means ridiculous to speak of similarity or dissimilarity or even identity of structure, in view of the fact that the efforts of geographers, since well before Mercator, have tended to reduce to a minimum, for example, the distortions made inevitable by the transition from the sphere to the plane. As to gestures and diagrams, the main reason for not going into the problems they pose is precisely that their complexity rules out any quick solution. But it would not be difficult to find, amongst all the various different sorts of diagrams, some examples where the structure of the diagram does indeed *imitate* the structure of its object.

No such modelling or imitation is however to be found in *meaningful languages*. Although we have been able to locate a certain sort of elementary structure in language we cannot find in facts or states of affairs any elements that could correspond to the elements of discourse.

308

As Adam Schaff writes:[70] "the relations between the elements of a sentence are not analogous to those between parts of the world". After he had given up the project of making the simple elements of discourse *(names)* correspond one-to-one to the simple elements which make up the totality of what there is *(objects)*, Wittgenstein denounced in the *Philosophical Investigations*[71] the falsity of the simplistic idea that the whole world is ordered into categories of perfectly distinct objects even before man looks at it. The inventory we have tried to provide above of the different sorts of nominalisation seems to show clearly that, far from there being any pre-existent correspondence between object and name that makes naming and nominalisation possible, it is rather – and not so surprisingly – *naming* and *nominalisation* that make names possible and articulate the very boundaries of the objects named.

On this point the most meticulous and at the same time most far-reaching criticism of the thesis that there is some similarity between expression and the state of affairs expressed is, in our opinion, that of Bolzano in his *Wissenschaftslehre*.[72] Nearly all the arguments on this point that are to be met with today, scattered throughout the writings of logicians and linguists, are to be found gathered together in this work and systematically ordered, though presented, it is true, in a somewhat scholarly manner which will blunt the curiosity of some. Although Bolzano's criticisms do not bear directly on the relation between what we have called 'expression' and object but between the latter and what he calls *'Vorstellung'* (representation, presentation), the sense of this latter term within his semantics is such that we can apply without hesitation his criticisms to the relation between *signifier* and *object signified*. Bolzano shows first of all that there are two possible ways of taking the relation of signifier and object signified as a relation of similarity. One may try to make the parts of the expression correspond either to

expressions for the parts of its object

or to

expressions for the properties of its object.

Neither possibility works.

That expressions for the parts of the objects cannot correspond to the parts of the expression is shown by

(1) the existence of genuine names which, however, are distinguished by the fact that they have no object, or least no real object, for example *nothing* or *a round square;*

(2) the existence of expressions that mention objects only negatively, for example *a country without mountains, a book without engravings;*

(3) the existence of expressions whose parts, far from designating parts of the object designated, designate an object of which the object designated by the expression forms a part, for example, *the eye of the man* or *the top of the house.*

In order to show that it is equally impossible for parts of an expression to correspond to expressions for the properties of the object, Bolzano establishes first of all that to certain constitutive elements of the proposition there corresponds, strictly speaking, no property of the object, and, secondly, that to certain essential properties of the object there corresponds no constitutive element of the expression. Bolzano supports the first assertion by referring to the existence of the expression 'which' whose fundamental role within certain nominal expressions we have already had occasion to note. It is impossible to find in the object a part or even a property that might correspond to 'which'. In support of his second assertion Bolzano can draw on mathematics for numerous examples of expressions which do not contain any mention of the totality of properties, which are sometimes infinite in number, of the objects they designate. His second assertion is also confirmed by the possibility of referring to one and the same object with the help of two designations even though these contain no mention of any shared property.

Bolzano was certainly not the only philosopher to denounce the vagueness of that characterization of the relation of signifier and object described as 'agreement' ("das vieldeutige Wort 'Übereinstimmung'")[73] and its dangerous tendency to suggest that the basis of this relation was resemblance. The same consideration, expressed in almost the same terms, is to be found in Pfänder.[74] But Bolzano is the only philosopher to have hunted down tirelessly and in detail all the absurd consequences to which the assimilation of the structure of expression to that of the object may give rise, both at the level of designation of objects by names and at the level of the assertion of states of affairs by propositions.

For in order to show that a name is not the picture of the object designated it is not enough to say, as does Pfänder,[75] that the expression 'gold' – in contrast to what it designates – is neither yellow nor shiny and has no specific weight. The same point could, after all, be made about the relation between a map and the corresponding region. Further, objections of this sort are powerless against the claims of Wittgenstein in the *Tractatus,* where correspondence is sought at the level not of matter but of structure; a structure may remain identical across different matters which have absolutely nothing else in common.

Similarly, Bolzano writes,[76] to define the truth of a proposition as its 'agreement with things', means nothing at all until the nature of this agreement has been made precise; the truth of a proposition is "that peculiarity of a proposition in virtue of which the latter attributes to certain objects a property which really belongs to them", a sentence which only acquires its full meaning when the analysis of the structure of propositions – of the sort we have tried to undertake in this book – has first indicated how the means by which a proposition can accord this property to certain objects are to be understood. But Bolzano's point, we should not deceive ourselves, will doubtless seem 'to explain nothing' to those who are impelled by an unacknowledged substantialism to look in vain for the explanation of this relation where it cannot be found – in the domain of expressions, or in the domain of their objects, or in something common to both.

The Arbitrariness of the Linguistic Sign

Do the conclusions we have been led to above confirm that 'arbitrariness of the sign' which was described both by certain ancient Chinese philosophers and by certain grammarians of ancient India,[77] mentioned by Plato in the *Cratylus,* upheld by Aristotle, taken up by the nominalists of the Middle Ages and which found expression in Leibniz and Locke, was developed by Condillac, and was finally to emerge into the light of day in de Saussure? The question has no easy answer for, as *The Port-Royal Logic*[78] pointed out, "there is much that is equivocal in this word *arbitrary* when one says that the meaning of words is arbitrary".

'Arbitrary' clearly does not mean that "either the individual or society can arbitrarily change and choose the verbal signs of language".[79] Saussure never dreamed of denying "the social and historical character of language and of verbal signs".[80] The emphasis on the arbitrary nature of signs should not be confused with any crude denial of the fact that a sign "enjoys a social 'existence' which is independent of us and has a history which is independent of our conventions";[81] or that the formation of a sign may well be genuinely determined in this way. All of this is irrelevant.

The ambiguity is to be sought elsewhere. Arnauld and Nicole go some way towards removing the difficulty when they concede, "it is true that to connect such and such an idea with such and such a sound is purely arbitrary".[82] This is indeed one of the possible meanings of certain sentences of Saussure which are rendered somewhat obscure only by their level of generality: "the link connecting the signifier to the signified is arbitrary".[83] "The signifier is arbitrary with respect to the signified with which it has no natural, real connections."[84] Less obscurely, what this amounts to is the claim that there is a certain sort of arbitrariness involved in the second of the two levels of articulation; for what links a given *morpheme* to a given *combination of phonemes* is essentially arbitrary in that an element which itself has meaning (the morpheme) is made to correspond to a series of phonetic elements which have no meaning of their own. If understood in this way the thesis of the arbitrariness of the sign would be a way of emphasizing what is specific to the second level of articulation and distinguishing it completely from the first. It would amount to saying "that there is no resemblance, no natural relation, between a horse grazing in a meadow and the vibrations" corresponding to the sound we pronounce as 'horse'.[85] From this phonological point of view (if we ignore the special case of onomatopoeia) the only problem likely to arise for the linguist is not the arbitrariness of the sign but rather those rare cases where this arbitrariness is challenged by a certain consensus across languages.[86]

The thesis of the arbitrariness of the sign may also signify, that at the first level of articulation the connection between signifier and signified is not that to be found obtaining between a copy and the original, in other words the structure of the linguistic sign is not to be identified with the structure of the object designated. But here at this first level of articulation the *arbitrariness* we are trying to pin down enters in two different ways; and it is not enough merely to oppose these to the arbitrariness we have shown to belong to the second level of articulation; they must, in any scrupulous analysis, be carefully distinguished from one another.

The first of these two sorts of arbitrariness is due to the fact that our experience of nature is never experience of objects that are already distinct from one another and to which, because of some *natural* designating link, morphemes would correspond, differing only from language to language in virtue of their phonetic guises. On the contrary, every linguistic system carves up the continuum of our experience in its own way, and it is this we may describe as arbitrary. Thus for example linguists have often stressed[87] that:

– there are many different ways of carving up the colour spectrum; unlike the majority of Western languages, which distinguish a range of colours much richer than the seven so-called *basic* colours, certain languages divide up the entire spectrum into two colours. In general, the number of colours and the boundaries between them vary from language to language;[88]

– where English uses the term 'wood' both for an area covered by trees and for the substance used for burning and building, other languages have distinct morphemes for each of these uses or re-group these uses differently;

– the distinctions established in English between, on the one hand, a pond, a loch, a lake, a sea, an ocean and, on the other hand, a brook, a stream, a river, give way in other languages to quite different distinctions;

– most Indo-European languages understand under a term such as 'uncle' both the 'patruus' (paternal uncle) and the 'avunculus' (maternal uncle), for which the Romans, by contrast, had no common term;

– in Navaho there is no morpheme designating the simple action *to go* but as many different morphemes as there are ways of going somewhere – on foot, on horseback, in a vehicle, at a walking pace or at a gallop. This arbitrariness in our ways of carving up reality is the reason why, in Martinet's words,[89] "to learn a language is not to apply new words to familiar objects but to familiarize oneself with new ways of analysing the objects of our linguistic communications".

But there is a second sort of arbitrariness at this first level of articulation, with its own distinct source. In order to understand this it is important to remember that if, as we have seen, natural languages are universal in the sense that there is nothing which cannot be expressed in them, they express what they express by grammatical or lexical means.[90] The fact that it is possible to express lexically what other linguistic systems express simply in grammatical terms makes it difficult and perhaps impossible to describe a grammatical framework that is indispensable to every language. Structures such as the distinctions between the singular and the plural, the definite and the indefinite articles, reference to the speaker or to the interlocutor, reference to the time of speaking, although they find grammatical expression in many languages, can be expressed just as effectively, albeit somewhat more clumsily, without any recourse to grammar.

313

The second sort of arbitrariness we want to identify pertains, then, to the manner of determination of the conceptual categories that a linguistic system *chooses* – if one may use this word – to supply with a form of grammatical expression. The word 'arbitrary' here means that when one passes from one language to another the conceptual categories that are grammaticalized also change. This is the second reason why to translate a text in a foreign language into one's native language is 'to make experience articulate once again, according to the pattern with which one is familiar'.[91]

Thus there are at least three ways in which the linguistic sign may be arbitrary. And when Saussure writes that "one cannot see what would prevent the association of any arbitrary idea with an arbitrary sequence of sounds" or when he stresses "the freedom to establish any relation whatsoever between phonic matter and ideas",[92] these expressions can signify so many different things that it makes no sense to agree or disagree with Saussure here. Is it true that "in language there are only differences"?[93] Such sallies, we fear, only retain whatever depth they may possess as long as those who use them continue to confuse the different levels we have distinguished. That language, from the first level of articulation upwards, contains a "play of linguistic oppositions"[94] and that these are respected and exploited by grammar is a point, already encountered above, that is beyond any doubt. Similarly, in our perceptual experience the law of contrasts leads us to isolate objects and states of affairs which become the themes of our referring acts and of our statements. But although none of this can be doubted, it is equally certain that there is nothing in all of this to justify the lapidary simplicity of Saussure's 'only'.

We are here perhaps making the mistake of treating as though they were scientific analyses the pedagogical sallies of an author whose principal aim was to lift his discipline out of the rut in which he found it. Let us therefore simply say that, at the level of inquiry which has been adopted throughout the present work, we have found nothing which might encourage us to regard the differential elements of language as linguistic atoms destined to come together in different, combinatorially determined ways. To say that "what is normally called 'a fact of grammar' ... always expresses an opposition between terms"[95] is, we think, to be both somewhat vague and somewhat hasty.*

Notes

[1] Aristotle, *De interpretatione*, 1, 16a.

[2] Cf. R. Jakobson, "Closing Statements", 1960.

[3] B. Malinowski, "The Problem of Meaning in Primitive Languages".

[4] Sapir, "Language", in *Selected Writings in Language, Culture and Personality*, 1949, p.16.

[5] Jakobson, ibid.

[6] Sapir, ibid., p.16.

[7] Sapir, ibid., p.16.

[8] *Geist und Kultur der Sprache*, Heidelberg, 1925, p.30, quoted by Gelb, 1969, p.254.

[9] *Langue et fonction*, p.32. The reductionism revealed by this expression is even more explicit in other passages. For example,

> The fundamental function of human language is to allow each person to communicate to his fellows his personal experience. By 'experience' must be understood everything that man feels or perceives, whether the stimulus come from within or from without, whether the 'experience' takes the form of a certainty, of a doubt, of a desire or of a need. Communication with others may take the form of an assertion, a question, of a request or of an order without ceasing to be communication. (*La linguistique synchronique*, 1970, p.9)

It cannot be repeated too often that assertion cannot be reduced to the communication of a certainty, nor a question to the communication of a doubt, nor an order to that of a desire.

[10] Ibid., p.10.

[11] Martinet, *Éléments de linguistique générale*, p.179.

[12] Martinet, *Langue et fonction*, p.32.

[13] Martinet, *Éléments de linguistique générale*, p.179.

[14] Serrus, 2nd part, ch.3, p.245.

[15] Martinet, *Éléments de linguistique générale*, p.6.

[16] Ibid.

[17] The distinction suggested here between *descriptive grammar* and *normative grammar* is not unrelated to the distinction made in many classical works – for example, Beauzée's *Grammaire générale, ou exposition raisonnée des éléments nécessaires à l'étude de toutes les langages*, Paris, 1767 between a *general grammar*, "the reasoned science of the unchangeable and general principles of language", and a *particular grammar*, "the art of applying or relating the customary and arbitrary institutions of a particular language to the general principles of Language". (Cf. also Chomsky, *Cartesian Linguistics*, p.53). The two distinctions do not, however, coincide:

(1) For Beauzée general grammar is descriptive: it is a *science;* a particular grammar is normative: it is an *art*. This is almost certainly due to the fact that Beauzée connected the notion of a particular grammar with the naturally normative attitude of the grammarians of his time, whereas when we speak of descriptive grammar we have in mind the contemporary grammarian's desire for objectivity.

(2) Beauzée sees general grammar as a "science ... of unchangeable principles", whereas we regard it as an *inventory of possibilities*. As possibilities they may of course be *unchangeable*, but this word is not very suitable to designate the situation that arises when one or other of these possibilities comes into or goes out of play.

[18] We have taken these descriptions from Serrus, 2nd part, ch. 3, p. 245.

[19] As Jacques Bouveresse writes in his "Langage ordinaire et philosophie":

> We can only deplore in absolute terms the lack of precision of a system of descriptive predicates if we can confront it trans-linguistically with a pre-existing system of properties which we want it to represent or represent more faithfully. When a vocabulary is criticized for being inexact, the reproach is probably always based in the last analysis on a more or less explicit form of Platonic realism: we are thought to be able to apprehend behind the screen of our vague and changing linguistic expressions a world of universals made up of realities that are perfectly precise and unchangeable and which must serve as a measure or standard for the task of adjusting and correcting our language (in: *La parole malheureuse*, p.335).

[20] Serrus, ibid., ch.2, p.157.
[21] Carnap, *Logical Syntax, §2, p.8.*
[22] Ibid.
[23] Husserl, *Logical Investigations,* V, §12, Eng. trans., pp.517f.
[24] Chomsky, *Cartesian Linguistics,* pp.60, 73.
[25] This is how M. Joos characterizes the 'Boasian' tradition in North American linguistics. Quoted by Chomsky, op.cit., p.24, n.47.
[26] *An Introduction to Generative Grammar,* Amsterdam, North Holland, 1973 ch.6, pp.299ff.
[27] Chomsky, *Cartesian Linguistics,* pp.57f.
[28] Serrus, 2nd part, ch.3, pp.244f. The following quotations in the paragraph are all taken from this part of Serrus' book.
[29] Op.cit., p.277.
[30] Op.cit., p.145.
[31] Leonard Bloomfield, *Language,* p.20.
[32] *Introduction to Generative Grammar,* ch.6, pp.299ff.
[33] For, Ruwet explains, "at first sight there is no more semantic reason for forbidding these sentences where the manner-adverbial is doubled than for admitting sentences like 'personne n'a rien vu nulle part' (no one saw anything anywhere) where it is the negation that is repeated, in co-occurrence with each of the indefinite pronouns". In order to agree with Ruwet on this point it would be necessary to attach a very strong sense to the expression "at first sight". (Ibid.)
[34] Ruwet adds here an interesting remark that takes care of a very simple objection (p.301): "I will assume throughout this discussion that sentences with 'broken intonation', such as *Pierre aime beaucoup Marie, avec passion* (Peter loves Mary a lot, with passion) are generated – by a transformation of a conjunction followed by the ellipsis of the common elements – from two simple sentences: *Pierre aime beaucoup Marie and Pierre aime Marie avec passion".*
[35] This repetition may nevertheless have a meaning in certain exceptional cases on which we cannot dwell here. Let us note simply the French idiomatic expression *un peu et même beaucoup.*

In addition, it is obvious that the adverbial locution *a little* may have either the meaning we have given it here, in which it is implied by *a lot,* or a meaning in which it excludes *a lot.* In the latter case *a little* might be more clearly expressed by saying *a little and only a little.*
[36] As is shown by the example of the conjunction *or* that we have discussed at the end of ch.8, pp. 240–43 above.
[37] Carnap, *Logical Syntax,* p.52.
[38] Ibid., Preface, p.xv.
[39] "Vor uns liegt der offene Ozean der freien Möglichkeiten". Ibid., p.xv.
[40] Aristotle, *De interpretatione,* 1, 16a.
[41] Arnauld and Lancelot, p.41.
[42] Ibid., 2nd part, ch.1, pp.65f.
[43] Ibid., p.66.
[44] Ibid., p.66.
[45] *Bulletin de la société française de philosophie,* 1912, p.59.
[46] *The New Cratylus,* p.69, quoted by Ogden and Richards, *The Meaning of Meaning,* p.264, n.1.
[47] Serrus, 3rd part, ch.3, p.505.
[48] Ibid., 2nd part, ch.5, p.374.
[49] Ibid., 1st part, ch.4, p.84.
[50] Ibid., 2nd part, ch.4, p.307.
[51] Frege, "On the Scientific Justification of a *Begriffsschrift*", as trans. in Bynum, ed., 1972, p.97.

316

[52] *Principia Mathematica,* vol.I, "Introduction", p.3.

[53] Ibid., ch.1, p.26.

[54] Cf. Tarsky, *The Completeness of Elementary Algebra and Geometry,* 1967, p.33.

[55] *Principia Mathematica,* vol.I, "Introduction", p.8.

[56] "Such functions are not excluded from our consideration and are included in the scope of any general propositions we make about functions; but the particular functions of propositions which we shall have occasion to construct or to consider explicitly are all truth-functions". *Principia Mathematica,* ibid.

[57] Cf. J.-L. Gardies, *Essai sur la logique des modalités,* 1979.

[58] Aristotle, *De interpretatione,* 1, 16a.

[59] Here we summarize in particular sentences 3.12 and 3.2 of the *Tractatus.*

[60] For example, Bolzano mentions the Hegelian claim that logic "contains the thought insofar as it is identical with the thing and the thing inasmuch as it is identical with pure thought" which seems to him to be devoid of any reasonable meaning; and he replies to it as follows: "the thought of a thing, and the thing itself, which is thought in such a thought, are in my view always different from one another, even in the case in which the thing about which we think is itself a thought". (Bolzano, §7.) Similarly Bolzano mentions the following passage from Hegel's *Logic:* "Nothing is according to its nature the same thing as being. Nothing is thought, represented, talked about: it therefore *is*". And he replies to it quite innocently: "In my opinion, what is designated first and most immediately by the *word* 'nothing' is certainly something, namely the idea nothing. It is true of this idea, as Herr Hegel says, that it is thought of and talked about. But this idea has this peculiarity that, unlike most other ideas, one cannot point to an object that it represents. This is why one cannot say that nothingness itself (as a sort of object) is represented, but simply that the concept of *nothing* may be represented". (Ibid., §9).) As in the case of many of Bolzano's analyses one can equally well regard what he says either as a collection of extremely banal remarks or as the anticipation by a genius of contemporary views of semantics (we have Tarski, in particular, in mind).

[61] 1966, ch.1, pp.10–13.

[62] Ogden and Richards (ibid., p.11), whose choice of vocabulary we have adopted here, also suggest saying that the symbol *symbolizes* the representation, that the latter *refers* to the object, and that the symbol *stands for* the object. If one wants at all costs to apply the same term *truth* to each of these three relations then it becomes apparent that there is a change of meaning from one case to the next: the contradictory of *truth* is in each case something different:
- for the symbol-object relation the relevant opposition is that between truth and *falsehood;*
- for the representation-object relation it is that between truth and *error;*
- for the symbol-representation relation it is that between truth and a *lie* or *misunderstanding.*

[63] Russell, *Logic and Knowledge,* London: Allen and Unwin, 1956, p.197.

[64] Cf. Tullio de Mauro, *Ludwig Wittgenstein, his Place in the Development of Semantics,* Dordrecht: Reidel, ch.4, pp.25f.

[65] *Tractatus,* 4.011.

[66] *Tractatus,* 4.011.

[67] Cf. above, p.285.

[68] Ogden and Richards, op.cit., p.254.

[69] Quoted by H. Hubien, 1968, p.115 from Ryle, "Systematically Misleading Expressions", in: Flew, A. (ed.), *Essays on Logic and Language,* Oxford: 1951, p.34.

[70] *Langage et connaissance,* suivi de *Six essais sur la philosophie du langage,* tr. Claire Brendel, Paris: Anthropos, 1969, p.212. It is all the more remarkable to find Schaff dealing with this theme, since he thinks that language is in some way the reflection of reality; but

317

the reflection of reality in language does not consist in the fact that the relations between the parts of a sentence correspond to relations between determinate elements of reality... The reflection of reality in language, the modelling of reality by language, does not consist either in the fact that language constitutes in some way or other a 'picture' or 'image' of reality in the sense of a direct replica of this reality [which would be contained] in the *form* of linguistic expressions (their sounds). (*Introduction à la sémantique*, p.305).

71 *Philosophical Investigations,* Oxford: Blackwell, 2nd ed., 1958, §47.

72 Cf. Bolzano, §§63f, pp.78–83. Since we cannot possibly reproduce Bolzano's long criticism in its entirety, we summarize it in the following pages, leaving out those arguments that are too closely bound up with the particular features of Bolzano's system, which as such suffer from the weakness that every system has and which could not, in any case, be expounded without a detailed account of the whole of Bolzano's semantics.

73 Bolzano, §44, p.57; cf. also §42.

74 *Logik,* 1963, pp.80f, 131.

75 Ibid.

76 Bolzano, §44, p.57.

77 Cf. G, Mounin, 1967, pp.61, 69.

78 *La logique ou l'art de penser,* Part 1, ch.1, p.33.

79 Schaff, *Langage et connaissance,* p.328.

80 Schaff, *Introduction à la sémantique,* p.186.

81 Ibid.

82 *La logique ou l'art de penser,* p.33.

83 Saussure, *Cours,* ch.1, p.100.

84 Ibid., p.101.

85 Martinet, *La linguistique synchronique,* p.20.

86 We are here referring to the fact that even languages that are otherwise very far apart nevertheless contain the same designation for father and mother in child language; cf. Jakobson, "Why 'Mama' and 'Papa'?", 1960.

87 Cf. Martinet, *Eléments,* pp.11f and *La linguistique synchronique,* p.12; Schaff, *Introduction,* pp.319f; *Langage et connaissance,* pp.26, 86f; Hjelmslev, *Prolégomènes,* pp.71ff.

88 "The part of the spectrum covered by the French word *vert* [green] is, in Welsh, cut by a line which takes in part of the area that in French is covered by the term *bleu* [blue] ... and the boundary marked in French between *vert* and *bleu* does not exist in Welsh; also missing from Welsh is the boundary between *bleu* and *gris* [grey] as well as that which in French opposes *gris* and *brun* [brown]. On the other hand, the area represented in French by *gris* is split into two parts in Welsh, such that one half corresponds to the area called *bleu* in French and the other to that called *brun*". (Hjelmslev, ibid., p.71.)

89 *Eléments,* p.12.

90 Sapir, *Selected Writings;* Jakobson, "Boas' view of grammatical meaning"; Schaff, *Langage et connaissance,* pp.81f; Martinet, *Eléments,* pp. 36f.

91 Martinet, ibid., p.37.

92 Saussure, *Cours,* ch.2, p.110.

93 Ibid., 2nd part, ch.4, p.166.

94 Ibid., p.168.

95 Ibid.

* [I should like to thank Barry Smith and Peter M. Simons for their help in preparing this translation. -Tr.]

Bibliography

Abelard, Peter	*Dialectica,* ed. by L. M. de Rijk, Assen: van Gorcum, 1956.
Ajdukiewicz, Kazimierz	"Syntactic Connexion", first publ. in German, 1935, Eng. trans. by H. Weber in S. McCall, ed., *Polish Logic,* Oxford: Clarendon, 1967, pp.207–31.
Aristotle	*The Works of Aristotle,* ed. by David Ross, vol. I, *Logic,* Oxford: Clarendon, 1928, referred to as: *Categoriae* and *De interpretatione.*
Arnauld, Antoine and Lancelot, Claude	*Grammaire générale et raisonnée,* repr. Paulet, 1969; Eng. trans. by J. Rieux and B. E. Rollin as *The Port-Royal Grammar,* Paris – The Hague: Mouton, 1975.
Arnauld, Antoine and Nicole, Pierre	*La logique ou l'art de penser,* new edition, Delalain, 1864, Eng. trans. by J. Dickoff and P. James as *The Art of Thinking,* Indianapolis: Bobbs-Merrill, 1964.
Austin, J. L.	*How to Do Things With Words,* Oxford: Clarendon, 1962.
Bally, Charles	*Linguistique générale et linguistique française,* 3rd ed., Bern: Francke, 1950.
Bar-Hillel, Y.	"A quasi-arithmetical notation for syntactic description", *Language,* 29, 1953, 47–58.
Blanché, Robert	*La logique et son histoire d'Aristote à Russell,* Paris: Armand Colin, 1970.
Bloomfield, Leonard	*Language,* New York: Holt-Rinehart-Winston, 1933.

Bocheński, J. M. *Ancient Formal Logic,* 4th ed., Amsterdam: North-Holland, 1968.
A History of Formal Logic, 2nd ed., New York: Chelsea, 1970.

Bolzano, Bernard *Grundlegung der Logik, (Wissenschaftstheorie I/ II),* Hamburg: Meiner, 1963; partial Eng. trans. by R. George as *Theory of Science,* Oxford: Blackwell, 1972.

Bouveresse, Jacques *La parole malheureuse. De l'alchimie linguistique à la grammaire philosophique,* Paris: Éditions de Minuit, 1971.

Buyssens, Eric *Les langages et le discours,* Brussels: Office de publicité, 1943.

Carnap, Rudolf *Introduction to Semantics* and *Formalisation of Logic,* 4th and 5th ed., Cambridge, Mass.: Harvard University Press, 1961.

Logische Syntax der Sprache, Vienna: Julius Springer, 1934. Eng. trans., *The Logical Syntax of Language,* London: Routledge and Kegan Paul, 1971. Referred to as: *Logical Syntax.*

Chomsky, Noam "The Formal Nature of Language", Appendix A to H. M. Lenneberg, *Biological Foundations of Language,* New York: Wiley, 1967. Referred to as: Chomsky, "The Formal Nature of Language".

Syntactic Structures, Paris – The Hague: Mouton, 1957.

Cartesian Linguistics, New York: Harper and Row, 1966.

Chomsky, Noam and Miller, George A. "Introduction to the Formal Study of Natural Languages" in R. D. Luce, *et al.,* eds., *Handbook of Mathematical Psychology,* New York: Wiley, 1963, 269–321. Referred to as: Chomsky and Miller.

Curry, Haskell B. and Feys, Robert
Combinatory Logic, vol.I, 2nd ed., Amsterdam: North-Holland, 1968.

Donzé, Roland
La grammaire générale et raisonnée de Port-Royal, contribution à l'histoire des idées grammaticales en France, Bern: Francke, 1967. Referred to as: Donzé.

Flew, Anthony
ed. *Essays on Logic and Language,* Oxford, 1951.

Frege, Gottlob
Begriffsschrift und andere Aufsätze, 2nd ed., with notes of Husserl and Scholz, Hildesheim: Olms, 1964. Referred to as: Frege, *Begriffsschrift;* Eng. trans. of ch.1 in P. Geach and M. Black, eds., *Translations from the Philosophical Writings of Gottlob Frege,* Oxford: Blackwell, 1970. Referred to as: Geach and Black. The essay "Über die wissenschaftliche Berechtigung einer Begriffsschrift" is translated in T. Bynum, ed., *Conceptual Notation and Related Articles,* Oxford: Clarendon, 1972.

Funktion, Begriff, Bedeutung, fünf logische Studien, Göttingen: Vandenhoeck und Ruprecht, 1962; referred to as translated in Geach and Black.

Grundgesetze der Arithmetik, 2 vols., repr. Hildesheim: Olms, 1962, partial Eng. trans. of vol.I by M. Furth as *Basic Laws of Arithmetic,* Berkeley: University of California Press, 1964. Cf. also extracts in: Geach and Black.

Gardies, Jean-Louis
Essai sur la logique des modalités, Paris: PUF, 1979.

"Une particularité du raisonnement juridique: la présence de fonctions complétives", *Logique et Analyse,* 53–54, 1971, 63–69.

Geach, Peter and Black, Max, eds.
See: Frege

321

Gelb, Adhémar | "Remarques générales sur l'utilisation des données pathologiques pour la psychologie et la philosophie du langage", in *Essais sur le langage, présentés par Jean-Claude Pariente,* Paris: Editions de Minuit, 1969, 227–56.

Gentzen, Gerhard | *The Collected Papers of Gerhard Gentzen,* ed. by M. E. Szabo, Amsterdam: North-Holland, 1969.

Gilson, Etienne | *Linguistique et philosophie. Essai sur les constantes philosophique du langage,* Paris: Vrin, 1969.

Hilbert, D. and Ackermann, W. | *Grundzüge der theoretischen Logik,* 5th ed., Berlin-Heidelberg-New York: Springer, 1967; Eng. translation as *Principles of Mathematical Logic,* New York: Chelsea, 1950.

Hjelmslev, Louis | *Prolégomènes à une théorie du langage,* Paris: Minuit, 1971. Eng. trans. as *Prolegomena to a Theory of Language,* Madison: University of Wisconsin Press, 1969.
Le langage, Paris: Minuit, 1966.

Hubien, Hubert | "Philosophie analytique et linguistique moderne", *Dialectica,* 22, 1968, 96–119.

Hughes, G. E. and Cresswell, M.J. | *An Introduction to Modal Logic,* 2nd ed., London: Methuen, 1974.

Humboldt, Wilhelm von | "Lettre à M. Abel Rémusat", in Wilhelm von Humboldt's *Werke,* vol. V, Berlin: B. Behr, 1905.

Husserl, Edmund | *Logical Investigations,* 2 vols., trans. of 2nd ed. by J. N. Findlay, London: Routledge and Kegan Paul, 1970.
Formal and Transcendental Logic, trans. by D. Cairns, The Hague: Nijhoff, 1969.

Jakobson, Roman | *Selected Writings,* Paris and The Hague: Mouton, 1960, etc. Referred to as SW.

"Boas' view of grammatical meaning", in: SW, II, 489–96.

"Why 'Mama' and 'Papa'?", in: SW, I, pp. 538–45.

"Shifters, Verbal Categories and the Russian Verb", in: SW, II, 130–47.

"Closing Statements: Linguistic and Poetics", in T. Seboek, ed., *Style in Language,* Cambridge, Mass.: M.I.T. Press, 1960, 350–77.

Child Language, Aphasia and Phonological Universals, Paris-The Hague: Mouton, 1968.

Kalinowski, Georges   "Sur les langages respectifs du législateur, du juge et de la loi", *Archives de philosophie du droit,* 19, 1974, 63–74.

Kneale, W. and   *The Development of Logic,* Oxford: Clarendon, Kneale, M.   1968.

Kotarbiński, Tadeusz   "Notes on the development of formal logic in Poland in the years 1900–1939", Introduction to S. McCall, ed., *Polish Logic,* Oxford: Clarendon, 1967, 1–14.

Kuroda, S.-Y.   "Edmund Husserl, *Grammaire générale et raisonnée* and Anton Marty" in *Foundations of Language,* 10, 1973, 169–95.

Lenneberg, E. H.   See: Chomsky.

Leśniewski, Stanislaw   "Grundzüge eines neuen Systems der Grundlalagen der Mathematik", *Fundamenta Mathematica,* 14, 1929, 1–81.

Łukasiewicz, Jan   *Elements of Mathematical Logic,* trans. from Polish by O. Wojtasiewicz, New York: Macmillan, Oxford: Pergamon Press, 1963.

"On the History of the Logic of Propositions", first published in Polish in 1934, Eng. trans. in S. McCall, ed., *Polish Logic,* Oxford: 1967, 66–87.

Luschei, Eugene C.   *The Logical Systems of Leśniewski,* Amsterdam: North-Holland, 1962.

Malinowski,   "The Problem of Meaning in Primitive
Bronislaw   Languages", appendix to C. K. Ogden and I. A. Richards, *The Meaning of Meaning,* London: Routledge and Kegan Paul, 1966, 296–336.

Martinet, André   "La double articulation linguistique", *Travaux du Cercle linguistique de Copenhague,* 5, 1949, 30–37; repr. in A. Martinet, *La linguistique synchronique.*

Eléments de linguistique générale, Paris, Armand Colin, 1970; Eng. trans., *Elements of General Linguistics,* London: Faber, 1964.

A Functional View of Language, Oxford: Clarendon, 1962.

La linguistique synchronique, Paris: PUF, 1970.

Langue et fonction, Paris: Denoël, 1970.

Mauro, Tullio de   *Ludwig Wittgenstein, his Place in the Development of Semantics,* Dordrecht: Reidel, 1967.

Montague, Richard   *Formal Philosophy,* New Haven and London: Yale University Press, 1974.

Mounin, Georges   *Histoire de la linguistique des origines au XXe siècle,* Paris: PUF, 1967.

Ogden, C. K. and   *The Meaning of Meaning. A study of the influence
Richards, I. A.   of language upon thought and of the science of symbolism,* 10th ed., London: Routledge and Kegan Paul, 1966.

Panfilov, V. Z.   *Grammar and Logic,* Paris – The Hague: Mouton, 1968.

Pariente, Jean-Claude   "Grammaire, logique et ponctuation" in: *Études sur le XVIIIème siècle,* "Textes et documents" Société française du XVIIIème siècle et Association des publications de Clermont II, 1979, 105–120.

Partee, Barbara, ed.   *Montague Grammar,* New York–San Francisco–London: Academic Press, 1976.

Pfänder, Alexander   *Logik,* 3rd ed., Tübingen: Niemeyer, 1963.

Plato   *Sophist* trans. by F. Cornford in F. Cornford, *Plato's Theory of Knowledge,* London: Routledge and Kegan Paul, 1966. Referred to as: *Sophist.*

Prior, Arthur N. and Prior, Mary   "Erotetic Logic", *Philosophical Review,* 64, 1955, 43–59.

Prior, Arthur N.   *Papers on Time and Tense,* Oxford: Clarendon, 1968.

"Postulates for Tense-Logic", *American Philosophical Quarterly,* 3, 1966, 1–9.

Time and Modality, Oxford: Clarendon, 1957.

Reinach, Adolf   *Zur Phänomenologie des Rechts. Die apriorischen Grundlagen des bürgerlichen Rechts,* Munich: Kösel, 1953 and in Reinach, *Sämtliche Werke,* Munich: Philosophia Verlag, textcritical ed. forthcoming. Eng. trans., *Aletheia,* Vol. III, 1984.

Rescher, Nicholas   *Topics in Philosophical Logic,* Dordrecht: Reidel, 1968.

Rijk, L. M. de   *Logica modernorum,* Assen: van Gorcum, 1972, 2 vols., the second in 2 parts.

Rosser, J.   *Logic for Mathematicians,* New York-Toronto-London: McGraw-Hill Book Co., 1953.

Russell, Bertrand   *An Inquiry into Meaning and Truth,* London: Allen and Unwin, 1940.
"Logical Atomism" in *Logic and Knowledge,* ed. R.C. Marsh, London: Allen and Unwin, pp. 323–43.

325

	The Principles of Mathematics, 2nd ed., London: Allen and Unwin, 1937.
Ruwet, Nicolas	*An Introduction to Generative Grammar,* Amsterdam: North-Holland, 1973. Original French edition, Paris: Plon, 1967. Referred to as: Ruwet, *Introduction.*
Ryle, Gilbert	"Systematically Misleading Expressions", in: Flew, A. (ed.), 1966, pp.11–36.
Sapir, Edward	*Selected Writings in Language, Culture and Personality,* ed., D. G. Mandelbaum, Berkeley: University of California Press, 1949.
	Language, New York: Harcourt, Brace and Co., 1921; also in ed. Mandelbaum.
Saussure, Ferdinand de	*Cours de linguistique générale,* Paris: Payot, 1966. Eng. trans. by W. Baskin, *Course in General Linguistics,* New York: Philosophical Library, 1959.
Schaff, Adam	*Introduction à la sémantique,* trans. by G. Lisowski, Paris: Anthropos, 1969.
	Langage et Connaissance suivi de *Six Essais sur la Philosophie du Langage,* trans. by C. Brendel, Paris: Anthropos, 1969.
Searle, J. R., ed.	*The Philosophy of Language,* Oxford: Oxford University Press, 1971.
Serrus, Charles	*Le parallélisme logico-grammatical,* Paris: Alcan, 1933. Referred to as: Serrus.
Staal, J. F.	*Word Order in Sanskrit and Universal Grammar,* in *Foundations of Grammar,* supplementary series vol.5, Dordrecht: Reidel, 1967.
Stahl, Gerold	"Un développement de la logique des questions", *Revue philosophique de la France et de l'étranger,* 88, CLIII, P.U.F., 1963, 293–301.

Tarski, Alfred   *The Completeness of Elementary Algebra and Geometry,* Centre National de la Recherche Scientifique, Institut Blaise Pascal, 1967.

"The Semantic Conception of Truth and the Foundations of Semantics", *Philosophy and Phenomenological Research,* 4, 1944, 341–76, repr. in L. Linsky, ed., *Semantics and the Philosophy of Language,* Chicago: University of Illinois Press, 1952, 13–49.

Introduction to Logic and to the Methodology of Deductive Sciences, with new material, Oxford: Oxford University Press, 1965.

Logic, Semantics, Metamathematics. Papers from 1923 to 1938, trans. by J. H. Woodger, Oxford: Clarendon, 1956.

Wachowitz,   "Against the Universality of a Single Wh-
Krystyna, A.   Question Movement", *Foundations of Language,* 11, 1974, 155–66.

Whitehead, Alfred N. *Principia Mathematica,* 3 vols., 2nd ed., Cam-
and Russell, Bertrand bridge: Cambridge University Press, 1963.

Whorf, B. L.   *Language, Thought and Reality,* Selected Writings, Cambridge, MA: M.I.T. Press, 1957.

Wittgenstein, Ludwig *Philosophical Investigations,* Eng. trans. by G.E.M. Anscombe, 2nd ed., Oxford: Blackwell, 1958.

Tractatus Logico-Philosophicus, Eng. trans. by D. F. Pears and B. F. McGuinness, London: Routledge and Kegan Paul, 1961.

Wright, Georg   "Quelques remarques sur la logique du temps et
Henrik von   les systèmes modales (sic)", *Scientia,* vol.102, Nov.-Dec. 1967, 1–8.

The Logic of Preference, Edinburgh: Edinburgh University Press, 1963.

327

Index of Names and Subjects

abacus 53, 124
Abelard 251, 261
absurdity *(Widersinn)* 18f., 23, 41, 279, 281
accident 208
Ackermann, W., 229, 244
active/passive 115
adjective 21f., 37, 45f., 79, 123, 128, 174, 177, 185–187, 190-92, 209f., 255
– attributive186
adequate 306
address 159, 173
adverb 9, 30, 46, 69, 119, 140, 148f., 174, 253–58, 260f., 297f.
Ajdukiewicz, K., 42, 60, 68–70, 73–78, 81, 85f., 136, 201, 203, 244, 248, 255f.
affirmativ 68, 258, 260
Albertus Magnus 251
algebra 14, 53, 112, 301
– of classes 240
– of propositions 240
algorithm 53, 56
alternation 23, 36
ambiguity 74, 77, 93, 95, 114, 117, 144, 148, 157, 178, 189, 197, 203, 223, 226, 278, 280, 282, 301, 312
Anselm of Canterbury 101
anteriority 266f.
antinomy 18, 44f., 47, 152
– semantical 48, 61
– syntactic 61
– logical 61
anti-psychologism 296
antonym 115
apodictic 19
appellative 159, 173
Apollonius 156
a-priori 18f., 41f., 88, 101, 115, 116, 153, 168, 174f., 194, 204, 263, 292–99

arbitrary 14, 105, 115, 118, 148, 195, 269, 298f., 311–14
argument 45, 68–77, 79–83, 86–89, 91, 95, 102–3, 107f., 110–19, 121, 124, 125, 129, 134, 136f., 141, 148, 153f., 167–71, 174, 180, 186–92, 196–99, 202, 210f., 222, 224f., 248f., 254–57, 259, 264–66, 304f.
Aristotle 17f., 36, 39, 63, 66f., 83f., 90, 96, 99, 120, 123, 135, 169, 183, 208, 250f., 286, 301, 303, 306, 311, 315
arithmetic 14, 52, 123, 295, 299, 305
Arnauld, A., 66, 83, 106, 120f., 123, 145, 150, 152f., 160f., 173f., 188, 199f., 209–11, 245, 257, 261, 301, 312
article 177f., 313
articulation
– double 11, 312
– first level of 11–14
– internal 21
– natural 11
– second level of 12, 14
aspect 263ff.
aspectualizer 263–66, 272f., 279f., 282
assertion 64f., 91, 168f., 201, 222f., 228, 237, 258, 260, 268f., 280, 285, 315
attention 28, 113, 118, 126, 134, 217, 219, 230, 237, 287
attitude 156
attribute 104
Aussagenkalkül 229
Austin, J.L., 159, 173f.
automatic procedure 73f.
Avicenna 40
axiom 33–35, 271
axiomatic 295
– constructions 18

329

– method 16

Bacon, R., 300
Bally, C., 197
Bar-Hillel, J., 69, 73–78, 81–84, 188
Baylis, C.A., 244
Beauzée, N., 85, 315
Bennett, A.A., 244
Benveniste, E., 197
Bhartṛhari 26
Black, M., 60f., 121, 123
Blanché, R., 258
Bloomfield, L., 153f., 294, 316
Boas, F., 149
Bocheński, I.M., 245, 251, 261
Bolzano, B., 21, 45f., 61, 64, 84, 91,
  97, 120, 122, 135–38, 151f., 168f.,
  175, 188, 209f., 212, 227f., 243, 257,
  305, 308–10, 315f.
Bonaventura 306
Boolean algebra 99f., 213
Boswell, J., 123
Bouveresse, J., 315
Bréal, M., 151
Bühler, K., 286
Buyssens, E., 165
Bynum, T.W. van, 124

calculation 33, 52–56, 74, 124, 282, 286
calculus 53, 55f., 99f., 121, 158, 185,
  220, 258, 304
– functional 91
– of predicates 91
– of names of states of affairs 223f.,
  229
– of proposition 24, 27f., 33–35, 38,
  56, 92, 95, 121, 164, 166, 219–24,
  228–33, 238–40, 245
– universal 55
Callimachus 233
Campanella, T., 190
Cantor, G., 43
Carnap, R., 30f., 33, 38, 45, 50f., 55,
  60–62, 119, 122, 125f., 150, 167f., 170,
  174, 205f., 212, 235, 244–46, 272, 284,
  292, 300, 316
Carroll, L. 16, 39, 155, 166, 174

Cartesian coordinates 152
categoreme 79, 177
categorematic 39f., 60, 65–66, 77f., 89,
  108, 121, 176, 202f., 206, 208f.
category 21, 119f., 124, 149, 178, 257,
  262, 314
– semantic 147, 212, 244
Chomsky, N., 25–32, 37f., 46, 58, 61f.,
  157, 173f., 211, 261, 293f., 300, 315f.
class 42f., 45, 99, 101f., 111, 187, 213
code 127
common sense 33, 58, 101
communication 33, 50, 53–56, 102,
  105, 110, 112, 117, 148f., 157f., 162,
  173, 185, 213, 230, 242f., 286–89,
  295, 299–301, 315
– radio 13
– universal 55
competence 28
compounding
– primitive forms of 21
complement 57, 89, 115–17, 125, 187,
  196f., 212, 252
completeness 36
comprehension 102, 105, 192f., 197,
  230f., and see intension
concept 183, 197
conditional 158, 173
Condillac, E.B. de, 311
conjunction 23, 28, 35–37, 40f., 55, 68,
  71, 75, 84, 101, 131, 163, 192, 199f.,
  203f., 213–22, 224, 230–33, 236–40,
  266, 268f., 273f., 280
conjunctive combination 22
connective 68, 84, 215, 220, 224, 230,
  234–36, 243, 258, 266f.
– material 235–36
– strict 235–36
– syntactical 68–70, 72, 84
connectedness 267
consignificantia 39
consistency 36
constative 173
construction
– ergative 94
content 205, 258
– intentional 100

330

- of judgment 194, 225f., 233, 258
- propositional 248, 259
- stroke 225, 228
context 31, 42, 47, 67, 74f., 81, 87, 98, 147, 170, 185, 196, 202, 241, 250, 255, 263, 280, 290, 299
contrast 16, 132
converses 113
coordination 213f., 216f.
copula 41, 90, 95–97, 101–5, 120, 152, 186, 250–52, 303
correct/incorrect 306
correctness
- grammatical 19
- syntactic 24, 26, 31, 33
countersense *(Widersinn)* 19, 23
counting 37
Couturat, L., 147, 300f.
creativity 28
Cresswell, M.J., 261
Curry, H.B., 84

deep structure 158, 198, 293
definition 35
- recursive 34, 38
demonstration 54
Demosthenes 154
Descartes, R., 53
description 180, 291
designation 64–66
determiner 177, 196
dicent 83, 228
Diodorus Cronus 233, 245
Diogenes Laertius 156
discourse 300f., 305–8
- apophantic 63
- declarative 63
- indicative 65
disjunction 35f., 70, 131, 217, 237, 266, 300
- exclusive 192
- inclusive 192
- material 237
- strict 237
disjunctive combination 22
domain 116
Donaldson 301

Donatus 106
Donzé, R., 60, 122, 145, 150, 152, 173, 211
dual 148, 154
Dumarsais, C.Ch., 257, 261

economy 31, 74, 100, 149, 213
elements 12–14, 111
- recursive 27f.
Encyclopédie 157, 300
epithet 186
equality 99
equivalence 23, 35f., 167, 192, 230, 280
essence 21, 194, 221, 259
- law of 21, 40
Estienne, R., 96, 198
Euclid 18, 52, 294, 297
event 118, 187
exclusion 23
existence 96, 98
expression 25ff.
- finite 29
- incoherent heap of 42
- incomplete (*ergänzungsbedürftig*) 84
- literal 38
- meaningful 20, 23–25, 30, 38, 44
- metaphorical 38
- phonic 11
- tautological 34
- well-formed 26f., 29, 34f., 43, 72, 74
extension 105, 122, 166, 192f., 197, 213, 230f., 236, 304

Feys, R., 84, 261
Findlay, J.N., 36, 175
Flew, A., 317
formalization 29
formula
- well-formed 30, 33
Frege, G., 18, 35, 43, 52, 60, 86f., 89, 91, 95–99, 113, 119, 122–24, 148, 207, 209, 212, 224–29, 244f., 252, 258, 302f.
function 50ff., 76, 86–91, 95, 102–04, 107, 110, 112, 117f., 122, 125, 128, 134, 138, 169, 180, 182, 190–91,

196f., 199, 210, 239f., 286–90, 304f.
- conative 286, 288
- distinctive 287
- domain or range of 76
- emotive 286
- expressive 286, 288
- incantatory 286
- magical 286
- numerical 86
- phatic 287f.
- propositional 88, 122
- technical 289–90
functor 45, 62f., 68–77, 79–82, 84f., 87–89, 107f., 112, 115, 117, 119, 124, 136f., 139, 142, 153, 167f., 186–89, 192f., 202–4, 210f., 222–25, 242–45, 248, 253–56, 258
- functorial 69, 82, 136, 141, 189, 248, 253–57, 264
- nominal 68f., 79f., 189, 202
- propositional 68–71, 80, 82, 84, 88, 136, 141, 188, 192, 210, 224, 229, 243, 249, 253f., 256–58, 264
- quotation 203f.
- temporal 139f.

Galileo, G., 297
Gaza, Th., 156
Geach, P., 60, 61, 121, 123f.
gender 146f., 149f., 155
generation 38
Gentzen, G., 34
geometry 294–97, 303
goals 287f.
- of language 50f., 284
Göttingen School 229
grammaire générale et raisonnée 20
grammar, 11, 14, 16, 18–20, 25–29, 39, 47, 49, 56, 59, 63, 74, 185, 249, 257, 282, 284–86, 291, 305, 313f.
- context-dependent 58
- context-free 58
- descriptive 291, 315
- empirical 299
- general 206, 294, 315
- generative 29, 47f., 293
- hierarchy of 58

- ideal 284, 291
- normative 291, 315
- particular 315
- philosophical 44, 49, 294
- pure 14, 16, 37, 42, 107, 109, 113, 115, 118f., 125, 139, 148, 159, 215, 263, 292, 294–97, 299, 302
- pure logical 20, 39, 111, 214
- rational 14, 16, 20, 42, 107, 109, 118f., 125, 139, 148, 263, 296f.
- real 74
- recursive 27
- traditional 79
- universal 37, 296
grammatical 16f., 31, 43, 282
- combination 41
- construction 249
- meaning 40
- symbol 39
grammaticality 29f., 39, 45–47, 59, 74, 82, 244, 263, 271, 281, 283, 297
grammaticalness 32, 58
- degree of 58

Harris, J., 165
Hegel, G.W.F., 306, 317
Heinrich, E., 84
Heyting, A., 283
Hilbert, D., 229, 244
Hjelmslev, L., 61, 154, 318
Hubien, H., 249, 317
Hughes, G.E., 261
Hugo, V., 80
Humbert, J., 174
Hamblin, C.L., 261
Humboldt, W.v., 26, 29, 106, 122, 301
Husserl, E., 18–24, 29f., 36f., 39–47, 57, 60f., 64, 66f., 77, 83f., 89f., 93, 108f., 120, 123, 156–58, 172, 175–77, 181f., 189f., 193–95, 197, 202–4, 207–12, 221–23, 226, 244, 281, 292, 296, 302, 316
hypothetical combination 22

ideal type 199f., 289
identity 96, 98f., 270, 299
ideogram 13, 53f.

– logico-mathematical 13
idéologues 300
implication 23, 70, 101f., 112, 192, 204, 226–29, 232–38, 245f., 266, 279
– material 232–34, 236–38, 246
– – of facts 234
– – of propositions 234
– strict 233–34, 246, 253f.
– – of facts 234
– – of propositions 234
incompatibility 19, 41, 192, 254
inclusion 96–99, 102, 122, 235
individual 98f., 107, 123, 128, 130, 147, 161, 174, 178, 182, 184f., 190–92, 196, 200, 209–11, 213, 254, 303f
Indo-European languages 27, 30, 45, 47, 63, 78, 86, 94f., 100f., 103f., 114, 127–29, 131–34, 139–41, 147ff., 151–54, 159f., 165, 177, 185f., 188, 207, 215, 219, 230–32, 242, 248, 255, 293, 298, 313
infinitive 107, 158, 186, 195f.
information 66, 109, 287
insertion 26
intelligibility 33, 41, 59
intension 105, 122, 167, 230f.
intention 109, 204
intentional 64, 109, 194, 197, 221
interpretability 29–31
intimation (*Kundgebung*) 39
intuition 23, 29, 44, 86, 100f., 296
– about linguistic form 31
– of meaning 29
intuitive 28, 246
– meaning 44
– rationality 43
invention 53
iota-operator 181, 19
Irson 107
Ishimoto 254

Jakobson, R., 38, 127, 150f., 153, 174, 286, 315, 318
Jaśkowski, S., 38
Joos, M., 316
judgment 91, 121f., 224–27, 291
– stroke (*Urteilsstrich*) 225, 228

Kalinowski, G., 174
Kant, I., 306
Kneale, M., 261
Kneale, W., 261
Kotarbiński, T., 84
Kuroda, S.-Y. 36, 84

La Fontaine 240
Lalande, A., 121
Lambert, J.H., 61
Lancelot, C., 83, 119, 121, 123, 145, 150, 152f., 160f., 173f., 188, 199, 209–11, 257, 261, 301
Langford, C.H., 244
language, 11–14, 284–89, 301
– artificial 32, 54, 132, 307
– colloquial 48f., 56
– everyday 17, 48, 61, 75, 89, 126
– formalized 16, 25f., 29, 31, 33, 49f., 53f., 56, 71f., 74, 76, 78, 135, 139f., 179, 249
– historical 28
– meaningful 308
– mimetic 308
– modern 171
– natural 14, 16, 25–28, 32f., 49f., 56, 58f., 69, 74, 78, 86f., 95, 97f., 100, 112, 114, 136, 139, 141, 143–45, 150, 168f., 179, 231, 236f., 249, 279, 282, 300, 313
– non-artificial 54
– ordinary 23, 26, 28, 37, 45, 48, 52f., 55, 71, 135, 179, 192, 204, 213, 219, 231f., 236f., 240, 242
– rationalized 175
– scientific 44, 126, 135
– spoken 28, 207, 268, 285f.
– vernacular 72, 74
– written 28, 207, 285f.
law (principle)
– of the excluded middle 43, 56, 166
Leibniz, G.W., 209, 311
Lenneberg, E.H., 37
Leśniewski, S., 23, 30, 43f., 46, 49, 60, 64, 68f., 84f., 98–100, 122, 158, 209
Lewis, C.I., 233, 235, 244f., 252
Lewis, D., 85

Locke, J., 311
logic 16, 18, 20–22, 33f., 47, 59, 282, 286, 303–5
– absolute 35
– of description 189
– erotetic 166, 173
– intuitionist 35, 283
– mathematical 86, 284
– minimal 35
– modal 233
– three-valued 34f.
– two-valued 34f.
logico-grammatical parallelism 302
Łukasiewicz, J., 23f., 34, 36–38, 48, 60, 70, 72, 84, 112, 215, 229, 245
Luschei, E.D., 61, 122, 209, 211

maieutic 52, 54
Malinowski, B., 287, 315
manner 260
Martinet, A., 11, 12, 14, 94, 114, 120f., 124, 152–54, 288, 313, 315
Marty, A., 60
Marx, K., 174
mathematical
– framework 284
– heritage 303
mathematics 303f., 310
mathesis universalis 55
Mauro, T. de, 317
Mauss, M., 173
McCall, S., 60
McGuiness, B., 83
meaning 14, 19, 22, 29, 32, 38, 42, 50, 66, 113, 117, 176, 202f., 269, 285, 292, 298, 306, 311f.
– category (Bedeutungskategorie) 39f., 68, and see semantic category
– dependent 40
– domain of 22
– full, entire 40
– intuitive 44
– literal 38
– metaphorical 38
– nominal 21, 37
– primitive forms of independent 21
– pure morphology of 19

– realm of 42
– theory of the forms of 42
meaning-elements 21
meaning-form 18f.
meaningful
– elements 12
– expression 30, 34, 38
meaningfulness 29f., 32, 35f., 44
meaning-structure 21
meaning-whole 67
Megarian School 232
Meillet, A., 121, 154
membership 96–101, 103f., 122, 138, 213
Menander 154
Mercator, G., 308
Meredith, 254
mereological 122
message 11, 13f., 51, 66, 127f., 288
metalanguage 49, 61, 140, 152, 243, 258
metalinguistic 100, 159
metaphor 59, 146
method
– recursive 21
Miller, G.A. 37, 62
modal 251–53
– functor 251, 253
– logic 117
– proposition 251f., 264, 271f.
modality 172, 175, 248, 250–52, 258–60, 272, 280
– de dicto 250–53, 258f.
– de re 250–52, 259
– functorial 260
– objective 260
– propositional 260
– subjective 260
modification
– primitive forms of 21
moneme 11, 12, 66
monism 101
Montague, R. 84f., 261
mood 50, 63, 155–75, 186, 195, 197–99, 286
– concessive 160 f.
– constative 173
– consultative 162–64, 173f.

– dubitative 166f., 171, 173, 175
– hortative 162f., 173f.
– imperative 155, 158, 161–65, 186, 201, 287f.
– indicative 63, 121, 135, 155–57, 159, 164f., 172f., 186, 197–200, 211, 267, 286f.
– interrogative 158, 161, 165ff., 171, 199
– 'invitative' 162, 164
– operative 186, 200
– optative 155, 160f., 201, 286f.
– performative 159, 173f., 286f.
– permissive 164
– precative 162–64, 173
– vocative 159, 173
Morgan, A. de 182
morpheme 11–13, 66, 312f.
morphological 126, 138, 152, 159, 198, 201, 211
– distinction 241
morphology 145, 157, 198, 200
Mounin, G., 122, 318
Mozart, W.A., 285
Mulligan, K., 9
music 285, 307
musical notation 307

name 22, 37, 45f., 49, 57f., 60, 63, 65–69, 77f., 80f., 83, 85, 89f., 107–10, 135, 137, 146f., 152, 176–212, 221f., 225, 304, 309f.
– abstract 195
– adjectival (nom adjectif) 176, 208f.
– common 183f., 188
– definite common 182
– indefinite 184f., 209f.
– of classes 190, 193
– of proposition 243f.
– positing/non-positing 178–81, 183f., 186, 199f., 209
– proper 109, 137, 147, 178–81, 186, 201, 207, 209
– substantive (nom substantif) 176f., 208
natural deduction 34, 36
necessity 172, 250, 252, 254, 258, 292

negation 23, 68, 75, 84, 152, 192, 213, 220, 223–25, 227–30, 234, 236, 241, 243, 257f., 260f., 266, 276
– of a fact 230
– of a proposition 75, 230, 258
Nicod, J., 240
Nicole, P., 245, 312
no-class theory 102
nominalisation 93, 188, 190–97, 201–204, 209ff., 309
– of the predicate 190, 195, 210
– of the proposition 188, 209
– of a statement 211
– of the verb 210
nonsense (Unsinn) 17, 22, 281
normative 290
noun 30, 41, 44f., 138, 152f., 177, 257
– abstract 197
– adjectival 208f.
– common 41, 78–81
– phrase 194, 197f.
– substantive 208
number 126, 147–49, 155

objectifying act 172, 175
Ogden, C.K., 84, 244, 306, 317
onomatopoiea 12, 312
optical 13f.
– system 13
oratio
    enunciativa 198, 200, 211
– imperativa 174
– optativa 174
– ordinativa 198, 200
– precativa 174

Panfilov, V.Z., 121, 123, 174
Panini 26
Pariente, J.-C., 85
Parmenides 101
Partee, B., 85, 260
participle 107, 137, 158, 185f., 209
particular 252
Patañjali 26
Patzig, G., 122
Peano, G., 61, 112
Pears, D., 61, 83

Peirce, Ch.S., 66, 83, 228
perception 12, 108, 111
perceptual
– privilege 116
– stability 108
performance 28
person 127f., 149f., 155
Peter of Spain 251
Pfänder, A., 93, 120f., 310
pheme 83
Philo 232
phoneme 12f., 66, 149, 212, 312
phonetic 14
– elements 84
– type of writing 54, 61, 285
physiology 29
picture 307f., 310, 318
place 138, 260
Plato 17f., 36, 65f., 83, 89f., 106, 119, 122, 154, 315
Polish School 68
Port-Royal Grammar 29, 65ff., 83, 90, 119, 121, 127, 137, 143, 145, 150, 156, 185, 190, 209, 257, 293, 297, 300
Port-Royal Logic 90, 104, 108, 119, 211, 302, 311
positing/non-positing (*setzend/nicht-setzend*) 175, 212
position (of a sign) 13, 73, 84, 112, 285
possible 250
possibility 46, 250, 252, 254
– combinatorial 12
– objective 19
pragmatic
– basis 280
– dimension 74
– reason 282
– uselessness 280
Prantl, K. 92, 244
predicate 81f., 91, 108, 186, 188, 192–96, 201f., 208–10, 213, 248, 250–52, 254
– calculus 91, 270–72
– of predicate 191
predication 120
predicator 68, 84, 252, 257, 259
principle of tolerance 300

Prior, A., 140, 142, 152, 173
priority, see anteriority
Priscian 39, 90, 96, 156, 173
probability
– degrees of 46
process 110f.
Proculus 246f.
pronoun 107, 127–30, 153
– demonstrative 137
– imperative 174
– interrogative 167f.
– personal 127–29, 134
– reflexive 134
– relative 138, 188
property 107, 147, 190, 193, 197, 204, 208, 254, 266, 268, 309f.
proposition 11, 19, 21f., 26, 37, 39f., 46, 60, 63–70, 72, 74, 76, 79, 81, 85–88, 90–96, 99–101, 104f., 117, 137–40, 155f., 170ff., 189ff., 192f., 196f., 199, 202f., 205, 207f., 211, 214–18, 220, 223–25, 228–39, 244–46, 248–53, 258f., 261f., 268–70, 273–76, 278f., 304f., 307, 310f.
– causal 221f.
– completive 9, 258, 305
– compound 220
– constituent 221
– deontic 265
– disjunctive 222
– elementary 68, 182f., 220, 228
– hypothetical 221f.
– imperative 158
– impersonal 91–93, 120, 126, 259, 272
– indicative 158
– interrogative 109
– intransitive 115
– modal 251f., 265, 272, 275
– negated 84
– subordinate 216, 228
– temporal 265
– tenseless 126
– well-formed 47
propositional
– argument 68, 76, 258, 261
– calculus 23, 70, 95, 112, 133, 192, 215, 219, 221, 223f., 237, 258

– content 248, 259
– form 24, 41, 195
– function 122
– functor 68–70, 82, 136–41, 188, 210f., 224, 243, 249, 254, 257f.
– modality 260
– negation 75, 258
Protagoras 156
Proust, M., 287
psychological 114, 214
– possibility 113
– reason 132
– significance 187
– structure 299
– truth 107
psychologism 158, 296, 299
psychologistic 157
psychology 29, 158, 217, 296

qualifier 266, 268
quantification 114, 129, 143, 147f., 252, 266
quantifier 140, 143, 148
quantity 260
Quine, W.v.O., 244
quotation marks 201f., 204, 207, 222, 243

Ramsey, F.P., 61
rationalisation 173
rationalism 158, 299, 305
– grammatical 29, 261, 292, 301f.
– of the seventeenth and eighteenth centuries 20, 29
rationality 59
recursive 38
– definition 23, 34, 38
– rules 27f., 32
recursivity 28, 37f.
reduction 91, 101, 103f., 158, 213, 261, 272, 288, 302
reductionism 158, 315
redundance 187
redundancy 31
Reinach, A., 173f.
relation 92
– theory of 255

relative clause 27, 80, 185
representation 91
Rescher, N., 253, 261
rheme 83
Richards, I.A., 84, 244, 306, 317
rigour 31, 74, 111, 274, 304
Rijk, L.M. de, 261f.
Romanticism
– German 301
Rosser, J.B., 206, 212
rules 14, 26, 27, 55
– grammatical 29, 34
– of detachment 218
– of inference 33f.
– of well-formedness 33
– recursive 27f., 32
Russell, B., 35, 43–45, 60f., 92, 97, 102, 107, 112, 124, 148, 180f., 209, 228f., 233–36, 246, 255, 303f., 307f., 317
Ruwet, N., 29, 37, 47, 62, 194, 211, 293, 297f.
Ryle, G., 308, 317

Sapir, E., 90, 94, 149, 287, 315, 318
saturated (*gesättigt*) 89
Sätze an sich 227
Saussure, F. de, 61, 132, 289, 311f., 314, 318
Scaliger 90, 106–9
Schaff, A., 309, 318
Schlegel, A.W., 300
Schröder, E., 97, 255
Searle, J., 173
security
– operational 54
segmentation 12, 14, 219
semantics 11, 12, 32, 49, 74f., 198, 238, 249, 263, 272f., 277, 280, 282, 294, 297, 304–6, 309
– category (*semantische Kategorie*) 39, 41–46, 58, 68f., 85, 88f., 304
semaphore 13
seme 83
semi-grammatical sentences 58
sense (*Sinn*) 18, 20, 42, 43, 46, 65, 67, 95, 99, 103, 114, 158, 189, 223, 241, 249, 251, 276, 291

– generic 178
– unity of 41
sentence (string of symbols) 25, 42, 69,72, 208, 217
– nominal 123
– verbal 123
Serrus, Ch., 111, 120, 122–24, 137, 152, 173, 210, 294, 302, 315
set 192f.
sex 149
Sheffer, H.M., 220, 242f.
– -stroke 240
sign 11–13, 31, 39, 54, 65, 100f., 173, 185, 215, 225, 228, 285, 301, 303, 306, 311f.
– systems of 12, 14, 32, 55, 288
significance
– logical 116
significant
– sub-domain of the 19
– terms 18
similarity 309
Smith, B., 174
sociology 29
space 51, 265
spatio-temporal 118f., 121, 126, 137f., 179, 212
spoken word (*parole*) 52
Staal, J.F., 37
stability 51f.
Stahl, G., 173
state 187
statement 64, 66, 206, 208, 314
state of affairs (*Sachverhalt*) 64f., 115, 181, 193, 197, 199f., 203f., 208, 220–25, 229, 231–33, 235, 243–45, 257–58, 286, 304, 306f., 314
– names of 227f.
statistical frequency 46
Stoics 18, 159
structural description 38
subject 67, 86, 104, 114
– –attribute couple 105
– –copula-attribute 110f.
– –copula-predicate form 90f., 120
– grammatical 295
subjunctive 158, 186, 197–201, 211, 267

subordination 96, 213f., 216–18
subordinative conjunction 215
substance 123, 208
– –accident form 105
substantive 107, 176, 186
– verb 96f., 104
substitute 22, 42
substitution 17, 41, 46, 55, 100
succession 50, 113, 124, 214, 219, 268
suppositio materialis 202
supposition
– logical 205
– linguistic 205
surface structure 293f.
Swift, J., 86, 284
syncategorematic 39f., 65–68, 89, 108, 202, 206
syntactic 16f., 44, 74f., 249, 279, 282, 300
– coherence 18
– consideration 18
– correctness 24, 33
– rules 17, 23, 300
– verification 69f.
syntax 19, 28, 32f., 38, 58, 85
system
– logico-mathematical 19f., 23
Szabo, M.E., 38

Tarski, A., 23, 42, 44, 48, 60f., 88, 205, 208, 212, 237
tautology 34
tense 119, 126, 135–39, 141, 143–47, 149, 152, 155, 164, 174, 211, 271
that-clauses 248
Theophrastus 251
theorem 34f., 105, 133, 140, 164, 220, 271
theory of types 43, 89, 97, 107, 122, 147, 153, 209
Thomas Aquinas 251f., 261
thought 306
time 51, 126, 135, 139, 141–44, 260, 265–68, 271ff., 295, 302, 313
– density of 267f., 271f., 275–78, 280f.
transcription
– alphabetic 13

transformation 33, 48, 53–55, 72f.
triad 148
true/false 16–19, 43, 47, 56, 86, 153, 157, 169, 195, 214, 216, 221f., 227, 231, 273–77
truth 16, 19, 135, 211, 217f., 225, 227, 236f., 265f., 274, 304, 311f.
– formal 18
– table 34f., 223f., 229, 238
– value 26, 81, 166, 168, 175, 304
Twardowski, K., 84

Ueberweg, F., 93
universality 48, 54–56, 58, 292, 299

validity
– pure theory of 19
value 86, 263
Vendrye 121
verb 30, 40, 45f., 60, 66–68, 76, 86, 88–90, 104, 109–11, 116, 119, 124, 138, 146, 148, 150, 175, 186, 191f., 194–97, 210f., 264, 269, 271, 281f.
– impersonal 89, 92f., 95, 122
– intransitive 115

– phrase 197
– transitive 75
verbalism 52
verification 71
– semantic 266
– syntactic 69f.
Viète, F., 53

Wachowicz, K.A., 174f.
Walter, G. 121
Walter, H. 121
Warsaw School 23, 66, 84, 229, 244
Weber, M., 173, 289
well-formedness 32, 45, 56, 168, 281
– rules of 33
wh-question 167, 170
Whitehead, A.N., 92, 107, 180f., 209, 228f., 246, 303f.
Whorf, B.L., 153
Wiggins, D., 122
William of Champeaux 261
William of Sherwood 251
Wittgenstein, L., 65, 83, 244, 306–10
Wright, G.H. von, 141, 255, 261

By the Same Author

Essai sur les fondements a priori de la rationalité morale et juridique, Bibliothèque de philosophie de droit, Paris: L.G.D.J., Pichon et Durand-Auzias, 1972.

La logique du temps, Paris: PUF, 1975.

Essai sur la logique des modalités, Paris: PUF, 1979.

Pascal entre Eudoxe et Cantor, Paris: Vrin, 1984.